Global Music Cultures

Oxford University Press
Digital Course Materials
for

Directions for accessing your
Oxford University Press Digital Course Materials

Global Music Cultures
An Introduction to World Music

Bonnie C. Wade
Patricia Shehan Campbell

Carefully scratch off the silver coating to see your personal redemption code.

This code can be redeemed only once.

Once the code has been revealed, this access card cannot be returned to the publisher.

Access can also be purchased online during the registration process.

The code on this card is valid for two years from the date of first purchase. Complete terms and conditions are available at learninglink.oup.com

Access Length: 6 months from redemption of the code.

Your OUP digital course materials can be delivered several different ways, depending on how your instructor has elected to incorporate them into his or her course.

BEFORE REGISTERING FOR ACCESS, be sure to check with your instructor to ensure that you register using the proper method.

VIA YOUR SCHOOL'S LEARNING MANAGEMENT SYSTEM

Use this method if your instructor has integrated these resources into your school's Learning Management System (LMS)—Blackboard, Canvas, Brightspace, Moodle, or other

Log in to your instructor's course within your school's LMS.

When you click a link to a resource that is access-protected, you will be prompted to register for access.

Follow the on-screen instructions.

Enter your personal redemption code (or purchase access) when prompted.

VIA OXFORD learning link

Use this method if you are using the resources for self-study only.
NOTE: *Scores for any quizzes you take on the OUP site will not report to your instructor's gradebook.*

Visit oup.com/he/wade-campbell

Select the edition you are using, then select student resources for that edition.

Click the link to upgrade your access to the student resources.

Follow the on-screen instructions.

Enter your personal redemption code (or purchase access) when prompted.

VIA OXFORD learning cloud

Use this method only if your instructor has specifically instructed you to enroll in an Oxford Learning Cloud course. **NOTE:** *If your instructor is using these resources within your school's LMS, use the Learning Management System instructions.*

Visit the course invitation URL provided by your instructor.

If you already have an oup.instructure.com account you will be added to the course automatically; if not, create an account by providing your name and email.

When you click a link to a resource in the course that is access-protected, you will be prompted to register.

Follow the on-screen instructions, entering your personal redemption code where prompted.

For assistance with code redemption, Oxford Learning Cloud registration, or if you redeemed your code using the wrong method for your course, please contact our customer support team at **learninglinkdirect.support@oup.com**
or 855-281-8749.

OXFORD
UNIVERSITY PRESS

Global Music Cultures

AN INTRODUCTION TO WORLD MUSIC

EDITED BY

Bonnie G. Wade

Patricia Shehan Campbell

New York   Oxford
OXFORD UNIVERSITY PRESS

Oxford University Press is a department of the University of Oxford.
It furthers the University's objective of excellence in research, scholarship,
and education by publishing worldwide. Oxford is a registered trade mark of
Oxford University Press in the UK and certain other countries.

Published in the United States of America by Oxford University Press,
198 Madison Avenue, New York, NY 10016, United States of America.

© 2021 by Oxford University Press

Library of Congress Cataloging-in-Publication Data

Names: Wade, Bonnie C., editor. | Campbell, Patricia Shehan, editor.
Title: Global music cultures : an introduction to world music / edited by
  Bonnie C. Wade, Patricia Shehan Campbell.
Description: [First edition.] | New York : Oxford University Press, 2020. |
  Includes bibliographical references and index.
Identifiers: LCCN 2020010424 (print) | LCCN 2020010425 (ebook) | ISBN
  978-0-19-064364-5 (paperback) | ISBN 978-0-19-064366-9 (epub)
Subjects: LCSH: World music—Analysis, appreciation. | Music appreciation.
Classification: LCC MT90 .G56 2020 (print) | LCC MT90 (ebook) | DDC
  780.9—dc23
LC record available at https://lccn.loc.gov/2020010424
LC ebook record available at https://lccn.loc.gov/2020010425

Printing number: 9 8 7 6 5 4 3 2 1
Printed by LSC Digital, Inc.,
United States of America

Brief Contents

Contents

PART 1   Understanding the Basics of Music

CHAPTER 1   **Pitch, Melody (Pitches in Succession), and Rhythm (Managing Time in Music)   4**

CHAPTER 2

Harmony (Simultaneous Pitches), Texture (How Musical Parts Fit Together), and Form (The Structure of a Piece) 18

CHAPTER 3

Understanding and Classifying Musical Instruments 32

PART 2   The Pacific and Asia

CHAPTER 12

Music in Egypt: Creating and Maintaining a Vibrant Islamic Presence in Day-to-Day Life   **182**
SCOTT MARCUS

PART 3   Africa

CHAPTER 13

Music in Ghana: Dagaaba Xylophone Music in a Ritual Context   **202**
JOHN DANKWA AND ERIC CHARRY

CHAPTER 14   **Music in South Africa:** Language, Race,
and Nation   **216**
GAVIN STEINGO

PART 4   **Europe**

CHAPTER 15   **Music in Spain:** *Flamenco*, between the Local
and the Global   **232**
**SUSANA MORENO FERNÁNDEZ AND
SALWA EL-SHAWAN CASTELO-BRANCO**

CHAPTER 18   **Music in Brazil:** *Samba*, a Symbol
of National Identity   **298**

JOHN MURPHY

Preface

Global Music Cultures is a new textbook for courses that introduce students to an array of musical styles and practices found in locations around the world. The approach taken in the book, however, is both geographic and thematic. Discussion of music and culture is thoroughly integrated in ethnomusicological fashion as each author pursues a uniting theme for the book, namely, an understanding about music that people—*people everywhere*—make music meaningful and useful in their lives. Thus, the approach taken in the book is both geographic and thematic, with discussion of music and culture thoroughly integrated in ethnomusicological fashion.

To set the stage, we editors introduce ourselves as music scholars and teachers, and then in chapters 1 and 2 introduce the essential elements most used in the sonic expressive medium commonly recognized as "music"—pitch, melody, harmony, rhythm, texture, and form. It becomes quickly evident that common ideas are put to work in ways quite different (as well as similar) through the creative imagination of humankind. Chapter 3 illustrates the same sort of creative imagination found in the construction and use of an assortment of some basic types of musical instruments that occur throughout the world. In chapter 4, the editors step back to introduce the sorts of topics of interest in the field of ethnomusicology in general—topics such as music and structures of power, the relevance of the past in the present, and the musical results of cultural interfaces. Each of chapters 5 through 20, authored by a specialist ethnomusicologist, is a case study focusing on one country/island/ethnic group where they have conducted field research, and where they have come to understand how some particular musical styles or practices have been made meaningful and useful in the lives of the people who create or practice it. To achieve flow through the book, introductory material in all the opening chapters is brought to bear in the case studies. In addition, the case study chapters are ordered geographically by regions of the world, beginning with the Pacific Ocean region and working westward.

The selection of case studies for this new book correlates largely with that for the already-published *Global Music Series* that consists of twenty-seven volumes—little books—written as textbooks for the field of ethnomusicology. To learn more about the Global Music Series, please visit https://global.oup.com/us/companion.websites/umbrella/globalmusic. That series provides a ready-made answer to the oft-raised question from instructors of introductory courses as to where they and students can go to learn more about musical material and ideas that are tantalizingly introduced in a single chapter format. The authors of the case study chapters in *Global Music Cultures* have drawn somewhat on their volumes but tailored the chapters here according to the focus of this book and the nature of the course for which it is intended. Much material is new.

One aspect of the selection of case studies for both this book (and the Series) had to do with the inclusion (or not) of any musics other than non-Western. A percentage of the reviewers of this book at the manuscript stage said that they would not be likely to assign the chapters on Ireland and Spain, that the "space" would more usefully be devoted to non-Western cultures. Thus, an explanation for our decisions is in order. Our reasons for including even explicitly Western European musics are primarily three: 1) We wish to make the point that the customary practice of excluding "the West" from "the world" in world music textbooks reinforces the unfortunate division of human cultures into those of "the West" and "the rest" —or into "what is familiar" and "what is exotic." The reality of globalization that has been experienced for many centuries by peoples all over the world, however, argues against the practicality (not to mention accuracy) of that binary sort of thought in the sphere of music. 2) One of the purposes of this and other world music textbooks is to introduce the field of ethnomusicology, and ethnomusicologists do not limit the field in that geographic manner. The ways of approaching music study along with the deeply grounded values of the field lead us to focus research on music anywhere. The uniting theme of this volume—that people make music meaningful and useful—pertains to people everywhere. 3) Furthermore, courses that focus only on musics in Western cultures rarely present the repertoires included here.

A significant goal of this text is engagement. Engagement of students with the editors and authors is sought by a relatively informal style of writing and reference to some personal moments in our work that have affected us. Also, engagement of the authors directly with the students as well as engagement of the students directly with the musical traditions being studied is facilitated through interactive listening guides and through activities interspersed in the text that are intended to guide students in self-study—ideally in advance of class.

Acknowledgments

Our engagement with the Higher Education Division of Oxford University Press has been long-standing and fruitful for us as individual scholars/teachers and for the field of ethnomusicology. Initiated in 1999 with editor Maribeth Payne, we have worked with a sequence of editors and OUP editorial assistants; the creation of this book can be credited to editor Richard Carlin whose idea it was. In the final stage, we are grateful for the support of Editor of Music and Art Justin Hoffman and Assistant Editor Olivia Clark.

We wish to thank some individuals for contributing to the book in ways that are often hidden: Elsa Ray, who compiled the composite Glossary with its many words from numerous languages; and graduate students Juliana Cantarelli Vita and Skuli Gestsson, who assisted with early stages in the development of assorted digital materials.

We want to express gratitude to the authors of the case study chapters who generously agreed to work on the project, although it would take much thought and considerable patience as we learned together how to create this very different spin-off from the *Global Music Series*. In alphabetical order, they are Eliot Bates, Salwa El-Shawan Castelo-Branco, Brian Diettrich, Gavin Douglas, Susana Moreno Fernández, Lisa Gold, Dorothea E. Hast, Frederick Lau, Scott Marcus, Robin Moore, John Murphy, John-Carlos Perea, George Ruckert, Stanley Scot, and Daniel Sheehy. Authors new to the project (for whom we give many thanks) are Eric Charry, John Dankwa, and Gavin Steingo.

List of Reviewers

Libby Allison, Berklee College of Music
Dawn Avery, Montgomery College–Rockville
Elizabeth Clendinning, Wake Forest University
Janice Dickensheets, University of Northern Colorado
Joshua Groffman, University of Pittsburgh–Bradford
Ramona Holmes, Seattle Pacific University
Inderjit Kaur, University of Michigan
Siv Lie, University of Maryland
Sheri Matascik, Maryville College
David McDonald, University of Indiana–Bloomington
George Murer, CUNY Hunter
Austin Okigbo, University of Colorado–Boulder
Brittney Patterson, University of Montevallo
Rose Pruiksma, University of New Hampshire
Marty Regan, Texas A&M University
Kendra Salois, American University
Natalie Sarrazin, SUNY College at Brockport
William Stacy, Missouri State University
Jeffrey van den Scott, Memorial University of Newfoundland
Jittapim Yamprai, University of Northern Colorado
Two anonymous reviewers

Introduction

This volume is a text for a "world music survey" course. However, it does not cover all the music that you could hear around the world. After all, the world is the planet that we and a whole lot of other people inhabit—the great globe of cultures and communities that reside on six habitable continents. In so much geographical space, our ways of thinking and doing and feeling and relating to each other became diverse a very long time ago. In this book, we offer you a few glimpses of the great diversity of music that humankind has produced over many centuries in many different regions of the world.

The contents of this textbook are derived from the work of scholars in the field of **ethnomusicology,** or the study of the world's music (see chapter 4). From the field's beginning in the mid-1950s, ethnomusicologists have travelled all over the globe, intent on documenting the musical performances that they could find (see Figure 0.1). What they have encountered is both a great deal of commonality and

ACTIVITY INTRO.1

To put yourself into this picture, take the time to explore these questions.

- What comprises your "world"? Has your world included intersection with other peoples, other countries, and other natural environments? Who is "other" in your experience, and why do you consider them "other"? What is your sense of yourself in relation to other people?
- What is "other music" in your experience? Will the contents of this book be largely unfamiliar to you, filled with "others"?
- What is "the world" of the persons sitting next to you or some rows behind or in front of you in the classroom? Introduce yourself to someone, to discover if their world and yours—including the music that each of you appreciates—are mostly similar or different in some ways—or in many ways. Do any overlapping musical interests stem from experiences in the family, community, or through the media?

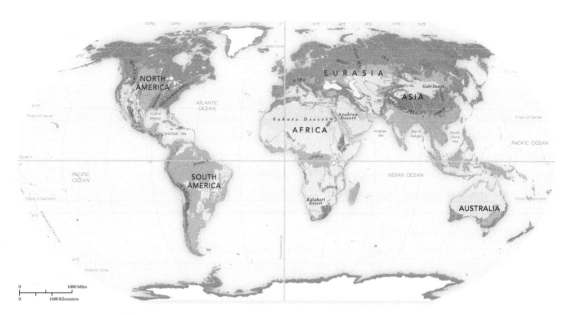

≡ **FIGURE 0.1** Map of the World.

difference in types of musical instruments; how melodies, rhythms, and harmony are created; and many other musical elements. Similarities are easy to hear, but differences are sometimes off-putting to us when we've been raised with certain expectations about musical performance. On the other hand, doesn't it happen that we might just love something heard for the first time without having the foggiest idea about why?

Ethnomusicologists understand that being *open to* and being *attracted to* different musical styles are not the same, of course. We are accustomed to listening to music of any and every sort, but each of us pursues what pushes at

ACTIVITY INTRO.2

What music do you absolutely love, absolutely abhor, won't even give a try, find "kind of" enjoyable or interesting? Make several lists of artists, genres, styles, and sources. Take a stab at explaining those reactions to yourself.

us—as aesthetically pleasing, as exotic perhaps, as intriguing or important to understand. Significantly, however, our aim is not only to learn about the music that fascinates us as individuals but equally what the makers and consumers of other musics consider to be important. Ours is a people-oriented field. This book is intended to introduce you to a number of different peoples and their musics.

How We Came to Study Global Music

≡ **FIGURE 0.2** Bonnie C. Wade.

You might wonder how we came to engage with different styles of music. I, Bonnie Wade (Figure 0.2), have had a longtime interest in the musics of Japan and India. My students always ask how on earth I came to love these musical traditions, so here's the story for you—in a nutshell. I grew up as many people in my generation did: studying piano, singing in a church choir, loving to dance, and generally enjoying music. First, I dreamed of becoming a concert pianist. When the reality hit me in high school that that was not going to happen, I switched my goal to being a professor of music history. That meant being a professor of the history of European art music only—the music I considered "my music."

Until, that is, generous friends treated me to a trip to Latin America when I was between my junior and senior years in college. I was too poor to go otherwise and, besides, I had never even considered visiting Latin America. During my trip, I experienced an epiphany: a life-changing experience. I was standing at the edge of an Andean mountain precipice near Cuzco, Peru, when up from the chasm below floated music like none I had ever heard before—a flute melody that didn't fit my musical expectations. But it was beautiful! What struck me most that day was that no one in my years of music study had ever mentioned "other" music to me. Granted, recordings were relatively few in those days (that's hard for you to imagine, I know), but I hadn't even considered listening to other varieties of music easily heard on the radio. I suddenly realized that that was not acceptable. Travel would open my ears and mind much farther when—between college and graduate school (for ethnomusicology)—I headed with two friends to Asia on what would become a lengthy adventure as we worked our way to lands south and west to experience a good deal of the world.

≡ **FIGURE 0.3** Patricia Shehan Campbell.

I, Patricia Campbell (Figure 0.3), tell my students of my earliest memories of family meals where parents, grandparents, aunts, uncles, and cousins, all fired up from their intake of calories, would shift from conversations to singing—anything: folk tunes, popular tunes, show tunes, dance tunes, all sung a cappella or with the radio, records, and at the piano. Similar to Bonnie, I studied piano, sang in the church and school choirs, and leaped at every opportunity to dance and listen to music alone and with friends. I was drawn as much to the Irish-American tunes of my grandfather and his friends as to the polka bands that played regularly at family weddings. I was enamored of the weekly "ethnic radio" programs devoted to Czech, Hungarian, Polish, and Slovenian music that I heard on the family radio, and was captivated by the high lonesome sounds that came crackling out of WWOV bluegrass programs in Wheeling, West Virginia.

In college, I studied music and how to teach it. I became a school music teacher, honing my lessons to fit curricular standards of European art music that should be listened to, taught and learned, sung and played, in school. It was not until I happened upon a summer course in ethnomusicology that I realized that *my* music—all of that music of my earlier experiences—was as beautiful as I'd always thought, and that it qualified for experience and study by the children I was teaching. The floodgates opened, and I learned of the music that ethnomusicologists studied, through their field recordings as well as through my visits to parts of Africa, Asia, the Americas, and Europe. I became convinced that all the world's musical expressions were worth knowing; and that they just required taking the time to listen; to understand reasons why people sing, play, and dance the way they do; and to recognize the commonalities and distinctive ways of people's expressions in music across so many cultures.

Structure of the Book

Global Music Cultures is about both commonalities and differences in the music heard in widely separated spots on the planet. As an entryway for you (considering that this might be your first course about music), this Introduction and part 1 are devoted to the similarities found across musical styles. This Introduction acquaints you with the unifying theme of the book. Part 1 introduces you to the basics of music wherever in the world it might be found:

- Chapter 1 covers pitch, melody, and rhythm (time)
- Chapter 2, harmony, texture, and form
- Chapter 3, musical instruments

After reading these chapters, it should be obvious that—while some basic elements are common to all musics—human creativity has resulted in variations (i.e., differences), as people have seen opportunities for "doing things my way."

Part 1 concludes with chapter 4, which introduces you to the field of ethnomusicology. Following a very brief history, we review some perspectives on world music and key themes that we will study throughout this book: the dynamic tension between musical continuity and change; and connections between musical expression and identity. A glimpse at types of sources for study and also research methods precedes consideration of how one might put the study of world music to work.

The remainder of the book is devoted to case studies of musical ideas and practices in different regions of the world. Organized by geographical regions, these case study chapters take us in part 2 to the Pacific region, East Asia, Southeast Asia, South Asia, West Asia, and the Middle East; in part 3 to Africa; and in parts 4 and 5 to Europe and the Americas. In selecting the case study chapters in this text, we have drawn mostly on the series of short textbooks that we edited for the *Oxford Global Music Series* (GMS), written by specialist ethnomusicologists to offer greater depth than a book such as this can offer. Should you be hooked by something in the case study offered by one of the GMS authors here, you can use the related book to further your study.

The Theme of This Book: Music that is Meaningful and Useful in Our Lives

From our studies of world music, ethnomusicologists recognize that—wherever they might be—people make music meaningful and useful in their lives. That basic reality provides the unifying theme of this book. Whoever the people are, whatever they consider "music" to be, however they make music or otherwise experience it, whatever meaning it has for them, and however they have made it useful, *people make music meaningful and useful in their lives.* To understand this theme better, let's consider each of its parts:

- the people who make and enjoy music
- what constitutes "music" itself
- how we define "meaning" and "use" in relation to music

People

People who make music meaningful and useful in their lives include those who *make* music themselves, and also individuals who *involve themselves* in music in other ways that can be vital in a musical culture. Consumers of music—patrons like yourselves possibly—are prime examples of the latter. Here we'll think first about music makers and turn to non–music makers next.

Music makers are many sorts: individuals and groups; children, youth, young adults, and older persons; women, men, and trans and non-binary individuals; amateurs and professionals. They are people who make music only for themselves—such as those who sing in the shower or secretly sing along while listening to their favorite recordings. They are also performers, people who make music purposefully for others. Music makers are also people who make music because they have to (as part of school or church group, for instance, or as street musicians hoping to earn enough for food and shelter) and people who do so simply for enjoyment.

What questions might we raise about music makers globally? We might ask whether music makers are regarded in any particular way in a particular place—as the term "musician" as opposed to "music maker" might imply. At one end of a spectrum, some societies expect people who make music to be specialists—born into the social role, or endowed "by nature" with a special capacity, or having achieved a high level of knowledge and competency. For example, a great many musicians in India's culture are considered to be specialists (see chapter 10). The *guru* (Sanskrit, Hindu culture) or **ustad** (Urdu, Muslim culture) occupies a special place, having attained a high level of musical knowledge and competency. A *guru/ustad* in music has the role of teacher and guide, responsible for transmitting the musical ideas, practices, and values of Indian music. At the other end of that spectrum, in some societies it is assumed that the practice of music is a human capacity and that all people will express themselves musically as a normal part of life. They will sing, dance, and play as readily as they walk, talk, and participate as members of their families and communities.

Asking questions about people who make music can lead to insights about their musical and social worlds. Who makes music? With whom do they make music? Who is permitted to be a teacher? Who learns music from whom? Who is permitted to perform where? Who can perform for whom? Who plays which instruments, and why? Do music makers have high cultural status (i.e., is their music-making highly valued by a group) or high social status (i.e., a prominent ranking in their society) or both? Is anyone prohibited from making or even listening to some particular type of music, and if so, why? Racial discrimination and gender are two possible reasons (see chapters 14 and 19).

ACTIVITY INTRO.3

Make an inventory of music makers who you know, including friends, family, and yourself. For each person in your inventory, consider whether or not you would categorize them as "a musician," and why or why not. That will clarify what your sense of "a musician" is, and whether or not "music maker" might not a more useful word for considering a bigger picture.

Further, focus in on two of the questions we've raised and consider the musical experience of individuals you have listed from those perspectives. Do you, for instance, know anyone who has been discouraged from studying a particular instrument? Or making a particular type of music? If so, why might they have been discouraged? Conversely, was anyone particularly encouraged to study or make a particular instrument or kind of music and if so, why?

Thus far, we have written about "people" as if music makers/musicians are the only people who make music meaningful and useful. Recently, another word has come into use by ethnomusicologists that takes us into another way of thinking. The word is "*musicker*." It comes from the word "*musicking*," which was introduced by sociologist Christopher Small. Instead of thinking of music as a *thing*, wrote Small, it should be thought of as an *activity*, something that people do. Small defined "musicking" as taking "part, in any capacity, in a musical performance, whether by performing, by listening, by rehearsing or practicing, by providing material for performance (as in the act of composing), or by dancing" (1998, 9).

Ethnomusicologists have extended the use of the word "musicking" beyond just the activities involved in producing musical sound. They've used the term "musicker" to refer to everyone involved in the production of music: from recording technicians to sales persons who promote it, as well as patrons of musicians, not to mention consumers for whom music is produced. In any case, the activity of "musicking" puts "people" together with "music."

Music

What is "music" anyway? A special category in the greater world of sounds, for sure. Is "music" whatever results when a group of people exercise their creative imaginations to use sound in some way that is different from the way they use sound for speech? Perhaps so, but the fact is that no one definition of "music" exists for all human cultures.

Definitions of music are *culturally specific*—that is, developed by individual groups over time. Here are just two examples:

- The ancient Greek word for "music" was adopted into the Arabic language as **musiqa**, but in the Islamic world view, it has been used in a more specific way (see chapter 12). The mellifluous recitation of the sacred **Qur'an**—which many non-Muslim listeners have categorized as "music"—is not considered by Muslims to be *musiqa*. Moreover, *musiqa* has carried different meanings. In present-day Egypt, *musiqa* is used to refer to music whose purpose is (worldly) entertainment, as distinct from music/sound phenomena that are explicitly religious, as in recitation of the Qur'an.

- In Balinese music culture, the concept of "music" is context specific. Rather than sweeping categories such as sacred and secular, **repertoires** (groups of pieces that are linked in some way) of the many instrumental ensembles and vocal practices are each named and associated with their specific functions (see chapter 9).

The word "music" generally is used in American culture to imply "something beautiful." We've all exclaimed "That's not music!" when encountering sounds we consider to be "just noise." Generally, this judgment is made solely on the basis of the quality of sound that is produced for a particular type of music, with the idea that musical sound should always be a beautiful sound. That brings us to **aesthetics**, which addresses what makes a sense of beauty, here specifically the beauty of musical sound. In American culture, the expression "that's music to my ears" suggests that one has heard something one wants to hear, or something beautiful. What made the sound beautiful for one person, however,

ACTIVITY INTRO.4

Think back to comments you have heard about musical sound that reveal a judgment on what is beautiful or not—comments such as "You have a terrible voice!"

To articulate your own ideas about musical aesthetics, select one recording in your playlist that

you really like, and then find a different version of the same song that you really don't like. Try to figure out why, in both cases. Another time, share the two versions with friends in order to discover that what is musically beautiful, or appealing, to one listener may not be so to another listener.

might very well not be appreciated by someone else—someone in your own world, even, perhaps someone of an older or younger generation. Music is more likely to be enjoyed when it is understood through repeated experiences as a listener, singer, and player.

Meaning

That music is meaningful—considered to have implied or explicit connotations or significance—no one doubts. Furthermore, a piece of music can be meaningful with or without sung text (or lyrics).

The meaning might be easy to understand if there is a text. Indeed, melody set to words constitutes much of the world's music. Perhaps that is because just about everyone, in every place and time, sings, with or without an instrument. Further, people everywhere in the world understand that music can heighten the expressivity of a text—as in the case of blues, gospel, or Spanish flamenco.

Particularly for music without a text, there have been great debates over whether its meaning resides in the musical materials themselves or is ascribed to them by someone for some particular reason. Is it literally the melody of "Taps" that connotes sadness over the loss of and respect for the deceased for their service to the country? Or is the association made because it is often played at funerals? Does "Amazing Grace" create a solemnity of sorts, a reflective feeling, a sense of reverence and homage, because of the words? Or does the melody itself, without words, convey a devotional tone due to its long affiliation with worship services?

Music can also derive meaning through its associations with key moments in our lives. One reason that we continue to love (if not get stuck in) the popular music of our adolescent years is that we first hear that music when we were experiencing love and other emotions as intensely as adolescents do. Twenty years from now, chances are that Lin-Manuel Miranda's "Helpless" (from *Hamilton*) and Ed Sheeran's "The Shape of You" may be meaningful for one generation of listeners as were songs like "And I Love Her" by the Beatles and Whitney Houston's "I Will Always Love You" to others. It is not only the style of the music that stays with us but also the embedded memory of the meaning it had at that crucial time in our lives.

The meaning of music might be individual or communally agreed on. Furthermore, one item of music can assume new meaning and hold multiple different meanings. In her book, *Music in America*, Adelaida Reyes illustrates through one song—"We Shall Overcome"—how it not only could assume new meanings, but also new functions, and even mark different identities. "We Shall Overcome" was originally a Christian church hymn: C. A. Tindley (1851–1933), who became

America's first important African American gospel songwriter, had written it for his congregation. In the 1960s, it was adopted by the civil rights movement and became an anthem associated with the African American struggle for equality and freedom from discrimination.

The song can take on different meanings in different contexts. Reyes recounts her experience some years ago attending a Thanksgiving Day celebration in Oxford (United Kingdom) when even such a clearly situated song underwent transformation—with shifting senses of community and meaning to individuals as well as to a community. As she recalled it:

> In the presence of other Americans and guests from the local and international community (mostly Europeans and Africans), one Anglo-American after another stood up to describe their connection to the Pilgrims. Then an African American began to sing "We Shall Overcome." Immediately, the other guests who knew the song joined in. In no time, the one voice had become a rousing chorus. I had to guess that when he began, the singer had intended the song to call attention to his difference from the earlier speakers and to the fact that, though American, he, as an African American, had no connection to the Pilgrims. As the other Americans joined in, the song assumed new meaning. The emphasis shifted from the difference that the African American singer was signaling to the shared meanings that "We Shall Overcome" has for all Americans. Finally, as the non-American guests added their voices, the scope of the song's meaning expanded beyond the boundaries of one national ideology. The non-Americans may just have been joining in on a party activity. But they may also have been expressing solidarity with the African American individual who initiated the singing in the narrow context of that Thanksgiving celebration. Alternatively, they may have been expressing solidarity with what he stood for in the wider context of racism and universal human rights. (Reyes 2005, 56)

Use

There is no question that music is used by people to accomplish some things. It may be used

- Socially, as a mode of interaction or to create a context for interaction
- Politically, to control whether to separate or to unite
- Spiritually, for sacred expression and worship
- Economically, to make a living
- Medically and/or psychologically, for soothing or healing

ACTIVITY INTRO.5

Through the history of the United States, there have been many moments when songs have been used to express social protest. Many concerns were raised musically during the 1960s—support for equal rights for African Americans and other racial and ethnic groups; objection to or support of the Vietnam War; and many, many others. Songs were written that addressed environmental concerns and women's rights in the 1970s and 1980s, the LA riots in the 1990s over the acquittal of police officers in the beating of Rodney King, the war in Iraq in the 2000s, and recent uprisings concerning travel bans and immigration issues. New music rises even as old songs are recycled in the continuing impulse to protest human rights, gender and racial equity, and war.

However, it is important to update the power of music as expression of protest. Locate at least two examples of protest song in the country between Fall 2016 and the present moment—ideally, expressing opposing opinions as is appropriate in a democratic society.

A frequent use for music with text is the license it gives musicians to say something not permitted in ordinary speaking. That is the case with Miriam Makeba's "Click Song," where even her choice of the very language used—one that incorporates clicks—is heavily laden with political meaning pertaining to apartheid-period South Africa (see chapter 14).

Music makers are not the only people for whom music is useful in life. Listeners are, after all, most of the world's musically involved population. Focusing

ACTIVITY INTRO.6

Some people do not realize the use of music in their lives; it is "just there." Saying that they are not interested in music at all, it turns out that they regularly listen to music in their cars, occasionally go to a performance, dance on a date, exercise with a listening device, or study with music to block out other sounds.

Think about how you use music in your life—and why. It might be that you do more musicking than you realize! Surprise yourself, too, as you recognize that you may be humming along with the tunes in your ears, tapping out the beat, and even matching your stride to the spirit of the music you are listening to.

specifically on use permits us to think about the needs and intentions of any persons for whom it is useful.

Another sort of aesthetic expectation rests in the desire for expressivity through some musical means. For many people, the highest value of music is placed on **affect**, that is, its capacity for expressivity—that it prompts us to feel emotion, has the power to move our hearts, minds, and bodies. Spanish flamenco music is about that—enabling aficionados to experience a transformation in feeling evoked by expression of intense emotions through singing, guitar playing, and dancing.

Bibliography

Small, Christopher. 1998. *Musicking: The Meanings of Performing and Listening.* Middletown, CT: Wesleyan University Press.

Global Music Cultures

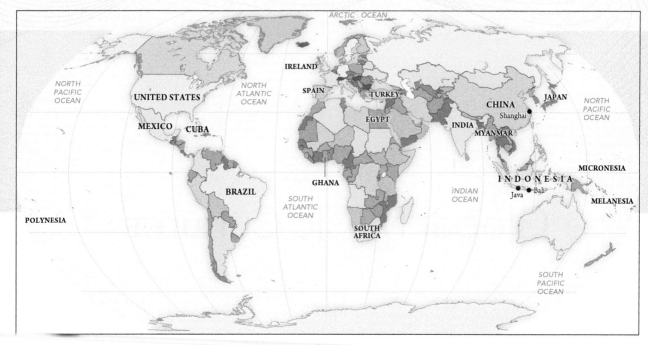

≡ **FIGURE I.1** Countries and regions whose musical traditions are explored in the text.

PART 1

Understanding the Basics of Music

1

Pitch, Melody (Pitches in Succession), and Rhythm (Managing Time in Music)

Chapter Contents

Introduction

In this chapter, we'll explore some basic concepts about music, particularly pitch (sometimes called a "note"), melody (a succession of pitches), and rhythm (the organization of time in music). We will explore these concepts using familiar Western musical examples, along with some examples drawn from less familiar or even perhaps utterly unfamiliar musical traditions that we will be studying in this text. This will give us a broader understanding of how to appreciate music from different cultures and also help us develop a common vocabulary for describing these many traditions.

≡ **Layaali Arabic Music Ensemble.**

Pitch

The term "**pitch**"—whether referring to the high-pitched screech of brakes or the low-pitched rumbling sound of a deep bass voice—is a relative quality of "highness" or "lowness" of sound. "Musical pitch" usually refers to some purposefully placed sound on a continuum from low to high. Pitch is the basic element in **melody**—generically defined as any selection of pitches in succession. It is also the basic element in **harmony**—generically defined as two or more pitches heard simultaneously (see chapter 2).

Selecting Pitches

People around the world have made some very different choices about pitch for their music-making: how many pitches they want to use, whether or not they want to be precise about pitch placement (frequency of sound vibration), and other features. A number of different systems have been developed, and a few are illustrated in case studies in this textbook.

Pitch Placement and Intonation

Pitch placement in most music within European-derived practice lies within a system that is likely to sound "natural" to you because you hear it constantly as part of your everyday soundscape. Pitches are named, and the named pitches (A, B, C, or do-re-mi, etc.) are expected to lie at some precise place, that is, at a precise **frequency** (the number of times a sound vibrates per second). By agreement in recent times, the pitch called "A above middle C" on the piano is set to vibrate at 440 **Hertz** (or 440 times per second; abbreviated as "hz"). A musician who produces pitches at the desired frequencies of a system is said to have "**good intonation.**" An ideal once held by musicians of European classical music was to have "**perfect pitch,**" meaning that an individual could identify the letter-named pitch whenever hearing music or even produce a desired pitch at its proper frequency out of the blue, without reference to an instrument to check. Instrumentalists in an ensemble such as an orchestra must be sure that their instruments are "**in tune**" with the other instruments.

Whether a musician adheres to that pitch placement in the European-derived system, however, can vary. For an opera singer or an individual member of an orchestra or chorus, correct placement is very important. Some popular musicians use audio processors (called "phase vocoders") that correct pitch in vocal and instrumental performances. However, one of the things that makes a performer unique is the way he or she alters pitch to create a unique sound: think of a blues guitarist like B. B. King who purposely "bent" a note to expressively change its pitch or the way a violinist like Hilary Hahn uses vibrato and other effects when playing. In fact, it is far more useful to "have excellent **relative pitch**"—the ability to sing a pitch in reference to any another. That is certainly the case if you want to enjoy music made by people in spots around the globe who have different senses of intonation. A sensible, flexible way to think about "good intonation" is to appreciate musicians' exceptionally good aural memory, in whatever pitch system they may use.

Two other entirely unrelated practices have developed a different approach to tuning. In Turkish studio-produced contemporary recordings of traditional folk music (see chapter 11) and Balinese *gamelan* ensembles (see chapter 9), a desired "shimmering" sound is produced by purposefully setting pitches of pairs of instruments intentionally and precisely "out of tune" with each other. In each case, of course, there must be a definite idea about "in-tuneness" against which "out of tuneness" is measured.

Setting the Pitch

Who sets the pitch? Someone has to! The manufacturers of fixed-pitch instruments need some reference to use when they are building the keyed woodwind instruments of European tradition and of pianos. Artisan craftspersons such as the highly respected makers of bronze *gamelan* instruments in Balinese tradition (see chapter 9) need a different understanding of pitch from that of the German violin makers. And individual musicians—such as a bowed-lute player of Turkish **kemençe** or **saz** (see chapter 11) or a player of the North Indian plucked-lute **sarod** (see chapter 10), for instance—need an understanding of their culture's approach to establishing pitch. They will tighten or loosen their instrument's main strings to certain expected pitches, then place fingers along them to produce other melodic pitches. Obviously, a vocalist in any tradition is responsible for control of pitch.

Naming Pitches

For communication about music and as an aid to memory, it is convenient to assign names to pitches. This has been done in various places around the world, using syllables, numbers, or letters.

Syllables. Syllables have been used to refer to pitches in the European system for a very long time: *do, re, mi, fa, sol, la,* and *ti* (or *si*), in ascending order. As the children in the classic Broadway musical *The Sound of Music* are given a singing lesson, the song "*Doe* a deer, a female deer," refers to these syllables, as in "*Ray*, a drop of golden sun; *me*, a name I call myself." In fact, this system (called **solfege**) is used for teaching music around the world. It has been widely adopted through West

Asia and the Middle East, where musicians are masters at singing and sight-reading in solfege.

In India as well, from ancient times, syllables have been assigned to seven pitches in ascending order: *sa, ri* or *re, ga, ma, pa, dha*, and *ni*. Those pitches are called *sargam*. In some Indian vocal practices, singers might use those syllables as **vocables** (text syllables without linguistic meaning) as they improvise melody. The syllables are also useful for notating melody. George Ruckert provides notation for the main phrase of the instrumental composition that is performed in "Rāg Chandranandan" (Audio Example 1.1), a performance that is featured in **chapter 10**. "Translated," the pitches as notated are shown in Musical Example 1.1.

MUSICAL EXAMPLE 1.1 Mukhṛā with Transnotation.

Letters. In the European system, letters as well as syllables are used for naming pitches. Adopted from the Greeks, via the Romans, c. 500 CE, the letters in ascent are A, B, C, D, E, F, and G.

Numbers. Numbers are used in music in at least two different ways. One use is to indicate pitch (1 = *do* fixed to pitch C in the French system, 2 = *re*, etc.). The other use is technical, instructing musicians how to play a piece of music—where to place their fingers on a stringed instrument, for instance. This is the case with the notation system called **tablature**. Tablature is used to notate music

ACTIVITY 1.1

Listen to "Rāg Chandranandan" (Audio Example 1.1 from 0:27) to familiarize yourself with this melody—both its pitches and its rhythm. Follow the melody as it is notated in Musical Example 1.1. Listen enough times that you can sing the melody, using the *sargam* syllables as "text."

for the Chinese **guqin**, an ancient zither-type instrument (Figure 1.1; see chapter 6).

Figure 1.2 shows the tablature for the beginning of a piece for *guqin*, "Flowing Water." Chinese-language texts (musical and textual) are read starting at the right side of the page and following the characters in each column, from top to bottom. In Figure 1.2, the title of the piece, "Flowing Water," is written at the top of the far right column, and the label for section one is given in the next column toward the left. The musical notation begins at the top of the third column, toward the middle of the page. Basically, the notation specifies left- and right-hand playing techniques and the strings on which they are to be executed.

Perhaps most importantly you should think about what this notation does and does not tell you. Each time the notation is used, the player renders it according to his own **dapu**, a process of realizing or interpreting the notation in sound.

Melody (Pitches in Succession)

Pitches placed in succession create a melody. To appreciate melody, we need to understand how pitches relate to each other—namely, the distance between pitches. The English-language term for that distance is "**interval**." Intervals are more important in European music than in any other in the world because they emphasize harmonic relationships (the sounding of simultaneous pitches). Before considering harmony in chapter 2, we need to explore how intervals function in melody.

Intervals

Intervals are so important in European music theory that they are given names. Two factors are involved in their naming.

One factor is *quantitative*: the number of pitches that the interval spans. Figure 1.6 shows a keyboard with the white keys labelled A, B, C, D, E, F, and G. Ascending from A to B involves two pitch letters; the interval from A to B is thus called a *second*. Going up from A to C spans across A, B,

FIGURE 1.1 Seven-stringed plucked long zither *guqin*. The prefix "gu" literally means "old" or "ancient" and is used to imply that the instrument has a long history. The thirteen white studs on the fingerboard are harmonic points that also function as guides for the right-hand finger. Stud 1 is on the far right, and stud 13 on the far left.

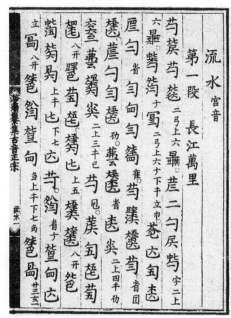

FIGURE 1.2 Tablature notation of "Flowing Water" for Chinese long zither *guqin*.

ACTIVITY 1.2

Locate the string numbers in the characters in Figure 1.2. Figure 1.3 shows the Chinese numbers used to indicate the strings of the instrument. Copy those numbers to give yourself a visual sense of them.

In Figure 1.2, count to column 5 from right to left. To get you started, here are the string numbers in the first five characters of column 5, from the top down: 3 & 4, 2, 3, 4, 3. Now try to identify those string numbers in the large characters for the whole of column 3 from the right, that is, from the beginning of the piece. (Small characters written to the right in a column refer to an action to be taken after the main pitches have been played, such as downward pressing of a string to raise the pitch).

As you can see, the numbers are embedded within the character, surrounded by indications of playing techniques. Using Figures 1.4 and 1.5 as a guide for these in column 3, you can see how the player is instructed to play each pitch.

Once you understand this notation, try copying the first column of melody to experience the flow of it.

At the beginning of the piece (column 3 from the right in Figure 1.2), these right-hand techniques are required.	
勺	Middle finger pulls the string.
ﾌ	Thumb pulls string with nail.
乇	Thumb pushes the string and comes to rest against the next string without sounding it
早	"Chord" from two simultaneous techniques
厂	Index finger pushes string with tip of fingernail, twice in succession.

≡ **FIGURE 1.4** Right-hand techniques on the Chinese long zither *guqin*.

Numbers indicate the string(s) on which the technique is executed.	
一	1
二	2
三	3
四	4
五	5
六	6

≡ **FIGURE 1.3** Chinese numbers.

勺	Middle finger pulls string 1.
戾	Thumb pulls string 6 with nails.
毯	Thumb pushes string 6.

≡ **FIGURE 1.5** Left-hand techniques on the *guqin* combined in notation with string numbers.

and C (i.e., three pitch letters), so the interval is called a *third*, and so forth. The interval from one pitch to another pitch with the same letter name spans eight pitch letters and is thus called an octave (*octo-*, "eight"), as in A to the next higher (or lower) A.

≡ **FIGURE 1.6** Keyboard with white keys named.

The second factor involved in the naming of intervals in the European system is *qualitative*. Intervals can have different sizes: minor and major seconds, for example. Return to Figure 1.6 to the keyboard with its white and black keys. Between any two adjacent keys there is a distance measured as a **half step**. Between F and the black key between F and G, there is a half step (a minor second); and between that black key and G, a half step. Between F and G, therefore, the distance adds up to a **whole step** (a major second). A half step equals a minor second; a whole step equals a major second. Figure 1.7 charts the intervals in one octave, with the number of half-steps within each. The octave is subdivided into twelve half steps.

Some pitches may have two different names. What is the pitch called that is a half-step up from F? Answer: F sharp, notated F#. What is the pitch called that is a half-step down from G? Answer: G flat, notated Gb. F# and Gb are at the same pitch frequency but named according to the pitch above or below in the succession of F G A B C, and so forth.

Some musical systems use **microtones**, intervals that do not match those of the European system of whole steps and half steps. For example, microtones are a feature of Arab music, which is based on a theoretical scale of twenty-four pitches per octave (see Chapter 12). The system includes all the twelve pitches per octave that coincide with those of Western music, but it adds an additional twelve pitches per octave by subdividing the intervals into quarter steps. This creates "half-flat" intervals—a half-flat second, half-flat third, and the like—and likewise "half-sharp" intervals. No musician would ever play the twenty-four pitches in succession; rather, the system just supplies a greater variety of possible pitches from which seven are selected on which to base a melody. You can hear a half-flat third and a half-flat seventh in a recording of an Islamic "Call to Prayer" (Audio Example 1.2).

Scales

Theorists and practitioners in a number of musical systems think about melodic material in terms of **pitch sets**—groups of pitches. One clear way to articulate a set of pitches is to present them as a **scale**, in straight ascending or descending order. When one hears a scale, the focus can be on the pitches or on the intervals formed by the distances between the pitches. The European system focuses largely on the intervals.

The most prominent scale type in the European system is **diatonic**: seven pitches with distinctive distribution of whole and half

# of half steps	Interval name
0	Unison
1	Minor 2nd
2	Major 2nd
3	Minor 3rd
4	Major 3rd
5	Perfect 4th
6	Tritone
7	Perfect 5th
8	Minor 6th
9	Major 6th
10	Minor 7th
11	Major 7th
12	Perfect Octave

≡ **FIGURE 1.7** Intervals in the European System.

steps. The two most prominent diatonic scales are the **major scale** and **natural minor scale**. Those two are distinguished by the distribution of whole and half steps:

Major scale:

W W H W W W H

Natural minor scale:

W H W W H W W

If you have grown up where Europe-derived music is all around you, and you are asked to sing seven pitches straight up and down, you will probably automatically sing a major scale. Call the pitches "do-re-mi-fa-sol-la-ti/si-do" and you will have replicated the starting pitches of each phrase of "Doe a deer, a female deer; ray, a drop of golden sun" and further.

Pitches of a minor scale are the basis for the Cuban **son** "*La Negra Tomasa*" (Audio Example 1.3).

The scale produced from the pitch selection for Spanish *flamenco* music, however, features an interval larger than a whole step: namely, an **augmented second** (aug2) that consists of three half steps. The intervals of that seven-pitch scale are H W/aug2 W/H W H W W. In a melody, the third degree of the scale can be either a half or whole step from the second degree (see Figure 1.8). Among *flamenco* musicians, this scale is referred to as the "**Andalusian mode**" (see chapter 15).

Melodic Mode

If any pitch in a pitch set is considered more important than others—being given some functional role in a melody such as "this is the pitch the melody should end on" or "this is the pitch that the melody should keep coming back to"—then you are dealing with a **melodic mode** rather than scale. In Myanmar, for example, music for the treasured arched harp (*saung*) is based on five primary notes and two secondary ones. A particular melodic mode is determined by assigning one pitch to be the **tonal center**; the other pitches are determined in relation to this center (see chapter 8).

Tonic is the term in the European system of music that is given to the tonal center—the most important pitch—in a set. Hierarchy among pitches of a set is so important in the European system that three other pitches are designated as more important functionally than the rest. The important pitch that is five pitches up from the tonic is called the **dominant** (the second most important pitch). The pitch located four pitches up from the tonic is the **subdominant** (third most important; see chapter 2).

Some—but not all—ethnomusicologists find the term "tonal center" more useful than "tonic" when speaking of the fundamental pitch in a number of other systems, including that of music for the Burmese arched harp.

Degrees	1		2		3		4	5		6		7
Intervals		H		aug2 or W		H or W		W		H		W	W

≡ **FIGURE 1.8** The Andalusian Mode.

Melodic mode, then, encompasses three characteristics:

1. A selected pitch set
2. Pitch function assigned to certain pitch(es)
3. Usually (but not always) hierarchy among the pitches

In some melodic systems, however, a melodic mode can have other meanings. It can suggest extramusical ideas as well, such as a mood or an association with time of day or season, and musical characteristics such as a distinctive melodic motive. Some examples include *rāga* of North India (see chapter 10), *makam* of Turkey (see chapter 11), and *maqam* of Egypt (see chapter 12). Audio Example 1.5 illustrates the Turkish *makam* Hijaz, with its six basic pitches of A Bb C# D E G and the tonal center on A (see chapter 11).

Rhythm (Managing Time in Music)

The general term used to describe the way people manage time in music is **rhythm**. Two common definitions of rhythm are "the systematic arrangement of musical sounds, principally according to duration"; and "a strong, regular, repeated pattern of movement or sound." While rhythm has to do with durations of musical sounds, these definitions are too restrictive when considering the management of time in music globally. Not all ways of managing time are systematically organized or based on regularized repetition of patterns. We briefly explore some examples here that you will study further later in the text.

Free Rhythm

As the term implies, **free rhythm** describes music with little or no sense of predictability about the organization of time. Free rhythm in world musical traditions can serve two purposes:

1. To express meaning and emotion.
2. To set apart a section of a composition to introduce melodic elements.

ACTIVITY 1.3

Listen to *"Saung Gauk"* (Audio Example 1.4). Do your best to distinguish the seven pitches in the set, and try to determine which pitches are primary and which are secondary. Further, try to identify which pitch is the tonal center in the melodic mode this piece is based on. Sing it softly as you listen, and notice how often the tonal center appears.

In the Irish tradition, solo and unaccompanied singers of **sean-nós** songs use free rhythm to express the meaning and emotion of a song text; this can be heard in "*Úirchill a' Chreagáin*" ("Creggan Graveyard"; Audio Example 1.6).

In Indian classical music, an improvised, unaccompanied prelude in free rhythm will begin a vocal or instrumental performance. The length of that prelude (*ālāp*)—the purpose of which is to focus solely on melody—will vary from under a minute to fifteen or twenty minutes, depending on the performance context and genre. In "Rāg Chandranandan," the prelude is only 26 seconds long (listen again to Audio Example 1.1).

Purposeful Organization of Time

Most music, however, is purposefully organized in terms of time. At the most basic level, music is organized in terms of **pulse (or beat)**. Beyond that, ways to manage time are amazingly diverse in practices around the globe.

Pulse/Beat. The two terms "**pulse**" and "**beat**" are interchangeable for most music. They refer to the consistent, equal-length durations of time such as we hear in the ticking of an analogue clock or see in the passage of time on a digital one. In Audio Example 1.7 of percussion parts similar to those heard in the Brazilian samba "*Se Foi Bom Pra Você*," (Audio Example 18.2), the rhythmic layer of the *surdo*, a large double-headed bass drum, is keeping a steady beat.

The term "beat," however, does not equate to "pulse" in every musical practice. The term "beat" has multiple meanings in Native American powwow music (see chapter 20). "Ruffle beat" indicates that each member of the drum group strikes the instrument, although not necessarily at precisely the same moment, to create a rumbling effect, while "straight beats" indicate a regular pulse 1/2/1/2/1/2, with the second beat somewhat accented. In Turkish folk music, a beat might be a short beat or a long beat, differing in duration (see chapter 11).

Distinctive Rhythm Patterns. Accenting (or **stressing**) a beat in some way—placing a louder percussive stroke on or somewhere between beats, for instance—is an important way to create distinctive rhythm. This can be heard in Audio Example 1.7—a repetitive rhythmic pattern with accents played on the *surdo* and *pandeiro* (see Figure 1.9). The **pandeiro** is a tambourine with metal jingles in the frame; its pattern appears to be steady sixteenth notes (subdivision of one beat into four equal units), but accents on certain of them create a distinctive rhythmic pattern. A capital letter X indicates an accented stroke.

By sounding the instrument at irregular moments, a third distinctive rhythm pattern produced by the *samba de morro* ensemble is contributed simultaneously by the players of the *tamborim* (a small tambourine without metal jingles in the frame) or *cuíca* (friction drum with a stick through

Beats	1	2		1	2	
Surdo	x	X		x	X	
Pandeiro	X x x X X x x X			X x x X X x x X		

≡ **FIGURE 1.9** Rhythm pattern played by the *surdo* and *pandeiro* in Audio Example 1.7.

ACTIVITY 1.4

Listen several times to Audio Example 1.7. Because there are four percussion instruments, you need to listen carefully to hear the steady 1-2-1-2 pulse being played on the lowest-sounding of the four instruments, the *surdo*. Listen until you can easily feel the basic beat.

the head). It too is repeated through the selection. Because the sounds of those ensemble percussion instruments are distinctive, the three rhythms can be heard by someone with a practiced ear (see Figure 1.10).

The rhythm patterns of the *pandeiro* and *tamborim* are called **syncopated**. That means that stress comes between the beats (termed "**offbeat**").

As if this organization of time were not enough, yet another rhythmic layer is added to this texture: that of the singer whose vocal line floats above the rhythm instruments, following the speech accents of the lyrics.

Polyrhythm. The multiple layers of rhythms that we have described in the *samba de morro* ensemble is an example of **polyrhythm**, a musical texture of multiple rhythmic patterns performed simultaneously. It is characteristic of a good deal of music in the African diaspora, including African American, Afro-Cuban, Afro-Brazilian, and other African-influenced Latin American practices—and of other musical practices as well.

Meter

A regular recurring grouping of beats such as the two-beat units of Audio Example 1.7 is termed **meter**. Globally, meters come in many sorts of lengths and configurations. Some, but not all, are distinguished by a recurring pattern of stresses or accents.

Duple and Triple Meters. Quantitatively, the simplest meters have two or three beats/counts; the former is called "**duple**," the latter is called "**triple**." Each unit of two or three counts constitutes a **measure** or **bar**—terminology from Western music notation that puts vertical bars (measure bars) between the units of time in a meter.

Meters with multiples of two counts are also considered to be duple meters: units of four counts, for instance. It is common for a four-count unit to feel like it comprises two sub-units (2 + 2), owing to stress being put on count 3 in addition to the expected strong stress placed on count 1 (called the

Beats		1	2		1	2	
Surdo		x	X		x	X	
Pandeiro		X x x X X x x X		X x x X X x x X	
Tamborim		x x x x		x x x x	
Cuíca		X x x		x X x x	

≡ **FIGURE 1.10** Additional rhythm pattern played by the *tamborim/cuíca* in Audio Example 1.7.

downbeat). Duple subdivisions of the beats is assumed, as in the rhythm patterns in the Brazilian *samba de morro*. The great majority of popular dance musics—*rhumba*, techno, and house, for example—are in duple meter. The waltz, however, is in triple meter.

Compound Meter. The jig of traditional Irish dance offers an example of another kind of meter in the Western cultural sphere. Called **compound meter**, it consists of recurring groupings of beats, but with each beat consisting of a subgroup of three pulses with equal duration. An easy way to feel this is by saying "*ra*-shers-and *sau*-sa-ges," with equal duration of each syllable and accents on "ra" and "sau." This is 6/8 meter; it can be heard on "Garrett Barry's Jig" (Audio Example 1.8).

Asymmetrical Meter. An **asymmetrical meter** has subdivisions that are not all the same length; a typical example has subdivisions that vary between two and three beats. Asymmetrical beat structures are especially important in the metric system of Turkey, called *usul*; they often match dances where there is a sequence of steps that bring the dancer on and off balance. Each asymmetrical beat structure has a name. *Devr-i hindi* is the name of the particular structure used in the Turkish language folksong "*Bu Dünya Bir Pencere*" (Audio Example 1.5). The beat structure is broken down into 2+2+3, although it is easier to think of it as having three beats, two short followed by one long. To tap the pattern for *Devr-i hind*, on your thighs: you'd tap left-right-right to correspond to the short-short-long subdivisions. Singers performing this repertoire often wave their hands in time with the structure. Musical meter in Turkey is very much connected to the body, whether the steps of the dancers or the hands of the singer or the audience.

Metric Cycles. In musical practice, when a metrical unit is systematically brought to an end on the next count 1, those meters are considered to be metric cycles. Many group a larger number of beats, as in the case of North Indian classical music. In North Indian classical music, many of the meters (called *tāla*) group a relatively larger number of beats (see chapter 10). The favorite *tāla*, **Tīntāl**, has a

ACTIVITY 1.5

Listen again to Audio Example 1.7. With colleagues, try to produce the *samba de morro* polyrhythm with three groups clapping the three rhythms. It is best to start with everyone together learning to tap out each one of the rhythms. It will take a good bit of practice to put them all together. Continue to try to create this polyrhythm with the recording, then without the recording to slow it down or tighten it up, and then with the recording again.

recurring cycle of sixteen beats, with four subdivisions of four beats each (therefore a duple rhythm): 4 + 4 + 4 + 4. Because musical tradition dictates that musical units end on the next count 1, *tālas* are considered to be cyclical groupings. Like North Indian classical music, most (but not all) types of Spanish *flamenco* music are organized in meter (called **compás**) that is performed cyclically There are a number of *flamenco* metric cycles, each characterized by total counts in the cycle and a specific distribution of accents that are emphasized through rhythmic, melodic, and harmonic changes (see chapter 15).

Tempo

The term "**tempo**" comes from the Italian term for "speed," and so describes the pace of the music. Some music is faster or slower than others, determined by a composer or a performer, or perhaps by how the music is used, such as for dancing or working. Once a tempo is established, it might change in the course of a selection by **acceleration** (speeding up) or **deceleration** (slowing down) or possibly fluctuation (**rubato**). In the case of the *samba* rhythm demonstrated in Audio Example 1.7, the speed is set by the need to coordinate musicians and dancers. Once set, it is the musical role of the player(s) of the *surdo* drum to keep the tempo steady.

ACTIVITY 1.6

Study the notation of the basic melody of the folksong "*Bu Dünya Bir Pencere*" (Musical Example 1.2). It might help you get the "limping" feel of this metric structure. Better yet, ask colleagues who can read the notation to sing the melody on some vocable while you do the tapping motions. "Limp" the feeling in your feet, stepping the "short-short-long" in place and around the room. Try to avoid actually counting out the seven-beat structure.

MUSICAL EXAMPLE 1.2 "*Bu Dünya Bir Pencere*" melody notation.

2

Harmony (Simultaneous Pitches), Texture (How Musical Parts Fit Together), and Form (The Structure of a Piece)

Chapter Contents

Introduction

Now that we've explored melody and rhythm, we'll discuss three other important terms that will help us better understand the musics of the world. All of these terms have different meanings in different cultures, although they are all derived from

≡ **ZO gospel choir performing at the open air theater in Vondelpark, Amsterdam.**

Western musical theory. We'll discuss *harmony* (the simultaneous sounding of two or more pitches), *texture* (the quality of sound created by the relationships among the musical parts), and *form* (how a musical work is structured).

Harmony (Tonal System)

When multiple pitches are heard simultaneously, their relationship can be called "harmonic." To encompass all the musical practices around the world, the term "harmony" needs to be understood broadly.

The idea of a **harmonic system** that emphasizes the relationships between chords (see below) gradually emerged in European musical practices from the Renaissance period. That **tonal system** has gradually come to be used in European-influenced cultural spheres to the point where it is now a shared musical "language" in locations on five of the seven continents and on many islands around the planet.

However, other senses of harmony can be found in different cultures. We will explore these various approaches to harmony through examples that we study in more detail later in this text.

Naming Simultaneous Pitch Relations

Multiple people singing or playing the *same* part simultaneously are said in European musical terminology to be "in unison"; thus, this is called a **unison** harmony. This musical practice occurs quite frequently among the Chuuk peoples of the South Pacific islands, where singers highly value this precise unison singing as a socio-aesthetic value (see chapter 5). Likewise, in singing Theravada Buddhist texts in Burmese tradition, all participants follow the identical text, melody, and rhythm with no individual or distinct music (Audio Example 2.1). As with the Buddhist philosophy behind the chant, the self (the individual voice) is regarded not as an individual but simply as part of the whole, a part of something greater (chapter 8).

Relationships between simultaneously sounded *different* pitches are named by the distance between the pitches. You already know these terms: seconds, thirds, and so forth (see chapter 1). Intervals larger than an octave are called ninths (i.e., an octave plus a second), tenths, elevenths, and so forth.

Chords

Intervals stacked vertically (or, produced simultaneously) in the European tonal music system are usually understood to form **chords**. Recalling the naming of the diatonic pitches of 1 to 7 (see chapter 1), a chord built on pitch 1 is a **tonic chord** (written in Roman numerals, I); likewise, a chord built on pitch 5 is a **dominant chord** (V); a chord built on pitch 4 is a **subdominant chord** (IV); and so forth. The use of those chords is called **functional harmony**. Not surprisingly, these chords constitute a hierarchy in the music that is the same as the pitch hierarchy discussed in chapter 1: the tonic chord is all-important; the dominant chord and subdominant chords are next in importance.

Chords in the tonal system consist of three or more pitches. The most basic type is a **triad**, so called because it consists of three pitches: the upper two of which are a "vertically" stacked third and a fifth, respectively, above the bottom pitch (or "**root**" of the chord). If the interval formed by the bottom pitch and the pitch a third above it is a major third, the chord is a **major chord**. If the interval formed by the bottom pitch and the third above it is a minor third, that is a **minor chord**. A major tonic chord is indicated in writing as "I," but a minor tonic chord is indicated in writing as "i." Whether major or minor, the tonic chord is particularly significant at ending moments (**cadences**) in a piece of music—at the end of a section perhaps, but certainly the end of a whole piece.

Chord Progressions

A sequence of chords is called a **chord progression**. In much tonal music, common practice guides which chord is likely to follow a given chord. The subdominant chord (IV) is likely to be followed by the dominant chord (V) or the tonic chord (I or i), for instance; the dominant chord (V) is likely to lead to the tonic chord (I or i). Chord progressions of countless songs use just two or three of those chords.

In its most basic form, African American blues uses a I, IV, and V chord progression. In most songs, this **blues progression** repeats in every verse, providing

ACTIVITY 2.1

Working with at least two colleagues, count together as you sing up from pitch 1 to 5 (place pitch 1 anywhere that is comfortable for all of you). Then, saying the numbers, together sing just 1, 3, and 5 (leaving out 2 and 4). Sing 1-3-5-3-1 (ascent and descent) until it feels easy. Then split up the pitches among you so that someone is singing each of them. When you sing them simultaneously, you are producing a triad. Build more triads, stacking third and fifth pitches above several different root pitches.

a stable underpinning for the flexible parts that are built on it. Stripped to its simplest and earliest form, the blues progression is

I   I   I   I
IV   I   I   I
V   V   I   I(V)

This progression is common to blues musicians such as B. B. King, Robert Johnson, Bessie Smith, Muddy Waters, and Keb' Mo'. These blues-flavored chords can also be heard in the work of more recent popular musicians, including Eric Clapton, Ben Harper, Led Zeppelin, Bonnie Raitt, the Rolling Stones, Stevie Ray Vaughn, and ZZ Top.

Other cultures also use basic chord progressions as a means of building their vocal music. The Cuban *son* genre uses the same blues progression of I-IV-V chords, against which a lead singer might improvise brief phrases or perhaps insert a longer couplet or quatrain before the group repeats the chorus (see chapter 17).

Key

Determining the **key** of a piece of music involves identifying its tonic pitch (1, I) in terms of acoustics—that rate of vibration (cycles per second, or **Hertz**) of a string, column of air, or other sound-producing body—that produces a pitch in the standardized **pitch frequency** system of A, B, C, D, E, F, G (where A = 440 **Hertz**). If the tonic pitch is located on C, the music is in the key of C: C major or minor. The composer of a piece of tonal music will specify the key in which the piece is intended to be performed.

In many, many ensemble practices, members of the group will negotiate the key in which they will play a selection, no matter what key might have been originally designated. That can happen if a singer in the ensemble is more comfortable singing in a lower pitch range—in the key of A rather than C, for example. All members of the ensemble must be sufficiently skilled to instantly play the piece in a different key if needed—a process called **transposition**. Musicians who have the knowledge of tonal harmony that this requires and are sufficiently skilled on their instrument are highly regarded in the Mexican American *mariachi* tradition, among many others (see chapter 19).

Harmony in World Fusion Music

Some chords are described as "harmonically ambiguous." They often consist of just the 1 and 5 pitches, without the defining third that would indicate whether a chord was a major or minor one. There are other harmonically unstable chords that can be formed (e.g., using three pitch classes, as in 1-flat 2-4). Using these chords is an imaginative means by which musicians can refer to the European system of functional harmony without following its expectations. "*Bu Dünya Bir Pencere (Marsis)*," a studio arrangement of a Turkish-language folk song, is one example (see chapter 11). In Audio Example 2.2 at 0:16 and 0:30, harmonically ambiguous chords are **arpeggiated** (their pitches played successively rather than together) and can also be used as "**power chords**." The term "power chords" is derived from heavy metal rock music. Here it refers to the overtracking of multiple instruments playing the same chords simultaneously to produce a "powerful," oversaturated sound. In this Turkish example, these chords are not used with any implication of a typical tonal harmonic progression such as I-IV-V.

Tone Clusters

The music of some cultures features sets of simultaneously sounded pitches that, unlike Audio Example 2.2 from Turkey, make absolutely no reference to the tonal harmonic system. They are referred to as **tone clusters**. Traditional Japanese court music (*gagaku*) played on a wind instrument (an aerophone) called the *shō* (see chapter 7; Video 7.1) is one prominent example. In the *shō* part, the bottom pitch of a cluster of pitches that are sounded together and an occasional single pitch in the musical part correspond to melodic pitches played on other instruments in the ensemble. The effect of the cluster is that of a complex chord played on an organ, sustained for several counts, which gradually changes to another cluster. The *shō*'s part is important to the sound of the ensemble; without it, the texture becomes very sparse.

Texture

As used in Ethnomusicology, the term "**texture**" refers to the relationships among multiple parts whether in performance practice or in a piece of composed music. There are many possibilities, spanning from precise unison to seeming chaos. Another way to think of it is music with no harmonic dimension at one end of a continuum to music in which the harmonic dimension is paramount at the other end. When one considers musics outside of the European or Europe-influenced systems, the number of possibilities for relationships among musical parts explodes, causing many ethnomusicologists to avoid analyzing music in terms of texture altogether. We will explore several of these possibilities, beginning with music with no harmonic dimension.

Performing One Melody

Monophony. Melody only—without any other musical part—whether performed as a solo by one person or by multiple people in unison is termed **monophony.** Here are three examples that you should review: "Monks singing *sutras*" of Theravada Buddhist texts in Burmese tradition (Audio Example 2.1), Irish traditional *sean-nós* ("old style") songs in free rhythm (Audio Example 2.3), and the melodic Islamic Call to Prayer that is issued from mosques five times every day (Audio Example 2.4). There are many other examples of monophonic performance in this textbook. Both solo and group monophony are illustrated by the Native American powwow song "Straight Intertribal" that begins with one singer alone who is followed quickly by a group of singers performing in unison (Audio Example 2.5).

Heterophony. When multiple musical parts of one melody are performed in slightly different versions simultaneously, the texture is called **heterophony.** This is found frequently in traditional East Asian musics. The Chinese piece "*Zhonghua liuban*" is one example performed by a **Jiangnan sizhu** instrumental ensemble (Figure 2.1). Although the musicians in Audio Example 2.6 follow the same melody, each individual produces creative variations of the tune, making the music organic and eliminating monotony. The melody can be transformed by elaborating or simplifying the basic skeleton melody—by adding ornaments, trills, and short melodic embellishments, for example, while maintaining the structure of the piece. A musician's competence and skills are measured by the ability to improvise in response to the playing of the other musicians and the overall musical context.

Heterophony in Balinese **gamelan** music is created in a different way: The whole melody is not in any one part but performed as the sum of the parts. The density of the part played by any one instrumental section of the *gamelan* (ensemble) is stratified: Musicians on the smaller, higher-pitched instruments play rapid figurations that embellish the slower moving skeletal melody played on the larger, lower-register instruments (Figure 2.2).

The rapid figurations in "*Gangsa kotekan norot*" from the final section of the **gamelan gong kebyar** composition "*Jaya Semara*" demonstrate another

≣ **FIGURE 2.1** Jiangnan sizhu "silk and bamboo" ensemble associated with the Jiangnan region of China in the proximity of Shanghai. Instruments from left to right clockwise are *pipa, yangqin, erhu, dizi, sheng, bangu* and clapper, *erhu, erhu,* and *qinqin*; 2006.

possibility for performing a single melody communally (Audio Example 2.7). Here, the pitches of a very fast figuration are distributed among the musicians—in this case, between two groups of musicians who are playing the smaller higher-pitched instruments in the ensemble. In order to produce the complete elaborating figuration, these parts must be coordinated in interlocking fashion; this is called **kotekan**. Author Lisa Gold discusses this in greater detail in **chapter 9** on Balinese *gamelan* music.

Performing One Melody with Some Other Pitched Part(s)

Much of classical North Indian vocal music is also heterophonic, featuring a soloist and another melody producing instrument that "shadows" the soloist. This second instrument is played by a musician whose role is to follow even improvised

ACTIVITY 2.2

Listen to Audio Example 2.7 *"Gangsa kotekan norot."* This demonstration excerpt begins with a lower-pitched instrument playing a four-pulse skeletal melody as a reference, while a time-keeping gong keeps the beat. Then the playing of two higher-pitched instruments begins—first one, then the other—with different parts. The two parts are then put together for the composite, complete elaborating figuration.

melody closely, or to improvise or repeat something just heard in order to give the soloist a short break after a cadence. This "shadowing" role provides another example of the musical texture of heterophony. But, as you can hear in *"Tarānā"* (Audio Example 2.8), another instrument is added to the ensemble for the express purpose of sounding a recurring pitch *Sa* (and usually one other pitch appropriate for the melodic mode)—a **drone** to ground the melody. Some North Indian instruments like the long-necked plucked lutes ***sitār*** and ***sarod*** incorporate drone strings in their construction so that the drone is always present.

Multiple Melodies (Polyphony)

Polyphony is created by simultaneously combining multiple relatively independent melodies. Polyphony need not be performed by multiple musicians. In Burmese music for both the arched harp (***saung***) and ***patt waing*** 21-drum set, one musician performs two melodies simultaneously. On the harp, melody is played by plucking with the first finger of the right hand while a secondary melodic line is played with the thumb (Audio Example 2.9). The player of the *patt waing* 21-drum set sits in the middle of a circle formed by the instruments, usually articulating a primary melody with the right hand while the left plays a supporting melody (Audio Example 2.10).

Melody and Chords (Homophony)

When the texture is one of melody accompanied with chords, or primarily chords created by all the musical parts, it is called **homophony** (literally, "same voice"). This is the primary texture found in European classical and popular music. Homophony is likely the most widespread texture in music making, due to centuries of European colonizing around the world, which was then reinforced through the spread of Western popular music.

One example of a piece with homophonic texture in world music is the twentieth-century Japanese *"Haru no Umi"* composed by ***koto***-ist Michio Miyagi as a duo for the traditional zither-type instrument on which he performed and the vertical flute ***shakuhachi*** (Video 2.1). *"Haru no Umi"* ("The Ocean in Spring") is often performed by duos of European instruments such as guitar and flute or piano and violin. The chords of the homophonic texture are mostly broken up—the pitches played in succession either ascending or descending (**arpeggiated**)—but the texture is homophonic nevertheless.

The dissemination of European harmonic practices through the process of Christian missionization was directly responsible for the adoption of harmony among the Pacific islanders of Chuuk. Chuukese especially value both sacred and secular group songs in which they freely add multiple vocal parts to create

ACTIVITY 2.3

Create a playlist of some of your favorite music. Take some time to find a few selections that are homophonic. To check your analysis, read the definition of homophony here to a couple of friends and listen to a couple of your selections together. Do they agree?

a chordal texture. A single vocalist may begin singing but then will be joined by others who freely add harmonic parts based on taste or experience. The choral homophonic texture created by finely integrated harmonies can be heard in a secular welcoming song *"Áách Kapwongen Etiwa Áámi"* (Audio Example 2.11). The homophonic texture is emphasized by the synchronized movement of the voices and by the rhythmic drive of the amplified electronic synthesizers that are ubiquitous instruments in Chuukese popular song. (See chapter 5.)

A quintessential example of homophony in popular music is "The Click Song" performed by influential South African singer Miriam Makeba (Audio Example 2.12). Makeba recorded this song after leaving South Africa and moving to New York. It became a major hit, perhaps thanks to its combination of the exotic "clicking" sounds from the South African language of the lyrics with an easy to understand Western harmonic accompaniment (see chapter 14).

Form

Musical form refers to the overall structure or plan of a piece of music. However, for this term to be useful to describe the variety of musical styles heard around the world, the question must immediately be asked: What is "a piece of music"—or, as some would put it, "a musical work"?

What Is a Piece of Music?

In many musical practices "a piece of music" is considered to be a "finished item" that has been created by someone with the expectation that it will be reproduced by every music maker with no or little changes made to it. That is the idea about a good deal of notated music in the European classical tradition, for instance, despite the reality that, in performance, some flexibility is expected of the music maker(s)—variations in phrasing, speed, or dynamics, perhaps—which is regarded as "interpretation." Almost all Japanese musical practices—whether contemporary works by Japanese composers or traditional pieces that would have been transmitted carefully through generations, even orally—also adhere to this rule. In fact, even interpretation is avoided in performance practice of historical Japanese pieces such as *"Rokudan"* (Video 2.2).

From these examples, it should be clear that the idea about "the piece" is entangled with ideas about performance practice. Take the example of the Irish **jig**, a tune composed most often in two sections (A and B) of predetermined length that will be carefully transmitted within a community of music makers. However, the performer of a jig knows that the performance tradition not only permits but expects ornamentation to be added to that tune (Audio Examples 2.13 and 2.14, two versions of "Garrett Barry's Jig").

In Chuukese singing, the tune is known by all, but each person will learn by experience how to contribute to turning a tune into a rich chordal texture on the spot (Audio Example 2.11). The Chinese *Jiangnan sizhu* practice expects that everyone will know the tunes in the genre's repertoire but will play them in individual ways to create a spontaneous, heterophonic, ensemble texture (Audio Example 2.6).

As you can see, "a piece" might be "finished," but—even if it is notated—the amount and the nature of the flexibility that is exercised in its performance varies widely from practice to practice. In light of this, ethnomusicologists are likely to extend the idea of musical form to encompass the plan for performance of "a piece" as well as "the piece itself."

ACTIVITY 2.4

Pretend you are a composer. That is to say, you intend to create a "piece" of music. What do you need to think about? Is this just for you to sing or play or do you need to consider what multiple music makers might contribute? What length do you want the piece to be? Do you want to model your piece after some existing piece, and if so, what is the plan of that piece? Further, what might your plan be for the performance of your piece? That might influence the length it needs to be, or the number of performers and other considerations.

Make a list of such factors as these that you need to think about, and begin to make a plan for your own piece.

The Structure of a Finished Work

There are many different ways to create a "finished" work of music. One can compose a piece through

- Creating new material from beginning to end; the Western music term for this is **through-composed**.
- Breaking the piece into sections; one example of a way to do this results in "call-and-response" form.
- Following the structure of its text; the chanting of Theravada Buddhist monks is broken into sections based on the stanzas of its text. The singers dramatically stretch out the last line of text, then pause for a moment before the clap of a punctuating instrument resolves the phrase (Audio Example 2.1).
- Giving each member of an ensemble in turn a chance to solo.

Creating Sections in a Piece Balinese compositions often use contrasting sections as a musical structure. As author Lisa Gold explains in chapter 9, the classical three-movement form such as that in *"Sinom Ladrang"* (Audio Example 2.15) is likened to the human body: its opening section is considered to be the head; its middle section, the torso or "main body"; and the final section, the feet. A progression in mood and pacing are based on these divisions:

- The head is short, with themes clearly presented, and a regular pulse, beginning fast and slowing down to settle into the tempo of the next movement.
- The main body has the longest metric cycle of the piece, permitting melodic and thematic development. Played in a slow, stately tempo, it always features an identifying fixed sequence of drum patterns.
- The feet have a shorter metric cycle, probably condensed melodic material from the main section, and fast tempo that accelerates to a climax before the piece ends.

Compositions such as *"Jaya Semara"* for the more recent Balinese *gamelan gong kebyar* (Audio Example 2.16) maintain this three-part form, but add to it another means for creating sections within a piece: namely, highlighting individual instrumental groupings within the large ensemble so that sections are formed by contrasts in the timbres and pitch registers of the instruments. Compositions come to a dramatic end with an explosive section in which all parts perform together in an asymmetrical, syncopated melody.

A special form of breaking a composition into parts is known as **call-and-response**. In this form, a leading vocalist or instrumentalist will perform a musical line, and then a group will "respond" to it. While we in American culture often automatically associate this musical structure with African American and other African diasporic musical practices, it occurs in many other practices as well. On the Pacific islands of Chuuk, exclamatory chants serve as a means to galvanize the men of the village for a difficult task at hand, such as moving canoes across the beach, carrying large bowls of pounded breadfruit, or lifting up heavy breadfruit logs. A group of men respond to the exclamatory chant of a leader, answering him with short punctuated phrases, often in rhythm with or repeating the last words of the leader.

Form in Performance

It is important to understand that none of these structural forms are followed exactly in most traditions. Performance practice allows for considerable variations on these basic structures, giving richness and variety to different musical expressions. Two examples from different cultures help illustrate how form might be modified in practice.

In traditional *flamenco* (see **chapter 15**), a composition (*cante*) consists of several verses (*coplas*) alternated with short guitar interludes (*falsetas/variaciones*). A flexible structure is shaped in the course of performance, however, where singers often improvise. A *cante* typically begins with a guitar introduction that establishes the metric cycle, tempo, tonality, and mood (Audio Example 2.17). The singer usually follows with a short vocal section in which the voice is warmed up and that singer sets the mood for the *copla* by improvising on syllables (vocables) like "*Ayayay*" (*ayeo*). The singer then structures the performance of the *coplas* in an open-ended manner—as she or he wishes. The accompanists perform solo *falsetas/variaciones* between verses, enhancing the vocalist's expression of intense emotions. Following the final *copla*, the guitarist closes with cadential patterns characteristic of each *cante* (song type).

ACTIVITY 2.5

By this time, you will have become quite familiar with several of the audio examples that you will hear again when studying these individual musical traditions. To review what you have learned about each of them musically, create a list of the examples that you have found in the text. Organize the list in any way you like—by culture of origin and selection title, for example. Add to your list each musical point that has been made about these examples in chapters 1 and 2. You are on your way to understanding commonalities and differences in music found in locations around the globe.

The structure of the urban Cuban *son*—or more specifically, the structure of a performance of the Cuban *son "La Negra Tomasa"* from the 1930s—is sectional (Audio Example 2.18). The two contrasting sections show the hybridity of the genre. The initial section—a **strophic song**/verse section known as the *tema, verso,* or *canto*—derives from European models; strophic song refers to a song tune that is repeated while the text changes. The second (and final) section, called *montuno*, consists of call-and-response vocals and many instruments repeating melodic riffs or rhythmic phrases. This structure and texture based on cycles lends itself to open-ended improvisation. As in much Afro-Latin repertoire, the *montuno* structure is derived ultimately from African models.

3

Understanding and Classifying Musical Instruments

Chapter Contents

Introduction

Around the world, people have created countless and varied musical instruments throughout time. They have ranged from a sound-making source from nature such as a leaf or a piece of wood—or the human voice or body—that is put to use without modification, or a more contrived object that has required creative thought and technological manipulation. When people design and craft instruments, they are producing items of **expressive culture**—that is, objects that are useful for the expression of cultural beliefs and values, for instance, or for some function such as signaling in warfare, or for entertainment or trade—as well as **material culture** (the object itself). Likely to be taken wherever people have gone, instruments also provide evidence of cultural diffusion in historical times and in current globalization. There being countless and varied instruments, it is inevitable that we compare and contrast them in terms of their construction, their expressive cultural meanings, and their functions.

☰ **Electric guitars at the Willie Nelson Museum in Nashville, Tennessee.**

Instruments as Physical Objects

Think first about instruments as physical objects—the way two instruments are constructed. Are the violin/fiddle and the acoustic guitar constructed alike? Yes, in some ways they are. Most basically, they both have strings; but further, they both consist basically of a body and a neck. How about a piano and the fiddle/guitar? At that same basic level of construction, the piano too has strings and a body, but no neck. Picture a basic drum kit. At the most basic level of construction, those drums are more or less like each other. But the cymbals? They are totally different (Figure 3.1).

To think about instruments as physical objects and particularly on a global scale, we ethnomusicologists make reference to them first in terms of basic types. Faced with new knowledge and specimens gathered from around the world in the period of world colonialization, nineteenth-century European scholars who wanted to organize a museum collection turned to a system that had been devised in ancient India for classifying instruments into four basic types. The criterion used for distinguishing the types was the primary medium for producing sound. In the twentieth century, two further types (five and six) were added to this most widely used system. Technical names were developed for these instruments using the Latin suffix "-phone" to indicate "sound."

Some instruments defy classification into this most basic categorization, of course, being of hybrid construction; for example, the electric guitar, which is both a chordophone and, with its characteristic amplification, an **electronophone**.

≡ **FIGURE 3.1** Image of basic drum kit.

ACTIVITY 3.1

To accustom yourself to thinking of instruments as physical objects by this system, flip through this book and make a list (making note of the page number) of the basic type of about twenty-five of the musical instruments that appear in graphics—to the extent that you can tell from the illustration. That is step 1, but you will quickly realize how basic that typology is and how much more detail you need to note about an instrument's construction to compare it with other instruments of the same type.

Primary medium for producing sound	Example	Name
1. The vibrating body of the instrument itself	The metal plate of a cymbal or gong	**Idiophone**
2. A vibrating membrane	The head of a drum	**Membranophone**
3. A vibrating string	A fiddle, guitar, or piano	**Chordophone**
4. A vibrating column of air	A trumpet or flute or voice	**Aerophone**
5. Electricity	An electronic organ or keyboard	**Electronophone**
6. The human body	Handclapping, body slap	**Corpophone**

Classifying Subtypes of Musical Instruments

Obviously, scholars needed to devise a system of subdivisions within the basic instrument types for the classifying to be helpful. Idiophones are subdivided into subgroups by the playing technique required—striking (Cuban *claves*, thick sticks of rosewood that are struck together) and plucking (Zimbabwe's *mbira*, or thumb piano, whose thin metal prongs are pressed and plucked), for instance. Membranophones are subdivided by shape: cylindrical, bowl, waisted/hourglass shaped, for instance. Chordophones are subgrouped by construction details, the most common of which around the world are (a) **lutes** (distinguished by the strings running along a body and a neck) and (b) **zithers** (without a neck, instead the strings running along almost the full length of the body). Two of the subdivisions of aerophones are **flutes** (on which a stream of air is directed against an edge of the instrument) and **reeds** (on which a piece of reed has been placed at the head of the instrument or inside).

ACTIVITY 3.2

Return to your list of instruments pictured in this book and to the graphics. Working from the previous paragraph, add to your list the identification of whatever subdivisions for idiophones, membranophones, and chordophones you can discern from the graphics. (This can be more difficult to tell from a photo of an aerophone.) You will be well on your way to thinking about instruments as physical objects.

Classifying Vocal Types

Classifying voice types has been of interest mostly in European-based practices. There, attention has been given in choral music to dividing parts based on the **range** (span) of pitches a singer is asked to produce (classified from high to low as soprano, alto, tenor, and bass). For soloists, **tessitura**—the most comfortable range for a given singer and that in which they present the best vocal quality—has been the subject of most attention. The expectation that a singer will probably expand a naturally comfortable range only slightly is a European, culture-specific idea about the use of the voice.

Equally culture specific is an expectation that a singer will systematically work to expand their range beyond the comfort zone. In North Indian classical music, the ideal is to sing in three **pitch registers** (areas within a pitch range, in this case high, middle, and low), displaying a range that is considerably wider than most people's "natural voice." The same can be said for Japanese traditional vocal practices, wherein a very wide range is expected, to the extent that it is sometimes impossible to discern if a female or male is singing.

Other Ways to View Musical Instruments as Physical Objects

Aesthetic Value. Another perspective on instruments as physical objects is to regard them as aesthetic items. Examples of this are a drum inlaid with mother-of-pearl, a harpsichord lid embellished with painted flowers and birds, an ornamental rosette of decorated wood around the sound hole of a guitar, and the wooden body of a grand piano gently undulating around a hidden sturdy steel frame.

Technology. Instruments have always been items of technology as well. It takes only the experience of trying to make one to appreciate the extent to which that is true. However, it took mass production and the burgeoning popularity of electronic instruments to make most of us think of them in technological terms. Is not "the technology" a member of the band? That leads to yet another perspective on instruments—as items of commodity, to be manufactured, marketed and sold. Worldwide distribution by the giant Japanese instrument manufacturers of Yamaha and Kawaii are cases in point.

Physical Characteristics. Instruments have their own idiomatic physical characteristics that greatly affect the music that can be made on them and also make demands on the players. One important factor determined by physical characteristics is the length of the decay once a sound has been initiated. On some instruments, the decay will be relatively rapid, and sustaining a sound means developing a specific performance technique or physical tool. The sound produced by a string will die away quickly, but it is possible to sustain a pitch on a bowed lute

ACTIVITY 3.3

With colleagues, prepare a short show-and-tell to demonstrate the length of decay on a range of instruments and techniques used to sustain a sound.

Or, with colleagues, prepare a short presentation on a variety of vocal qualities that are cultivated in places around the globe.

with repeated bowing across the string, and on a plucked lute or zither by repeated plucking or striking. On a wooden-keyed xylophone, repeated rapid striking of one key will sustain a sound. Singers work on their breath control, as do players of aerophones—particularly those instruments such as flutes and horns without a mechanism such as the bladder on a bagpipe for storing air. Conversely, the long decay of the sound of a bell or a gong or a key on a **metallophone** (percussion idiophone-type instrument with metal keys) must be coped with. One possibility is to assign a sparse musical role to those instruments in an ensemble in order to avoid a muddle of sound, while another possibility is to develop damping techniques.

Timbre. The last perspective on instruments as physical objects to be suggested here is that of **timbre**—the character or quality of sound produced by an instrument or voice, whether naturally or by intentional cultivation. Herein is one of the marvels of human imagination because there are so many different sounds preferred by so many different people, even on the same instrument type. What can and has been done with the human voice—a physiognomy that we all share—is a case in point. Just think of the different vocal qualities cultivated by a variety of your favorite singers, by punk artists as opposed to blues stylists, by opera singers in the European sphere as opposed to artists of Chinese opera, by Spanish singers of flamenco, by Native American powwow singers, by Siberian throat singers, by singers of bluegrass and old-time country music. The reasons *why* people prefer and cultivate such different sounds is of endless fascination to ethnomusicologists.

Instruments as Expressive Culture

As we have noted, when people design and craft instruments, they are producing items of expressive culture—that is, items that by meaningful association or function are useful for expressing their ideas, beliefs and values, and emotions in everyday life—meaningful association with spirituality, for instance, or useful for displaying one's economic status.

Extramusical Associations

Some instruments carry extramusical associations so clear and strong that the mere sound or sight of them will transmit shared meaning to anyone in a knowledgeable group. An example that comes quickly to mind is the very large bass drum that undergirds the beat in marching bands at US football game halftime intermission shows. The bass drum is the largest version of a widely distributed type of membranophone—a cylindrically shaped, double-headed "**frame drum**" whose heads are wider than the width of the frame that holds them.

Perhaps the most widely distributed of such drums was the Turkish *davul* (see Chapter 11) that was disseminated by the Janissary military bands of the Ottoman Sultans whose transcontinental empire spanned the "Eastern and Western worlds" from 1453 to 1922. Transportable, played vertically with its deep and percussive sound, it was an instrument of war (Figure 3.2) and was recognized as such by Europeans such as the composers of early orchestral music when they incorporated it into the ensemble to specifically reference Ottoman Janissary, and therefore warlike, connotations. Although the bass drum in the marching band is no longer literally martial, the presence of it and the whole marching band phenomenon are

FIGURE 3.2 *Davul* drum from Turkey. This type of drum was disseminated through the world by the Janissary military bands during the Ottoman Empire.

associated with competitive events. That type of drum used in concert bands, orchestras, and also in a drum kit now have also (arguably) lost that initial martial association.

A bass drum of similar construction is played entirely differently by Native Americans in the context of a powwow and with significant, different meaning. Placed in the center of the powwow space with wide membrane up, its large size permits multiple men (usually) to sit around it so that all can play, and "a drum" becomes "the **powwow drum**" (see chapter 20). The drum is rich in symbolism and "sounds" the relationships between human beings and the world around them, reminding powwow participants that we—human beings—do not live in control of or apart from but very much in relation to and as part of the world.

Social/Cultural Status

Social class associations with particular instruments can be quite strong, with matching cultural status. In Japan, the piano holds a high cultural status (see chapter 7). When European music was being adopted in Japan in the nineteenth and early twentieth centuries, the piano was a rare item; only relatively wealthy persons could afford one or had the appropriate space in which to house one. By the time instruments became widely accessible from Japanese manufacturers such as Yamaha and Kawai, the piano had already accrued the prestigious socioeconomic associations that it still holds. Americans can understand this easily, thinking of grand pianos that sit unplayed in living rooms as a piece of furniture, transmitting visually the aura of high cultural status.

Conversely, in Cuban culture, historically a drum played with bare hands carried "primitive" associations; elites considered its performance unsightly. The popularity and dissemination of the *son*—the first popular music genre to incorporate

ACTIVITY 3.4

Two other types of associations with musical instruments that occur in cultures around the world are gender and location. Ideas about gender, for instance, sometimes dictate who may and may not play an instrument. As for location, if you think banjo, or **guqin,** or **didjeridu**, for example, where would you place them nationally or regionally or culturally? Think about these two types of association and come up with some examples of your own.

performance on a drum played with the bare hands and that became emblematic of Cuban culture—eroded that association to the point that it is almost unimaginable today (see chapter 17).

Musical Ensembles

If you think about it in the most flexible of terms, an "ensemble" can consist of anything. Instruments (including the voice) can potentially be put together in any way that people want. What has to happen, of course, is that at some point, some person(s) must decide what *will* be put together. When multiple people make music together, it is a socio-musical activity and—even if dictated by some individual in a position of power—certainly a mode of sharing expressive culture.

The first question to ask about an ensemble is about the instrumentarium (selection of instruments): What does it consist of? All the same type of instrument, as in choral ensembles; or within that, a choral ensemble comprised of singers of the same sex or mixed? All the same basic instrument type as in a string quartet or a steel band or a bluegrass group? Almost all the same basic instrument type as in a Balinese *gamelan* or a Mexican American *mariachi* ensemble or a West African percussion ensemble? A mixture of instrument types such as in an indie rock band, a North Indian classical musical ensemble, an orchestra?

In terms of ensemble sound that results from combinations of instrument types, peoples' preferences lie somewhere on a continuum from an ideal of a **homogeneous sound** (timbral similarity, as in a brass band) to a **heterogeneous sound** (timbral variety, as in an Irish traditional ensemble of fiddle, flute, guitar, and hand drum). Close to timbral similarity but on the continuum toward timbral variety are ensembles such as a string quartet whose instruments' sounds are basically similar but are distinguished by a difference in the pitch range.

ACTIVITY 3.5

The audio examples in this textbook's case studies amply demonstrate this continuum of ensemble sound ideals in musical cultures. Listen to at least four examples from different places on the globe and organize them on the timbral continuum).

ACTIVITY 3.6

Do you participate in a musical ensemble? If so, consisting of what? Would you say that your musical role is a flexible one or a consistent one—and if so, what? When your ensemble rehearses, what musical goals do you have in mind as a group—that is, what ensemble ideals are you striving for?

If you do not participate in an ensemble, ask these questions of a friend who does.

One last idea about ensembles. In some ensemble practices, an instrument can be designated to play a certain, consistent musical role. In Spanish flamenco, for instance, the role of the guitar has been to accompany the singing (and the *zapateado* rhythm of the footwork), although recently guitarists are performing as soloists. In Brazilian *samba* and Cuban *son* ensembles, particular instruments such as the *ganzá* or as **maracas** contribute a relatively constant rhythm throughout a given piece, while others (the *cuíca* or bongo) often vary their parts prominently. In many types of Afro-Latin repertoire, the rhythms performed even on melodic instruments are at least as important as the pitches they play. Generally speaking, in North Indian *rāga* music the roles of the instruments will include a melodic soloist (singer) or instrumentalist, a percussionist, and a producer of a constant drone.

On the other hand, in some ensemble practices such as the orchestra, an instrument's role can be quite flexible—anything a composer wishes it to be—so that a cello, flute, or trombone may play melody at one point and harmony at other times. In jazz, it is commonplace for the solo role to be passed among the players in a band.

4

Thinking about Global Music Cultures

Chapter Contents

Introduction

In the Introduction to this book, we described our own journeys and discoveries about world music and how we began to think about global music cultures. We also posed a few questions to start you thinking about your own experience of music found around the world. In the first three chapters of Part 1, we explored specific musical ways of addressing them, including the ways in which some people around the world have drawn on the basic elements of music—pitch, melody, rhythm, harmony, texture, and form—to shape concepts and create particular musical practices.

This chapter introduces you further to the field of *ethnomusicology* or the study of world music cultures. A very brief history is followed by commentary on some perspectives that have been—and are increasingly—of particular interest in the discipline in general as we pursue studies of global music cultures. Don't forget that "world music" includes a grand variety of people and their music, including you and yours. We also touch on research sources and methods—how we go about learning about world musics and what we do professionally with the knowledge we have gained. Finally, we suggest how the study of world music can enrich the lives of even those who do not chose it as a career.

The chapters to come are devoted to the thinking of the global music-makers themselves. For Parts 2, 3, 4, and 5, specialist ethnomusicologists have contributed case

≡ **Mongolian band**   The Hu combines traditional tribal music with the contemporary genre of heavy metal.

studies that introduce you to ways in which they have learned that people have made music meaningful and useful in their lives.

The Field of Ethnomusicology
A Very Brief History

When the term "ethnomusicology" was first coined in the mid-twentieth century, there was no such field of study. Previously, nineteenth-century European scholars had developed a new area of study called "comparative musicology." In that era of colonialism, comparative musicologists were interested in the origin of the whole human phenomenon of music, taking a scientific interest in classifying different musical instruments and particular traits of music. They wondered what "universal" features might be found in music from across the globe. Interest in *music cultures* gradually followed as they began to consider *why* musical traits or instrument types were shared in different parts of the world. Advances in recording technology made studies of music around the world ever more feasible.

The first appearance of the word "ethnomusicology" is credited to Dutch musicologist Jaap Kunst (1891–1960). Kunst studied music in Java, Indonesia, for many decades before publishing a book by the title *Ethnomusicology* in 1950; it included a remarkable bibliography that would serve as a solid foundation for a newly named field of study.

The broad geographic selection of the chapters of this textbook results from decades-long practice by ethnomusicologists of focusing their research on a selected part of the world—largely not in Europe and specifically not on European art music. "I am a South Asianist," I would say because I did research in and on India for a number of years. Others would self-identify in a similar way: "I am an Africanist" or "I am a Caribbeanist."

A geographic orientation was logical in a heady period of discovery of musics all over the globe. It led to the field being defined as "the study of non-Western music" until the late 1980s. However, this definition became increasingly misleading, as the geographic breadth of the field became assumed to include studies of music in European contexts (chapter 15 on Spain; chapter 16 on Ireland) and of Western music wherever it was disseminated in the era of colonialism or has been circulated by globalization (chapter 7 on Japan; chapter 5 on Chuuk in Micronesia).

What is particularly meaningful about the term "ethnomusicology," however, is the prefix "ethno," from a Greek word that indicates an emphasis on culture—namely, the study of music from the cultural and social perspectives of the people who make it. That means seeking to understand the ways in which cultural and social status and value come into play with regard to music (chapter 6 on China; chapter 10 on India; and chapter 18 on Brazil). It also addresses the relationship of music with senses of community (chapters 5 on Chuuk in Micronesia; chapter 16 on Ireland; and chapter 20 on music in Native America). Today, ethnomusicologists are likely to be less focussed on a specific location than with a particular research perspective or topic such as music and spirituality (chapter 9 on Bali; chapter 12 on Egypt; and chapter 13 on Ghana). The field is now being defined by the meaning of that prefix of "ethno"—not only the practice and theory of music but also the study of music from the cultural and social perspectives of the people who make it. A bit of historical perspective will help to explain the shift.

After World War II (after 1945), the world as it had been known in the long era of colonialism underwent a succession of huge social forces—each of which affected music in global cultures. To resist being colonized (chapter 7 on Japan), or to replace an empire (chapter 11 on Turkey), political organizing shifted to formation of modern nation-states. In these nationalistic drives, music was found (and is still being found) to be a useful tool, and that draws the attention of ethnomusicologists.

In the 1960s—a turbulent time around the globe—marginalized peoples began to stand up for their rights in organized and individual ways, often using music to express or amplify their messages (see chapter 14 on South Africa; and, for a more recent instance, chapter 8 on Myanmar). From this time—especially in the scholarly disciplines of the social sciences (anthropology and sociology) and in ethnomusicology—the issue of **representation** surfaced, raising question such as the following:

- Who has the right and the knowledge to represent (i.e., speak for) whom?
- Who is an outsider and who is an insider?
- Whose perspectives are brought to the scholarly table?
- Whose ideas and creativity are allowed to be the basis for comparative analyses—and allowed by whom (!)?

Lively discussions of these questions continue into the present. For example, in addition to studies of "music of the other," a number of ethnomusicologists choose to study their "own music" (chapter 20 on Native American powwow musical cultures).

In the late 1980s, the question of "which music was of sufficient value to be studied" expanded as scholars realized that a great deal can be learned about society and culture through popular culture studies. Study of popular music—that had been neglected in scholarship even by broad-minded ethnomusicologists—emerged from the shadows to take a significant position. Perspectives on popular music are unimaginably numerous: they range from issues of intellectual property rights, and development and use of technologies, to expression of national identity (chapter 13 on Ghana and chapter 18 on Brazil). Since the 1950s when the field was founded, then, ethnomusicological research has responded in diverse ways to cultural and political forces that are felt in many locations around the world.

Perspectives in the Study of Global Music

The Tension between Continuity and Change. Perhaps the most persistent interest in the study of global music cultures has been in people's responses to the dynamic tension between the following:

- The near-inevitability of change as new technologies arise and cultures come increasingly into communication with each other
- The desire to preserve musical ideas, practices, and/or individual musical works even as circumstances change

These are seldom either-or options for people, as both continuity and change are central to our lives. Learning *what* is or is not changed is one part of the work of ethnomusicologists, but understanding *why* people have made these decisions is another.

A number of factors have contributed to the tension between continuity and change in musical cultures. A major one has been migration. Immigrants settling in a new location are likely to bring with them their own musical traditions. Hundreds of studies of musicking in immigrant communities in the United States have explored the tension between preserving traditional cultures and either the necessity or desirability of change (chapter 19 on Mexican American mariachi). Those studies have provided insight into the lives of millions of Americans about whom we as individual Americans know little.

Migration of a different sort has been of concern for ethnomusicologists as well: that resulting when people are forcibly displaced from their homes. Forced slavery of course was a global force of magnitude, causing what is known as the "African diaspora." Its effects on music particularly in the Americas have been studied by an increasing number of ethnomusicologists (chapter 17 on Cuba; and chapter 18 on Brazil). But involuntary migration is a reality for humans to the present moment. According to the UN Refugee Agency, the number of displaced persons in the world's population is larger right now than ever in human history. These "displaced persons" include those internally displaced (IDP) who have found safety from conflict and violence somewhere within their own country, and refugees who have had to flee their homes to survive and seek asylum in another country. Like immigrants, displaced persons are likely to take with them familiar musical practices—ways of musicking—that help sustain them. Some ethnomusicologists have reported on efforts in receiving countries to help refugees through their trauma by creating opportunities to perform music together, even if the music is unfamiliar.

Sociopolitical pressures exerted on local peoples during the long period of colonization (chapter 7 on Japan; chapter 14 on South Africa; and chapter 16 on Ireland) and also formerly colonized residents' musical responses to the freedom of independence are other important factors in why and how musical traditions survive or change. Internal political struggles also can inspire preservation or change of musical cultures (chapter 6 on China). Through most of the chapters in this textbook, we will see how much music created in global music cultures is a reaction to this dynamic tension between continuity and change.

Music and Identities. A second persistent area of interest for the field has been the expression of identity through music. This expression ranges across numerous significant kinds of identity, usually of some group: ethnic (chapter 8), religious (chapter 8), national (chapters 11 and 18), regional (chapters 13 and 15), and others. Studies of ethnic/racial identity have morphed from predominance of "race" implying "black" (or in any case, not "white") to consideration of "whiteness" as well. Very recently, the reality that there is a great deal of mixed-race culture around the world is being acknowledged and explored.

Studies of **gender** (the ways maleness and femaleness are constructed in a context) emerged in the late 1980s, as it was acknowledged that, when gender was

ACTIVITY 4.1

Prepare for a class discussion on the continuing perspectives that ethnomusicologists have employed in their study of global music by reflecting on your own experiences.

- What do you consider to be your multiple identities—musical or otherwise?
- Has some sort of migration—displacement or otherwise—been a factor in your own or your immediate family's life; and if so, what sort?
- If so, has music been an element in that experience, and are you aware of tension between concern for preservation or desire for change on anyone's part? What have been the sources of the tension and the resolutions?

not mentioned, it could be assumed that the gender of focus was masculine. For a time, "gender studies" automatically implied a research focus on feminine music-making, but that is now complemented by attention to "masculinities." At present, we must still work toward a balance of attention to all genders in ethnomusicology, but progress has been made. Studies of **sexuality** emerged relatively recently, in response to social forces in a number of societies around the world and issues around representing peoples who have previously been ignored (chapter 19). Studies of sexuality focus on a human's capacity for sexual feelings, understood broadly and without precise definition as the ways a person might experience and express themselves sexually.

What began as studies of *identity* that presumed to speak for musicking among an entire group has largely turned into studies of *identities*, as we realize that individuals live with multiple identities: a mix and match of associations with music with meanings and uses that traverse many intersecting categories including religion, race, gender, sexuality, nationality, and regionality.

Sources and Research Methods

The *potential* major resources for ethnomusicological study are

- Aural: Recordings, broadcast media, live performances; one's own musical practice
- Visual
  - Manuscripts (i.e., handwritten)
  - Print sources as widely ranging as newspapers, diaries, court records, scholarly writing
  - Musical notations, whether transcription of sound into writing or transnotation from one system of notation to another
  - Media of multiple sorts from paintings, still photography, film (documentary, nondocumentary), video, internet
- Physical: Music-making
- Living people

For ethnomusicologists, two types of research methods have been particularly important: physical, that is, making music oneself; and learning from people. The perspectives gained from these two sources are irreplaceable.

Ethnomusicologists often study a musical instrument with a master practitioner from a musical culture. Playing a musical instrument can give you an appreciation of the physical talents needed to master it and how the construction of an instrument can pose constraints on music as well as possibilities for creativity. Learning from a master teacher also allows you to experience the social roles of teachers and students in the culture, share musical knowledge with fellow human beings, think about the responsibilities of solo or of ensemble music-making, and experience the possibility of personal expression through music.

The research method of learning primarily from people (including from master practitioners) is known as **ethnography**, an approach to research that originally came from anthropology. What has been considered to make a study ethnographic has changed through time, but it has been consistently thought of as "**fieldwork**." The early idea was that the scholar would reside with a group for a sustained period of time (likely, at least a year) in order to study it through participation and observation. **Participation** for an ethnomusicologist usually included music instruction and performance, and **observation** consisted of asking questions and holding discussions but also of hanging out and keeping copious, careful **field notes** for later reference. "Residing with a group" became a differently formulated research method when studies increasingly focused on urban contexts; but fundamentally, the research process is the same. Urban-based research blossomed in the 1990s when ethnomusicologists began to pursue growing interest in popular musics all over the world.

Given the emphasis on ethnographic research method, ethnomusicology has been tagged by a number of people as a field without, or having little interest in, historical study. What is more accurate is that most of the historical study done by ethnomusicologists has started from the present (what music is, means, and does *now*) and worked backward in time to understand—to the extent possible—how it got to be the way it is (see chapter 6 on China and chapter 7 on Japan). The study of change, after all, requires historical perspective. Historical studies by ethnomusicologists that focus entirely on the past are indeed relatively few to date, and a goodly number of those are produced by specialists in Asian traditions. The reality is that the nature of the sources that are *actually* (as opposed to *potentially* as listed above) available is a huge factor in the kind of study that an ethnomusicologist might pursue. Historical aural sources for much traditional music on the globe— and especially for improvisatory practices such as that discussed in chapter 10 on India—did not exist until the invention of recording technology.

The bottom line is that ethnomusicology is a study of music not only from the perspectives of theory and practice but also from the cultural and social perspectives of the people who make (or made) it. The case studies in this textbook exemplify that approach with a focus on ways in which people make music meaningful and useful in their lives.

ACTIVITY 4.2

Imagine yourself a prospective ethnomusicologist by experimenting with designing a research project. What piece of music, or kind of music, or musical group (or whatever) would you like to explore in some depth? What perspective are you interested in bringing to it? Those are the first choices you need to make to decide on the focus of a research project.

Formulate a statement of purpose, a goal of your project: "I want to learn about X by exploring it from the perspective of X."

With a project in mind:

- Devise a set of questions to address about your topic.
- Figure out how you would go about answering them:
  - o Identify likely sources. With whom would you need to speak?
  - o Where on the internet *and elsewhere* could you find information?
  - o In what order do you need to learn about what?
- Consider the practicality of logistics, were you to actually carry out this project:
  - o How much time would it require?
  - o Are the potential sources actually available to you?
  - o Would you be welcome to speak with potential interlocutors?
  - o Would you need to purchase tickets to performances?
  - o Would you need to make music—and if so, what would that involve?

To share your idea for a project with colleagues, write a formal proposal for carrying it out, using the answers to those questions as a guideline.

Putting Your Studies of World Music to Work

What opportunities do studies of world music offer you? The most obvious answer to this question would be a career in teaching. Diversifying the music curriculum has become important for many educational institutions—colleges and universities such as the one you are attending, and also schools at the K–12 level. Knowledgeable instructors are needed.

Outside of academia, there are many opportunities that are generally referred to as "applied ethnomusicology." In the legal profession, an ethnomusicologist's knowledge and expertise in intellectual property rights and copyright law is highly prized; in the medical profession, use of music in therapy and specializations such as working with the aged or the disabled is needed. Opportunities also abound in the music industry, for example, in production, retail, or marketing. And in arts administration, ethnomusicologists are employed, for instance, in concert venues. Ethnomusicologists work in a number of museums—as curators, as designers of exhibitions, and in outreach efforts. Grant writing for non-profit organizations has been important. Also, ethnomusicologists find work in community organizations such as non-degree-granting community music schools that foster amateur music-making; and civic institutions, such as park services, many of which plan regular cultural projects such as festivals. Each of these would involve you in continuing studies of diverse musical traditions and practices and the necessity for understanding social and cultural values of music.

Perhaps most important of all is the window into diversity that is offered by study of music. While modern genetics have proven that humans are one single, recently emerged and biologically fairly uniform species, the reality of human existence is that we are culturally diverse. As I heard one student put it, "We ARE diverse, so we might as well make peace with it and benefit from it. Doing that through music is a wonderful way."

On to the case studies.

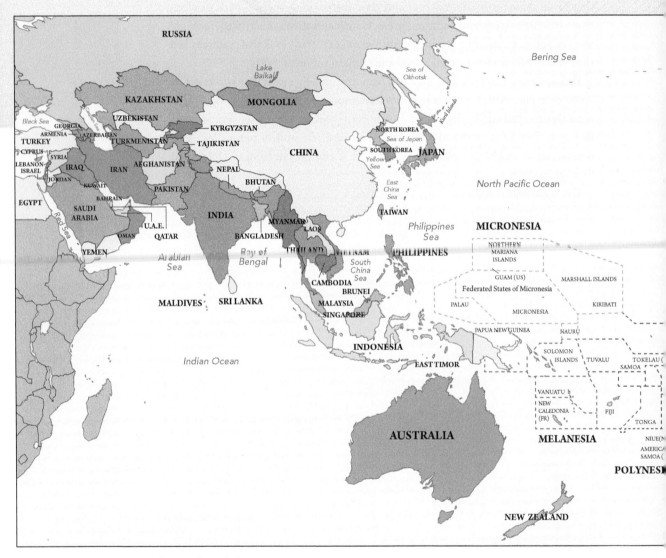

FIGURE II.1 Map of Asia and Pacific Region.

PART 2

The Pacific and Asia

5

Music in Chuuk (Micronesia)

Music and Dance in a Sea of Islands

BRIAN DIETTRICH

Chapter Contents

Introduction

This chapter takes you to one of the largest areas of the world but one that receives very little attention from the outside, relatively speaking: Oceania. The vast expanse of the Pacific Ocean covers nearly a third of the earth's total area. Dotted across this "water-world" are numerous groupings of islands that are home to a diversity of peoples and cultures. The islands fall into three large groupings—the "-nesia's": Micronesia, Melanesia, and Polynesia (Figure 5.1). In this chapter, we will focus on Micronesia in the northwestern Pacific; and within that large grouping, one particular group of islands known as Chuuk (Figure 5.2).

For peoples of Chuuk, music and dance are deeply meaningful as modes through which to express and maintain social and cultural values. Two of those values are introduced here:

1. **Rootedness to place**: The people of Chuuk have firmly rooted senses of belonging within the vast space of the Pacific Ocean, to their own ancestral islands, to the surrounding seas, and to others to which they are connected both historically

≡ **Performers from Pollap Island, Chuuk State, at the 12th Festival of Pacific Arts on Guam, 2016.**

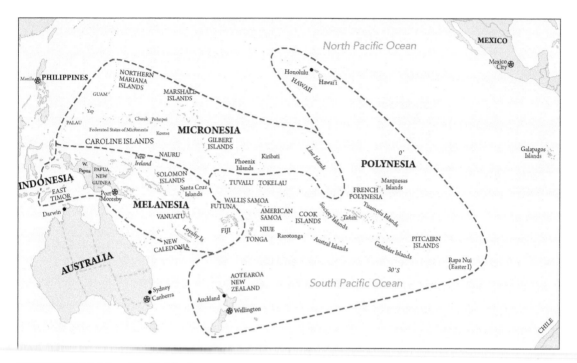

≡ **FIGURE 5.1** Map of Pacific Islands.

and most recently along the routes of global cultural flow (Diettrich, Moulin, and Webb, 2011).

2. **Communal affiliation**: The values of a shared community—such as within lineage groups and in villages, on individual islands, or within Christian denominations—play a fundamental role in Chuukese society and culture.

In this chapter, expression of both of those values will be illustrated through poetry, music, and dance first in moments of everyday local life: moments of engagement with the sea, ancestral ways, religious worship, and communal celebration. The chapter ends with a shift to exploration of ways in which place and belonging intersect with international encounters.

Chuuk

Encompassing forty-one islands, Chuuk is a state in the Federated States of Micronesia (FSM; Figure 5.2). Chuuk is a place of contrasts, with mountainous islands lush with vegetation and low sandy atolls dispersed over vast waterways and with numerous villages. Chuuk maintains the largest population in the FSM, and a

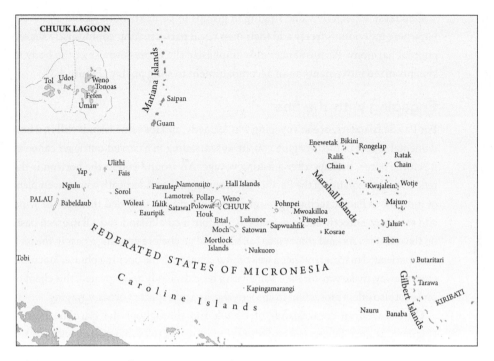

≡ **FIGURE 5.2** Map of Micronesia.

majority of its people resides on the island of Weno that includes the state's urban capital. The people of Chuuk share with other Micronesians a past marked by missionization and colonial administrations from Spain (1886–1899), Germany (1899–1914), Japan (1914–1945), and the United States (1945–1979)—historical enterprises that have shaped music and dance (Hezel 1995). In addition to the home islands, Chuukese communities are well established outside the FSM: on the island of Guam (Guåhån); in Hawai'i; and in the continental United States, where music is a means of expressing a shared identity abroad.

Musical Practices

Musical practices in Chuuk comprise a rich variety of locally distinctive styles and a complexity of global engagements. Music originates with poetry, the performance of which is a means of communicating and reaffirming social and cultural values, whether in oratory, recitation, song, or formal storytelling. The oldest vocal musics include rhythmically intoned speech and lyrical chants sung in unison or with leader–group structure (in form, **call-and-response**).

Chuukese especially value singing in groups in contexts both sacred and secular, where individuals freely add their own vocal part, creating communally shared chordal harmony. Performances also emphasize the expressive use of the body in synchronized movements as an accompaniment to sung poetry (Figure 5.3).

Engaging with the Sea

For Pacific Islanders, ocean voyaging was formerly, and for some islands still is, a fundamental aspect of life. Imagine you are at sea, sailing in a carved outrigger canoe as it returns home, perhaps after a fishing voyage. All around you to the horizon is the reflective blue expanse of the Pacific. The wooden canoe underneath you—an emblem of indigenous Pacific technology—glides easily with sail unfurled through the wind and sea spray. Directly ahead is your destination: a coral island and a flat, green oasis on these waters. As land comes into full view and just before entering a pass in the reef, an experienced mariner intones a welcoming chant with the opening phrase, "open the entranceway, make way for me." Sung with a lyrical melody and repeated, this chant of protocol also offers protection from *weriyeng*, a patron spirit of ocean voyaging.

On the western coral islands of Chuuk and throughout the Caroline Islands (Figure 5.2), specific musical and other sounding practices that engage with the sea

≡ **FIGURE 5.3** Dancers from the western islands of Chuuk State perform at a public celebration.

as place are strongly valued by these seagoing people. Delivered in **kapasen le mataw** (language of the sea), and especially known by **pélú** (master mariners), musical practices of ocean **wayfinding** (navigation) preserve sonic maps of stars and sea lanes between islands. They also index the sea life and past human experiences on the ocean.

Two excerpts of *kapasen le mataw* can be heard in "Navigators of Polowat" (Audio Example 5.1). The first excerpt is a lyrical chant about the story of legendary mariner Olap, intoned by the famous mariner from Polowat Island named Hipour. Along with Mau Piailug from Satawal Island and other Micronesian mariners, Hipour played a role in the revitalization of traditional Oceanic wayfinding in the twentieth century (Metzgar 2006; Diaz 2011). The second excerpt is a **rhythmic recitation** for new mariners delivered by the navigator Tawochu. The music of *kapasen le mataw* represents the close cultural relationships that Oceanic communities have forged with the surrounding sea, an environment of valued resources and cultural inspiration and a means of connection within the Pacific world (Diettrich 2018a). Understanding these relationships is all the more vital given the impending changes in the region brought by climate change and rising seas, which are critical issues for Pacific nations (Steiner 2015).

Engaging with Ancestral Ways

A vivid sense of rootedness to place is expressed through a broad category of music called **kéénún nóómw** (songs from the past) that the Chuukese associate with their ancestors and ancestral ways of life on the islands. Among the genres of songs from the past is **emweyir**, exclamatory chants for work: the work of lifting and hauling heavy objects, for instance. A performance of *emweyir* is a means to galvanize the men of the village for a difficult task at hand, such as moving canoes across the beach, carrying large ceremonial bowls of pounded breadfruit (Figure 5.4), or lifting up heavy breadfruit tree logs. The words of the *emweyir* called "Erééta

ACTIVITY 5.1

Micronesian and Pacific Island Wayfinding (Navigation)

View an excerpt of the film "Sacred Vessels: Navigating Tradition and Identity in Micronesia" about the island of Polowat by scholar and filmmaker Vicente Diaz (1997). What are the main issues presented in this excerpt, and what types of music-making are shown and heard? From watching this clip, describe five ways that the land and sea are valued within Micronesian communities.

≡ **FIGURE 5.4** Performance of an *emweyir* at the College of Micronesia, Chuuk Campus.

Meyinuku" ("Lift Up the Breadfruit Tree Logs"; Audio Example 5.2) are of particular interest because they map islands across the geographic region of Micronesia, starting with the island of Pohnpei, and including Kachaw (Kosrae) and
Pingelap in the FSM, and the atolls of Jaluit and Ebon and the Ratak island chain
of the Marshall Islands to the east (see Figure 5.1). As ancestral music, "Erééta
Meyinuku" constitutes a valued thread of cultural knowledge that links village life
in Chuuk with the wider region through practices passed down orally from the
ancestral past.

ACTIVITY 5.2

Using the map of Micronesia (Figure 5.2), working
your way from west to east, locate Chuuk, as well
as the islands of Pohnpei, Pingelap, Kosrae, and
Jaluit (Jālwōj) in Micronesia. Chose at least three
of them to investigate in a bit of detail by browsing
the web. Such sites as Wikipedia, Encyclopedia
Britannica, and local posts for tourism are informa-
tive. Your explorations will contribute to a better
understanding of the islands in the region.

When a group of men are working, the text is recited by a chant leader, and then the group responds with short punctuated phrases, often in rhyme, or with a **vocable** derived from the last word of the leader. "Eréeta Meyinuku" was recited to me in 2001 as a solo performance by the now late Meichik Amon, formerly from the village of Chukienu on the island of Tol in Chuuk Lagoon. Meichik sang both parts of the chant himself, but the text transcription indicates the separate parts for the leader and group.

Time	Text (Leader)	Text (Response)	Translation (Leader)	Translation (Response)
0:00	*Éwúruko wúrúúr,*	*wúrúúr,*	We haul it,	haul,
	éwúruko wúrúúr,	*wúrúúr,*	we haul it,	haul,
0:07	*wúrúúrún Fóónupi ii,*	*ii,*	hauling to Pohnpei,	(vocable)
	áchcha Nomwúnikachó,	*óó,*	moving to Kachaw Lagoon	(vocable)
0:11	*aa Raateka,*	*aa,*	to Ratak	(vocable)
	ii Seniwisi,	*ii,*	to Jaluit	(vocable)
0:14	*ee Pikiram e,*	*ee,*	to Pingelap	(vocable)
	aa Pón ó,	*óó,*	to Ebon	(vocable)
0:17	*aa Póppónóchiki,*	*ii,*	to little Ebon	(vocable)
	aa fisi pwe ii,	*ii,*	it is happening,	(vocable)
0.21	*aa fisi pwe aa,*	*aa,*	it is happening,	(vocable)
	aa fisi pwe ii,	*ii,*	it is happening,	(vocable)
0:24	*aa fisi pwe aa,*	*aa,*	it is happening,	(vocable)
	aa fisi sipwe apwasa,	*wehu!*	we will cheer it,	Yeah!

Worshipping through Music

Christian social and cultural values play a fundamental role in Chuukese society. The people of Chuuk mostly belong to either Catholic or Protestant churches but with growing affiliations of Seventh-Day Adventists, Pentecostals, and Mormons. For all, the church holds a central place in village life, not only as a site of worship but a center of communal and musical activity. At Sunday church services throughout Chuuk's villages singing is foremost in both the amount of time it occupies as

ACTIVITY 5.3

Listen to "Eréeta Meyinuku" first to recognize the call and response form and then to follow the text. If you can, sing the response to feel the participatory, rhythmic flow of the song.

well as the opportunity it affords for social engagement. The people of Chuuk also sing Christian songs regularly outside of church during celebratory days throughout the year, and where song and faith are a focal point for village social activity.

One church known for its exceptional singing and one that I have visited many times is Berea Evangelical Church in Nepukos Village on Weno Island. At the ten o'clock Sunday service, the interior of Berea church is hot and humid under the morning equatorial sun. As people gather, the space is filled with the sounds of their footsteps, the voices of children, and quiet, casual conversations. Shortly after ten o'clock, the service begins with **_kéénún namanam_** (Christian song), a term that refers to Christian music of any kind or context, including unaccompanied **hymns**. One favorite, locally composed hymn that is sung by the Berea congregation is called "_Nupwen Néwún Aramas_" ("When the Son of Man"), which affirms Chuukese Christian values:

Sipwe toonong lóón ewe fénúwen pwaapwa,	We will enter into the land of happiness,
fénúwen kinamwmwe,	the land of peace,
neeniyen chóón núkúúw iten Siises.	the place of the believers of Jesus.

A senior female who sits near the front of the church announces the hymn by its first phrase, which she sings confidently and loudly in a high register. Immediately after, the congregation joins with men and women breaking into separate parts. Everyone sings, with the full and intense sound filling the space and resonating powerfully in the church and outside into the village. Multipart hymns such as this one generally progress slowly, verse by verse, and vocal harmony is freely added according to the singers' taste and experience. The senses of what is beautiful and appropriate for choral singing in Chuuk, as in other Micronesian areas, are culturally determined and learned socially from active participation over time.

In addition to unaccompanied hymns, the Berea congregation, like that of other churches, sings newly composed songs accompanied by an electronically amplified keyboard, which is widespread in Chuukese musical practices.

Celebrating with Music and Dance

Celebratory performances held throughout the year or every few years are especially significant occasions for music and dance. One government event that I took part in was on the island of Fefen in Chuuk Lagoon, during which villagers and state representatives came together to celebrate the inauguration of a new state governor. This celebration lasted the full day and included continuous performances of choral songs, arrangements of popular music, and performances inspired by other Pacific Island dances. Traditional dances are especially valued in Chuuk as in most

Pacific Island cultures. These performances combine expressions of poetry, song, and movement; dancers wear special costumes and often scented oil or perfume.

Near the end of the day, a small group from Inaka village presented an especially valued genre of dance (Figure 5.5) called **pwérúkún faan maram** ("dances under the moon," or simply "moon dances") and also by the name **éwúwénú**. This dance is performed by a small group of seated men and women, both young and old, who arrange themselves in a half circle. The *pwérúkún faan maram* features alternating sections of chant and song, accompanied by gestures of the hands and arms and handclapping as part of its expressive and rhythmic elements.

For example, the poetry of a well-known song from the *pwérúkún faan maram* called *"Wúwa nómw wóón Fénú neey"* ("I am on my Island") describes a scene of traditional island life: being at home in a village and hearing the sound of laundry being washed by hand under the palm trees (Audio Example 5.3). The deep sense of place and belonging is expressed from the start in the title/first line, "I am on my Island." The lyrics convey a playful dialogue that takes place between two people: a man invites a woman to step outside, but she refuses, using a common metaphor in the banter of romantic relationships in Chuuk.

≡ **FIGURE 5.5** Performance of *pwérúkún faan maram* ("dances under the moon") on Fefen Island, Chuuk.

"Wúwa nómw wóón Fénú neey" (I am on my Island)

Performed by a Village group from Fefen Island

Recorded on Fefen Island, Chuuk State, Micronesia in 2006 by Brian Diettrich

Instrumentation: Vocals, hand claps and slaps

Time	Text	Translation	Something to Listen For
0:01	Wúwa nómw wóón fénú neey, wúfen ii rongorongo, púpúngúpúngún ttatangentangen an nemin sóópw neeyirúpwúng.	I am on my island, I walk and hear, the pounding and squashing, of a girl washing clothes at the ivory nut palm trees.	Women's voices, with sequence of claps and slaps as a clear means of setting the pulse of the song. In the background, adult men and children's voices can be heard talking, calling, and laughing. The voices (more women than men) are sometimes singing in unison and other times are harmonizing. On occasion, a male song/dance leader audibly calls out some of the phrases (quickly) ahead of the full group. Some of the shouted comments heard during the singing are in support of the performers.
0:27 (Repeat)	Wúwa nómw wóón fénú neey, wúfen ii rongorongo, púpúngúpúngún ttatangentangen, an nemin sóópw neeyirúpwúng.	I am on my island, I walk and hear, the pounding and squashing, of a girl washing clothes at the ivory nut palm trees.	
0:51	Nge pwata ko kese pwáátá kopwe toowuuw, wúpwe wúrenuk nee miney rekirek?	But why madam, you do not get up and come outside, so I will tell you my thoughts?	
1:07 (Repeat)	Nge pwata ko kese pwáátá kopwe toowuuw, wúpwe wúrenuk nee miney rekirek?	But why madam, you do not get up and come outside, so I will tell you my thoughts?	
1:24	Wúse túúfich, wúpwe pwáátá, wúpwe toowuuw, ngaang meyi semwmwen oo.	I am unable, to get up, to come outside, because I am not well.	
1:38 (Repeat)	Wúse túúfich, wúpwe pwáátá, wúpwe toowuuw, ngaang meyi semwmwen oo.	I am unable, to get up, to come outside, because I am not well.	
1:52			Choir heaves a collective sigh, then a high "whoo," which is a formulaic exclamatory ending in Chuukese performances.

Listeners gathered around the performers, sang along with the music, and adorned the performers with sprayed perfume and small gifts, including pieces of bright cloth. This is typical of celebratory events in Chuuk in which everyone takes part. Performances such as this one forge together villagers and visitors into the social fabric of community and place. Music and dance are thus a valuable means to bring people together in shared experience.

Participating in Global Flow

Chuukese people live outside their home islands on Saipan, Guam, Hawai'i, and in the continental United States. The value they give to place and belonging exists alongside their exposure to other people, ideas, and culture, including music and dance (Peter 2000). Contemporary Chuukese musical practices have been influenced by this cultural interchange, and in turn music and dance offer support and identity for communities abroad. We will discuss two examples of how this interaction has occurred, the first in popular music and the second in international festival performance. Both reveal the centrality of the sense of place and belonging even in circumstances of cultural and musical mobility.

Chuukese engage with a wide variety of global popular musics. Connections among Chuukese communities outside of the home islands play an important role in creating and disseminating this music, with new productions often coming from abroad (Diettrich 2007, 2016). ReChuuk, one of the earliest acclaimed popular Chuukese bands, produced some of their earliest successes from the island of Guam in the 1990s. One popular new Chuukese musical group is KFC (Kids from Chuuk), a group of four young Chuukese men who are also based on Guam. As Chuukese migration outside of the FSM has greatly increased over the past two decades, this mobility has continued to shape contemporary musical practice in Chuuk.

ACTIVITY 5.4

Explore dance in Chuuk further by watching Video 5.2, which shows a dance from the western outer islands of Chuuk performed by female and male students at the College of Micronesia as part of celebrations of local culture. As you watch, pay attention to the spatial layout of the performance, the gestures used by men and women, the attire of the performers, the melody of the example and the relationship between the men's and women's vocal parts; and also note the use of the exclamatory ending of the example.

While some Chuukese popular songs are based on older musical models, many more are influenced by current global styles, especially reggae, but also country, rap, and hip-hop. Chuukese artists create new lyrics, tunes, beats tracks, and textures; and they adapt elements from a variety of sources, including songs from other Micronesian and Pacific cultures, as well as American songs. Favorite love songs (*kéénún núkún*) are especially valued in Chuuk for their sentimental poetry and the expressive qualities of individual vocalists. Musicians distribute new favorite songs on locally produced CD albums, but they increasingly share music over mobile phones and on the web. With sometimes limited access to electricity or the internet in Chuuk, live performance remains a vital element for popular music in the islands.

Many popular songs feature solo artists or small groups, but new popular song is also the domain of community performances. New popular songs performed by village and island groups emphasize the shared, interactive practice of music and dance. An example is a welcoming song (*kéénún etiwetiw*) called "Áách Kapwongen Etiwa Áámi" (Our Welcome Greetings to You All, Audio Example 5.4). In the first phrases of the song, the sense of place and also engagement with the sea are expressed just as they were in older song styles. This will be clear as you follow the text in the Listening Guide as you listen to the recording.

This song was composed in 2006 on the coral island of Moch in the Mortlock Islands, south of Chuuk lagoon (see Figure 5.2). As this example demonstrates, the act of welcoming through song is an important expression of belonging. Moch is the smallest island in Chuuk, and this song plays with its identity by referring to its pass in the large surrounding reef. The song was performed by a seated and enthusiastic group of men and women to welcome visiting government officials from Chuuk, who traveled by ship to the event. "Áách Kapwongen Etiwa Áámi" demonstrates finely integrated choral harmonies, a precision in the synchronized movement of the voices, and the rhythmic drive of the electronic keyboards, ubiquitous instruments in Chuukese popular song. As they sat together closely in a group, the performers moved their upper bodies and heads in time to the energetic beat of the music—a shared presentation in voice and gesture that represented the hospitality and communal identity of the people of Moch.

Festival experiences offer a means to reflect on local culture practices, alongside those of others, in a shared environment. Like many peoples across the globe, Chuukese value time-honored forms of expression that emphasize their own cultural identity. Festival delegations use these standards for the selection of music and dance that will be presented. The Festival of Pacific Arts, a quadrennial

LISTENING GUIDE

"Áách Kapwongen Etiwa Áámi"

Performed by Mixed choir

Recorded on Moch Island, Chuuk State, Micronesia in 2006 by Brian Diettrich

Instrumentation: Vocals, accompanied by a synthesizer (with an in-built drum machine)

Áách Kapwongen Etiwa Áámi (Our Welcome Greetings to you all)			
0:01	*Áách kapwongen etiwa áámi* *chóón toolong lóón fénúyáách Moch.* *Sipwe áwáttiin etiwa* *kemi long loon*	Verse 1 Our welcome greetings to you all those who enter into our island of Moch. We will greatly welcome you all inside	Mixed choir (more women than men) sings a verse homophonically as the synthesizer sounds out chords (G, Am, C). Harmonies are tightly constructed, driven forward by the constant rhythm of the synthesizer and its percussion backdrop. The lyrics offer welcome to visitors from the state government to the island of Moch in 2006.
0:17	*taw chikichik o taw lapalap,* *éwúpwe fiti kich* *le mwareni péén mwosor* *meyi iiy péé pwechepwech,* *sipwe chuu lóón tong.*	Verse 2 from the small pass, the great pass, you will accompany us donning floral garlands from the *mwosor* tree with its white flowers, we will come together in love.	Verse 2 utilizes the same melody and harmony as Verse 1. The lyrics reference the floral garlands of fragrant white flowers from the tree *mwosor* (*Guettarda speciose*) that are presented to arriving visitors.
0:36		Synthesizer transition	
0:39 repeat		Repeat of Verse 1 (lyrics and music)	Listen for the repetition of the melody and harmony and try to follow along with the repeated lyrics.
0:54 repeat		Repeat of Verse 2 (lyrics and music)	Listen for the repetition of the melody and harmony and try to follow along with the repeated lyrics.

1:14		Synthesizer transition	
1:16		Verse 3	Verse 3 utilizes new melodic and harmonic material and new lyrics. The words make reference to assistance from the state government, with the governor of Chuuk State and other officials in attendance and listening to the song. Listen for the men's sigh ("oh") that has been worked into the lyrics in this verse for added effect.
	Oh, akatong mesemesen fénúyaach	*Oh, to feel sympathy to the face of our island*	
	a resin le kuta,	*searching and searching,*	
	ita iyan epwe kuna	*so it will be recognised*	
	me iyan chomong álillis,	*as a place in need of great assistance,*	
	pwe epwe ngasaló.	*so that we can sigh in relief.*	
1:40 repeat		Repeat of Verse 3 (lyrics and music)	

celebration that brings together peoples and cultures from throughout the region of Oceania, is a prime example. The 2016 Festival of Pacific Arts that took place on the island of Guam, for example, was especially important for people from Chuuk, given both the ease of accessibility to the island from Chuuk and the Chuukese communities already residing on the island.

At the Guam festival, the men of the Mortlock Islands performed a *tukuyá* (stick dance), an iconic traditional dance from Chuuk and its surrounding coral islands. In this genre of performance, a group of men, including a lead chanter, recite traditional poetry as they move in different choreographed formations and rhythmically strike carved wooden staves of opposing dancers (Figure 5.6).

ACTIVITY 5.5

Explore the variety of Chuukese popular musics on YouTube, starting with the search criterion of "Chuukese music," then search using the names of musicians such as Relinda Kansou, Ozeky, Pintong (Bintong), and others, as well as the bands Re-Chuuk and Kids from Chuuk. Your goal is to find and describe at least three different styles of popular music, keeping track of where you find each style.

━ **FIGURE 5.6** Stick dance performance by a delegation from Chuuk State at the 12th Festival of Pacific Arts, Guam.

The percussive recitation of the poetry joins with the continuous striking of the staves to create a driving and energetic performance as the men progress through various spatial arrangements, while sitting, kneeling, and standing. Audio Example 5.5 presents an excerpt of the *tukuyá* performance at the festival on Guam. The extract of the poetry transcribed below is heard at 0:32 and is repeated.

Ttiti mwacheeche	Continuously moving stick points,
réélong sápetiw	reaching downward,
réélong sápeta	reaching upward,
raa mwo ókkóóna	they descend,
wókuno chee pwérúk	the moving sticks of the dance.

Broadly similar stick dances performed by other Micronesian peoples suggest historical exchanges of music and dance, but specific communities locally value the dances for their unique aspects of language, performance, and historical contexts. For the people of Chuuk and especially men, stick dances represent a primary means of conveying links with the ancestral past through shared group participation.

ACTIVITY 5.6

Watch the video "Chuuk Team, College of Micronesia-FSM Founding Day 2015" (Video 5.3). It illustrates performances by Chuukese students at the celebration on the island on Pohnpei. On the site, the first four minutes of the video show a contrasting type of dance by young women. The link provided here is an excerpt of the *tukuyá* (stick dance) from 7:55 to 13:02 that you should watch. Observe how the dance is performed, the different positions and use of space, the movements of the dancers, and the rhythmic chanting recited throughout. In what way is the performance focused on both agility and synchrony?

Conclusion

This chapter has explored the rich variety of musics and dances practiced by the people of Chuuk State in the Federated States of Micronesia. In these islands, people find music meaningful particularly through its close linkage to place and community. The musical selections in this chapter illustrated this sense of rootedness to land and sea, to village and church, and to special events of communal celebration. Senses of space and of belonging are also expressed in examples of cultural interchange, through global popular musics, and in performances at festivals. In this sea of islands (Hau'ofa 1994), people make music meaningful and useful in their lives, throughout the blue Pacific and in global movements across new horizons.

Bibliography

Diaz, Vicente M, director. 1997. *Sacred Vessels: Navigating Tradition and Identity in Micronesia.* 1997. Video, 28 min. Directed and written by Vicente M. Diaz; produced by Christine Taitano DeLisle and Vicente M. Diaz. Guam: Moving Islands, Inc.

Diaz, Vicente M. 2011. "Voyaging for Anti-Colonial Recovery: Austronesian Seafaring, Archipelagic Rethinking, and the Re-mapping of Indigeneity." *Pacific Asia Inquiry* 2 (1): 21–32.

Diettrich, Brian. 2007. "Across All Micronesia and Beyond: Innovation and Connections in Chuukese Popular Music and Contemporary Recordings." *The World of Music* 49 (1): 65–81.

Diettrich, Brian. 2016. "Virtual Micronesia: Performance and Participatory Culture in a Pacific Facebook Community." *Perfect Beat* 17 (1): 52–70.

Diettrich, Brian. 2018a. "A Sea of Voices: Performance, Relations, and Belonging in Saltwater Places." *Yearbook for Traditional Music* 50: 41–69.

Diettrich, Brian. 2018b. "Summoning Breadfruit" and "Opening Seas": Towards a Performative Ecology in Oceania. *"Ethnomusicology* 62(1).

Diettrich, Brian, Jane Moulin, and Michael Webb. 2011. *Music in Pacific Island Cultures: Experiencing Music, Expressing Culture.* New York: Oxford University Press.

Hau'ofa, Epeli. 1994. "Our Sea of Islands." *The Contemporary Pacific* 6 (1): 148–161.

Hezel, Francis X. 1995. *Strangers in Their Own Land: A Century of Colonial Rule in the Caroline and Marshall Islands.* Honolulu: University of Hawai'i Press.

Metzgar, Eric. 2006. "Carolinian Voyaging in the New Millennium." *Micronesian Journal of the Humanities and Social Sciences* 5 (1/2): 293–305.

Peter, Joakim. 2000. "Chuukese Travelers in Our Postcolonial Horizon." *Asia Pacific Viewpoint* 41 (3): 253–267.

Steiner, Candice Elanna. 2015. "A Sea of Warriors: Performing an Identity of Resilience and Empowerment in the Face of Climate Change in the Pacific." *The Contemporary Pacific* 27 (1): 147–180.

6

Music in China

Recalibrating Musical Heritage in a Radically Changing Society

FREDERICK LAU

Chapter Contents

Introduction

This chapter takes you to an extraordinary place: China, the largest nation in the area commonly referred to as East Asia (Figure 6.1). The long history of China and the tremendous changes experienced there especially since the beginning of the twentieth century illustrate the point of this chapter: namely, that people ground the uses and meanings of music in place and time. When circumstances change, people's ideas about the existing music and practices are likely to change in some ways. They might even decide to abandon some practice that is no longer relevant. I am calling this process of change "recalibration," which involves changes among the relationships of people, music, time, and place.

≡ Traditional pavilions in Yu Yuan Gardens, Shanghai, China.

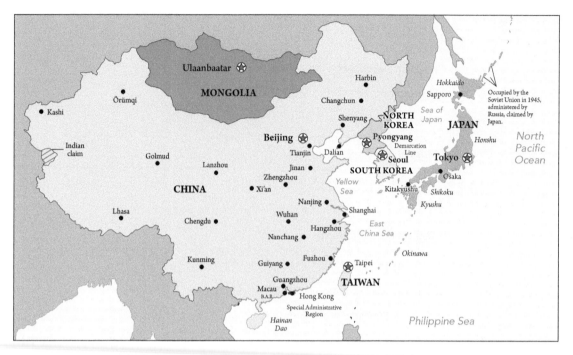

≣ **FIGURE 6.1** Map of East Asia.

To trace processes of recalibration, I have selected two contrasting traditional musical practices that remain current in China today:

1. The ancient solo tradition of the plucked, long, zither-type chordophone *guqin*. Through most of its history, *guqin* has been considered the pinnacle of Chinese musical heritage.
2. The nineteenth-century instrumental ensemble tradition of *Jiangnan sizhu.* This tradition is representative of musics associated with particular regions of the huge country.

The contrasts between these two musical traditions are striking, in terms of music, place, and time:

1. Music: *Guqin* is a solo form of music, while *Jiangnan sizhu* is played by an ensemble.
2. Place: *Guqin* has been embraced nationally, but *Jiangnan sizhu* is only locally known.
3. Time: *Guqin* is an ancient tradition, and *Jiangnan sizhu* is historical, but, relatively speaking, much more recent.

What each tradition has meant and how each has been used through time are the stories that are told in this chapter.

Because China's history is so long, and the *guqin* tradition is so ancient, this chapter will include a good bit of historical discussion. After introducing you to the history of China in sweeping terms, I will introduce you to *guqin* and *Jiangnan sizhu* as musical practices, then track the recalibrations of each during different historical eras. In addition, you will learn about the recent "new traditional music" that involves further recalibrations.

China

China (see Figure 6.2) emerged as one of the world's earliest civilizations in the fertile Yellow River basin in the North China plain. It is now the world's second largest country by land area, with a present population of c. 1.4 billion. It has the longest combined land border in the world—13,743 miles from the mouth of the Yalu River to the Gulf of Tonkin. China's 9,000-mile-long coastline along the Pacific Ocean is bounded by the Bohai, Yellow, East China, and South China Seas.

China's landscape is vast and diverse: ranging from the Taklamakan and continuingly expanding Gobi deserts with their high plateaus in the west; to the arid north; to subtropical forests in the wetter south. While in the north on the edges of the Inner Mongolian Plateau, broad grasslands predominate, southern China is dominated by hills and low mountain ranges. In western China loom six major mountain ranges including the Himalayas, Karakoram, Pamir, and Tian Shan that separate China from much of South and Central Asia; Mount Everest lies on the China-Nepal border. The country's lowest, and the world's third-lowest, point is the dried lake bed of Ayding Lake in the Turpan Depression. The Yangtze and Yellow Rivers—the third- and sixth-longest in the world, respectively—run from the Tibetan Plateau to the densely populated eastern seaboard. In the central east lie the Yangtze and Yellow River deltas. In eastern China, extensive and densely populated alluvial plains lie along the shores of the Yellow Sea and the East China Sea.

For most of its history, China was ruled politically by a series of imperial dynasties; from 1700 BCE to 1911 CE, when the imperial system ended, 3,611 years had passed. The last dynasty—the Qing—ended after 267 years, that is, longer than the United States of America has been an independent nation. (Perhaps you have seen the movie, *The Last Emperor*, which dramatizes its ending in the early twentieth century.) During the twentieth century, rapid changes occurred, and China

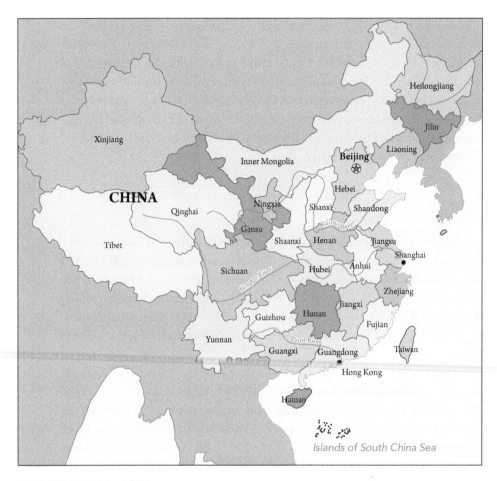

≡ **FIGURE 6.2** Map of China.

went through a series of different governments (Lau 2008). In a nutshell, these were the following:

1. The Republic of China (1912–1949). The system of imperial rule gave way to the founding of a Republic of China in 1912. China had been being pressured for trade from encroaching European countries and the United States. In the late 1910s and early 1920s, Chinese students and intellectuals challenged old customs, bringing on a large-scale effort to reform Chinese culture through Western learning—including Western music.

2. The Maoist period (1949–1976). Wracked by widespread civil war from 1945, the Republic of China succumbed in 1949 to the Communist Revolution led

by Mao Zedong. Mao declared the creation of the People's Republic of China (PRC) on October 1 of that year. Radical change resulted, as Chairman Mao took steps to shift China from a hierarchical imperialist organization of society and culture to a classless, popularist, communist one. In this period, music was put to the purpose of sustaining the revolution and furthering the aims of the government.

3. From 1978 into the twenty-first century. A different Communist future opened for China when a new economic policy—called the Open Door policy—was initiated in 1978, opening up the country to investment for foreign businesses. Consumerism, with which we associate China today, engulfed society, causing some drastic—and in the case of *guqin* and instrumental ensemble practice, perhaps surprising—recalibrations in the sphere of music in the twenty-first century.

Musical Practices

Guqin, a Solo Instrumental Tradition

The *guqin* (formerly referred to as *qin*) is one of the oldest Chinese instruments (Figure 6.3). Archaeological discoveries confirm that that particular form of long zither existed as early as the fifteenth century BCE (during the Shang dynasty). For centuries, it was the instrument of the **literati**: culturally elite scholar-bureaucrats of Imperial China. The literati followed the great philosopher Confucius (551 BCE to 479 BCE), who felt that China's elite should avoid practicing music professionally and instead focus on abstract writing about music's place in the universe and ideas about right and wrong conduct. The literati disparaged cultural practices of subordinate social groups, including professional musicians. The *guqin* was to be played by members of the elite literati class, such as Confucius himself, each for his own self-cultivation, and for each other. Thus, the practice was meaningful and useful for a specific set of people. Who those people were in the society established a sense of *guqin* music as elitist—a sense that, as you will learn, has persisted to the present.

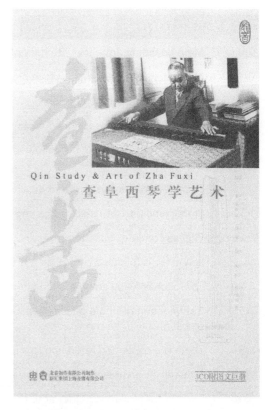

Qin Study & Art of Zha Fuxi
查阜西琴学艺术

≣ **FIGURE 6.3** Front cover of the historical recording set of *Qin* [*Guqin*] Study and the Art of Zha Fuxi.

"Yiguren" (忆故人) [Recalling an Old Friend]

Performed by Zha Fuxi (1895–1976)

Recording location and year: China, October 2016, historical recording set of *Qin [Guqin] Study and the Art of Zha Fuxi.*

Instrumentation: *Guqin*

Listen to the excerpt of *"Yiguren"* ("Recalling an Old Friend"; Audio Example 6.1) from a historical recording performed by *guqin* master and scholar Zha Fuxi (1895–1976). Pay particular attention to the tempo and nuances of the right hand plucks and left hand glides across and along the strings, as well as the makeup of the melody. In your own words, how would you introduce and characterize this unique music to someone who has never heard it?

Time	Something to Listen For
0:01	Melodic theme appears, with harmonic tones played alongside pressed tones.
0:17	Melodic theme played an octave higher, with harmonic tones.
0:35	Partial melodic theme appears.
0:43	A descending "pressed tone" is played.
0:47	Low pitches are prominent, followed by the sound of fingers sliding and scraping on strings.
0:55	Pitches continue, sustained, then silence, then scraping on strings.
1:10	From static pitches rises a sustained pitch, followed by a pitch a fifth higher.
1:25	Pitches continue close together and then an octave or more apart, sustained.
1:39	Low pitch is followed by a pitch a fifth higher.
2:00	Low pitch is followed by a pitch a fifth higher.
2:05	Continuation of single pitches in succession, played in higher and lower registers, sometimes with harmonic tones.
5:31	There is a continued reference to a lower drone pitch as a higher melody proceeds.
5:55	A metallic-percussive quality sounds from two strings.
6:02	Two strings played together at the octave.
6:28	Sliding pitches are played at different registers.
7:11	Glissando.
7:32	Glissando.

Jiangnan Sizhu: An Instrumental Ensemble Tradition

Although *Jiangnan sizhu,* like *guqin,* is music practiced by a social group for their own self-cultivation, its music, performance context, and type of elite status are entirely different from those of the *guqin* heritage. *Jiangnan sizhu* is a major musical genre of the Jiangnan region. It originated from Anhui, Jiangsu, and Zhejiang provinces, and most notably in and around the city of Shanghai (Figure 6.2). Historically popular in both urban and rural areas, it was developed to its present form in the mid-nineteenth century (in the late Qing dynasty period) by an emerging local urban elite, performed by and for the enjoyment of its community of performers (Witzleben 1995, 9; Yuan 1987, 291–292; Jones 1996, 270).

As in other Chinese regional musics, the instrumentation of a *Jiangnan sizhu* ensemble consists of three groups of commonly used instruments, as shown in Figure 2.1.

1. Strings: **erhu** (bowed spiked lute/fiddle with two strings)
    pipa (short-necked, pear-shaped, plucked lute with four strings)
    qinqin (small, short-necked, round-bodied, plucked lute with three or four strings)
    yangqin (trapezoidally shaped, hammered zither/dulcimer)
2. Winds: **dizi** (side-blown bamboo flute with membrane)
    xiao (narrow, end-blown flute with notched rim)
    sheng (free reed mouth organ)
3. Percussion: *bangu* (small, stick-played frame drum)
    ban a pair of wooden clappers

In *Jiangnan sizhu* practice, each instrumentalist in the ensemble plays the same melody while simultaneously varying the melody according to individual preference and in response to other players' melodic lines. The texture of this music is called **heterophony.** This way of playing has been characterized as the defining feature of *Jiangnan sizhu* playing.

Musical Recalibrations across Time
In the Period of the Republic of China (1912–1949)

Like many facets of traditional knowledge, the popularity of the *guqin* was eclipsed in this period. Out of favor, *guqin* survived only as an esoteric art form for a privileged few traditionalists. *Jiangnan sizhu,* however, continued unaffected by cultural changes because it was a genre practiced by "commoners"—a local, urban elite—rather than by imperialist elites.

LISTENING GUIDE

"Zhonghua Liuban"

Performed by a group of musicians in Shanghai Teahouse

Recorded by Frederick Lau in Shanghai, August 1986

Instrumentation: *Jiangnan sizhu* ensemble (silk and bamboo): *pipa, yangqin, erhu, dizi, sheng, bangu, qinqin,* and clappers

While listening to "*Zhonghua liuban,*" try to hear multiple sounds of the types of instruments.

Time	Something to Listen For
0:01	Two beats on the wooden clappers lead to sustained tones played on all instruments of the ensemble and most prominently heard here is the sound of *erhu* (bowed lute), *dizi* (flute), *sheng* (mouth organ), and *pipa* (plucked lute).
0:02	Something to listen for: All instruments have settled in on the tempo and finding their role......
0:06	Moving melody is sounded on *erhu* over sustained tones and plucked tones of *pipa* (plucked lute).
0:14	*Dizi* emerges to lead the melody upward in register.
0:20	All four instrumentalists (*erhu, dizi, sheng,* and *pipa*) have settled in, finding their role as contributors to melody and sustained tones.
0:24	Two melodies are played simultaneously on *dizi* and *erhu,* with pitches intertwining pitches in and around one another.
0:30	Plucked sound of the *pipa* can be heard as a means of indicating phrases, or reminding listeners of important pitches (and home tones).
0:41	*Dizi* player adds a faster-moving, melodic flourish.
0:48	Two melodies intersect again, coming from *dizi* and *erhu.*
0:51	*Dizi* emerges melodically, followed by the *erhu*'s melodic weave.

ACTIVITY 6.1

Listen again to my field recording of the entire piece of "*Zhonghua liuban*" (Audio Example 6.2). Then, listen to the skeleton melody of "*Zhonghua liuban*" for the purpose of learning to sing it. Listen several more times to the entire piece, focusing in turn on each instrument. Notice how the melody of each instrument is derived from the skeleton melody.

What had happened? During this period, Western music, techniques, instruments, pedagogy, and aesthetics were introduced to China. The first Western-style national music academy was established in Shanghai in 1927 by German-trained music scholar Xiao Youmei (1884–1940). China also saw the first systematic approach to the study of traditional music and instruments implemented by Liu Tianhua (1895–1932) at Peking University, the leading educational institution in the country.

As new musical knowledge and concepts from the West made their way into Chinese society, discussions of how to transform and reinvigorate China's traditional music became hot topics in both scholarly and popular circles (Wang 2005; Jones 2001). There were heated discussions about how to ground the uses and meanings of music in the new social circumstances, and which music should be favored. The cultural purists who decried the death of traditional music in the face of the encroaching popularity of Western music wanted to protect its originality and integrity (Wang 1999), that is, preserve it. Others saw opportunities to experiment and create new forms in order to rejuvenate traditional music and ensure its continuity.

New compositions, musical practice, concepts, aesthetics, and theories of music began to circulate widely, as traditional music was combined with Western music in order to "jazz up" and "modernize" traditional music (He 2002). Newness in sound was created by the use of Western harmonic language and instrumentation. A new generation of composers—such as Zhao Yuan Ren (1892–1980), Huang Zi (1904–1938), and He Luting (1903–1999)—began to compose music that captured the hearts and minds of their contemporaries. Some of the new "invented" practices quickly became traditions in their own right by virtue of their popularity and visibility. They would eventually become the foundation for developing Chinese music from the second half of the twentieth century and beyond.

In the Maoist Period (1949–1976)

In the decades after the declaration of the creation of the PRC from 1949, the Maoist government put music to use in support of workers, peasants, and soldiers in order to support and promote the newly adopted communist ideology. Internal resistance to control of China's culture by Mao was perhaps inevitable, as radical change takes time to be absorbed: change from an ancient hierarchical imperialist idea about the organization of society and culture to a classless, popularist, communist one. As a result of a struggle for power between Mao and his enemies, a ten-year period of political struggle called the Cultural Revolution (1966–1976) saw Mao taking drastic steps to prevent China from regressing into a traditionalist, elitist society. During the Cultural Revolution, with the goal of preserving "true" Communist ideology in the country, Mao organized urban youths into Red Guards and encouraged them to attack all traditional values and bourgeois behavior and ideology. Most traditional Chinese music and also Western instruments were banned. *Guqin,* seen as the icon of China's feudal past, was an explicit target of Mao's 1974 political campaign against Confucianism. The Cultural Revolution ended with the death of Mao and the arrest of his strongest four supporters (called the Gang of Four) in 1976.

The Maoist government supported the development of "traditional music" (**minzu yinyue**) by creating new music academies and conservatories throughout the country. The government also instituted a system of professional musicians who were assigned to perform in newly formed government organizations such as song and dance troupes; music ensembles; cultural workers' troupes; and traditional orchestras at the local, county, and provincial level. Under the state-sponsored music system, public concerts and performances were plentiful and well-funded, and the careers of musicians were secure. For the academically trained professional musicians, this political recognition effectively reversed the low status that professional musicians had held since the time of Confucius. At the same time, what those institutions did, in effect, was to create a standardized "Chinese music."

From 1978 into the Twenty-First Century

When the Open Door policy was initiated in 1978, the demands on music and musicians changed again. From the 1980s, the state no longer considered it useful to support music; state-run troupes had to secure their own funding for survival. Musicians were dislodged from job security. Two seemingly contradictory music trends emerged. On the one hand, the Maoist-period, standardized traditional music lost its appeal among general audiences, especially the younger generations who saw these artistic expressions as remnants of the past. On the other hand, as consumerism engulfed society, music became key in a reactionary longing for innocence and antiquity.

I came into the field of Chinese music at the cusp of this watershed moment. When I first arrived at Shanghai Conservatory in the late 1980s to conduct my ethnographic field research, I met older Western-trained musicians whose careers has been set under the Maoist system and also younger musicians rushing to seek alternative ways to survive the harsh reality of a market-driven performing world. The regard for traditional musics was not high. I was told that *guqin* was still not popular among young people, and only a handful of students were playing it. The most often cited explanation was not a political one but that the sound of the instrument is too soft for stage performance, and the instrument had not been as modernized and developed as other instruments of traditional music had been. As for regional music such as *Jiangnan sizhu*, the "artists among the folk" (*minjian yiren*) who practiced them were disparaged by those in the academy as untrained and unskilled, and unprofessional. Considered crude and unpolished, their music begged to be developed and transformed by professionals—injected with innovation and creativity.

Early in my field research, however, I learned that not all musicians were facing the turmoil of socioeconomic pressure and its demands for changing values. During my first week in Shanghai, I was invited to attend an evening gathering to celebrate the mid-Autumn Festival with several teachers and foreign students from the Conservatory. Hosting this event was an active local music club located in the old part of the city of Shanghai. We arrived at the Hu Xin Ting (Pavilion at the Middle of the Lake), a teahouse situated in the heart of the Yu Yuan Garden, a modest mansion built in 1559 during the Ming Dynasty by a local elite and official (Figure 6.4). After being seated near the upstairs window of the pavilion, we were treated to a performance of local music: "*Jiangnan sizhu*, Silk and Bamboo music from south of the Yangtze River, popularized only in Shanghai and nearby regions," as it was explained.

FIGURE 6.4
Shanghai's Hu Xing Ting "Pavilion in the Middle of the Lake."

The entire evening was filled with camaraderie, conversation, tea, and laughter accompanied by the soothing sound of *Jiangnan sizhu*.

Musicians took turns playing. About ten to twelve at a time were invited to take their place at the table in the middle of the room. On the table was a collection of Chinese instruments. The musicians told us that this evening was a perfect occasion to hear this beautiful music just as it used to be when this music was performed for entertainment and self-enjoyment. They started with the piece "*Zhonghua liuban*," called "*zhong ban*" for short among the musicians. They played without a conductor and from memory. That was my first time experiencing *Jiangnan sizhu* performed live. I could sense a deep and meaningful attachment of the practitioners to their local regional music, something that was missing from the "Chinese music" performed by professional musicians. I was captivated by the sentiments invoked by the interwoven musical lines and the skills and attention with which the musicians manipulated the melody.

As a participant observer of *Jiangnan sizhu* music in Shanghai, I glimpsed the importance of music in and as social life for its practitioners—a community of musicians, commonly known as **minjian yiren** (literally, "artists among the folk"). As ethnomusicologist Thomas Turino puts it, "The performing arts are frequently fulcrums of identity, allowing people to intimately feel themselves part of the community through the realization of shared cultural knowledge and style and through the very act of participation together in performance" (2008, 2). These cultural insiders hold views about their music that contrast with what is presented in textbooks and by professional musicians outside of the clubs.

These *minjian yiren* sometimes play down their status by presenting themselves as an exotic folk culture or a slice from the past. They have internalized the social bias toward regional culture as peripheral to national culture, which tends to confine regional music to marginal status. While proud of their tradition, practitioners can be sensitive to the image of the wider public toward it and themselves. For instance, when the 1987 New Year celebration featured the resident group at the *Wenmiao* (Confucius Temple) performing an all-day-long concert of *Jiangnan sizhu* music, contrary to their casualness and chattiness at weekly informal gatherings, the musicians conducted themselves solemnly and even "professionally" at this staged concert.

Contemporary Recalibration of the *Guqin* and *Jiangnan Sizhu* Traditions

Attention to *Jiangnan sizhu* grew from the 1980s, and its status was gradually elevated as sound recordings, concerts, and printed scores became readily available. Communities have been built around many neighborhood *Jiangnan sizhu* clubs. *Jiangnan sizhu* became a cultural icon of the Jiangnan region and a source of cultural pride for the city of Shanghai, which has bolstered its reputation by large-scale events celebrating regional culture and identity (Figure 6.5). An international competition in 1987 officially announced the importance of this genre for the city of Shanghai.

In 2005, the city of Shanghai formed the Shanghai Association of Jiangnan Sizhu for research, preservation, and systematization of the traditional repertory. It organizes concerts and master classes and encourages new compositions and the general promotion of this music (Figure 6.5). The formation of the Association solidified the traditional meaning of *Jiangnan sizhu*, but it also transformed this regional tradition into an icon of China's enduring cultural traditions. Is this not evidence that the uses and meanings of music are grounded in time and place?

In the late twentieth century as well, the *guqin*'s legacy was reassessed as part of a shift toward learning old things and hearkening back to Confucianism. In 1983, the People's Music Publishing House in Beijing released two volumes of music entitled *Guqin Quji* (*Anthology of Guqin Repertory*; Figure 6.6). Al-

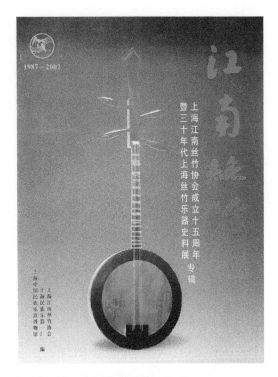

FIGURE 6.5 Cover of the event program commemorating the 15th anniversary of the establishment of the Shanghai Association of Jiangnan Sizhu.

though this press had published many collections of music and instruction books for traditional instruments, this was the first time that the elitist *guqin* music was featured. In addition to providing traditional abbreviated-character *guqin* notation (see Figure 1.2), the volume also featured transcriptions in staff notation of pieces performed by famous twentieth-century players. It was the first systematic approach to publishing *guqin* music in a modern edition.

Remarkably, that ancient, iconic instrument of China, the *guqin*, has seen its restoration to a position of high cultural status. The *guqin* has drawn the attention of a range of *guqin* lovers and laypersons through concerts and other events, the publication of scores, and reissues of old recordings as well as new commercial or privately issued recordings since the 2000s.

With the call by UNESCO for world recognition of intangible cultural heritage, the international implications for countries whose musical heritage carries value for all of humankind were not lost on the Chinese government. In 2006, the

≡ FIGURE 6.6 Book cover of *Guqin Quji* (*Anthology of Guqin Repertory*).

Chinese Intangible Cultural Heritage (ICH) Protection Center was founded. Many local and regional offices were set up to collect items from each region that would then be submitted to the central government for recognition. The implementation of the Center has elevated many well-known, little-known, and regional genres such as *Jiangnan sizhu* from quaint artifacts to national treasures. Armed with its long documented history, *guqin* was a logical early choice for recognition as a national treasure; its addition to the UNESCO list confirmed its significance for China culture.

"New" Traditional Music

Whereas in the early years of the twentieth century, traditional music was "updated" through the overt use of Western harmonic language and instrumentation, in the twenty-first century, the quality and the extent of new elements are different. Recent trends tend to transform not only the appearance but the core of what is defined as traditional: new music grounded in a new time and "place," called literally new traditional music (***xin minyue***).

We see, for instance, a new style of ensemble utilizing traditional instruments and repertory but accompanied by a rock beat and presented in glamorous stage presentations, a sort of contemporary rendition of traditionality with hyped-up sights and sounds. This style gives the impression of "newness" by avoiding traditional sounds and settings. Musicians are transcending national, local, and political boundaries to create a sense of cosmopolitanism and international pop sensibility—the trademark of global fusion music.

ACTIVITY 6.2

The UNESCO Intangible Cultural Heritage convention of 2004 is having tremendous impact on the arts in many countries of the world. To inform yourself more about this, study the site at https://ich.unesco.org/.

A remarkable phenomenon in the twenty-first century is the increase of girl bands performing with Chinese traditional instruments. These bands carefully cultivate their image, appearance, and presentation. While their collective image is refreshing, sensual, sharp, and innovative, it relies on the use of selected Chinese motives and elements in their fashion and design. Among the most famous of these groups nationally and internationally are the Oriental Angels (OA). Established in the summer of 2003, OA is an ensemble made up of five outstanding young female musicians who are graduates of the Shanghai Conservatory of Music. They cultivate a hyperfeminine style with specially designed costumes and choreography for each performance—a far cry from the traditional music presented by song and dance troupes of the 1970s. Their publicity uses phrases like "oriental charm" and "elegant beauty" to describe the group's presentation. In the words of one of its members, Li Jie, "when we stand on stage and [are] faced with foreign friends, what we represent is Chinese folk music and China. We are confident to bring honor to the Chinese people" (Lau 2017, 122). In other words, they are consciously cultivating a unique group persona in addition to their music.

Another way in which the group is trying to cultivate an image different from that of traditional performers is through an eclectic repertoire. In their DVD recording "Oriental Angels," the group featured seven pieces of music: two of them drawn from the traditional repertory, one arrangement of a Romanian folksong, and three original compositions. The seventh piece is a 1940s Shanghai pop song.

ACTIVITY 6.3

Search for a video of the musical group Oriental Angels' performance of "Dream of the Angels" on YouTube or your preferred streaming service. Make note of the performers' appearance and stage presentation. Pay close attention to the eight-bar melodic phrase and chordal accompaniment that is played first on **paixiao** (a set of end-blown bamboo pipes of different lengths bound together), then on *erhu* and *dizi*. Identify and classify the stringed instruments; compare their musical parts and prepare a statement about their musical roles in this piece. Finally, compare this music to the *Jiangnan sizhu* music that was discussed earlier (Audio Example 6.1.)

For the second example, "Spring" (based on a Romanian folksong), pay attention to the texture—simple accompaniment and the unison playing on *erhu*, *yangqin*, and *dizi*. Compare and contrast this music with "Dream of the Angels" and *Jiangnan sizhu* music.

Another girl band you might want to investigate independently is Twelve Girls Band (Lau 2008, 159).

Final proof of the grounding of meanings and uses of music in time and place involves the revered *guqin*. As noted, its relevance once resided solely in the everyday life of the elite literati class of ancient China. Currently, however, *guqin* is seen as a tradition relevant in anyone's everyday life—as a tool for finding tranquility, an antidote to a chaotic contemporary lifestyle marked by a quest for material goods, wealth, and instant gratification; and characterized by competition, chaos, and greed. Playing the *guqin* has begun to be associated with a back-to-nature and new-age kind of lifestyle as well as with Chinese medicine, health, meditation, relaxation, and spiritual advancement. To make it accessible, one promotional website suggests that people do not need to achieve perfection in their playing; anyone can simply improvise, playing the *guqin* any way they want. The goal is to bring the sound of the *guqin* into one's life, and through repetition to integrate sound with bodily involvement to gradually alter one's frame of mind and ways of thinking. *Guqin* has been recalibrated with fresh meaning and use.

Conclusion

Despite drastic changes in social and economic systems over the last 100+ years, and despite the popularity of global cultural forms in China, traditional musics continue to thrive. With the changing political environments, however, meanings, uses, and practices of music have changed. If we accept that music is grounded in time and place, then a new China would no doubt produce more new kinds of music.

Introducing Western instruments or incorporating a rock beat into a traditional repertory as a marker of cosmopolitanism, reviving *guqin's* former glory and elevating it to the status of repository of a nation's intangible cultural heritage, and playing a regional genre as a feature of community and regional pride on a global stage are all articulations of new uses and meanings for existing cultural practices and traditions. When we accept processes of recalibration as a given and embrace a flexible concept of traditional music, we are able to accept ingenuity, innovation, and creative impulses that underlie the music we hear in the twenty-first century as the Chinese people make music meaningful and useful in their lives.

Bibliography

He, Xiaobing. 2002. "新民乐:传统音乐的 "改版" [New Traditional Music, an Altered Version of Original Traditional Music]." 音乐周报 [*Music Weekly*] 3 (October–November).

Jones, Andrew F. 2001. *Yellow Music: Media Culture and Colonial Modernity in the Chinese Jazz Age*. Durham, NC: Duke University Press.

Jones, Stephen. 1996. *Folk Music of China: Living Instrumental Traditions*. Oxford: Oxford University Press.

Lau, Frederick. 2008. *Music in China: Experiencing Music, Expressing Culture*. Oxford: Oxford University Press.

Lau, Frederick. 2017. "Celestial Music, Glamorous Angels: Girls Glitzing up and Traditional Chinese." In *Music in China Today: Traditions, Contemporary Trends*, edited by Bernhard Hanneken and Tiago de Oliveria Pinto, 111–130. Berlin: Verlag für Wissenschaft und Bildung.

Turino, Thomas. 2008. *Music as Social Life : The Politics of Participation, Chicago Studies in Ethnomusicology*. Chicago: University of Chicago Press.

Wang, Tong. 1999. "对" 大同乐会"在现代国乐演进中的认识" ["Towards Understanding the Role of Datong National Music Association in the Development of National Music"]. 南京艺术学院学报 *[Journal of the Nanjing Arts Academy]* 2.

Wang, Yuhe, ed. 2005. *Zhongguo Jinxiandai Yinyue Shijuan (1901–1949) [Historical Sources of Contemporary Chinese Music]*. Beijing: Renmin yinyue chubanshe [People's Music Publishing House].

Witzleben, Lawrence. 1995. *"Silk and Bamboo" Music in Shanghai: The Jiangnan Sizhu Instrumental Ensemble Tradition*. Kent, OH: The Kent State University Press.

Yuan, Jingfang. 1987. *"Minzu Qiyue [National Instrumental Music]."* Beijing: Renmin Yinyue Chubanshe [People's Music Publishing Company].

7

Music in Japan

Encounters with Asian and European Traditions

BONNIE C. WADE

Chapter Contents

Introduction

Japanese music has been profoundly affected by encounters and sustained interface with other musical traditions from both Asian (continental and island) and European cultural spheres (Europe and the Americas). This has occurred in a three-step process of (1) learning and adopting musical ideas and items from other cultures; followed by (2) selective assimilation; and then (3) indigenization (Japanization) of them. Thus, in modern Japan, two deeply cultivated, historically grounded cultures exist. Musicians (including composers) can draw from these traditions: traditional Japanese aesthetics, forms, instruments (De Ferranti, 2000), and practices; and also Western aesthetics, forms, instruments, and practices. Not surprisingly, many musicians have responded to the opportunity to create new music that draws on both traditions. Call it *fusion, hybridity,* or *syncretism,* it is a creative process that is challenging to pull off successfully but sometimes works really well. Significantly, the process of interfacing has become multidirectional, as Japanese musicians are now participating in musical

≡ **Cherry blossoms at night in Nakameguro, Tokyo.**

flows throughout the world: sending musical ideas and items out as well as taking them in (Wade, 2014).

This chapter will introduce you to the most significant musical ensemble tradition that resulted from the early Asian encounters: *Gagaku*, a form of Japanese court music. That is followed by study of a solo musical tradition—for *koto* (long plucked zither with thirteen strings, or more; Wade, 1994)—that resulted from the indigenization process. Further, two twentieth-century compositions created by individuals drawing on both Japanese and Western musical traditions demonstrate not only successful hybridity but also ways in which Japanese musicians have made musical encounters useful and meaningful for their culture and beyond.

Japan

Japan is an archipelago of several thousands of islands (see Figure 7.1). It is situated across the Sea of Japan off the east coast of East Asia, with nearest neighbors Korea, China, and Russia. Honshu, home to the major cities of Tokyo, Kyoto, and Osaka, is the largest of the islands and features Mt. Fuji, the tallest mountain in the country. The other main islands (Kyushu, Shikoku, and Hokkaido) are also mountainous, with forests that cover 70 percent of all the land.

Contact between Japan and other Asian cultures began very early. Archaeological records document movement of peoples across the Sea of Japan in the fourth, fifth, and sixth centuries CE (Figure 7.1). The first recorded visit of musicians to Japan was by eighty performers from Korea's Silla kingdom in the year 453. Because Korean culture was heavily influenced by China, Korea was also a conduit through which elements of continental civilization were introduced to Japan: Buddhism and its music in the sixth century, for one significant example. Buddhism became a vehicle for the transfer of much Chinese culture to Japan, just as Christianity would serve as one vehicle for the transfer of elements of European civilization to Japan a millennium later.

Direct Japanese contact with China was longstanding by the sixth century when the Japanese began to take concerted steps to transplant elements of the continental culture. That process escalated in the seventh century because the Chinese Tang court (618–907)—located at the eastern end of the overland Silk Road for trade across the continent of Asia—had become one of the most powerful, sophisticated, and cosmopolitan cultural centers in history. Large embassies were sent from Japan to China, accompanied by students of Buddhism and of Chinese history and literature, painting, music, and other subjects. Although the Japanese language is unrelated to the Chinese language, the Chinese writing system was

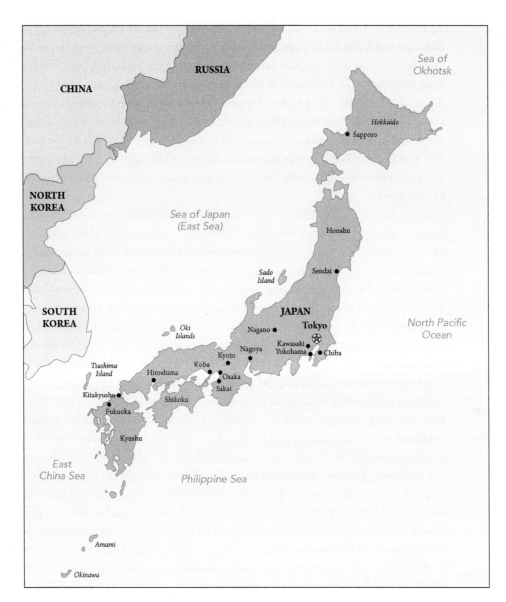

≡ **FIGURE 7.1** Map of Japan.

adopted by the Japanese, along with selected Chinese ideas, tastes and systems, court ceremonials, and most pertinently here, musical instruments and pieces performed on them.

Contact between Japan and Europe began when nations and mercantile companies sent traders to the islands in the sixteenth century. Missionaries were often on board the ships, intent on the spread of their particular brands of European cultures, and Japan's first experience with European music came with music for their worship. To ward off politically threatening foreign ideas, however, Christianity was banned in 1588; and in the Tokugawa period (or Edo era, 1600–1868) the policy of the Tokugawa *samurai* (warrior) clan's government was one of nearly complete isolation. For about 250 years, Japan turned mostly inward, a feudal society more or less unto itself, with political and economic power held by the military clan in Edo (Tokyo) while successive emperors languished in the old capital of Kyoto, powerless in poverty. As a result, European music was almost entirely extinguished.

In the first half of the 19th century—in the late Tokugawa period—European, British, and also American presence was felt ever more insistently, as the system of global colonialism threatened the independence of more and more of the world's peoples. For Japan, isolation became increasingly difficult to sustain. In addition, the islands had been experiencing considerable internal turmoil, as regional clan leaders sought to secure their places in whatever structure would emerge from efforts to dislodge the weakening Tokugawa clan. On the evening of July 8, 1853, Commodore Matthew Perry—commander in chief of the US Naval forces stationed in the East India, China, and Japan Seas—sailed into the entrance to Tokyo Bay. Outside influences could no longer be ignored.

Japan's new leaders understood that, without some kind of fresh internal structure and cohesion, there was a real possibility that it would become yet another colonized area. The strongest clan leaders chose to modernize, to learn from those who held power in the world, and thereby fend them off. (This is the "fight fire with fire" solution.) The year 1868 officially marks a drastic change: the long-powerless emperor was reinstated to the top of the political hierarchy, and a new era—the Meiji period (1868–1912)—began. Japanese leaders orchestrated an effective process of studying and adopting the tools for modernizing their country, similar in many respects to the way they had studied and selected from Korean and Chinese civilizations in the first millennium. Embassies were sent abroad to systematically survey aspects of European and American societies, from imperial celebrations to public school systems. The economy was shifted from agriculture to industry, causing rapid urbanization. Understood to be the basis of the modernizing process, universal education was instituted with a governmentally managed school system that became an effective tool for communication with the population as a whole. Thus, Japan began its amazingly rapid rise to an extremely powerful, contemporary nation-state.

ACTIVITY 7.1

A thorough explanation of the ancient court music as it has survived to the present is available on the video *Gagaku: The Court Music of Japan.*

Instruments that play pieces imported from China are demonstrated in Video 7.1 in the following order: *gagaku biwa, koto, taiko, shōko, kakko; ryūteki; hichiriki;* and *sho.* Finally, the full ensemble is heard. As you study the video, pay particular attention to the *koto,* the long plucked zither. Its musical role in the ensemble is quite sparse. When the full ensemble plays, the *koto* is difficult to hear because it blends with the *gagaku biwa* (short-necked ovoid-shaped plucked lute). Nevertheless, as you will learn, the *koto* would become the instrument with the most enduring importance in Japanese traditional music.

Musical Developments

Gagaku: Japanese Court Music

The most significant musical effect on Japanese culture of early interface with other Asian cultures was the importation from China of musical instruments and music played on them during the Tang period. First useful in Japan for performance of specific repertoires of pieces for life in the court context, the instruments of the *gagaku* ensemble—varieties of aerophones, membranophones, idiophones, and chordophones—were each slowly disseminated beyond the court context and were gradually assimilated as instruments for a variety of styles of indigenous Japanese traditional music.

Indigenous Traditional Musics

In the Tokugawa period (from the seventeenth through the mid-nineteenth centuries), much of the music we know as "traditional Japanese music" was created by male performer-composers. They functioned in various spheres of the society outside of the languishing court, greatly contributing to burgeoning cultural activities. The **shamisen**—a long-necked, three-stringed, plucked lute—was commonplace for many types of music of the lower social groups in society (Figure 7.2). Popular theatrical forms (**kabuki** and **bunraku**) catered to the common people in towns and cities; for each of them, *shamisen* players and singers provided an integral (but stylistically distinctive) musical component (Johnson 2010). A unique

≡ **FIGURE 7.2**
Enjoying the Cool on the Riverbed at Shijō. Harada Keigaku, Japanese, active about 1850–1860.

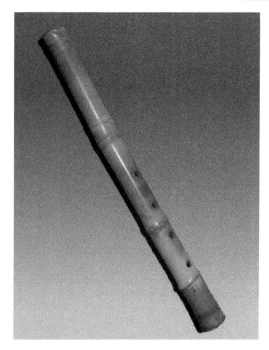

≡ **FIGURE 7.3** *Shakuhachi,* Nineteenth Century.

musico-dramatic style, the rarified **Noh theater**, was patronized by the top class of *samurai* elite (Wade 2004). In the religious sphere, the Fuke subsect of Zen Buddhism swelled with out-of-work *samurai*, all of whom had to play the **shakuhachi** (wide, end-blown, bamboo flute with notched rim) as part of their religious practice (Figure 7.3). Repertoires of chamber music—song accompanied on *shamisen* and/or *koto*—were composed and taught only by governmentally licensed, blind, male musicians to members of the families of feudal lords (Figure 7.4) and wealthier segments of urban populations (merchants). Amateurs among *shakuhachi* players could join *koto* and *shamisen* players for a trio chamber ensemble. There were no venues such as concert halls for music recitals open to the public, so that chamber music was literally that—music to be played in private contexts. Each type of music was meaningful to a particular segment of society.

Western Music

More than a thousand years after *gagaku* was adopted in Japanese culture, another musical adoption would occur as an equally significant effect of the process of cultural interface (Epstein 1994). In the design of the new educational system in the second half of the nineteenth century—a system designed to be classless as in the United States—Meiji national cultural policy dictated that music would be included in the new primary level curriculum, just as it had recently been in the state of Massachusetts. For Japanese leaders, the reasons were not aesthetic; rather, music was regarded as useful. In selecting Western music for the medium of musical instruction, the educational sector was following the example of the military and of a "ceremonial style of governance" that had been witnessed by Japanese guests in European courts who had been entertained with music. Bands attached to foreign armies had appeared to Japanese observers to be a factor conducive to maintaining discipline and raising morale. In the new primary level curriculum, music was deemed valuable for the spiritual and physical health and character formation of the pupils (Figure 7.5).

≡ **FIGURE 7.4** *Descending Geese of the Koto Bridges* (*Kotoji rakugan*), from the series *Eight Views of the Parlor* (*Zashii hakkei*), Torri Kiyonaga, Japanese, 1752–1815.

The adoption of Western music was useful for another reason in the process of modernizing the culture. While the various repertoires of traditional Japanese music were associated with particular segments of society, an entirely new music could be taught as every Japanese person's music, and it could therefore be an expressive cultural space for all citizens in the new nation-state. One further reason was unfortunately a negative one. In deliberating the choice of school music, an official statement of 1879 reveals one of the most devastating effects of the colonial system of power, namely, a belief in the superiority of the culture of the more powerful in a system of unequal relations. After listing a set of choices from which a musical choice would be made, a conclusion was reached: "It will, therefore, be far better to adopt European music in our schools than to undertake the awkward task of improving the imperfect oriental music" (cited in May 1963, 52–53). Although foreign powers never colonized Japan on Japanese soil, such ideas were transmitted—and believed. Music was thus literally a tool useful for building a national community, with new songs on

≡ **FIGURE 7.5**
Japanese children
singing "God Save
the King," 1922.

Western models or set to Western tunes but praising their own emperor and inspiring loyalty. Thus began the thorough enculturation of all Japanese people into Western music.

The positive reception in Japan of music from Western cultures since the second half of the nineteenth century has meant that a rich variety of music and music-making is carried on there. The metropolitan area of the capital, Tokyo, alone now supports no fewer than ten professional orchestras. Jazz has been a consistent presence from the first half of the twentieth century. Throughout the country, amateur choral singing is very popular among young people in school clubs from primary level through university, and an enormous number of people continue to sing in choruses as adults. Wind bands, too, flourish as school activities. One need only think of the name Yamaha to understand the significant place of musical instrument manufacture in the economy, and the name of Sony that undergirds a huge entertainment industry both locally and globally. The importation, enthusiastic reception—and practice—of musics from classical to folk to popular from everywhere is simply a given in contemporary Japanese life, as it is globally. Japanese people make Western music meaningful and useful in their lives in many group and individual ways.

Creative Contributions by Individual Musicians

Three examples are offered here by which to introduce you to some elements of both traditional Japanese music and music in the modern era. They focus on the creative contributions of individual musicians: **Yatsuhashi Kengyō**, a *koto* player in the sixteenth century who set music for that instrument on an entirely new, popularized path; **Michio Miyagi**, a *koto* player in the first half of the twentieth century whose interest in fusion music earned him the title of "father of modern *koto* music"; and **Keiko Abe**, a creative superstar in the world of *marimba* (a xylophone—set of tuned wooden bars, each with a resonator pipe below to amplify the sound) who exemplifies the outward direction of Japan's international interface.

Yatsuhashi Kengyō and Historic Music for the *Koto*

Although the playing of the *koto* had been taken up beyond court culture by the sixteenth century, the physical construction of the instrument had been left essentially intact. In the seventeenth century, a talented, blind male musician, Yatsuhashi Kengyō (1624–1715), created compositions for solo *koto* (for *koto* only, without song) that took a huge step toward *koto* music as it is known today: in a very real sense, *koto* music was indigenized and "popularized." Leaving behind Chinese-derived *gagaku* melodic modes, Yatsuhashi Kengyō adopted melodic practice from players of the *shamisen* (see Figure 7.2)—that instrument in the sphere of popular music—to create a new set of pieces. One of them, titled **"Rokudan"** ("Six Sections"), not only endured from the seventeenth century but is among the few traditional pieces that every Japanese school child learns about at present. "Rokudan" is also the piece toward which many young women work in their *koto* lessons, as the goal for sufficient musical achievement for a good marriage.

"Rokudan" illustrates several characteristics of traditional *koto* music (Audio Example 7.1). A kind of motion I describe as "flowing ongoingness" is a trait of much melody that is not accompanying song. Rhythmically, no meter is intended in traditional *koto* music, although listeners with ears experienced with Western music are likely to hear it as metered. Pieces (and/or sections of pieces) begin slowly and usually gradually accelerate, with a slowing at the end. In addition, although there are patterns that recur in this music, there is no such thing as development of thematic motives or even many clear phrase breaks as the melody flows on. The melody is intimately linked to the tuning to which the movable *koto* bridges are set—created for the most part by the plucking of consecutive strings. Finally, in this style there is a straightforward rendering of the melody, without exploiting dynamic range or other expressive techniques. Even if, unlike "Rokudan,"

ACTIVITY 7.2

Listen to Audio Example 7.1, "Rokudan: Section 1," at least three times, each time focusing on one of these traits: (1) "flowing ongoingness" (just try to find phrase breaks where you could sneak a breath if singing); (2) lack of a metric pattern of recurring stress on designated beats; and (3) straightforward, unemotive presentation of the melody. This recording offers only the first of the six sections.

To introduce you further to the *koto* as an instrument, one tuning, and several playing techniques for this type of traditional music, link to the video "Introduction to the Japanese *koto*" that was made for this chapter by San Francisco Bay Area *koto* artist, Shoko Hikage. The video ends with a performance of the entire "Rokudan" in which the pattern of tempo is fully displayed.

a composition includes song (self-accompanied on *koto*), the emotive expression lies in the text, not in the musical setting.

Michio Miyagi: "The Father of Modern *Koto* Music"

Michio Miyagi (1894–1956) played a key role in the integration of Western influences into Japanese *koto* music. Miyagi was born in the Meiji era when the movement for modernization was in full swing and Western music was being aggressively introduced. Growing up in the foreign section in the trading city of Kobe as the son of a clerk of a foreign company, he was continually exposed to international culture. When he was blinded by disease during childhood, it was decided that he should enter the field of music—one of the few occupations available to the blind. From age 8 he was apprenticed to traditional musicians to study *koto* and *shamisen* intensively. After only three years of training, he became a professional musician at age 11, because his father, now working in Korea, was seriously injured by burglars. Miyagi had to become an assistant for his teacher in order to support himself and his grandmother in Kobe. At age 13, however, he had to leave Kobe for Korea to care for his father and do his best to support his father and a brother there. Good teachers of the traditional type were not available in Korea at that time, so he could no longer study performance. He began to teach what little he had learned of *koto* and *shamisen*. To increase his options and the number of students, he taught himself to play *shakuhachi*. Miyagi's short period of study contributed to his becoming a performer-composer: growing tired of playing the limited number of pieces he had been privileged to learn in traditional study and living outside the traditional music world of Japan, he took the opportunity to compose his own music much earlier in his career than was typical for other musicians.

Miyagi's early exposure to Western music was reinforced in Korea. Having befriended amateur *shakuhachi* players among the members of a Western military band in Seoul, he heard many band concerts and became familiar with those instruments. He listened avidly to Western music on imported recordings. Encouraged by a friend to go to Tokyo where both traditional Western music and Japanese music could be heard, although in two fairly distinct musical worlds, he left Korea as a 21-year-old professional musician. After two years of struggling, he gave a recital in 1917 featuring pieces composed during his Korea period. While those pieces were close to traditional *koto* music, they were sufficiently different to capture the attention of the nontraditional music enthusiasts. Encouraged by that success, Miyagi began a period of intensive study of European music theory, composition, violin and piano, and general European culture and literature. And, unusual for a musician whose roots were in the highly in-group-oriented world of traditional music, he studied Japanese instruments with which he was unfamiliar. With all of this training, he began serious experimentation with a synthesis of European and traditional Japanese musical elements in new works.

Significantly, in 1930, Miyagi was hired as a member of the faculty of the most significant institution for music in Japan: the Tokyo School of Music, which would become the Tokyo National University of Fine Arts in the first half of the twentieth century. Able to interact with well-trained students of Western music there and aware of the burgeoning interest in music for large ensembles, he composed many syncretic pieces, some for *koto* with chorus and some for large ensembles of Japanese instruments—both startling innovations from the perspective of traditional *koto* music. For *koto* he experimented with metered pieces, even writing in triple meter that is so utterly non-Japanese, songs whose melodies were really "tunes" in the Western-music sense; use of instruments as chordal accompaniment to songs he composed in the European system of harmony; and also pairing of Western and Japanese instruments. While *"Haru no Umi"* ("The Ocean in Spring" (Video Example 7.4)), his most enduring syncretic work in musical terms, was composed for *koto* and *shakuhachi* in 1929, it has been performed on a variety of instruments—*koto* and violin, for instance, and for piano and flute.

LISTENING GUIDE

"Haru no Umi" by Michio Miyagi

Performed by Shirley Muramoto (*koto*) and Kaoru Kakizakai (*shakuhachi*)

Recording location and year: Berkeley, CA, 2014

Instrumentation: *koto, shakuhachi*

Time	Something to Listen For
0:01	*Koto* plays arpeggiated figures
0:08	Melody by *shakuhachi* over *koto*'s continued arpeggiated chords
0:32	*Shakuhachi* repeats opening of melody
0:42	Sustained flute pitches over *koto*'s active plucking of thirds
0:54	Single *shakuhachi* pitches, emphasizing octaves, with and without *koto* accompaniment
1:12	Lyrical melody by *shakuhachi* with steady *koto* accompaniment
1:24	*Shakuhachi* melody continues while *koto* becomes more active, rhythmically dense
1:41	*Koto* plays melody, with embellishments by *shakuhachi*; gradually roles switch so that *shakuhachi* rises to melody while *koto* recedes to accompaniment
2:06	New lyrical *shakuhachi* melody ensues, with *koto* accompaniment that features sustained and running pages, occasional imitation of the melody
2:35	*Shakuhachi* leaps an octave to a new section, with *koto*'s greater harmonic density
2:47	*Shakuhachi* is imitated by *koto*, followed by the two instruments joining together in a falling, then rising, passage
2:58	*Shakuhachi* and *koto* alternate between call-response and melody-and-accompaniment
3:23	Low-pitched *koto* "solo" of melody and accompaniment
3:32	Re-entrance of *shakuhachi*, with *koto* playing in response, leading to resumption of lyrical melody with accompaniment (2:06)
3:52	*Shakuhachi* leaps an octave, leading to a slowing of the tempo, call-response between *shakuhachi* and *koto* and an active passage together, followed by melodic fragments by one or both instruments
4:34	*Shakuhachi* and *koto* in close melody to harmony correspondence, leading to a gradual decrease in tempo
4:44	*Koto* plays solo passage consisting of descending passage (loudly played), glissando, and a passage of strummed chords that decrease in speed

Time	Something to Listen For
5:00	As at the beginning, the *koto* plays arpeggiated chords, and then is joined by the *shakuhachi*'s melody
5:41	Sustained flute pitches over *koto*'s active plucking of thirds, reminiscent of the passage at 0:42
5:55	Single *shakuhachi* pitches, emphasizing octaves, with *koto* accompaniment, reminiscent of 0:54
6:00	*Shakuhachi* plays short phrases, immediately imitated or otherwise responded to, softly and delicately by the *koto*
6:16	*Shakuhachi* plays high-pitched passage, solo, that features repeated pitches, a slight acceleration, and then slowdown of tempo
6:27	*Shakuhachi* and *koto* begin anew a section of melody and accompaniment
6:38	Greater density of *koto* accompaniment as the *shakuhachi* continues its soaring melody in a gradually decreasing tempo
6:54	Final melodic figure as a statement of closure, with a slow arpeggiated *koto* ending
7:05	*Koto*'s final chordal strum

ACTIVITY 7.3

Rewatch the video performance of "*Haru no Umi*" (Video 7.4) performed by Shirley Muramoto Wong (*koto*) and Kaoru Kakizakai (*shakukuhachi*). After studying the performance on the video, review what you have learned about traditional *koto* music through "Rokudan." Compare the similarities and differences that you see in the two performances.

Keiko Abe, Superstar in the World of Marimba

Keiko Abe's personal history illustrates the process of interface with other cultures in Japanese music. It also provides an example of ways in which Japanese musicians are participating in musical flows throughout the world: sending music out as well as taking music in. Born in Tokyo in 1937 to a doctor father and artist mother, Abe attended a mission school for junior high school; there, at age twelve, she encountered the missionary Lawrence Lacour, who "brought marimba to Japan" (Abe personal communication, May 11, 2001). Attending Tokyo Gakugei University in music education, she graduated with an MA at age 22, still playing percussion. Her professional performing career began when composer Isao Tomita (associated with synthesizer music) needed a percussionist who could make organ sounds on a marimba. Because Lacour had played hymns on marimba, that was no problem for her.

However, Keiko Abe wanted to turn the marimba from "just a part of percussion" into a solo instrument. She commissioned pieces at first, and her career was launched with an award-winning record in 1968. Interested in improvising, she came to America in 1977 to find musicians with similar ideas; in the meantime, her playing was beginning to attract a following in Japan. To really "make it big," Abe decided to commission pieces from the best Japanese contemporary composers. Among them was Minoru Miki, who, after hearing her play the **concerto** (a piece for solo instrument and orchestra) she commissioned from him, remarked to her that the American marimba she was using did not fit her musicality. "You need to develop it more," she reported his having said. So Abe asked the Yamaha company to help; Yamaha "gave me an engineer to work with," she said modestly. The significant result was a five-octave marimba with a deep sound (Yamaha Marimba YM-6000). With it, her career skyrocketed; she has toured North America, Europe, and Asia repeatedly, made many recordings, and was the first woman inducted into the Percussive Arts Society Hall of Fame. On November 1, 2001, from Grand Rapids, Michigan, Yamaha announced a Keiko Abe signature set of mallets. Abe's artistry, her creativity, and her technological innovations are among Japan's gifts to the international community in music.

Abe's composition, "Dream of Cherry Blossoms" (Audio Example 7.2) invokes the familiar tune "***Sakura, sakura***" (Cherry Blossoms) that is likely to automatically remind international audiences of Japan. In many American music textbooks, "*Sakura*" is taught as *the* tune to represent Japan.

Composing for the Japanese as well as an international audience, Keiko Abe begins her "Dream of Cherry Blossoms" with tonal material that does not come from Japanese tradition before she introduces "Sakura"—a tune whose pitch selection is traditional. While the tune of "Sakura" is fragmented in the composition and represented in many variations, it is always clear. According to the liner notes of Abe's recording (on her own label), the song text expresses how, after full bloom, the petals of the cherry blossoms are blown away from the tree, creating a blizzard by gusts of the spring breeze—which I personally experienced and found to be

LISTENING GUIDE

"Dream of Cherry Blossoms"

Performed by Keiko Abe: From *Marimba Fantasy—the Art of Keiko Abe*

Recording location and year: Tokyo, 1998

Instrumentation: Five-octave marimba

Time	Something to Listen For
0:01	Pulsating single high pitch, repeated
0:07	Additional pitch, sounding once, while pulsating, single high pitch continues
0:14	Sequence of broken chords, descending, sounding below the repeated pulsating pitch
0:21	Pulsating high pitch drops out as broken chords emerge
0:24	Melody of "*Sakura*" sounds over the broken chords in a 3-3-2 rhythm that interfaces with a duple feeling in the lower-pitched accompaniment
0:44	Melody is fuller with addition of second pitch for each pitch of the melody, a fourth lower and in slight anticipation of the melody pitches
0:58	Melodic rhythm is rhythmically altered, sounding faster
1:05	Chromatic section that shifts the melody away from its earlier key, through an exploration of pitches in various keys
1:28	Pitches in close proximity of one another (an interval of a second apart) are emphatically repeated
1:34	Fragments of melody appear in lower pitches, below the fast-moving accompaniment
1:43	Slowing of tempo to a shaking tremolo sound, to a stop
1:48	Emphatic lower-pitched melody (call) followed by higher-pitched response, twice
1:56	Buildup, soft to loud, slower to faster, tonal to less tonal/more chromatic sound
2:06	Sustained tremolo to a grand pause
2:13	Soft and slow tremolo chords giving way to melodic fragment in tremolo style
2:38	Loud melodic leap, echoed softly, sounding again at different pitch levels, with scalar passages to surround and close section
3:00	Short section of accented and gradually accelerating passages
3:08	Cadenza begins with arpeggiated, "broken" chords rising upward, and then cascading downward

continued

Time	Something to Listen For
3:26	Emphatic open fifths (call) followed by response, reminiscent of 1:48, with further call-response sections to follow
3:50	Return to the melody, with brief phrases in between
4:10	Soft pulsating clusters, through contrasting fast passage to soft pulsating clusters
4:18	Melodic fragments "dressed" with seconds
4:26	Broken chords under repeated pulsating pitch, reminiscent of 0:14
4:32	Melodic fragments over repeated pitch and lower-pitched open fourths and fifths
4:38	Pulsating, single high pitch, repeated, with broken chords, softening, slowing, fading away yet with a feeling of continuance

emotionally gripping when it suddenly happened in a *sakura* grove in Washington, DC. Whereas in traditional Japanese song performance, expression of the meaning of a text is left to the words themselves and not to the musical setting of the text, Abe draws on Western musical means of expressing the meaning—changing dynamics and tempo and dramatic playing techniques. The Listening Guide is here for your close listening.

ACTIVITY 7.4

The Wikipedia site on "Sakura" (particularly the section on symbolism) is a very good one for understanding the meanings of "*sakura*" in Japanese culture. On the site of the International Shakuhachi Society, you can find a reliable history of the song "*Sakura, Sakura*," text translation, and information on other examples of fusion settings of the melody.

At my request, Shoko Hikage performed "*Sakura, sakura*" (Video Example 7.5) because its pitch selection is very close to the pitches of the *koto* tuning (*hirajoshi*) that she demonstrates. Watch her video to learn the melody so that you can hear it in Keiko Abe's composition "Dream of the Cherry Blossoms" (Audio Example 7.2).

On YouTube, you can find a number of sites that reference "*Sakura, Sakura*." Search to find a contemporary musical version of it that remains so close to the tune that, unlike in "Dream of the Cherry Blossoms," you hear little or nothing to suggest that the version is a piece of fusion in terms of musical material.

Conclusion

This chapter has addressed the profound effect on Japanese musical culture of interface with others—both Asian cultures in the first millennium and Western cultures from the late nineteenth century. Through some of the encounters and effects of them, Japanese people have made musical interface useful and meaningful for themselves in multiple ways.

Bibliography

De Ferranti, Hugh. 2000. *Japanese Musical Instruments*. New York: Oxford University Press.

Epstein, Ury. 1994. *The Beginnings of Western Music in Meiji Era Japan*. Lewiston, NY: Edwin Mellen Press.

Johnson, Henry. 2010. *The Shamisen: Tradition and Diversity*. Leiden: Brill.

May, Elizabeth. 1963. *The Influence of the Meiji Period on Japanese Children's Music*. Berkeley: University of California Press.

Wade, Bonnie C. 1994. "Keiko Nosaka and the Twenty-Stringed Koto: Tradition and Modernization in Japanese Music." In *The Musicological Juncture: Essays in Honor of Rulan Chao Pian*, edited by Bell Yung and Joseph S. C. Lam, 184–198. Cambridge, MA: Harvard University Press.

Wade, Bonnie C. 2005. *Music in Japan: Experiencing Music, Expressing Culture*. New York: Oxford University Press.

Wade, Bonnie C. 2014. *Composing Japanese Musical Modernity*. Chicago: University of Chicago Press.

8

Music in Myanmar (Burma)

Expressing Commonalities and Differences

GAVIN DOUGLAS

Chapter Contents

Introduction

Myanmar (formerly Burma), the westernmost country in mainland Southeast Asia (Figure 8.1), is home to an ethnically diverse population who practice several different religions. Its political structure is also complex. It goes without saying that such a diverse context encompasses many different expressive traditions, among them:

- Religious music: Buddhist chant and music for spirit possession ceremonies
- Two historical traditions that remain relevant in the present: music for arched harp, and the *hsaing waing* outdoor instrumental ensemble.

The settings and inspiration for these musical performances are equally diverse. The performance of Buddhist chant occurs in a monastery, as part of expressing religious belief. Another type of performance occurs at an outdoor event called a **pwe**— a Burmese term that refers broadly to a festival, ritual, theater, offering, or party.

≡ **Traditional Burmese Musicians Performing on the Xylophone (*Pattalar*) and arched Harp (*Saung Gauk*).**

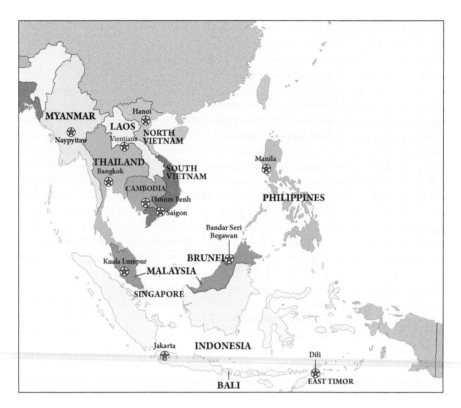

≡ **FIGURE 8.1** Map of Southeast Asia.

Finally, music is playing an increasing role in response to oppressive governmental authoritarianism. As in other cultures we've studied, people in Myanmar have used music meaningfully—as illustrated in this chapter—for the purpose of asserting their commonalities and differences.

Myanmar

Bordered by India and Bangladesh to the west, China to the north, and Thailand and Laos to the east, Myanmar stretches 1,200 miles from the snowy Himalayan mountain range to the tropical waters of the Andaman Sea (Figure 8.2) The expansive basin of the Irrawaddy River that bisects the country is home to Myanmar's largest ethnic group, the **Bamar** (or **Burman**), who make up 65% of the country's 53 million people. A horseshoe of mountains around the edge of the country is home to many of the non-Bamar populations, who speak approximately 100 languages and identify with more than 130 ethnic groups.

The early political history of Burma was characterized by periods of strong empires separated by periods of less organized rule. The first empire under the Burman peoples was founded in the eleventh century. Over a succession of Burman dynasties through the nineteenth century, the cultural power of the Burmese court had limited impact on the mountainous peripheries. As one moved farther from the capital or the palace, the administrative, economic, and cultural influence diminished such that many of the hill tribes had only a distant relationship to them. Throughout history to today, then, the traditions of the lowland Bamar and those of the other 35% of the country's population have contrasted sharply.

Dynastic kingdoms were followed by periods of colonial rule in the nineteenth and twentieth centuries. The nation-state of Burma took its present borders under British colonialism. Burma was a major theater in World War II between the Allied (British and American) forces and the Japanese. Groundwork for independence was laid by a valiant hero, General Aung San, who gained the trust of many of the disparate ethnic minorities, unifying the diverse country to push out the British. Newly independent after the war but rocked by civil wars, the government was taken over in 1962 by a military regime that chose isolation of their new country over international cooperation. The autocratic state would be challenged by periodic ethnic insurgencies and pro-democratic uprisings. Only in 2011 did the military dictatorship cede power to a democratically elected government.

≡ **FIGURE 8.2** Map of Myanmar.

Musical activity of all types during the period of military control reflected and influenced the political struggle. After the 1962 military coup, new censorship laws forced all printers and publishers to register works with the Press Scrutiny Board. Aggressive restrictions were imposed on the contents of all published literature and recordings for anything potentially injurious to state ideology, the economy, or security. The censorship laws were significant obstacles for all musicians and songwriters, as any lyrics or musical styles that threatened public order were considered suspect (Douglas

2005). For decades, many journalists, writers, artists and musicians were arrested for breaking these laws. The laws produced significant paranoia in the music industry and subsequently led to a high degree of self-censorship because a rejection from the Scrutiny Board could lead to the loss of an entire recording project.

Religious pluralism is an aspect of Myanmar's diversity. Although close to 85 percent of Myanmar residents practice Buddhism, it is not the only religion practiced in the country. In the largest city of Yangon, one can stand on the steps of a famous Buddhist shrine—the Sule Pagoda—and hear prayer bells ringing along with monks chanting *sutras* (blessings and prayers) into microphones amplified on loudspeakers. Across the street to the east, the bells of Immanuel Baptist Church invite the Christian community to worship. From the west, the Muslim call to prayer can be heard from loudspeakers at the Cholia Jama Mosque. A short walk from the Sule Pagoda can take you to several Hindu temples, a Catholic church, and a Sikh temple. Religious sound is part of the urban social soundscape. There are a greater number of Buddhists in the country's population than those who are ethnically Bamar/Burman; its practitioners are ethnically diverse.

While religious plurality is present, religious tensions that challenge local and national stability are significant in Myanmar. The Kachin, Chin, and some **Karen** Christian communities have struggled with discrimination and abuse; and the human rights concerns and refugee crises of the Rohingya Muslims on the Bangladesh border have generated considerable international condemnation of the government.

Musical Traditions
Buddhist chant

The Buddhist religious tradition—**Theravada**—that is practiced in Myanmar links the culture to those of Sri Lanka, Thailand, and Cambodia. Theravada Buddhism, known as "The Way of the Elders," is one of the two main traditions of

ACTIVITY 8.1

To familiarize yourself somewhat more with Burma/Myanmar's recent political situation, browse the following significant individuals and events: Aung San (the independence hero); his daughter, Aung San Suu Kyi (Nobel laureate, political prisoner, and current de facto leader); 1988 (massive pro-democracy uprising that was brutally suppressed); and the Saffron Revolution (monk-led protest of 2007). Search for information on the variety of ethnic groups; the **Karen**, **Rohingya**, **Shan**, Kachin, and Chin to name a few of many.

Buddhism (the other being Mahayana that was disseminated from India to Central and East Asian cultures). The title "Way of the Elders" reflects the reverence for tradition and the order of monks (*sangha*) that distinguishes Theravada. The practice strongly emphasizes the texts associated with the Buddha that are recorded in the ancient Indian language of *Pali*. The shared philosophies, cosmologies, views on enlightenment, texts, and histories provide a common set of principles for Theravada Buddhists throughout much of mainland Southeast Asia.

The strong emphasis on the original Pali text in the Theravada tradition has resulted in a sound of chant that is quite conservative in its expression in comparison to many Chinese, Japanese, or Tibetan styles of Buddhist chant. Rather than chant style being used to distinguish ethnicities in this Buddhist context, all are united in the Theravada practice. Rhythm is steady and often phrased around the line of text, pitch variety is usually quite limited, ornamentation is restricted, and the presentation of the text is very **syllabic** (i.e., one note per syllable). Text should always be accessible to the listener.

Theravada Buddhist philosophy distinguishes between chant and music on the grounds that music is inappropriate to the habits of someone pursuing a religious life. The Seventh of the Ten Buddhist precepts, adopted by all devoted Theravada Buddhists, asserts that one should refrain from music, theater, and perfumes. In practice, this principle has many interpretations. The general consensus turns on the degree of attachment that such activity cultivates and distracts from the religious pathway.

Music to Call the *Nats*

While musical instruments (with the exception of ritual markers like bells) are not found in Theravada Buddhist practice, they are found in spirit possession ceremonies. Intertwined with Burmese Buddhism is a tradition known as the **nat** cult; particularly popular in Upper Myanmar, it blends with Buddhism without conflict. *Nat*s are animistic spirits, belief in which predates the arrival of Buddhism. They are largely acknowledged to be the spirits of "green" unjust deaths, such as murders, and accidents. *Nat* spirits are engaged at **nat pwes** where offerings of money, food, alcohol, and music facilitate communication. Failure to acknowledge and honor the *nat*s may result in bad luck, poverty, failed crops, and the like.

Spirit possession ceremonies include particular songs to cultivate a trance-inducing atmosphere. The sonic canvas for the ritual calling is the **hsaing waing** ensemble from the early Burman court music tradition that flourishes still. The *hsaing waing* is generally played outdoors in loud festival or ritual contexts. While the *hsaing waing* ensemble performs at a *nat pwe* in a similar manner to the court ensemble, the repertoire is unique to that ritual context.

Musics from Historic Ethnic Bamar Court Traditions

"Traditional" Burmese music, the roots of which are found in the dynasties of the Burmese kings (i.e., in the culture of the ethnic Bamar), has been transmitted from the period of the last Konbaung dynasty (1752–1885). Unlike Theravada Buddhist practice, these traditions have either an instrumental soloist or a small ensemble. Musical ensembles feature little in the way of doubling of instruments and little unison or synchronicity of parts. This is best illustrated through the *hsaing waing* outdoor instrumental ensemble and the music for the **saung gauk** (arched harp).

During the era of the military dictators, the court traditions were invoked for the purpose of suggesting a common national identity both internally and outside of the country. Exercising censorship to discourage avant-garde, experimental, and fusion musics, government patronage since the 1990s created new contexts including new arts universities and national competitions for the performance of traditional Burmese music. The *hsaing waing* and *saung gauk* also enjoy a measure of popularity and prominence on national radio and television.

The *Hsaing Waing* Ensemble. The *hsaing waing* ensemble is the most commonly used outdoor ensemble in Myanmar (Audio Example 8.1). Most troupes today make their living playing for various types of *pwe*. The host of the *pwe* will hire a troupe (inclusive of singers and comedians), set up a stage on the road in front of their home, and invite everyone in the neighborhood to attend. Even in urban Yangon, a *pwe* will block traffic for the night, starting around 8:00 p.m. and going on until sunrise. Today, all instruments will be amplified through loudspeakers, which adds lots of reverberation and distortion to the sound.

The *hsaing waing* ensemble consists of six to ten players on membranophones, idiophones, and aerophones. The basic core of the ensemble consists of a **patt waing** (literally, "drum circle"), a set of twenty-one double-headed, elongated, barrel-shaped drums that are suspended vertically inside a circular frame (Figure 8.3). It is complemented by a **kyi waing** (literally "copper/bronze circle"), a tuned set of bronze gong chimes/pot gongs resting horizontally on a circular rack. Each of these sets is played by a single musician—the drums played by hand, the bronze pot gongs played with a stick beater. The third main melodic instrument is the **hne** (a wooden, double-reed aerophone). Its name is pronounced with a slight nasalization at the beginning, like the English word "hmm."

The twenty-one drums of the *patt waing* are fine-tuned with a tuning paste called **patt sa** (literally, "drum food"). This paste is added to or subtracted from the top heads of the drums, allowing them to be tuned precisely with bell-like tones of clear, exact pitch for playing melodies. The player sits in the middle of the circle and usually performs the primary melody using the right hand while the left plays supporting,

FIGURE 8.3 Tuned drums of the *hsaing waing* ensemble.

polyphonic, pitches. The *kyi waing* player produces truncated versions of that melody. The *hne* player will add to the melodies with his or her own idiosyncratic version of the tune, thereby creating a **heterophonic** texture (Garfias 1985).

ACTIVITY 8.2

"*Pabawin Thachin*" is a song by the famous *hsaing* leader Sein Be Da. It is here performed by the troupe of Mandalay-based Shwei Daung Myaing.

Listen to the example multiple times, but note first the contrasting timbres of the instruments. Instruments additional to the core three include the *maung* (a set of tuned gong chimes/pot gongs resting horizontally on a rack in a straight row), *patt ma* (large, double-headed, barrel-shaped drum), *chauk lon batt* (a less numerous set of tuned drums), *wa let kouke* (bamboo clappers), and *lingwin* (cymbal pair).

Finally, listen closely for the two parts played on the *patt waing*: the main melody in the right hand and a supporting melody in the left, creating a polyphonic texture. Then note the heterophonic relationship between the *patt waing* melody and that of the *hne*.

LISTENING GUIDE

"Pabawin Thachin"

Performed by the *hsaing waing* troupe of Shwei Daung Myaing

Recording location and year: Field recording in Myanmar, 1974, by Robert Garfias

Instrumentation: *hsaing waing* ensemble, consisting of *patt waing* (circle of twenty-one drums), *kyi waing* (circle of small bronze gongs), *hne* (quadruple reed), *maung zaing* (gong rack), *chauk lon batt* (set of six tuned drums), *patt ma* (large bass drum), **si** (bells), and *wa let kouke* (large bamboo clapper)

Time	Something to Listen For
0:00	Male voice calls out as the *patt waing* (drums) and *kyi waing* (gongs) sound intermittently; *si* (bells) sound metallically.
0:06	Male singer and *patt waing* begin a brief melody that descends and rises again.
0:14	*Patt waing* and *hne* play similar versions of the same melody; *kyi waing* keeps a fundamental and steady rhythm, and *si* (bells) and *wa* (clapper) enter.
0:22	Ensemble plays at an ever-increasing tempo.
0:28	Tempo increases to a rapid pace.
0:50	As the tempo decreases, the *patt waing* pattern changes, now striking twice each time it is played.
0:54	Tempo of the ensemble increases again, then stops.
1:02	Male singer enters with the earlier brief melody that descends and rises again, as instrumentalists decrease their tempo and volume.
1:12	Singer becomes more expressive, partly singing and partly shouting.
1:30	Singer varies his speaking and singing, softly and then loudly.
1:37	*Hne* plays melodic interlude.
1:42	Singer returns, speaking and singing.
1:55	*Hne* plays melody, joined prominently by *patt waing* and drums.
2:10	Tempo increases to a rapid pace.
2:28	Tempo decreases briefly, then returns to previous fast tempo.
2:30	*Kyi wang* and other instruments move into a new rhythm, and the emphatic slapping of the *wa let kouke* can be heard as musicians bring the music to an abrupt close.

The *patt waing* player is the musical and organizational leader of the ensemble, and the troupe will often take the name of that player. Though traditionally male, female *patt waing* players are increasingly found in the contemporary *hsaing waing* contexts such as national competitions and the state universities (Lu 2009).

The *Saung Gauk* (Arched Harp). In contrast to the loud and boisterous outdoor ensemble, the Burmese *saung gauk* is the most prominent instrument in the court traditions for intimate, indoor, chamber or solo music (Figure 8.4). Over the last three centuries, it has become a national icon, reproduced today on stamps, currency, and in miniature reproductions for sale at tourist boutiques. Its standardized gold, red, and black design gives it a prestigious association with the royal palace (which is also awash in gold, red, and black). Buddhist imagery also is found in the very design of the instrument. The extension of the long neck beyond the strings is ornamental and ends in the figure of a stylized lead of the *bodhi* tree, the tree under which Buddha attained enlightenment. Players of the *saung* sit like the Buddha, under the *bodhi* tree, while they play.

The harp is constructed from a hollowed-out piece of wood. The fourteen to sixteen nylon or silk strings of the modern harp stretch from the deer- or goatskin-covered body to red silk cords and then are tied with a pinch knot onto the neck of the instrument. Modern guitar tuners are quickly replacing the traditional silk chords for quick tuning.

Both *saung* players and the *hsaing waing* use the same modal system (Audio Example 8.2). The seven-tone scale has five primary pitches and two secondary. Mode is determined by the placement of the tonic pitch and by the relative arrangement of the five primary pitches. On the *saung,* the strings are generally tuned to the five primary pitches, with the secondary ones achieved by pinching

≡ **FIGURE 8.4**
Saung gauk (arched harp).

the string with the thumb of the left hand. (The left hand—with some virtuosic exceptions—does not pluck the string). Melody is played by plucking with the index fingers of the right hand while the secondary melodic line is played with the thumb in much the same way that the parts were divided between right and left hand on the *patt waing*.

Recognized rhythmic patterns are articulated on the *si* and *wa*. All are organized in duple meter with the *wa* beat emphasizing the most important beat in the cycle. Each pattern is very simple on the surface but there may be great fluctuations in pulse, as

ACTIVITY 8.3

As you listen to the *saung gauk* recording "In Praise of the Burmese Harp" (Audio Example 8.2), try to produce the pitches of the mode yourself. Note also two accompanying percussion instruments:

si—two small metal bells struck against each other, and *wa*—a slit node of bamboo or pair of stubby wooden sticks that is held by the singer (see Figure 8.5).

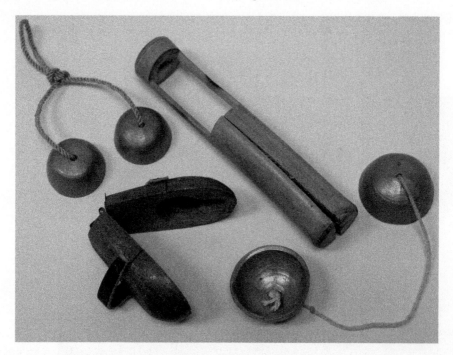

≡ **FIGURE 8.5** Two sets of *si* (bell) and *wa* (clapper).

LISTENING GUIDE

Saung Gauk ("In Praise of the Burmese Harp")

Performed by U Myint Maung (*saung*) and Daw Yi Yi Thant (singer)

Recording location and year: Yangon, Myanmar, January 2000

Instrumentation: *Saung gauk* (harp), vocals, *si* (bells), and *wa* (small bamboo clapper)

Time	Something to Listen For
0:00	The player of *saung gauk* (harp) plucks an opening passage, beginning at a high pitch and cascading downward.
0:11	*Saung gauk* is joined by *si* (bell) and *wa* (clapper), instruments that mark the beats. A common rhythmic pattern **na yi si** is heard as the sound of two bells, rest, and clap, depicted as x x – o. The destination and most important beat is the *wa* clap. Some performers and scholars label the *wa* beat 4, while others call it beat 1.
1:17	*Wa* dramatically holds the final beat while the harpist finishes the phrase.
1:30	Female voice sings melody, in small range, with slides and scoops, and with sustained pitches at phrase-endings; while the harpist continues to play. The words refer to the radiant color of the sandalwood tree, glowing red, the noble golden harp's delicate sound: *"Zabuyaung kun thane' hkan mye'soun hlyan, maun hywei saung mya hcu than."*
2:18	Female voice and *saung gauk* repeat the earlier stanza, with the vocalist stretching out the poetic verse.
3:01	Female voice and *saung gauk* begin a new stanza.

pieces speed up and slow down. *Na yi si*, the most common pattern, is a four-beat rhythmic pattern of two *si* beats, a rest, followed by a *wa*. Other frequent patterns include *wa let si* (simple alternation) and *wa let amyan* (simultaneous *si* and *wa* on every beat). When notated, the *si* is usually marked with an X and the *wa* with an O (see Figure 8.6).

Na yi si:	‖: X X – O:‖
Wa let si:	‖: X O X O:‖
Wa let amyan:	‖: x/o x/o x/o x/o:‖

FIGURE 8.6 *Na yi si* notation.

ACTIVITY 8.4

Do an online search for video examples of both the *hsaing waing* ensemble and the *saung gauk* to reinforce the sounds and the playing styles of both examples of court-related music. Be ready to share the examples you find with your classmates.

Music in Performance
Chant in Theravada Monasteries

In most Theravada monasteries, ritual time and daily practices are in great measure signaled through sounds, such as the patterned sounding of log drums, bells, gongs, and chants. Chant in the Theravada monastic context serves multiple purposes for both the order of monks and the laity. It serves as prayer, as meditation, and as a form of protection. It is also a mark of education and authority among monks and devout laity. While chanting may be done solo, it is usually a group activity where large portions of the Pali text are collectively rehearsed and memorized (Audio Example 8.3). The memorization of texts consumes a large portion of any monk's time. All participants follow the identical text, melody, and rhythm with no individual or distinct musical part. As with the Theravada Buddhist philosophy behind the chant, the self (the individual voice) is regarded not as an individual but simply as part of the whole, a part of something greater.

While Buddhist chant may sound like "music," it is often not referred to as such in the monasteries. One can readily find monks in the Theravada world who refute the assertion that their chanting is "music" or "singing." In contrast, on the other hand, during my own fieldwork in Myanmar, Thailand, and Cambodia, I frequently met monks who wanted to discuss music with me and even invited me into their monasteries to make recordings. One can surely find monasteries where the approaches to music are both more liberal and more orthodox (Douglas 2017).

Music in a *Pwe*

In recent times, people in Myanmar have used music meaningfully for the purpose of sounding assertions of both commonalities and differences. A short vignette demonstrates how both the common Buddhist identity but also the ethnic diversity of the hill areas can both be expressed musically even in the same event.

After spending the night in Taunggyi, a small city in the highlands of Shan state in Eastern Burma, I awoke at sunrise to the Call to Prayer from one of several mosques serving the small, but audible Muslim community. Later that day, a local pagoda festival (*paya pwe*) featured a dynamic display of ethnic expression by some of the local groups. A local patron had made a sizeable donation to the *Shwe Thu Htay Gon* Buddhist monastery by procuring a complete copy of the Tripitaka. The Tripitaka is the body of texts, written in ancient Pali language, that record the teachings of the Buddha. They are contained in approximately fifty volumes and are said to take two years to recite. Such an important and substantial gift was an opportunity for celebration. The Buddhist communities surrounding Taunggyi gathered to commemorate the event with music, dance, and food while the monks recited sutras to the donors and for the lay community. You can watch a video of this performance (Video 8.1).

ACTIVITY 8.5

Listen to the recording of the monks chanting at the Taunggyi pagoda festival (Audio Example 8.3). Note how many notes there are for each syllable of text; this is a syllabic style setting that maximizes understandability. To be sure you hear this, make a transcription of what you hear as the syllables of text; though you cannot understand Pali or even distinguish discrete words, the clear enunciation of the text should be apparent.

Each line of the chant is divided into phrases by a "sung" ending. Mark on your transcription where those endings occur.

Finally, focus on the pitches of the chant. Try and match the pitches and sing along using whatever syllables you wish or even humming.

While forty or fifty Buddhist monks began their chanting indoors, a procession of seven **Pa-O** musicians—a subgroup of the Karen ethnic group—approached the pagoda. Through speakers hung outside of the monastery, I could hear the chanting outdoors; layers of sound created a festival-like atmosphere. Each musician held a single gong, except for the last pair who held a large gong slung between them. They processed to the pagoda and took a position on one side of it. The steady, slow pulsation on the gongs (approximately 12 bpm) set a contemplative tone and was soon joined by a set of cymbals improvising to the measured gong pulses. An elderly male dancer moved to the front of the procession, arms raised high and then alternately thrust in the air at each pulse. The sound was clearly recognizable by all the locals as a Pa-O procession (Audio Example 8.4; Video Example 8.2). In addition, the Pa-Os' clothing—dark black or blue baggy trousers and jackets with colorful headscarves—was another unmistakable symbol of their group identity.

Midway through this performance, a loud clamor came from the other side of the pagoda seventy feet away. Faster pulses punched out by many gongs beating approximately 110 bpm heralded an ethnic Shan ensemble playing for a pair of dancers engaged in a stylized martial arts repartee (Audio Example 8.5; Video Example. 8.3). In addition to ten or so participants striking single handheld gongs, the ensemble was led by a pair of cymbals and a Shan *ozi*, a goblet-shaped drum as long as eight feet whose player improvised rhythmic ideas that interconnected with the cymbals.

The *Shwe Thu Htay Gon* pagoda festival was clearly a special event for the people of the region. The event combined food, dance, music, family, and friends and reaffirmed relationships between the monks and the community. A wonderful cacophony of sounds—chanting monks, Pa-O processional music, and Shan *ozi*, amidst the hustle and bustle of old friends reunited and children playing—performed difference and similarity simultaneously (Douglas 2013). All were sharing their common Buddhist identity while playfully asserting their unique ethnic identities.

Musical Responses to Authoritarianism

At the beginning of this chapter, I mentioned that musical activity of all types during the period of military control (1962–2011) reflected and influenced the political struggle. Musicians particularly responded to the oppressive official system of censorship. There were diverse artistic and scholarly reactions to government censorship: some were submissive, defiant, subversive, or evasive. Two notable responses include the absorption of foreign popular music styles with new lyrics written to reflect local concerns and the creation of new musical styles by refugees and non-Burmese musicians outside of the country.

Mainstream Burmese youth culture has actively absorbed foreign popular music from the United States, England, China, Korea, and Japan and put it to their own use. Burmese cover songs of international hits—known as **copy thachin** (literally "copy song")—are ubiquitous in the contemporary music scene. *Copy thachin* involve the recording of a popular hit with the melody and style of the original piece virtually identical to the original (Ferguson 2013). New lyrics are written in Burmese that often imitate the sound of the original language but bear little or no relationship to the original meaning. The re-conceptualization and re-signification of songs captures an international feel reframed in a heavily censored and authoritarian local context. Debates among musicians and scholars regarding the artistic value, originality, and cultural significance of *copy thachin* have raged since the 1980s. Myanmar's fast-developing economic and legal relationships with foreign networks (post-2011) will no doubt increase the controversy.

In addition, outside of Myanmar, Western pop stars and Burmese refugees have produced a growing body of Burma/Myanmar-related musics. Pro-democracy campaigns and festivals have enlisted international music stars to draw attention to the country's struggles; and many songs have been composed about or inspired by the pro-democracy activist and Nobel laureate, Aung San Suu Kyi, and her seventeen years of house arrest under the regime. Over the last twenty years, activist groups, often based in Thailand, have worked with foreign organizations to build

ACTIVITY 8.6

Search the web for "Burmese copy song" (*copy thachin*)
to hear voices of mainstream Burmese youth culture.

distribution networks to spread music, literature, graffiti, and other subversive material critical of the military dictatorship.

The 2010s relaxation of internet restrictions (specifically Facebook and YouTube) and the closing of the Censor Board is rapidly transforming the networks of music production and distribution. While the legacy of the military dictatorship is sharp in the memories of Myanmar's citizens, many are active in creating new, multiple, and diverse ways of making music useful and meaningful in their lives.

Conclusion

The people of Myanmar use music in multiple ways, including to reinforce their ethnic or religious ties; facilitate efforts to control the people and to unite the nation; resist the government; and connect internationally. This chapter highlights several traditions that actively sculpt the political, ethnic, and religious cultures in the country. The country is now in transition from years of isolationist military rule toward a democracy with powers precariously balanced between the army and elected representatives. Simultaneously, rapid changes in commerce, education, and media are liberating and disrupting the daily lives of residents. In the coming years, musicians will continue to make meaningful sounds to assert both commonalities and differences within the plurality that is Myanmar.

Bibliography

Douglas, Gavin. 2005. "Myanmar (Burma)." In *The Encyclopedia of Popular Music of the World*, Vol. 4, edited by John Shepherd, David Horn, Dave Laing, Paul Oliver, and Peter Wicke, 196–202. London: Continuum International Publishing Group.

Douglas, Gavin. 2010. *Music in Mainland Southeast Asia: Experiencing Music, Expressing Culture*. New York: Oxford University Series.

Douglas, Gavin. 2013. "Performing Ethnicity in Southern Shan State, Burma/Myanmar: The *Ozi* and Gong Traditions of the Myelat." *Ethnomusicology* 57, no. 2: 185–206.

Douglas, Gavin. 2017. "Buddhist Soundscapes in Myanmar: Dhamma Instruments and Divine States of Consciousness." *Proceedings of the 4th Symposium of the ICTM Study Group on Performing Arts of Southeast Asia*, edited by Mohd Anis Md Nor and Patricia Matusky, 11–15. Denpasar, Bali: Institut Seni Indonesia (ISI).

Ferguson, Jane M. 2013. "Buddhist Super Trouper: How Burmese Poets and Musicians Turn Global Popular Music into Copy Thachin" *Asia Pacific Journal of Anthropology* 14, no. 3: 221–239.

Garfias, Robert. 1985. "Development of the Modern Burmese Hsaing Ensemble." *Asian Music* 16, no. 1: 1–28.

Lu, Hsin-chun Tasaw. 2009. "The Burmese Classical Music Tradition: An Introduction." *Fontes Artis Musicae* 56, no. 3: 254–271.

9

Music in Bali

The Sound World of a Balinese Temple Ceremony

LISA GOLD

Chapter Contents

Introduction

This chapter introduces you to music in Bali, a tiny island province in the Republic of Indonesia (see Figure 9.1). Consisting of thousands of volcanic islands, Indonesia lies between the Indian Ocean and the Pacific Ocean in Southeast Asia. Bali has long been attractive to international visitors, not only due to its natural beauty but also due to its rich artistic culture in which music, dance, theater, and ritual are completely integrated. Poetry is sung and stories are told through music and dance. Ensembles are linked to dance forms and to enacted narratives. Balinese music itself is inherently theatrical, with the ability to move a community and shape a ritual event. In addition, Balinese identity and sense of history are deeply linked to the contemporary performing arts. Through performance, the past is played in the present.

≡ *Gamelan* **players at a public arts festival.**

The History of Bali

From early Bronze Age migrations to the present, Bali has been exposed to out-side influences. With each new cultural arrival, the Balinese have incorporated new elements of religious beliefs and cultural practices, synthesizing them with indigenous ones. Across the centuries, Indian Buddhist and Hindu culture, colonialism, tourism, and globalization have all contributed to Balinese culture in some way, with ancient traditions proving to be resilient. This chapter illustrates the meaningful link of music with Balinese sense of history and its contribution to community expression of deeply felt belief in spiritual powers.

Balinese trace much of their cultural heritage to the neighboring island of Java, a short distance directly west of Bali (Figure 9.1). Java was the center for a succession of Hindu kingdoms in Indonesia from roughly the fifth through the early sixteenth centuries. Hinduism was brought to Southeast Asia by religious scholars from

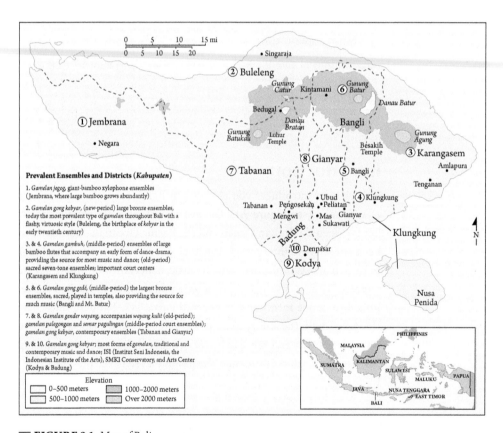

Prevalent Ensembles and Districts (*Kabupaten*)

1. *Gamelan jegog*, giant-bamboo xylophone ensembles (Jembrana, where large bamboo grows abundantly)

2. *Gamelan gong kebyar*, (new-period) large bronze ensembles, today the most prevalent type of *gamelan* throughout Bali with a flashy, virtuosic style (Buleleng, the birthplace of *kebyar* in the early twentieth century)

3. & 4. *Gamelan gambuh*, (middle-period) ensembles of large bamboo flutes that accompany an early form of dance-drama, providing the source for most music and dance; (old-period) sacred seven-tone ensembles; important court centers (Karangasem and Klungkung)

5. & 6. *Gamelan gong gedé*, (middle-period) the largest bronze ensembles, sacred, played in temples, also providing the source for much music (Bangli and Mt. Batur)

7. & 8. *Gamelan gender wayang*, accompanies *wayang kulit* (old-period); *gamelan palegongan* and *semar pagulingan* (middle-period court ensembles); *gamelan gong kebyar*, contemporary ensembles (Tabanan and Gianyar)

9. & 10. *Gamelan gong kebyar*; most forms of *gamelan*, traditional and contemporary music and dance; ISI (Institut Seni Indonesia, the Indonesian Institute of the Arts), SMKI Conservatory, and Arts Center (Kodya & Badung)

≡ **FIGURE 9.1** Map of Bali.

India along the sea and land trade routes from India to China. Cultural exchange between Hindu-Javanese and Balinese courts began around the ninth century and strengthened in the eleventh century when the Balinese-born King Erlangga became a powerful ruler of East Java. In the mid-fourteenth century, Bali became part of Majapahit, Java's last Hindu empire, and Balinese courts were modeled after those of Java. When Majapahit fell to the first Islamic Javanese kingdom of Demak in the late fifteenth century, many Hindu-Javanese nobility moved to the Hindu-Javanese-influenced courts of Bali where they supported artists, musicians, dancers, scribes, and poets. Rulers surrounded themselves with many ensembles that performed at elaborate royal spectacles as an assertion of the king's power and for religious purposes.

After centuries of local Balinese kingdoms warring for control, the Dutch began to take control of the island around 1846, but their influence was not widespread until 1906 and 1908 with the first and second *Puputan* ("the finish") massacres by the Dutch (Vickers, 1989; 1992). The Balinese royal courts gradually ceased to function as patrons of the performing arts. The Dutch government assumed this role, and, as a result, some of the court musical instruments were distributed to villages where many clubs were formed and supported by local community organizations. In the early twentieth century, in an attempt to make amends for their destructiveness, the Dutch instituted a policy of preservation of Balinese culture while simultaneously opening the island to the first Western tourists (Picard 1990, 37–75). Following several shifts in power, at the end of World War II in 1945, Indonesia declared its independence. It was officially recognized by the Dutch as a unified independent nation—the Republic of Indonesia—in 1949. In addition to regular village, temple, and court functions, the role of sponsorship of the arts was taken on by the national Indonesian and local Balinese governments in the 1960s.

Religious Practice in Bali

Through the succession of political shifts, Bali has remained a culture in which a deeply felt belief in spiritual powers is of primary importance. Today's "Hindu Bali" religion is a synthesis of pre-Hindu beliefs and practices with elements of Indian Hinduism and Buddhism that reached Bali from Java. Ancestor worship, animism, and the honoring of spirits and deities associated with cycles of nature, such as rice cultivation, link Bali to other indigenous cultures of Southeast Asia. This is expressed, for instance, in the spiritual sense of the natural environment of the island. Of Bali's four large volcanoes, the tallest, *Gunung Agung* (Great Mountain) is considered Mahameru, the Indian seat of the gods, transported to Bali. The cardinal directions are oriented from this spiritually powerful mountain, determining the placement of physical objects and events, including music, dance, and ritual activities. Toward the mountain, or "inward," is **kaja**, also the term for cardinal north; and toward the sea is **kelod**, also the term for cardinal south. The closer one is to *kaja*, the closer one is to the gods and spiritual purity. Toward the sea are demonic forces. The Balinese village, temple, and house compounds are laid out in relation to the *kaja/kelod* axis (toward the mountain or sea, respectively). Another volcano, Batukaru located further west, is also considered spiritually important for those living in western Bali. In addition, the east–west axis that follows the path of the sun also has significance. People feel most at ease sleeping with the head of the bed facing north or east.

The name "*Bali*" means "offering," aptly expressing a major means of expressing belief in spiritual power and of daily life: making, giving, and performing offerings to the gods. These offerings include flowers, incense, rice, fruit, and animal sacrifices, as well as music, dance, and theater. Ceremonies occur daily, to honor the living (rites of passage such as weddings, births, and tooth filings), the dead (such as cremations), sages, demons (such as purification rituals), and gods (such as temple ceremonies). Most religious practices require music of some kind, which can be heard from great distances. Ceremonies occur in and outside of temples, in home compounds, by the ocean, even along the roads.

Music in Bali

Music is also a major force for social cohesion. Once restricted to men born into musician families, very recently, girls, boys, men, and women, from any family, have begun to gain access to musical study and achieve high levels of musical proficiency. While there are many musicians that one could call "professional" (teachers and musicians who train others and perform and tour regularly), most musicians have other forms of employment, even the great masters of their tradition. The playing of music is regarded as a community activity that fosters group cohesion and social responsibility. Playing in ceremonies without pay, contributing to the community, is considered the most meaningful and personally satisfying context for performance (Gold, 2013; 2016).

Considering this deeply held belief, it is not surprising that Balinese music is primarily an ensemble practice. Players work together to produce a composite whole, with individuals selflessly contributing to a musical texture that is far greater than the sum of its parts. To show the association of music with spiritual power and its function as a force for social cohesion, this chapter will highlight ensemble music in the context of a temple ceremony (**odalan**). Of course, there are other, less sacred musical contexts for traditional music; and other musical genres practiced in Bali, including western-influenced music such as classical, jazz, rock, metal, grunge, ethnic fusion, and other popular musics (for which the term *musik* has been adapted from English) as well as a vibrant category of indigenously Balinese contemporary composition (termed *kontemporer*; see McGraw 2013). However, these musics are not considered appropriate or functional in temple ceremonies or other rituals.

In Bali, as in many places, the concept of music is context specific. Rather than a single category called "music," or "song," the numerous types of instrumental ensembles and their **repertoires** (groups of pieces that are linked in some way), as well as vocal practices, are named and associated with the specific functions that they fulfill. For example, one form of vocal chant is sung by a shadow puppet master when he brings a character to life; others are used for narration, dialogue, or to express moods. A different form of chant is sung by a congregation of worshippers to bond as a community and with the spirit world. Another form of chant is sung in reading clubs by specialists. They interpret esoteric texts by first singing the poems in their archaic language, then improvising solos that paraphrase them in the local Balinese language, thereby bringing the ancient texts up to date. No single term encompasses all of these vocal activities. The same holds true for instrumental music.

FIGURE 9.2 *Wayang lemah* (daytime ceremonial shadow puppet play) from a *mecaru* (purification) ceremony in Sukawati, Gianyar, 1992.

Figure 9.2 shows a *mecaru* (exorcistic purification) ceremony in Sukawati village in 1992. You can see in the foreground a daytime ceremonial shadow puppet performance in progress (**wayang lemah**), surrounded by people praying and watching. A shadow puppet master (**dalang**) manipulates the tree of life, a rawhide puppet that embodies the spirit of this ancient storytelling genre. It forms a link between the *dalang* and the world of the stories, accompanied by musicians seated at instruments behind him (**gamelan gender wayang**). Also shown are gongs from another music ensemble (**gamelan balaganjur**), played, often simultaneously, to summon, entertain, and ward off evil ground spirits, the main purpose of this village-wide ritual. As in many Balinese ceremonies, this one is observed by tourists.

The most striking thing about this ceremony was that it took place in *the* major intersection of an extremely congested north–south route, requiring people to redirect traffic, halting the ongoing pace of daily life. In this annual ceremony, the entire village participates in a multistaged ritual to cleanse the village, ending with a procession to the sea. This allows village life to continue undisturbed by the *bhuta*, "ground spirits," who are feasted with liquor, animal sacrifices, food offerings, and music. The participation of all the villagers demonstrates the social cohesion this ceremony creates. People have had to adapt this ancient ceremony to the modern world, surrounded by the sounds of automobiles and buses, exhaust fumes, and tourists—but it is no less powerful in its intent and function.

Instrumental Ensembles (*Gamelan*) and Instruments

Balinese music is primarily an ensemble tradition. This reflects the value placed on group identity over individual expression and, to a certain extent, the cooperative nature of Balinese social organization. The word **gamelan** designates certain types of indigenous Javanese and Balinese ensembles. The Balinese sometimes use a slight variation of this term, *gambelan* (from *magamble*, "to strike"), suggesting that the ensemble consists of instruments that are played by striking. However, the term is used for many *gamelan* types, including, for example, an ensemble of flutes (McPhee 1966; Gold 2001). (Because *gamelan* is the most commonly used name for these musical ensembles, it is used throughout this chapter.)

Gamelan is a collective term used for an entire ensemble of instruments of which there are some 30 distinct types in Bali. The different types accommodate a range of numbers of musicians from as few as two to as many as sixty or more. It is difficult to count the exact number of varieties because new ensembles are constantly created; older, nearly extinct ensembles are revived, while some are already extinct. Each type of *gamelan* has a name (e.g., **gamelan gong kebyar** or **gamelan gender wayang**) denoting the instrumentation, tuning system, repertoire, and function.

All the instruments in each ensemble are made by one *gamelan* maker. The maker will tune them together to a particular tuning system, but from ensemble to ensemble there is no standardized pitch. Each *gamelan* has its own unique timbre and feeling, even among ensembles of the same type. Thus, no two *gamelan*s can be played together. Instruments are tuned in pairs, with one slightly higher than the other. The resultant sound when struck together shimmers and is known as a "wave," as the tone undulates, much like the timbre of a gong, bringing life into the sound.

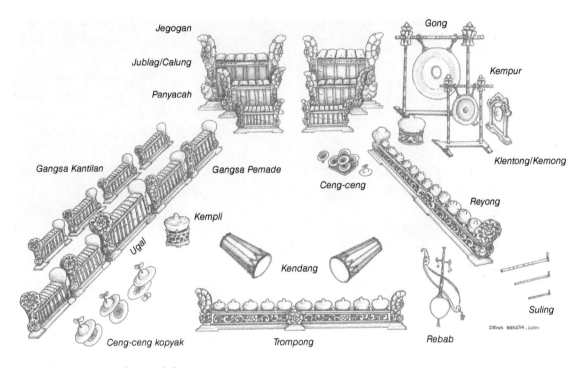

≡ **FIGURE 9.3** *Gamelan gong kebyar.*

As shown in Figure 9.3, which shows one type of *gamelan*, instruments are made from a variety of materials that produce a variety of timbres—primarily bamboo and bronze (with some that use iron), wood, or reeds. On the other hand, an ensemble might be comprised completely of instruments made of one type of material: an ensemble of bamboo flutes, for example, or of struck bamboo **idiophones**. Or an ensemble might be comprised primarily of instruments made of one type of material, but include others. In most ensembles, double-headed, conically shaped hand drums (**kendang**), played in pairs or solo by only one or two musicians, will lead the ensemble. Some idiophone ensembles also include vertical, end-blown, bamboo flutes of various lengths (**suling**); and occasionally one long-necked, bowed, spike lute (**rebab**) with a small resonating chamber covered in skin, and long, thin lateral pegs to tune its two strings (see Figure 9.3), adding a lyrical layer.

The majority of *gamelan* instruments are tuned bronze idiophones such as gongs, gong-chimes, and metallophones with bamboo resonators, along with drums and cymbals (Figure 9.3). A **gong** is a metal (here, thick bronze) disc that has been forged by hammering a deeply turned rim; on Indonesian gongs, a bulbous raised boss (for controlling vibration) is placed in the middle of the playing

≡ **FIGURE 9.4** *Gamelan gong kebyar* youth ensemble performing in Singapadu village *odalan*, 2015; from left to right: bowed lute *rebab*, vertical flute *suling*; front; gong chime *trompong*.

surface. The timbre of Indonesian gongs is deep and rich, with a highly valued, long, sustained tone and undulating pitch. Most gongs are suspended for playing with a padded mallet. The term "**gong-chime**" (also called "kettle gong") refers to a set of tuned gongs, laid horizontally on a rack with the raised boss facing up (in Figure 9.3, in front and on the right side; also Figure 9.4). These fulfill a melodic elaborating function. The most widespread type of ensemble, *gamelan gong kebyar*, is often referred to as *gamelan gong*, indicating the great importance of the gongs. It is the gongs that link Bali's *gamelan* to Southeast Asia's widespread ancient tradition of gong forging and its association with spiritual power and community.

Metallophones are instruments with keys/bars made of some sort of metal (as opposed to xylophones with keys/bars made of wood or bamboo). The bronze-keyed metallophones of Bali usually have bamboo tube resonators and are set in ornately carved wooden cases (Figures 2.2 and 9.3).

A **cymbal** is a slightly concave, round metal plate. The variety of cymbal in *gong kebyar* (called **ceng-ceng**, pronounced onomatopoetically as "cheng-cheng") is a single instrument consisting of a series of overlapping, small, bronze discs (cymbals) facing upward on a stand that is often a carved wooden turtle (related to an important Balinese origin myth). A single player holds a small cymbal in each

ACTIVITY 9.1

Gamelan Demonstration Video

Watch a video demonstration filmed in Ubud, Bali, in 2018, featuring Gamelan Yuganada, led by drummer I Wayan Sudirana. It shows how a composition is built through the combination of each of the individual parts. First, you hear an example of the time-keeping horizontal gong known as the *kajar* (1:23). This is an important reference point for all of the instruments. After this, the various-sized suspended gongs and their functions are introduced (1:51); the metallophone group is then presented (beginning at 3:10), starting with the low instrument group (*calung* and *jegogan*) that plays the skeletal melody and its abstraction.

The metallophones that play elaborating parts (***gangsa***) are shown (3:57), followed by the row of gong-chimes called the *reyong* (4:03) played by four players. At 4:22, other percussive instruments are introduced: *ceng-ceng* (cymbals) and kendang (drums). The paired tuning is introduced at 5:26. At 8:01 you will hear and see a demonstration of each of these layers in the context of an eight-beat melodic and gong cycle. Sudirana adds his drum part at 14:18 and leads the musicians as conductor of the ensemble, indicating to the others when changes in speed or dynamics are to occur.

hand and strikes the metal plates in percussive patterns that accentuate syncopations in the music in tandem with the drums and gong-chimes (in the center of Figure 9.3).

Temple Ceremonies (*Odalan*)

Each village or town contains at least three temples: a village temple; a temple of origins; and a death temple. Many others exist, such as a temple for high caste members of society. Each is devoted to a specific purpose.

A temple is composed of a series of walled courtyards, usually two or three, which set sacred space and time apart from the outside world (Figure 9.5). These walls represent borders between levels of spiritual purity. The courtyards are not concentric; rather, the concept of "inner" courtyard denotes a privileged position that is the closest to the *kaja* direction. This chapter's audio examples are drawn from performances that occurred in a temple of three courtyards: inner, middle, and outer.

A temple's *odalan,* celebrated every 210 days (one Balinese year in the Hindu-Bali cycle), marks the anniversary of the day it was first inaugurated. This often coincides

≡ **FIGURE 9.5**   Temple in relation to mountain; *Jaba* would be outside the temple in this case.

with the full moon; but each temple has its own anniversary, so they are scattered throughout the year. While temples are just empty structures consisting of several adjoining, walled courtyards open to the sky, within which are roofed ceremonial pavilions and shrines, during the *odalan* the temple is transformed into a colorful feast for the senses (Figure 9.6). Shrines, statues, and pavilions are wrapped in hand-painted gold-leafed cloth and incense wafts through the air and up to the gods. All sonic and visual space is filled, an ideal known as **ramé** (full, boisterous, active), in order for the ceremonies to be complete and successful (Dibia, 1982).

The order of events in the *odalan* generally follows this larger structure: a ritual purification and exorcism during which demons are invited to enter the temple and then are escorted out; an invitation to the gods and deified ancestors; an entertainment period of several days; and a send-off of the gods. Many stages include ritual processions with music delineating spiritually pure and less pure space and time. The congregation, led by priests, presents offerings of food, incense, prayer, and entertainment. A similar sequence is followed on a smaller scale for ceremonies occurring within a house.

≡ **FIGURE 9.6**
Temple during a Singapadu village *odalan*, here with women dancing for the gods, 2015.

Music plays a powerful role of accompanying the ceremony and affecting its dynamic shaping. The word *"ngiring"* describes music's function as "guiding along" and "accompanying" ceremonial and theatrical performance, illustrating a link in function and association. Music can summon, entertain, or escort out gods and evil spirits, as well as accompany humans in various activities from inspiring processions to inducing trance states or bringing dance and drama to life. Music has the ability to move people as a community and to act as catalyst during important points of ritual change (Gold 1998, 2005; Bandem and DeBoer 1995).

Gamelan Music in Temple Ceremonies

The types of *gamelan* (and therefore the genres of music) you might encounter in each of the three temple courtyards is linked to relative degrees of sacredness. Each genre is closely associated with specific time periods in Balinese history; the older the genre, the more sacred it is, thus determining its placement in the temple in its proximity to *kaja* and *kelod.*

In the *inner courtyard,* the performances are closely coordinated with the rituals of the Hindu priest. For an audience of gods who are the invited guests of the ceremony, women perform a slow, free-form dance (Figure 9.6). The slow temple music (*lalambatan*) is played by the powerful, large, bronze *gamelan gong gedé.* At the same time, a shadow master performs a daytime ceremonial shadow puppet performance portraying epics from the Indian past. The ensemble accompanying him is the delicate duo or quartet, *gamelan gender wayang* (Figure 9.2), tuned to an entirely different tuning system from that of *gong gedé* in striking juxtaposition (Gold 1992, 1998, 2005, 2013, 2016). These genres are considered to be from an "Old" period in Balinese history, predating Javanese influence.

In the *middle courtyard,* performances have a looser connection with the rituals. For an audience of gods and people, a dance drama of Old Javanese tales is accompanied by a *gamelan gambuh* (flute ensemble); or *legong* is danced by three little girls, accompanied by *gamelan palegongan*; or delicate music is played on the courtly *gamelan semar pagulingan,* for example. These genres are considered to be from a "Middle" period in Balinese history when Javanese influence was strongest.

In the *outer courtyard* (or, in the case of a temple with two courtyards, just outside the wall of the second courtyard), performances are for an audience of people for pure enjoyment. (However, gods are believed to be observing the entirety of the *odalan*; Dibia 1992). A *gamelan gong kebyar* may play flashy newer compositions or new dance creations from a "New" period in Balinese music from the early twentieth century to the present. All three contexts and ensembles old and new encompass what is considered to be Balinese "tradition."

ACTIVITY 9.2

Following the description of music in each court-yard, listen to each of these audio examples that I recorded with permission during my field research. With the exception of Audio Examples 9.1a and 9.1c, all are performed by Sanggar Çudamani, Pengosekan, Bali, directed by I Dewa Putu Berata.

Listen to each example to hear the components of the soundscape of a temple ceremony and the distinctive sounds of the different *gamelan* ensembles. Try to describe the layers of sound that you hear in each audio example, and to map the ensembles' placement in each of 2 the courtyards on the diagram and in front of the temple, where the "Jaba" (outer space) would be. (Figure 9.5). You can also search YouTube for video examples.

Remember, however, although recorded individually here (with the exception of 9.1a), these sounds would be occurring simultaneously, resulting in the ideal full, boisterous, active (*ramé*) soundscape. All sonic and visual space is filled in order for a ceremony to be complete and successful.

- In the inner courtyard
- In the middle courtyard
- In the outer courtyard or in front of the temple walls to the kelod

The Classical Form of *Gamelan* Pieces

Most classical pieces (such as those for the courtly ensemble, *gamelan semar pagulingan*) are composed in three parts. The form is likened to the human body, consisting of a "head" (**kawitan**), usually short and compressed; a "main body" (**pangawak**), a long cycle in a fluctuating slow tempo; and the "legs and feet" (**pangecet**), a lively ending section in a faster tempo. Audio Example 9.2 "*Sinom Ladrang*" is composed in this form.

Musical Texture in *Gamelan* Music

The **texture** in *gamelan* music (musical relationships between ensemble parts) is often called **heterophony** (from the root for "different voices"), as all the parts play either an abstraction or an elaboration of a single skeletal melody. This is typical of most pre-twentieth-century Balinese compositions, and many beyond.

As you can see in Video Examples 9.1 and 9.2, in Balinese *gamelan* music, the heterophonic relationship is **stratified,** with the pitch register of an instrument correlated to the density of the musical part. That is, the lower the pitch register of the instruments, the less frequently the players strike their instruments. Higher-pitched and lower-pitched instruments can be identified by the relative sizes of the instruments. The big gong is the lowest-pitched instrument and is

ACTIVITY 9.3

Listen to Audio Example 9.2 "*Sinom Ladrang*" again, this time from beginning to end for the purpose of recognizing the form of a classical piece. The "head" in this recording is from 00:00–1:49; the main body from 1:49–4:55; the "legs and feet" from 4:55 to its conclusion. If you want to listen at a far greater level of detail, a Listening Guide for "*Sinom Ladrang*" is available in the *Music in Bali* volume of the *Global Music Series* (Gold 2005). For now, you may watch Video Example 9.2 to see part of this piece performed.

"Performance of Selisir" Video
In this video, "Tabuh Selisir" is performed by Gamelan Yuganada, led by the musician, Sudirana. This is actually the piece from which the first section of "*Sinom Ladrang*" is taken. This first section is also known as "*Bapang Selisir*"; "*Bapang*" indicates the metric structure, and "selisir" indicates the melodic mode that favors pitches numbered in the tuning system as 1, 2, 3, 5, and 6.

Notice the eight-beat repeating melody played in the low *calung* instruments and punctuated by *jegogan* strokes. The main stress of the melodic cycle is marked by the largest gong, and the midpoint of the cycle is marked by a small gong that is struck with a hard mallet, allowing the sound to stand out. The *gangsa* group plays **kotekan** (interlocking parts; see chapter 2), and the row of gong-chimes is played by a soloist (*trompong*) who functions as a melodic leader, playing the introduction and embellishing the melody.

The whole ensemble is led by a drummer who cues dynamic contrasts, tempo changes, and rhythmic accents or breaks in the cycle known as **angsel**. An example of the *angsel* cueing begins at 0:37 where the drummer plays louder and initiates a specific drum pattern that cues the musicians that an *angsel* is about to occur. The sequence ends at 0:47 where you see the *gangsas* play a little grace-note pause. This repeats between 0:57 where the drummer gives the cue, and 1:07 where the *gangsas* insert the *angsel*, followed immediately by another one. At this point, the drummer speeds up the tempo, and the camera zooms in on the *trompong* player where you can see how he embellishes the melody. The drummer cues the slowdown to the end at around 1:40.

After viewing this video, you may return to Audio Example 9.2 "*Sinom Ladrang*" to hear that its first section (00:00–1:49) is a version of this piece, "*Bapang Selisir*." In Audio Example 9.2 ("*Sinom Ladrang*"), the "*Bapang Selisir*" section is developed to contain more *angsels* and an alternate melody interspersed between repetitions of this main eight-beat melody. This "*Selisir*" section is then followed by the main body and legs and feet taken from yet a different piece. This is a good example of how flexible "a piece" may be in Bali, with almost unlimited possibilities of how "a piece" may be performed.

struck the least frequently. Its role is to punctuate cycles of melody, with subsidiary smaller gongs marking smaller divisions of the cycle. The lower-pitched metallophones play a slowly moving, skeletal melody. The higher-pitched metallophones play rapid interlocking figures to embellish the skeletal melody.

Innovations in Twentieth-Century *Gamelan Gong Kebyar*

The three-part form and stratified heterophonic texture in *gamelan* compositions carry over to the present, with some striking innovations. An example of this balance of continuity and change can be heard in the twentieth-century style called *gamelan gong kebyar* (literally, "explosive" sound), which is the most ubiquitous and popular today. *"Jaya Semara"* ("Victorious Divine Love/Love Deity"; Audio Example 9.3), composed by I Wayan Beratha in 1964, features three striking innovations:

1. *"Jaya Semara"* begins and ends with an energetic section (a *kebyar* style **gineman** that replaces the "head" in the classic three-part form) containing a kebyar passage in which all parts move together in an asymmetrical, syncopated melody, a hallmark of the **kebyar** style.

2. In contrast to *"Sinom Ladrang,"* the stratified texture is split up in the first segments of the piece so that individual virtuosic instrumental sections of the ensemble are highlighted. This timbral distinction was innovative in the early twentieth century and has become another hallmark of the *kebyar* style.

3. A cyclic repeating section comprised of two types of **alternating interlocking** figurations (**kotekan**) embellishing a slower-moving, repeating melody functions as the *pangecet*, final section. (To review one of the types, return to Activity 2.2.)

You can follow the progression through these three parts in the Listening Guide. The basic idea of *kotekan* (interlocking figuration) is that while the low-instrument group plays the skeletal melody of a composition (**pokok**), two other main groups of instruments—**reyong** and *gangsa* (Figure 9.3)—create composite elaborating melodies by playing interlocking figuration. The *gangsas* play two complementary, interlocking parts: the **polos** ("basic," main part, usually plays on the beat); and the **sangsih** ("differing," fits into the spaces between *polos* notes).

The composite melody has a faster tempo than any player could execute alone. It is usually four or eight times as fast as the *pokok* melody, evenly filling in all sonic space to meet the aesthetic ideal of *ramé*. In order to play *kotekan,* each musician must hear their part in relation to the complementary part—as one composite melody—rather than in isolation. The player must damp the note just played to stop the vibration of the key, allowing their partner to strike a following note, so that the two are not sounding at the same time. One kind of *kotekan*—*gangsa kotekan norot* ("neighbor-tone interlocking")—was demonstrated in Activity 2.2. A second type—*gangsa kotekan nyog-cag,* "leaping interlocking"—is demonstrated in Audio Example 9.4: the *polos* part is heard first, then at 0:34 the *sangsih* part; then at 1:04 the composite.

The "neighbor-tone" interlocking figuration is also played by four musicians who sit at the *reyong,* a row of tuned kettles (gong-chimes). They must use an even

"Jaya Semara"

Performed by Sanggar Çudamani, directed by I Dewa Putu Berata

Recording location and year: Pengosekan, Bali, 2000, by Lisa Gold and Ben Brinner

Instrumentation: *Gamelan gong kebyar*

Section 1 *Kebyar Gineman*

This first section is a freestanding prelude, a metrically free, non-pulsed alternation of energetic, virtuosic "solos" that highlight each instrument group.

Time	Something to Listen For
0:01	*Kebyar* (a syncopated unison section, hallmark of this style) full ensemble plays.
0:07	*Reyong* (twelve horizontal gong-chimes played by four players) interlocking "solo" briefly interjects.
0:09	*Kebyar* full ensemble plays.
0:15	Drum interlocking briefly interjects.
0:17	*Kebyar* full ensemble plays.
0:30	*Reyong* interlocking "solo" briefly interjects.
0:34	*Reyong* interlocking "solo" #1 is featured.
0:48	*Kebyar* full ensemble plays.
0:56	*Gangsa* (metallophones with bamboo resonators) interlocking interjection is featured.
0:58	*Kebyar* full ensemble plays.
1:04	*Gangsa* interlocking brief melody ends with *kempur* (medium-sized, vertical, pitched gong).
1:08	*Ceng-ceng* cymbals articulate briefly.
1:11	*Reyong* interlocking "solo" #2 is featured.
1:23	Brief *kebyar* full ensemble plays.
1:26	*Reyong* solo #2 continues; drums, *ceng-ceng*, *kempur*, gong interject.
1:43	Lead metallophone (*ugal*) introduction to transition, followed by full ensemble.
1:52	Low-instrument metallophone group plays a transitional section alone: medium register (*panyacah*), one octave lower and playing at half the density (*jublag*), and the lowest and least densely played (*jegogan*), followed by entrance of full ensemble and two *angsels* (articulated breaks).
2:05	An extended drum solo is featured.

Section 2 *Pangecet*

Full ensemble enters, with *gangsa* alternating between two kinds of interlocking (*kotekan*): "neighbor-tone" (**norot**; Audio Example 9.5), and "leaping" (**nyog-cag**; Audio Example 9.4).

Time	Something to Listen For
2:31	(1) *Gangsa:* Neighbor-tone interlocking technique (with *reyong* entering louder than *gangsa*, all play softly, then all loudly, *angsel* or break).
2:53	(2) *Gangsa:* Leaping interlocking technique (with *gangsa* entering louder than *reyong*, all play softly, then all loudly, *angsel*).
3:13	Repeat (1) *Gangsa:* Neighbor-tone interlocking technique.
3:33	Repeat (2) *Gangsa:* Leaping interlocking technique.
3:54	Repeat (1), ending with loud dynamics of full ensemble, building momentum to the final section.

Kebyar (Ending)

Closure comes with a brief, climactic *kebyar* ending that recalls the opening.

Time	Something to Listen For
4:13	*Kebyar* full ensemble; notice its characteristic syncopated unison playing.
4:29	*Gangsa* interlocking interjection returns.
4:31	*Kebyar* full ensemble ends in a loud flourish.

more difficult damping technique: with a mallet in each hand, they strike one kettle while simultaneously damping the previous kettle. This can be heard in Audio Example 9.5.

The level of skill required to play these parts cleanly and at very high speed takes years to achieve.

Conclusion

Bali, Indonesia, has a rich artistic culture in which music, dance, theater, ritual, and visual arts are completely integrated. With many resilient ancient traditions, the contemporary performing arts are intrinsically linked to a Balinese sense of identity and history. Through Bali's history, religion has been of primary importance—in terms of deeply felt belief in spiritual powers expressed, for instance, in the spiritual sense of the natural environment of the island and through daily ceremonies as offerings to the gods including performances of music, dance, and theater. Vital to every ceremony, the playing of music is regarded by Balinese individuals as a community activity that fosters group cohesion and social respon-sibility. With such deeply held values, Balinese music is primarily an ensemble practice. Together players work to produce a composite whole, with individuals selflessly contributing to a musical texture that is far greater than the sum of its parts. We have seen how this occurs in the context of a temple ceremony. Most of these musics can also be performed in more secular settings on stages, for Balinese audiences and tourists alike, yet never entirely divorced from their meaningful as-sociations. You have studied an early example of *kebyar*, the predominant twenti-eth- and twenty-first-century *gamelan* style, and listened to some of its historical predecessors from which it draws musical ideas, in order to understand how the forces of continuity and change coexist in this musical practice. It is important to remember that the concept of "tradition" in Bali is flexible and inclusive of the contemporary, changing world.

Bibliography

Bandem, I Made, and Fredrik Eugene DeBoer. 1995. *Balinese Dance in Transition: Kaja and Kelod*, 2nd ed. Kuala Lumpur: Oxford University Press.

Dibia, I. Wayan. 1992. "Arja: A Sung Dance-Drama of Bali: A Study of Change and Transformation." PhD diss., University of California, Los Angeles.

Gold, Lisa. 1992. "Musical Expression in the Gender Wayang Repertoire: A Bridge between Narrative and Ritual." In *Balinese Music in Context. A Sixty-Fifth Birthday Tribute to Hans Oesch*, edited by Danker Schaareman, 245–275. Basel: Amadeus.

Gold, Lisa. 1998. "The Gender Wayang Repertoire in Theater and Ritual: A Study of Balinese Musical Meaning." PhD diss., University of California, Berkeley.

Gold, Lisa. 2001. "Bali." In *The New Grove Dictionary of Music and Musicians*.

Gold, Lisa. 2005. *Music in Bali, Experiencing Music, Expressing Culture*. New York: Oxford University Press Global Music Series.

Gold, Lisa. 2013. "Time and Place Conflated: *Zaman Dulu* (a Bygone Era), and an Ecological Approach to a Century of Balinese Shadow Play Music." In *Performing Arts in Postmodern Bali: Changing Interpretations, Founding Traditions*, edited by Kendra Stepputat: 13–78. Aachen: Shaker, 2013.

Gold, Lisa. 2016. "Musical Knowledge, Innovation, and Transmission Within the Eco-System of Balinese Wayang Performance." In *Performing Indonesia*, edited by Andrew McGraw and Sumarsam. Washington, DC: Freer and Sackler Galleries, Smithsonian Institution. https://asia.si.edu/research/performing-indonesia/transmission/.

McGraw, Andrew Clay. 2013. *Radical Traditions: Reimagining Culture in Balinese Contemporary Music*. New York: Oxford University Press.

McPhee, Colin. 1966. *Music in Bali: A Study in Form and Instrumental Organization in Balinese Orchestral Music*. New Haven: Yale University Press.

Picard, Michel. 1990. "'Cultural Tourism' in Bali: Cultural Performances as Tourist Attraction." *Indonesia* 49: 37–75.

Vickers, Adrian. 1989. *Bali: A Paradise Created*. Berkeley, CA: Periplus Editions, Inc.

Vickers, Adrian. 1992. *Travelling to Bali: Four Hundred Years of Journeys*. New York: Oxford University Press.

10

Music in North India

An Enduring Classical Musical Tradition

GEORGE RUCKERT

Chapter Contents

≡ **Indian musician Ravi Shankar (1920–2012; center) performs onstage at Northern Illinois University, DeKalb, Illinois, 1972.**

Introduction

This chapter introduces you to key ideas and musical practices that have endured for hundreds of years in Indian culture as a remarkable example of the relevance of music from the past for musical culture in the present. These ideas and practices have endured because they have been transmitted (i.e. "passed on") through a system of teaching and learning that itself has endured for many centuries.

Since about the thirteenth century, creative practices in expressing and using these ideas on the part of musicians in the northern part (Hindustan) and those in the southern part of the Indian subcontinent diverged sufficiently so that two separate classical traditions exist. This chapter focuses on musical practices in the northern system: Hindustani classical music.

In this chapter, I will address the perspectives of both teachers and students in that system and acquaint you with five ancient ideas that remain paramount in classical musical practice to this moment. Those ideas are the following:

1. The honored placed of music in the culture.
2. The organization of pitch as realized through the concept of *rāga*, or melodic map (see the section on "melodic mode" in chapter 1).
3. The organization of rhythm into metric cycles: a system called *tāla*. I will specifically focus on how this metric cycle is put to use as the framework for a favorite way to mark a musical ending (a **cadence**).
4. The use of syllables other than those in linguistically coherent song texts (i.e., vocables). This will be demonstrated through the **Hindustani** vocal/dance genre called *tārānā*.
5. The interweaving of fixed composition and "on the spot" realization in the structuring of a performance of a *rāga*. This structural idea will be illustrated through an emphasis on instrumental performance, including a performance by one of North India's most brilliant musicians, Ali Akbar Khan.

In North Indian speech, *rāga*—the term for the melodic idea—is usually pronounced as *rāg*; and *tāla*—the term for the rhythmic system—as *tāl*.

India

India is located in the geographic region of South Asia (Figure 10.1) that is home to the longest continuously flourishing civilization in the world. Having begun with the urban Indus Valley civilization of the third millennium BCE, it is younger only than the Mesopotamian civilization that ceased to exist long ago. India of today is bordered by eight neighboring countries: Pakistan to its west; China, Nepal, and

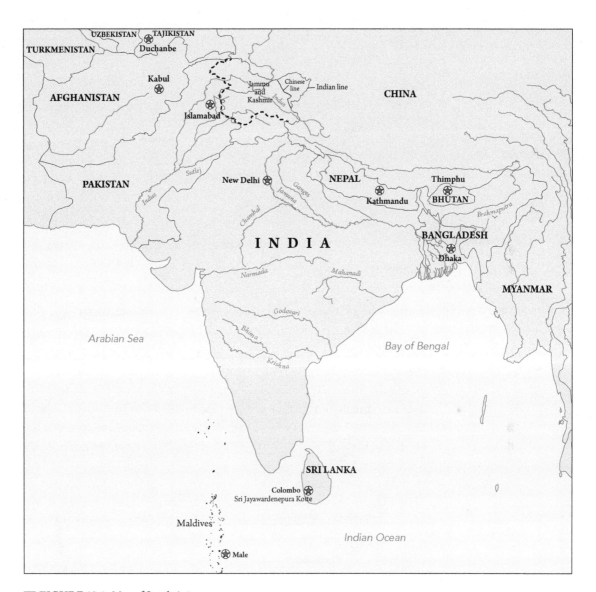

≡ **FIGURE 10.1** Map of South Asia.

Bhutan to the northeast; Bangladesh and Myanmar to the east; Sri Lanka and the Maldives to the south. Its Andaman and Nicobar Islands share a maritime border with Thailand and Indonesia.

India itself is located on a subcontinent that extends south from the continent of Asia (Figure 10.2). The subcontinent is bordered on its south by the Indian Ocean, on the southwest by the Arabian Sea, and on the southeast by the Bay of

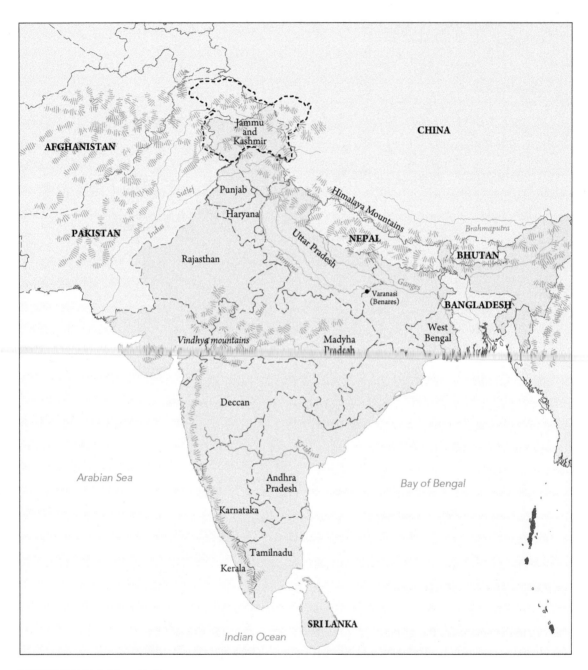

≡ **FIGURE 10.2** Map of India.

Bengal—into which drain the mighty Ganges and Brahmaputra rivers that originate in the Himalayan mountains to India's north. India is the largest country in South Asia. It is the seventh-largest nation by area in the world, the second most populous (1.3+ billion people), and the most populous democracy.

The culture has long been rich in ethnic and cultural diversity. Originally occupied by Dravidian peoples, it became home to others who entered from the northwest—most notably Aryan peoples who brought with them ancient Vedic culture and, many centuries later, groups from Central and West Asia in the Persian cultural sphere. India has more than twenty official languages among the numerous regional and tribal languages. Demonstrating their diversity, fifteen of them are "Indic" (from Aryan culture), four are Dravidian, and two are of the Tibeto-Burman language family.

Religion has been significant in this enduring culture. The oldest scriptures associated with the Hindu religion date back to the second millennium BCE. The first millennium BCE saw large-scale urbanization on the Ganges River, and the rise of the Buddhist and Jain religions. Several major political empires have flourished through time, including the Muslim Mughal empire in the sixteenth century CE, which was followed by British colonial rule when India was known as "the jewel in the crown." The entire continent had not been united politically until the British colonial era; under the British, English became the common language. The subcontinent achieved independence in 1947, at which time Pakistan and Bangladesh broke away to form nation-states separate from India.

Musical Ideas and Practices
Music's Honored Place in the Culture

The instrumentalist reaches down to pick up his instrument for the concert. But before doing so, a subtle touch to the forehead and heart in an age-old gesture of devotional respect for the instrument and the music acknowledges the ancient idea of **Nād Brahmā,** the divinity of sound itself. This is not necessarily a religious belief in the conventional sense, because in India musicians are Hindu, Muslim, Jewish, Buddhist, Jain, Christian, and even agnostic about religious issues. But from c. 1500 BCE, the idea that musical practice is a yoga leading to the highest enlightenment and internal realizations has been passed on to musicians of all varieties of religious backgrounds. Hence the concert will not be entertainment in a shallow sense but a demonstration of the honored and meaningful place music has had in this ancient civilization.

The Teaching/Learning System (*Gūru-shisyā paramparā*)

All musicians in the world of Hindustani classical music have the experience of learning with a master musician in the traditional system. The teacher (*gūru*) teaches the music directly through oral repetition: hear, repeat, practice, repeat, practice. Knowledge of melodic and rhythmic material is accumulated slowly along with technical abilities, to be executed with greater and greater refinement and discernment of the ear. The student is continually required to prove that they are ready for the next step.

In the past, the *gūru*'s repertoire was often a highly guarded treasure, and not simply distributed at the request of the student. As the traditional saying goes, "*Gūru kripyā binā koi nahī pave*"—"Without the blessings of the *gūru*, one gets nothing." Musical knowledge has therefore been useful as well as meaningful: in this centuries-old economic and social system, the *gūru* was a master in a professional guild, and admission to it was an economic guarantee of a livelihood in music. Therefore, in that rarefied atmosphere that protected the musical lineage as well as the professional world to which it led, to learn a new composition was an honor bestowed on the student. The years of slowly measured progress and refinement developed the students' patience, respect, and humility. The system has moved on to some extent, but unchanged is the bond that develops over the years between teacher and student in this tradition; one could even say that it is a sacred one.

Rāga: The Melodic Map

The concept of *rāg* is very elusive. Some *rāgs* are very broad in their possibilities for melodic elasticity and expansion, while others are quite narrow and restrictive. Each is named. Rather than asking you to direct your listening systematically to each of the general qualities common to all *rāgs*, I have written a list that outlines these qualities (Table 10.1) and will refer to some of the characteristics as I take you through a few listening examples. The *rāgs* featured in them are *Rāg* Adānā and *Rāg* Chandranandan. They are meant to be performed in the late night, and in the evening, respectively (see no. 7 in Table 10.1).

The melodic maps of *rāgs* are conveyed by a teacher who instills the student with both rigid patterns of composition and animating departures of improvisation. The balance of these two qualities takes a long time to learn, and often the musicians who do it best are quite mature—in contrast to younger performers who may keep audience interest through speed and dazzling technique.

≡ **TABLE 10.1** General Qualities Common to All rāgs.

1. A *rāg/ārāga* must have at least five notes and cannot omit **sa**.
2. Some form of **ma** or **pa** must be present as well.
3. Two forms of the same note adjacent to each other are rarely encountered.
4. A *rāg* uses a certain selection of tones; ones that are omitted are termed "forbidden" and cannot be used without destroying the *rāg*.
5. There is an as ascending and descending format for the series of pitches used in a *rāg*.
6. Many *rāgs* have strong tonal centers, called *vādi* and *samvādi*. Typically, these notes are a fifth apart. The **vādi-samvādi** do not substitute for the importance of the tonal center **sa** in a *rāg* and do not always function the same way for each *rāg*.
7. Certain moods are typically associated with each *rāg*, and often a time of day or season of the year.
8. Prescribed melodic movements that often recur, like catch phrases, identify the *rāg*.
9. There can be precise use of timbres and tonal shading, heightened by the use of microtonal pitches that vary from one *rāg* to another, lending particular character to the *rāg*. (Considering these variations, one cannot use blanket phrases such as "perfect tuning" or "Indian tuning" to refer to pitch placement.)

Tāla: The Metric System

In North Indian classical music, many of the meters (called *tāla*) group a relatively larger number of beats. The favorite *tāla*, **tīntāl,** has a recurring cycle of sixteen beats, conceptualized with four subdivisions of four beats each: 4 + 4 + 4 + 4; therefore it is a duple rhythm.

Musicians in that tradition learn to speak the *tālas,* with vocables for drum strokes. To speak *tīntāl* as played on the drum-pair called **tablā,** the vocables/ syllables are as shown in Figure 10.3.

The "dha" and "dhin" strokes, played on both left and right drums, produce a heavier, deeper sound than the "na," "tin," and "ta" strokes played on the right-hand drum only. Because musical tradition dictates that musical units end on a next count 1, *tālas* are considered to be cyclical groupings.

Tihāī: A Cadential Practice

A rhythmic practice that occurs a number of times in the recorded examples for this chapter is **tihāī** (literally, "one-third"); it is simply a rhythm pattern that is played three times. The conclusion of the third time through the pattern is usually timed

1	2	3	4	5	6	7	8	9	10	11	12	13	14	15	16	1
dha	dhin	dhin	dha	dha	dhin	dhin	dha	na	tin	tin	ta	ta	dhin	dhin	dha	dha

≡ **FIGURE 10.3** Vocables for speaking *tīntāl* as played on a *tablā*.

ACTIVITY 10.1

1. Practice speaking the *tīntāl* syllable pattern (Figure 10.3) without worrying about counting numbers or thinking about subdivisions. Then do it with one or two classmates until you can all speak the pattern easily. Ideally, memorize it.

2. Now you need to get comfortable with the quantitative structure of the *tāla*—the feeling of counting out sixteen, coming to completion on a next count 1, and the feeling of the four-count subdivisions. To do this as a knowledgeable musician would, you will need to do physical motions to embody the pattern: for this *tāla*, clap three times—on counts 1, 5, and 13. Wave to the side on count 9; as you will feel, that divides the cycle in half. Do the motions without counting until you are comfortable

with the pattern: clap clap wave clap/clap clap wave clap/.

3. Once comfortable, speak the numbers of the counts as you do the motion. Don't stop at the next count 1. Keep going through more cycles!

4. Replace the numbers with the syllable pattern while doing the motion pattern. If you can do that, you will have really learned *tīntāl*.

5. The final step is to hear the cycle in performed music. In "*Rāg* Chandranandan" (Audio Example 10.1), the *tāla* starts after the very brief prelude at 27 seconds. Listen to the melody to feel the beats and try to sense the *tāla* structure. While listening, try keeping the *tāla* with the claps and waves. If you lose your place, wait for the next clear count 1 to start again.

to coincide with the downbeat of a *tāl* cycle on beat 1—adding considerable interest to the performance and creating a cadence (ending to a musical unit or to the selection). In vocal and melodic instrumental music, the third occurrence of the pattern may come either on that downbeat or on whatever beat in the *tāl* cycle the composition begins on. The best way to recognize a *tihāī* is to engage with one yourself. In Activity 10.2, the phrase of drumming syllables "*Tete kata gadi gena dha*," is used to illustrate the structure of the practice.

The Musical Syllable (Vocable)

In addition to drumming patterns, vocables are important for conveying dance and instrumental rhythms. A sampling of the musicality of the recited syllables of drumming and dance has been created by dancer Joanna de Souza and drummer Ritesh Das. This performance—which we call the "Tongue Twister Recording" (Audio Example 10.4)—is composed of vocables and is both lyrical and exciting. The dance style is **Kathak**, one of the forms of classical dance in

ACTIVITY 10.2

Audio Example 10.2 "*Tihāī#1*" and Audio Example 10.3 "*Tihāī#2*" demonstrate two *tihāī* that can be created, for example, from the *tablā* stroke phrase "*Tete kata gadi gena dha*"—a five-count pattern.

"*Tihāī#1*": To make this demonstration recording for you, I chose to put one count between the first two occurrences; that count becomes part of the pattern. Played (or spoken) three times, the *tihāī* consumes seventeen counts (including the final count 1). Before listening to the recordings, speak the pattern several times, saying "rest" for the count after *dha* (-). The *Tihāī* comes to an end on the final *dha*, so you don't need to repeat "rest" there.

> *Tete kata gadi gena dha –*
> *Tete kata gadi gena dha –*
> *Tete kata gadi gena dha/*

Tihāī occur within a *tāl* cycle, and I am choosing here to put this one into *tīntāl* with a cycle of sixteen counts. To fit this particular pattern into *tīntāl* and come to an end on count 1, I need to begin it on a count 1. In "*Tihāī #1*" (Audio Example 10.2), my recitation begins with the common drumming pattern for *tīntāl* (see Figure 10.3) and then goes right

into the *Tihāī*. Listen to this several times and then speak it all with me.

To create "*Tihāī #2*" (Audio Example 10.3) I chose to speak the pattern right through without any count between the occurrences. That consumes only fifteen counts—not a full cycle of *tīntāl*. That allows me to have a little fun with it by putting two counts after the third *dha* and making that the pattern. I keep on going with the principle of three times through until the final *dha* comes out on a count 1. Before listening to the recording, speak that new pattern three times (without thinking about *tīntāl*), saying "rest rest" for the two-count separations.

> *Tete kata gadi gena dha Tete kata gadi gena dha*
> *Tete kata gadi gena dha - -Tete kata gadi gena dha*
> *Tete kata gadi gena dha Tete kata gadi gena dha - -*
> *Tete kata gadi gena dha Tete kata gadi gena dha*
> *Tete kata gadi gena dha/*

I start the recitation of "*Tihāī #2*" with the *tīntāl* drumming pattern and then recite the whole *tihāī*. Listen to this several times and then speak it all with me. Enjoy!

If you want to do more, see Ruckert 2004: 46–49.

North India, one in which rhythmic play is very significant. The drum, the *tablā*, is actually a pair of single-headed, hand-struck drums played by one musician: the left one, bowl shaped with a deep sound; the right one conical, the shape of two truncated cones bulging at the center and carefully tuned to higher pitch with a special paste.

Vocables are also used in Hindustani music for carrying melody or for melodic information. A formal vocal performance of a *rāg*, for instance, is usually begun with a prelude accompanied only on the drone-producing instrument, the **tān-pūrā** (plucked composite lute-zither chordophone), with the melody sung to vocables. Since ancient times, syllables have been used for tonal information, that is, for naming pitches: the syllables **sa ri** (or **re**) **ga ma pa dha** and **ni**. These syllables are referred to as **sargam**. Further, it is not unusual for a singer to sing a song whose linguistic meaning may not be fully articulated, as the vocalist may prolong the syllables of a song or combine them in a melodic passage in such a way as to completely obscure meaning. "Meaning" often becomes secondary to the sound of pitch itself. You will have experienced this analytically by doing Activity 1.1 in chapter 1.

Vocables in the Vocal/Dance Genre *Tārānā*

The rhythmic syllable is a prominent part of a genre of Hindustani vocal music, the **tārānā** . There are multiple sources for the syllables of a *tārānā* composition: the vocables used to carry the melody in the prelude to a vocal *rāg* performance; syllables from dance, from instrumental music, from **drumming**, and some others that are unique to the genre itself. A *tārānā* is often sung as a concluding item of a *rāg* performance because most are performed at a fast tempo and can be quite exciting. The example here is an excerpt from a very old and traditional *tārānā* in the late-night Rāg Adānā (Audio Example 10.5).

ACTIVITY 10.3

Listen to Audio Example 10.5 first to distinguish the instruments of the ensemble and then to hear the sectioning of the selection: the drone-producing *tānpūrā*, then the *tablā* played by Swapan Chaudhuri with the drone-producing *tānpūrā*, in the background, and a shadowing melodic instrument—the short, broad-necked, bowed lute *sārangī*—played by Ramesh Misra. A famous singer of light-classical styles, Asha Bhosle, begins with the first part of the composition: the first, lower, "home" section. At 0:55, a second, higher section begins. Division into these two sections—low and high—is a common way of structuring fixed compositions—and to a lesser extent, improvisation as well. To hear at a greater level of detail, follow the Listening Guide.

LISTENING GUIDE

"Tārānā in Rāg Adānā"

Performed by Asha Bhosle

Recording location and year: from Legacy, CD, AMMP Productions, 1996

Instrumentation: voice, sārangī, guitar, tānpūrā, tablā

Time	Something to Listen For
0:01	*Tānpūrā*, sounds first, fifth, and octave drone pitches in continuous plucking stream.
0:05	*Tablā* enters with a flourish, offering a short introduction to the *tāl* (*tīntāl*) by Swapan Chaudhuri that ends with a *tihāī* (three-part rhythmic cadence) that leads into the basic sixteen-beat drum pattern for *tīntāl*.
0:14	The female vocalist begins the "home" section, singing a text comprised of vocables accompanied by the *sārangī* and *tablā*. These vocables are traditional to *tārānā*: "o de ta na de re na ta dim ta dim, ta nan a na ta na de re na, tan nan a deri da ni tum deri da ni," and so on.
0:28	Vocalist repeats the first section, with *sārangī*, *tablā*, and guitar, played by Brian Goldon, ending with a vocally ornamental "wavering."
0:43	Instrumental interlude features *sārangī* on melody, with *tablā* and *tānpūrā*.
0:51	Vocalist returns with a short phrase that bridges the first and second sections, ending with a vocally ornamental "wavering" effect.
0:56	Vocalist begins the second and higher part of the composition, shifting into a higher register of pitches, featuring some fast-moving melodic passages.
1:09	Vocalist builds the melody to its highest pitch, followed by several brief rhythmic phrases.
1:16	Vocalist repeats the first section, ending with a vocally ornamental "wavering."
1:33	Instrumental interlude.
1:38	Vocalist returns with a short phrase (like 0:51).
1:54	Vocalist builds the melody to its highest pitch, followed by several brief rhythmic phrases (like 1:09).
2:27	The first section returns, and the tempo increases to a "wavering" vocal close.

Weaving of Fixed Composition and "On the Spot" Realization

In performance of both vocal and instrumental music, a musician can choose how to treat a composition. For example, the fixed composition of the *tārānā* in Rāg Adānā could be performed in concert just as you hear it, in its complete two-part form, or it could be expanded with improvisatory sections that would depend on the school and style of its singer. It could also be a training tool for tracing paths of the *rāg* (Table 10.1, nos. 5 and 8); that is a main teaching method for learning the maps of the melodic phrases of the *rāgs*. In the words of the master musician Ali Akbar Khan:

A composition is like a snapshot, you see. Like you go to your friend's house and see an album of the family pictures. From one picture of this cousin you get some idea of how he looks. But then you see many pictures of him and you start to get a more real image of that person. Like that you learn the picture of the *rāg*.
But still you won't know it until you practice and play it. Even now I am still learning about the *rāgs* every time I play.

Traditionally, instrumentalists learned the basics of *rāg* structure and how to build on it through "on the spot" realization through studying vocal techniques. Further, the basic idea of a full-blown performance of a *rāg*—that it starts with a focus on only a few pitches, expands into full pitch range, and then into a composition with faster and more rhythmic patterns—is reflective of vocal models that all instrumentalists have studied in past years. But in the last century, the instrumentalists have taken the tradition to new heights of expression, refinement, and technique. The newer music has been configured by the concert experience and its younger audiences. Its subtlety, power, and outreach have been greatly aided by electronic amplification and recording.

The Rise of Instrumental Music

In the last seventy or so years, instrumental music has risen in North India to the level of prominence traditionally accorded to vocal music—indeed, if not surpassing it in public interest, especially as the music has migrated to Western countries. Two instruments in particular—the *sitār* and the *sarod*—have been in the forefront (Figure 10.4); but the guitar, flute, and several others have also gained in popularity.

The **sitār** is a long-necked, plucked lute with a bowl-shaped gourd resonating chamber attached to the wooden neck. Its high metal frets are movable to accommodate the *rāg* being performed, and its metal strings that are plucked with metal

≡ FIGURE 10.4
Sitār player Ravi Shankar (second from left) and *sarod* player Ali Akbar Khan (far right) performing at The Concert for Bangladesh, New York City, 1971.

finger picks create a distinctive sound. It is a relatively recent instrument by Indian standards—having first appeared in the eighteenth century as a very small instrument resembling a Persian plucked lute then in use in the subcontinent (Miner 1993, 35). The instrument had become central to the musical image of North India by the late nineteenth century. As young women in Britain and America might have been expected to demonstrate skills on the piano, so the *sitār* became the rising middle-class image of culture and cultivation. Physical changes were gradually made such as the addition of drone strings and **sympathetic strings** (strings underneath the playing strings that vibrate in sympathy with the melody strings rather than being plucked). It reached its present form only in the late nineteenth to early twentieth century.

For many, the *sitār* now symbolizes the music of North India. The image of Ravi Shankar teaching Beatle George Harrison is iconographic: one of the great masters of "the East" reaching to "the West" through a young pop idol of the 1960s. While the *sitār* still holds some of that position, it is not an easy instrument to play, and frustrates anyone without a serious dedication to master it.

The **sarod**—an even later addition to the important instruments of North Indian classical music (introduced during the nineteenth century)—is also a long-necked, plucked lute, but its construction is entirely different from that of the *sitār*. Its slightly waisted-shaped, wooden resonating body is covered with goatskin. Its long, fretless neck tapers from wide at the body to narrower at the top and is covered with a smooth steel fingerboard over which the player slides the fingernails of the left hand. The sound produced on the *sarod* is deeper, more mellow than that of the *sitār*, although it too has metal playing, drone, and sympathetic strings. Credit for modifying the nineteenth-century instrument to the substantial form that we know today goes to a legendary twentieth-century musician,

FIGURE 10.5
Zakir Hussain
(center) and Ali
Akbar Khan (right)
performing at the
Berlin Jazz Festival,
1972.

Allauddin Khan (1862–1972). Allauddin Khan's son, the illustrious Ali Akbar Khan (1922–2009), is the featured sarodist in the rest of this chapter (Figure 10.5).

The *tablā* drum, originally relegated to mere accompaniment in ensemble with the *sitār* or *sarod,* is now highly regarded for its virtuosic literature and technique. It was introduced widely in Europe and America through performing tours of Ravi Shankar (Figures 10.0) (Shankar 1999) and Ali Akbar Khan, mostly accompanied by *tablist* Alla Rakha and then by his son, Zakir Hussain, who is now an international superstar and soloist on his instrument. The *tablā* is now also incorporated into many other ensembles east and west. Video 10.1 features a demonstration of the *tablā* played by Dr. Narenda Budhakar.

Ali Akbar Khan Plays *Rāg* Chandranandan on the *Sarod*

This section introduces the instrumental technique of weaving fixed and improvised performance through a famous *sarod* performance by one of its preeminent masters, Ali Akbar Khan (Figure 10.5). The recording is of the evening *Rāg* Chandranandan—a melodic mode of his own creation (see Ruckert 1994, 2001). Solos by the melodic artist and drummer alternate throughout the performance; a solo in Indian music can mean either one musical part alone, or a featured part even if other musical parts are present. Speed is thought of in relative terms: slow, medium, fast. There is likely to be a gradual acceleration of the speed from beginning to end of a performance. This *gat* is in *tīntāl* paced at slow speed.

First, I will walk you through the performance in considerable detail. For accessibility, the performance is heard here in five recorded excerpts, with portions of the thirty-two-minute-long selection edited out. The details are explained in the order they are mentioned in the basic Listening Guide that follows, and I suggest that you first read the explanations of the details without listening to gain a sense of the whole.

Excerpt 1 (Audio Example 10.1)

This excerpt is in three parts:

The *mukhrā*: After a quick introduction, Ali Akbar plays the first phrase (**mukhrā**) of the fixed composition (known generically as **gat**). The *mukhrā* also serves as a main phrase in improvisation and—structurally important through most of the performance—recurs as a cadential phrase that leads to the downbeat of a cycle of the *tāl*, here *tīntāl*. Rather than proceeding immediately to the rest of the *gat* melody, he stays with that first phrase but ornaments it for a few cycles of the *tāl*. The *mukhrā* of this *gat* should sound familiar to you, from your having learned while doing Activity 1.1; it is notated in Musical Example 1.

Vistār: An improvised developmental section played by the melodic artist in a *rāg* performance. The *vistār* might focus within just part of the wide range of pitch that can be produced on the instrument—in lower, middle, or high register. As in this recording, the artist builds the *vistār*s by increasing the range and rhythmic variety until the artist reaches and explores the upper pitch register of the *rāg*.

Tān: A melodic pattern used to expand the *rāg* in performance after the fixed composition. The term *tān* is often used in the sense of a fast, melodic run/flourish.

Excerpt 2 (Audio Example 10.6)

In this part of his performance, Khan plays with the rhythm. Including this type of improvisation in his *rāg* performance reveals Ali Akbar Khan's deep grounding in a particular genre of classical vocal music wherein rhythmic design is treated with this kind of rigor. The rhythmic articulation is deliberately composed to sound counter to the regularity of the *tablā* beats.

Excerpt 3 (Audio Example 10.7)

This excerpt features two sections:

Fast *gat*: A second fixed composition is introduced, this one in fast speed *tīntāl*. This *gat* is presented with its regular rhythmic pattern (1 2 3, 1 2 3 . . .) articulated by the sarodist's right-hand plucking patterns.

Larant: The final *tān* of this excerpt features a style called *larant*, using the repeated pitch *sa* as a springboard for neighbor-note motion around it.

Excerpt 4 (Audio Example 10.8)

This is an excerpt of the **jhālā** section of the *rāg*. The "sparkling" approach to the end of the performance is characterized by intensely fast repeated strokes on the instrument's high drone strings.

Excerpt 5 (Audio Example 10.9)

This excerpt from the conclusion of the performance includes two sections:

Sawāl-jawāb: A "question-answer" exchange between the two artists. Here the melodic soloist plays a rhythm, and the *tablā* player answers with an imitation, or a variation based on the same idea. The exchanges finally become shorter and quicker, until the performance ends with a thrilling *tihāī* played together.

Chakradār tihāī: In this performance, the *tihāī* is made all the more climactic with nine occurrences of the cadential figure, ending on high pitch *sa*.

A Visit with an Elderly Master

Having introduced you to the musical details in the practice of Hindustani classical music that were so carefully passed down to me as a student, I now will introduce you to my teacher for his perspective on the musical ideas, practices, and values in the North Indian tradition (Figures 10.4, 10.5).

In August 2000, I visited the home of my *guru*, Ali Akbar Khan **sahib** (respectful form of address), near his College of Music in San Rafael, California, where he taught for more than thirty years. He lived in a small house in those suburbs of San Francisco, north of the famous Golden Gate Bridge, with his wife and three children. He often received visitors in the evening at his home: If there is music to be taught, then one would come early; if not, then after 8 p.m. Though he passed away in 2009, I decided to write this account of my experience of him in the present tense.

His room is on the newly added second floor, above the clamor of his three kids with their neighborhood friends, whose vigorous American lifestyle contrasts with the sanctorum of the master's space. There is a couch and a chair in the spacious room, but the chief sitting area is the thick green carpet on which most of his guests seat themselves on the floor, "Indian style." On one wall is a large curtained bookcase that functions almost like an altar, where Khansahib keeps icons of many religions. There are also many photos and mementos of his more personal spiritual history and quest. This case will be closed when the room is used for informal meetings, parties, or conversations. Khansahib has received many distinguished

LISTENING GUIDE

Rāg Chandranandan*

Performed by Ali Akbar Khan (*sarod*) and Mahapurush Misra (*tablā*)

Recording location and year: Connoisseur Society, 1964 (Reissued on AMMP Productions, 1990)

Instrumentation: *sarod, tablā, tānpūrā,*

Excerpt 1

Time	Something to Listen For
0:01	After two strums of the open strings on his instrument, Ali Akbar Khan (AAK) plays several phrases from the *rāg* as introduction; this short style is known as *aochar ālāp*.
0:27	*Mukhrā* to the fixed composition (*gat*) in slow *tīntāl. Tablā* enters with short solo.
0:41	*Mukhrā* to *gat* returns, variation of *gat*.
0:55	*Mukhrā*.
1:04	*Vistār*, lower-mid register, ends with medium speed *tān*,
1:24	*Mukhrā* returns, *tablā* solo (two cycles).
1:56	Low register *vistār* gradually ascends to middle *ga*.
2:48	*Mukhrā* to *tablā* solo beginning with triplets, ending in fast duple rhythm.
3:17	*Vistār* is played in middle register.
3:47	*Tān* in style with mainly downstrokes of right hand with *tihāī* at 3:52, continues with *vistārs* to *antarā* (high register).
4:55	*Tān* ends with *mukhrā* at 5:21.

Excerpt 2
Jump ahead in performance to a section of rhythmic variation, first with offbeats; then mixed with right-hand stroke patterns, consciously maintaining the offbeat inflection.

Time	Something to Listen For
1:18	*Tihāī*, then *mukhrā*, ends this offbeat *tān*.

Excerpt 3
Jump ahead in performance to fast *gat* in *tīntāl*

Time	Something to Listen For
0:13	Second line of composition ending in *tān*-like flourish.

0:26	Variations of first line of *gat*.
0:47	*Tān* with downstrokes.
0:57	*Tān* continues in *larant* style, using the repeated *sa* as a springboard for neighbor-note motion around it.

🔊)) **Excerpt 4**

Beginning of *jhālā* section with repeated rhythmic striking of the high drone strings

🔊)) **Excerpt 5**

Beginning of *sawāl-jawāb* (question-answer) section with *tablā*

Time	Something to Listen For
1:56	Tightening of the responses begins.
2:39	Fast *jhālā*.
2:55	Fast *tān* finishing in *chakradār tihāī* (nine repetitions of the cadential pattern).

friends, dignitaries, students, and admirers in this room, and he receives guests with a cordiality that puts everyone at ease.

Well, almost at ease: I, for one, am never totally at ease with a man whose musical genius has awed and humbled me on hundreds of occasions. In his eighties, he could still produce music of spellbinding invention, lilting charm, fierce power, and profound sadness—all in one sitting. And he taught his tradition freely to everyone who sat in front of him, without regard to their pedigree or musical background, including the entire gamut of the repertoire of Hindustani music, from vocal music to instrumental, and from light-classical tunes to the most intricate and mathematical depths of the tradition. In the face of this understanding of this man's stature and gift to mankind, one cannot be casual.

With all that in mind, I volunteer my diffidence at having returned to California to play a program at his college—to perform on the very platform from which he has taught thousands of classes.

He laughs. "That is a good sign. A musician has to begin from a feeling of humility, or he will not find that mood." He pauses. We five or six visitors become silent, for this is an area of mutual interest to all of his students. "My father [Allauddin Khan] taught that music is like a prayer, you see. When you pray you cannot think, 'Oh, I am great,' 'I am doing all this and all that,' 'My runs are fastest,' and all that macho stuff. You won't get God's grace with that attitude . . . and your music will suffer."

A young student speaks up. "But Khansahib, so many musicians are playing that way. And what else can we do? We have to show the power and speed or else people will be bored."

"No . . . if you play in rhythm and in tune, God will help you. That is my point. If you start by thinking the other way, your music will be hopeless. *That* is boring music—box-office type music. Many people are doing that, but I don't think that way.

"When I was a boy, in those days people thought of the [classical] music as either *dhrupad* style or *khyāl* style [two vocal genres]. In *khyāl* style, they did not pay so strict attention to matters of purity in the *rāgs*, but *dhrupad* people always were very careful about those things."

Khansahib thoughtfully continued. "My feeling is, that the music is gradually going down and down . . . but it won't die . . . and one day it will come up again, just like it has happened before in history. Sometimes it became less, and people became aware of these things. But then somebody has to show them—what is going wrong—but nowadays the young generation has no idea about this, and the old maestros are not alive. But today the musicians have to tour all the time, and think about money matters, and entertainment. They don't really have the time to teach in the old way."

We students shuffled nervously and looked at each other in the sighing acknowledgment of the possibility that the great tradition was in an ebbing stage. After a silence, someone piped up, "But Khansahib, a lot of good things are happening, too. I heard you in New York on a recording. I didn't know, like, *anything*, but I was able to get on a plane and come to study with you. *That* couldn't have happened in the old days!"

"Yes, these kinds of things—television, recording, concerts—they are all improving a lot. The publicity matters are better, but at the same time the publicity can spoil the whole thing, and create the wrong idea in everybody's mind. In the old days these things were weak, but the music was more pure."

I mused about the life's work of this great artist sitting just before me. Of anyone I know, he certainly dedicated his life and time to passing on the tradition in the purest way he knew. I wonder if anyone in antiquity could have done a better job. Khansahib's journey through life took him from growing up in a feudal court in a traditional culture, suddenly being called on to address the modern artistic world, and finally landing amidst the headlong rush of the quilted society we collectively address as twenty-first-century America. It would be almost impossible for most people to address these circumstances of transgenerational, multi-artistic, and cross-cultural adjustment.

"This music is not just to entertain, it is really a pathway to God. And once you really get the right sound in your soul and mind, it is such a peaceful and pleasant feeling. That peace you cannot get anywhere."

Conclusion

This chapter has given you a glimpse into musical practices that have endured with an honored, meaningful cultural space in the oldest continuously flourishing civilization on the earth. The definition of "musical practices" has been extended here to include the system of teaching and learning that itself has endured for many centuries. Paramount musical ideas have been explored: the organization of pitch as realized through the concept of *rāga*, or melodic map; the organization of rhythm into metric cycles, the *tāla* system; the idea that musical syllables are useful for carrying rhythmic and pitch information and can be incorporated into musical creativity itself; and the structural principle in the performance of a *rāga* of interweaving fixed composition and "on-the-spot" realization. Focus has been on Hindustani classical music—the tradition that flourishes in the northern part of the Indian subcontinent, particularly instrumental performance of *rāg*, the *sitār*, *sarod*, and *tablā*; and finally, the artistry and views of master sarodist Ali Akbar Khan.

Bibliography

Miner, Allyn. 1993. *Sitar and Sarod in the 18th and 19th Centuries*. Wilhelmhaven, Germany: Florian Noetzl Verlag.

Ruckert, George. 1994. *The Music of Ali Akbar Khan: An Analysis of His Musical Style through the Examination of His Composition in Three Selected Ragas*. PhD diss., University of California, Berkeley.

Ruckert, George, general ed. 2001–. *The classical music of North India: The Music of the Baba Allauddin Gharana as Taught by Ali Akbar Khan at the Ali Akbar College of*

Music. Notations and explanatory text by George Ruckert. New Delhi: Munshiram Manoharlal Publishers.

Ruckert, George. 2004. *Music in North India: Experiencing Music, Expressing Culture*. New York: Oxford University Press.

Shankar, Ravi. 1999. *Ragamala: Autobiography of Ravi Shankar*. London: Genesis Publications.

11

Music in Turkey

Contemporary Recording of Traditional Music

ELIOT BATES

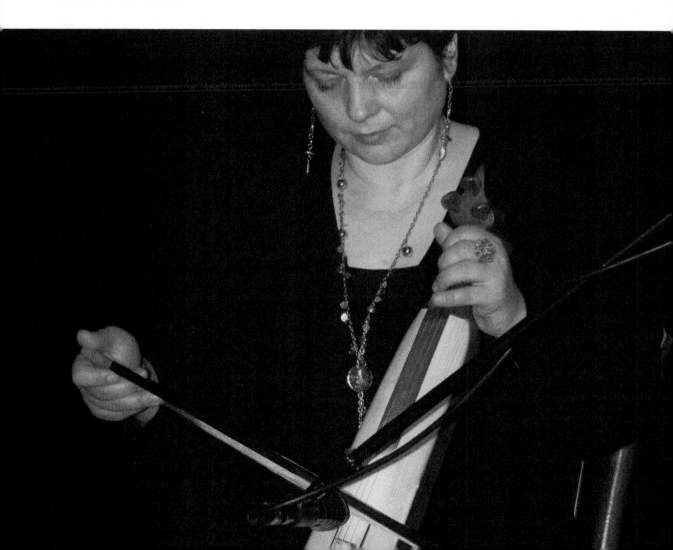

Chapter Contents

Introduction

Among the nations of the world at present, Turkey is one of few (Figure 11.1) that spans two continents—Europe and Asia—situated on land that once comprised part of the Hittite, Greek, Roman, Byzantine, and Ottoman Empires. The Ottoman Empire was founded in 1299 CE by Osman I, the leader of the Ottoman Turks in northwestern Anatolia, who consolidated rule among the many different Turkic tribes. In 1453, the Ottomans conquered Constantinople, the capital of the Byzantine Empire. By 1566, under the reign of Sultan Suleiman the Magnificent, the Ottoman Empire had expanded and developed into a multinational, multilingual empire controlling much of Southeast Europe (stopped, as it is said, "at the gates of Vienna"), also western Asia, and coastal North Africa. Following the Ottoman defeat in World War I and a brief period of European occupation, the Republic of Turkey was founded as a modern nation that identifies its geopolitical location as European and West Asian.

The vast expanse of Turkey encompasses numerous distinct ecosystems ranging from deserts to snow-covered mountains to dense rainforests. It is bordered on the west by Bulgaria and Greece, and on the east by Georgia, Armenia, and Iran. Much of

≡ İlknur Yakupoğlu performing *kemençe.*

≡ **FIGURE 11.1** Map of Turkey.

the northern border is the Black Sea, from which a narrow channel called the Bosphorus flows southward toward the Mediterranean Sea, separating the European and Asian sides of Turkey. (Regular ferry service provides easy transport from one side to the other.) With a population of just under 85 million (mid-2020), the territory houses nearly four dozen ethnicities. The only language officially recognized today is the modern Turkish language, but over twenty languages—including Turkish, Kurdish, Armenian, Greek, and Lazuri—belonging to several distinct language families continue to be natively spoken in Turkey.

When the modern Republic of Turkey was founded in 1923, intellectuals and political theorists wanted to create a unified sense of identity that was distinctly Turkish instead of Ottoman, and inclusive of the rural area on the West Asian side known as **Anatolia** (Figure 11.1). As in some other countries at the time, folksongs were regarded as a key tool. In Turkey, recording technologies, studio practices, and experiments with folksongs play significant roles in the process of instilling and reinforcing national values—a shared sense of Turkishness among all citizens in the Republic of Turkey, but also a national awareness of regional and local cultural differences.

Selecting which musics might accomplish these aims was challenging because Turkey is home to a rich diversity of musical traditions. In his research in the 1960s–1970s, Laurence Picken encountered over 1,000 indigenous folk instruments in rural Anatolia (Picken 1975) and that did not even include the several dozen instruments used for urban art music performance or the many foreign instruments that have been more recently adopted. Furthermore, all folksongs and instruments are specific to geographical regions, towns, or even places as small as a twenty-person village.

The unifying factor that was selected was language, modern Turkish—the official language of the new country. The government, universities, and folklore institutes began a project to collect and document whatever folksongs in Turkish could be found anywhere in the new nation, often modifying the lyrics of songs when they contained words that were not part of the modern Turkish language. The result was an archive of thousands of songs known as *türkü*. To this day, singing *türkü* is both useful and meaningful for instilling a sense of "Turkishness" among Turkish citizens.

Alongside the love of traditional songs and instruments, there has been a recording industry in Turkey since the late 1890s (contemporaneous with the development of industries in the United States and Europe). Since then, artists have experimented with the creative possibilities of recorded media and studio technologies (Bates 2016). If you pick up a contemporary album of Turkish music, there is a good chance you'll find one or more songs from the traditional repertoire, but arranged for a fusion of traditional and foreign instruments—drawing on musical styles ranging from modal jazz to heavy metal—and made with the latest in computer-based **Digital Audio Workstation (DAW)** technologies (Figure 11.2). Since the mid-1990s, songs from one region—the Doğu Karadeniz (Eastern Black Sea region)—have been particularly popular for this style of **arrangement** and recording.

≡ **FIGURE 11.2**
Photo of Kalan Stüdyo, where one of the examples in this chapter was recorded, showing the Digital Audio Workstation (DAW) along with other studio technologies.

This chapter illustrates how, when the new Republic of Turkey was founded, Turkish language folksongs became useful for instilling a unified sense of identity; and in the present, new studio-produced arrangements of folksongs continue to help reinforce national values. Those values include a sense of Turkishness for all citizens but also a national awareness of regional and local cultural differences (Bates, 2011).

By 2005, when I began conducting my research on arranged folk music and Istanbul's recording studios, a "Karadeniz genre" was emerging. At that time, it was striking to me how much of the musical content in arranged Karadeniz songs differed from archival field recordings, yet singers or lead instrumentalists sang or played these songs similar to traditional versions. For arrangements of Karadeniz songs, new artists tended to view three commercially successful experiments from the late 1990s as their major influences, copying aspects of previous albums while making new ones, or employing the same musicians who were responsible for creating the seminal works. These influences were the following:

1. Kazım Koyuncu (1971–2005), an ethnically Laz singer from the town of Hopa near the Georgian border (Figure 11.1), pioneered a style known as "Laz rock." Following Kazım's death, it was continued by Laz rock groups such as Marsis.
2. Fuat Saka (b. 1952) developed a jazz guitar style for playing Laz folk songs.
3. Singer Ayşenur Kolivar worked with the large, pan-Anatolian performing ensemble Kardeş Türküler to create recorded and stage arrangements of Hemşin, Lazuri, and Turkish language folksongs (the three primary languages in the region) for a large heterogeneous ensemble of Anatolian instruments featuring a full battery of percussion.

A dance song in the *türkü* repertoire, *"Bu Dünya Bir Pencere"* ("This World Is a Window") from the Karadeniz (Eastern Black Sea) region, is an example of how a traditional Turkish song has been subject to change through the new techniques of studio recording and arrangement. Three versions of *"Bu Dünya Bir Pencere"* illustrate this

ACTIVITY 11.1

Search on Spotify or YouTube for Kazım Koyuncu's live recording of "Tabancamın Sapini," Fuat Saka's recording of "Derule," and Kardeş Türküler's recording of the song "Golas Empula Yulun." What is similar among these three arrangements? What elements mark each as distinctive?

change: a basic rendering of the instrumental melody; and two contemporary arrangements, one by Şevval Sam and the other by the group Marsis. Through studying these two contemporary versions, we will explore how contemporary artists and audio engineers take traditional materials and reshape them for contemporary audiences, thereby contributing to maintaining the relevance of traditions in the present.

"Bu Dünya Bir Pencere," A Traditional Dance Song

Not much is known about *"Bu Dünya Bir Pencere"*; it is typically described as having "anonymous" authorship. It is a classic **horon** dance song, a form of line dance performed in the Black Sea region of Turkey (Figure 11.3). In its traditional form, it most commonly uses asymmetrical beat structures such as **devr-i hindi**, a three-beat (usually short + short + long) **usul** that is notated in 7/8. It can be accompanied by several different instruments, including the **kemençe** (a very short-necked, bowed lute, Chapter opening image), **tulum** (bagpipe without drone pipe, with two chanters), **garmon** (a small piano accordion), or **kaval** (an end-blown flute made typically of boxwood or fruitwood). The *horon* features a single melody and seven-syllable rhyming scheme. The lyrics of *"Bu Dünya Bir Pencere"* appear to be directly inspired by a much older poem by the Turkish mystic poet and humanist Yunus Emre (1238–1320), considered not just an important literary and religious figure but one of the important textual sources for the modern Turkish language. The song lyrics read:

Dereler akar gider	The streams go on flowing
Taşlari yıkar gider	They go on washing the stones
Bu dünya bir pencere	This world is a window
Her gelen bakar gider	All who come go on looking
Dere akar bulanuk	The stream flows and gets muddy
Köpüğünden alaluk	From its frothy bubbles it gets ruddy
Ha bu ışıklı dünya	Oh this radiant world
Oldu bize karanluk	It became dark for us
Enelum değirmene	Let's go to the mill
Öğütelum unlari	Let's mill some flour
Güneşe çevirelum	Let's turn to the sun
Bu karanlık günleri	These days of darkness

≡ **FIGURE 11.3**
Horon dancing done
in Istanbul.

At a basic level, the melody of *"Bu Dünya Bir Pencere"* can be represented through staff notation (Musical Example 11.1). This simple score offers a few important pieces of information:

a. The piece uses an asymmetrical beat structure, notated here as 7/8.
b. Asymmetrical beat structures are especially important in Turkey, and they often match dances such as the *horon* where there is a sequence of steps that bring the dancer on and off balance.

ACTIVITY 11.2

To familiarize yourself with the *horon* dance song *"Bu Dünya Bir Pencere,"* listen several times to the recording of the basic song (Audio Example 11.1). Try to hum along with the recording or even memorize the tune. The more familiar you are with it, the more you will be able to catch what's going on in the studio arrangements.

The *horon* line dance exists in many varieties. Search on YouTube for "Tahsin Terzi horon" and "Yusuf Cemal Keskin horon" to find live videos of *horon* dances being done to other melodies, in contexts outside, inside for weddings, and in classes given to young students of *kemençe*, a bowed lute prominent in and associated with the Karadeniz region.

c. The melodic mode of *"Bu Dünya Bir Pencere"* is called *Hicaz,* one of the most common modes throughout Turkey, the Arab world, and parts of Southeastern Europe.

MUSICAL EXAMPLE 11.1 Notation of *"Bu Dünya Bir Pencere,"* basic melody.

Beat Structure (or, Musical Meter)

The whole system of beat structures in Turkish traditional music is called **usul.** Many of the structures—each with a name—are asymmetrical. *Devr-i hindi,* the *usul* for *"Bu Dünya Bir Pencere"* (see chap. 1 on musical rhythms), has the asymmetrical structure of short-short-long beats (2 – 2 – 3). Musical Example 11.2 and Activity 11.3 will help you understand this rhythm.

MUSICAL EXAMPLE 11.2 Notation of an asymmetric *usul: devr-i hindi.*

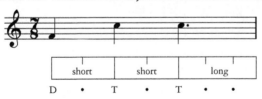

ACTIVITY 11.3

Speak and tap out the strong beats to the *devr-i hindi usul.* The spoken syllables are "düm – tek – tek," and you should tap "left – right – right" in time with the spoken syllables.

Melodic Mode

In Turkey, music is not structured around chord sequences and vertical harmony but rather around a system of melodic modes known collectively as the **makam** system. These are similar to the Western modes of major and minor except that instead of two, there are several hundred Turkish modes. The *makam* system specifies not only the pitches that musicians play but also contains rules concerning which pitches are emphasized and the overall shape of the melody.

Makam Hicaz, the mode in which "*Bu Dünya Bir Pencere*" was composed, is shown in Musical Example 11.3. Its distinguishing feature is the augmented second between the second and third notes of the mode, here between the B-flat and the C-sharp. It is also notable for a strong emphasis on the fourth note of the mode, in this case D. As for the overall shape of melody, Hicaz is defined as an ascending-descending *makam*, meaning that it starts low, ascends through the notes of the *makam*, then descends to the final pitch (known as the **durak**).

MUSICAL EXAMPLE 11.3 A scalar representation of *makam* Hicaz.

Contemporary Interpretations of "*Bu Dünya Bir Pencere*"

The nine-measure melody of "*Bu Dünya Bir Pencere*" can be sung in nine seconds, with the verse and chorus sharing the identical melody. Even with three verses and three choruses, the song takes less than one minute to perform. But by using contemporary recording and arranging techniques, short songs like this can be made much longer. To illustrate how this is done, you will study two arrangements of

ACTIVITY 11.4

Listen several times again to the recording of the basic melody of "*Bu Dünya Bir Pencere*" (Audio Example 11.1) to keep the beat structure of *devr-i hindi usul* and also to hear the melodic details of *makam* Hicaz.

"Bu Dünya Bir Pencere": one created by a well-known arranger for a solo singer (what I will refer to as "the Şevval Sam recording"); the other by the Laz (ethnicity) rock group, Marsis ("the Marsis recording"). Şevval Sam's version was on one of the top selling albums in Turkey in 2008. It was so well received that Marsis included their own take of the same song on their 2009 debut album.

The Şevval Sam Recording

A version of *"Bu Dünya Bir Pencere"* (Audio Example 11.2) was arranged for soloist Şevval Sam (b. 1973) by arranger Aytekin Gazi Ataş. Şevval Sam is a film actress and well-known performer of contemporary Turkish art songs in the Turkish language. She began singing Karadeniz-arranged folk music following a TV series role where she starred alongside pioneer Laz rock singer Kazım Koyuncu. Arranger Aytekin Gazi Ataş (b. 1978) is an Istanbul-based musician whose familial roots lie in the Eastern Anatolian city of Tunceli (Dersim) (see Figure 11.1). Ethnically Zaza and Alevi (Zaza is a linguistically defined ethnicity, Alevi a religiously defined one), Aytekin began his professional music career singing and playing *saz* (a long-necked, plucked lute) and percussion in the pan-Anatolian ethnic fusion group, Kardeş Türküler. Since 2004, he has worked as an arranger of numerous regional and popular genres of music. He is best known for arranging the music to the TV series *Fırtına* (a Black Sea–themed drama) and *Mühteşem Yüzyıl* ("Magnificent Century," a dramatization of the life of Sultan Suleiman the Magnificent and his wife Hürrem Sultan) and the feature films *Beynelmilel* and *Son Osmanlı*.

Recordings are heavily constructed and edited studio productions that have been largely created by professionals of the Turkish recorded music industry, including mix/mastering engineers and studio musicians. The engineer who mixed the Şevval Sam recording is Mayki Murat Başaran, one of the house engineers for the Kalan record label who mixes styles of music ranging from art music to Karadeniz music to TV drama scores. Tahsin Terzi, the *kemençe* player on this recording, is one of the most prolific performers of that instrument, and a first-call performer whenever that timbre is needed for a new recording. Studio musicians Nejat Özgür (*garmon*) and Neriman Güneş (violin/viola) are also proficient. None of these musicians are especially well known by the Turkish public, even as their recorded sound is familiar to everyone. (This mode of production, including the relative anonymity of the musicians who work within the industry, mirrors guild-based music economies elsewhere in the world, including the Hollywood and Bollywood film music industries.)

Part of Aytekin's signature sound is using a large ensemble of Anatolian folk instruments, notably the *saz* family of plucked lute-type instruments (Figure 11.4)

 **FIGURE 11.4** The *bağlama* is one of the *saz* family of instruments.

played in a "muted" style; a large backing percussion section; and subtle vocal sounds used as special effects. This song arrangement has a very "filmic" (film score) quality, enhanced by his use of drones, wind noise, and reverberant sound effects. Musical Example 11.4 provides a diagram of the introduction to this arrangement, one minute and forty-four seconds that precede the actual beginning of the first verse of the *türkü*. Sections A to G show its instrumentation and some other musical details.

Musical Example 11.4 shows consistent instrumentation from section C through G. However, each of the eight sections has a different ensemble sound, with between two and sixteen different instruments playing in any section.

One technique for creating four- and five-minute arrangements of a short song is shown in sections D and E in Musical Example 11.4: "*soru*" and "*cevap*" ("question" and "answer"). From very small fragments of the original melody, new sections are made. This technique was pioneered by the pan-Anatolian ethnic fusion group Kardeş Türküler; Aytekin often uses it to create new question-answer passages out of a couple of

MUSICAL EXAMPLE 11.4 Block diagram of the introduction to Şevval Sam's recording of "*Bu Dünya Bir Pencere*" arranged by Aytekin Atas; "pizzicato violin" refers to playing the violin by plucking a string rather than bowing across it; "*soru*" and "*cevap*" are "question" and "answer."

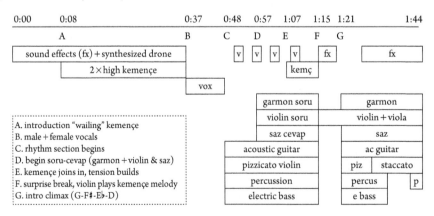

A. introduction "wailing" kemençe
B. male + female vocals
C. rhythm section begins
D. begin soru-cevap (garmon + violin & saz)
E. kemençe joins in, tension builds
F. surprise break, violin plays kemençe melody
G. intro climax (G-F♯-E♭-D)

ACTIVITY 11.5

Listen to the entire recording of Aytekin's arrangement to just get it into your ears (Audio Example 11.2). When the song *"Bu Dünya Bir Pencere"* actually begins, take note not only of the melody but the ornamentation as well. The ornamentation is appropriate to the Karadeniz regional style. Aytekin grounds the arrangement in the region by prominently featuring the traditional Karadeniz instrument, the *kemençe*. He also uses electric guitar, which of course is less regionally associated.

ACTIVITY 11.6

Listen as many times as it takes you to plot the changes in ensemble sound—however sketchily. Following the Listening Guide below this Activity may aid your listening.

notes extracted from the original song melody. In this arrangement, he invented a question-answer section (D and E), where the questions are performed on violin with *garmon* accordion and answered by plucked stringed instruments. The question phrase is a variation of the song melody's sixth measure (see Musical Example 11.1), but in the question-answer context it sounds entirely different. Aytekin uses this new phrase throughout the song, in passages between verses and choruses, and in leading up to verses. It becomes a "second theme" in the piece. In section F, it occurs as a solo violin interpretation for a surprising break.

Aytekin also created entirely new melodic material, in particular the dramatic last section (G) with the slowly descending melody characteristic of *makam* Hicaz.

ACTIVITY 11.7

Listen to the Şevval Sam recording (Audio Example 11.2) again, specifically to identify the question and answer technique and the introduction of new melodic material.

LISTENING GUIDE

"Bu Dünya Bir Pencere," Aytekin's arrangement

Performed by Şevval Sam, arranged by Aytekin Gazi Ataş

Recording location and year 2008, Turkey

Instrumentation: Vocals, *kemençe* (bowed lute), *saz* (plucked lute), violin, electric bass, acoustic guitar, electric guitar, *garmon* (accordion), percussion including *bendir* (frame drum), cymbals played with a wire brush, *cajón* (box drum), and "ocean drum"

Time	Something to Listen For
0:01	Initial drone opens the piece, along with the sound of a gunshot (1)
0:02	Further gunshots (2) follow.
0:05	A reversed "ocean drum" effect appears.
0:07	Two high-pitched *kemençe* play, beginning on a single pitch.
0:13	A distant howling sound appears over *kemençe*.
0:14	A trill on the *kemençe* is followed by more trills over drones and a descending melody.
0:21	A reversed "ocean drum" effect returns.
0:23	*Kemençe* plays short phrases interspersed with roars (or drum rolls).
0:32	Drum rolls lead into reverberated drum sounds.
0:37	A male and female voice enter on a melody in 7/8, in AABB form. *Güneşe çevirelum* *Bu karanlık günleri*
0:48	Drum rolls lead to entrance of full ensemble, continuing 7/8 via pitched percussive patterns played on violin, acoustic and electric guitar, vocals, and percussion.
0:57	Pitched rhythmic phrases play repeatedly, featuring violin and *garmon* over ensemble.
1:09	*Kemençe* joins, providing answer melodies.
1:15	Violin and viola are prominent (with a little electric guitar in background); the full ensemble drops out.
1:21	The full ensemble returns with bowed strings and melody performed on the *garmon*.
1:39	Pitched percussive phrases are played repeatedly.
1:43	A female voice performs the melody in AABB verse form (male voice joins at the end of the phrase). This phrase, like several others in the song, features a regional pronunciation that differs from standard Turkish (*taşlari*, instead of the standard *taşları*) and marks the piece as being Karadeniz. *Dereler akar gider* *Taşlari yıkar gider*

Time	Something to Listen For
1:54	Pitched percussive phrases are repeated.
1:59	A female voice sings on melody in AABB verse form. *Bu dünya bir pencere* *Her gelen bakar gider*
2:10	The full ensemble returns with melody.
2:14	Drum rolls sound as the full ensemble fades.

The Marsis Recording

Marsis's version of *"Bu Dünya Bir Pencere"* (Audio Example 11.3) is aligned with indie-rock arrangements, using layers of rock guitars, electric bass (as well as acoustic guitar), and contrasting drum-set patterns. Even in the shorter introduction of forty-two seconds before the song begins, the striking contrast in sound aesthetic is clear. As you can see in Musical Example 11.5, however, the *kemençe* bowed lute is featured prominently here as well, grounding the arrangement as Karadeniz. The use of *kaval* flute is distinctive to this version.

MUSICAL EXAMPLE 11.5 Block diagram of the introduction to Marsis's recording of *"Bu Dünya Bir Pencere."*

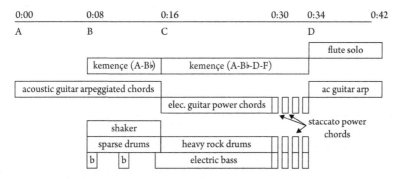

Influenced by the Şevval Sam recording, Marsis used the second theme that Aytekin had created as a *kemençe* melody in section B, although without the question-answer structure. As a standard practice of folksong arrangement, Marsis also invented new melodic, harmonic, and rhythmic material for sections C and D.

Structurally, while both arrangements feature a "surprising break," the surprises are different. Instead of Aytekin's solo violin break, for Marsis it is the *kaval*

LISTENING GUIDE

"Bu Dünya Bir Pencere," Marsis arrangement

Performed by Marsis

Recording location and year: 2009, Turkey

Instrumentation: Vocals, electric guitar, electric bass, drum set, *kemençe*, *kaval*, shaker

Time	Something to Listen For
0:00	Electric guitar plays arpeggiated chords.
0:08	*Kemençe* (bowed lute) enters with drum set, shakers, and bass, 7/8 meter.
0:16	Strummed electric guitar power chords, with electric bass and drum set, supporting *kemençe* on lead melody.
0:30	Drums, bass, and guitar switch to staccato power chords for transition to next segment.
0:34	*Kaval* flute offers a breathy, descending melody over the sound of an arpeggiated guitar.
0:42	Male voice sings melody, continuing 7/8, in AABB form, performed twice. *Dereler akar gider* *Taşlari yıkar gider* *Bu dünya bir pencere* *Her gelen bakar gider*
1:01	Several male voices sing melody in same form, with *kemençe*. *Bu dünya bir pencere* *Her gelen bakar gider*
1:10	*Kemençe* leads the instrumental ensemble in the melody that slowly fades away.

(end-blown flute) playing a brief improvisation with only guitar accompaniment (section D). This use of flute suggests that Marsis, too, has been influenced by film music soundscapes.

A striking difference between the introductions of the two arrangements is rhythmic. Aytekin's arrangement features a relatively seamless rhythmic groove produced by various hand percussion and pizzicato (plucked) violins. In contrast, Marsis interjects dramatic rock-style staccato power chords at the end of section C that break up the rhythmic groove that had been established. (For the explanation of power chords and staff notation of these, see chapter 2.)

Common Techniques Used on Both Recordings

While each of these recordings shows a distinctive approach to making a contemporary version of this traditional melody, both use techniques found on many contemporary Turkish studio recordings. In Istanbul, musicians do not play together in the studio; instead, they record their parts one at a time, listening back to different combinations of "plot" melody parts, prerecorded parts, and a steady click track. This practice began for pragmatic purposes: it reduced the expense of having a large number of musicians present at one time and also enabled the arranger and engineer to have more control over the parts after they were recorded. However, it quickly came to define specific musical aesthetics. Musicians often do not know what the arrangement will sound like until the album is released.

While most overdubbing is of distinct musical parts, there is one special kind of overdubbing known as **double-tracking** that produces a desired and distinctly audible effect. With double-tracking, the same musician overdubs the identical part of the same instrument, attempting to replicate the timing, tuning, and feel of the original part as closely as possible. Because it is impossible to exactly achieve, the result is a part that is subtly out of tune and out of time with the original, creating a "shimmering" effect known as *chorusing* that sometimes creates the illusion of multiple musicians performing at once. (It is called chorusing due to its acoustic similarity to a chorus of voices.) It is a difficult task to double-track parts in the studio, requiring a kind of performative expertise and real-time critical listening technique that stage musicians lack. This is partly why the musical economy of Turkey depends so much on studio musicians.

You can hear double-tracking clearly in two spots on the recordings. In the Şevval Sam recording (Audio Example 11.2), contrast Şevval Sam's vocal part beginning at 1:48 (single-tracked) with the verse beginning at 3:25 (double-tracked). In the Marsis recording (Audio Example 11.3), listen to the *kaval* (end-blown reed flute) solo at 0:34 (double-tracked).

The second effect that stands out in these recordings is the selective use of digital **reverberation** (or reverb for short). In an acoustic environment, reverb is the persistence of sound within a space; different qualities and lengths of reverb are why a performance in a concert hall sounds different from one in a practice room, a classroom, a cathedral, or an outdoor space. An increase in the amount of reverb increases the perceived distance between the listener and the sound source. Rather than representing one acoustic space, contemporary recordings often switch between quite distinct constructed acoustic environments (even imaginary ones such as in the Marsis recording), or even invoke different acoustic spaces at the very same time (as in the Şevval Sam recording).

In the opening passage of the Şevval Sam recording, the *kemençe* and the background "sound effects" layers are treated with a great deal of a long reverb, while in the first vocal passage at 0:37, the singers sound very close to the listener and there is very little reverb. When the groove begins at 0:45, certain parts in the mix sound very present and close (e.g., some of the high plucked strings), while the sound effects and some of the frame drums sound distant.

In the Marsis recording, the opening section features guitars with a small amount of reverb and a *kemençe* that has very little reverb and sounds very present in the mix. The tom drums in the drum set, however, are treated with considerable reverb that gives them extra sustain. When the *kaval* flutes (double-tracked, again) enter at 0:34 with their dreamlike melodic sequence, we hear the longest and most extreme use of reverb.

This creative play with space accomplishes several things at once. It demonstrates the artistic mastery of the arranger and the engineer of the song arrangement. It is also an essential part of the project of moving song arrangements beyond a simple representation of a temporally and spatially bounded performance. Finally, it aligns productions made in Turkey with the recorded aesthetics of albums and films made both within and outside of Turkey.

Conclusion

Songs such as *"Bu Dünya Bir Pencere"* gain their power and importance in Turkey due to their links with a shared regionally specific tradition. But studio productions of this music go beyond a simple representation of tradition, situating Turkey's traditions, and the *türkü* song form specifically, within globally circulating musical genres and recording studio practices. However, arrangements are not successful unless they continue to acknowledge regional and local cultural differences. In both contemporary arrangements of *"Bu Dünya Bir Pencere,"* it is clear that it is a folksong from the Doğu Karadeniz—the Eastern Black Sea region of Turkey. The prominent presence of the sound of *kemençe* alone identifies it as a traditional song from that region. The two singers' approach to ornamentation is also similar, showing that despite the musical genre influences that artists draw on, they tend to sing *türkü* using regionally appropriate ornamentation.

Bibliography

Bates, Eliot. 2011. *Music in Turkey: Experiencing Music, Expressing Culture*. New York: Oxford University Press.

Bates, Eliot. 2016. *Digital Tradition: Arrangement and Labor in Istanbul's Recording Studio Culture*. New York: Oxford University Press.

Picken, Laurence Ernest Rowland. 1975. *Folk Musical Instruments of Turkey*. New York: Oxford University Press.

12

Music in Egypt

Creating and Maintaining a Vibrant Islamic Presence in Day-to-Day Life

SCOTT MARCUS

Chapter Contents

Introduction

The population of Egypt is 90 percent Muslim, so it's not surprising that its music gains meaning, in good part, through its intersections with Islam. Musicians help maintain a vibrant Islamic presence in day-to-day life. However, since the beginning of Islam in the seventh century CE, there have been conflicting opinions about music in the religion. A number of factors have contributed to this conflict, among them a belief in maintaining a separation between the sacred and secular, the divine and the human. This controversy is often framed in terms of the permissibility of listening to music.

Those with a strong conservative religious bent see music as leading a person away from a life of proper religious devotion. For them, music is *ḥarām*, forbidden or unlawful in Islam (Marcus 2007). In general, Muslims believe that there should be a separation between the realms of prayer and more worldly musical manifestations. This understanding of a separation between the sacred and the secular is reflected by a rejection of musical terms when referring to the call to prayer. One does not,

☰ **An imām (the person who leads prayers in a mosque) giving the call to prayer from the Ibn Ṭūlūn Mosque in Cairo.**

for example, "sing" the call (*azān* in colloquial Egyptian Arabic); rather one "says," "gives," or "raises up" the call. Alternatively, a verb is created from the word *azān* itself: "to *azān*" (*yi'azzan*). Similarly, rather than applying the usual terms for singers of secular music, a singer of religious song is referred to as a *munshid*. Beyond the call to prayer, there are other genres of religious song in the sacred realm, such as sung religious poetry (*madḥ*) that praises God, the Prophet Muhammad, and other revered figures of Islam. We will hear examples of both genres in this chapter.

Despite the controversy over music and Islam, music has continued to flourish in numerous forms in Egypt and beyond. We will explore several different intersections of religion and music in popular culture—in performances by *zaffa* wedding bands, mid-twentieth-century "long song" repertoires of love songs and religious songs, and also music in the world of present-day pop stars—each of which helps maintain a vibrant Islamic presence in day-to-day life.

The Arab Republic of Egypt

Situated in the northeastern corner of the African continent, Egypt is part of the Eastern Arab world, a cultural region that extends from Egypt up along the eastern Mediterranean coast to Syria and Lebanon. Geographically it is transcontinental, with its easternmost area connected to Asia by a natural land bridge (the Sinai Peninsula) and now also by a constructed bridge over the Suez Canal that connects the Mediterranean Sea with the Red Sea (Figure 12.1). The country is bordered to the northeast by the Gaza Strip and Israel and to the east by the Gulf of Aqaba and the Red Sea. To the south lies Sudan, and to the west, Libya.

Egypt is home to one of the most familiar of the world's ancient civilizations: that of the pharaohs. Its later history is one of a succession of conquests both military and cultural. After the collapse of the pharaohs, Hellenistic culture was imported to Egypt under Greek rule. The Greeks were followed by the Romans, who in turn were followed by Byzantine Christians (Christianity having been introduced in the first century by St. Mark); Muslim Arabs in the seventh century; Ottoman Turks from 1517; the French in a 1798 invasion led by Napoleon Bonaparte; and British occupation in the nineteenth century. Independence finally was won in 1922. The present Arab Republic of Egypt was founded in 1953. Islam has been a presence for almost fourteen centuries, and has kept a vibrant presence in day-to-day life, with music and musicians playing a prominent role in making it and keeping it so.

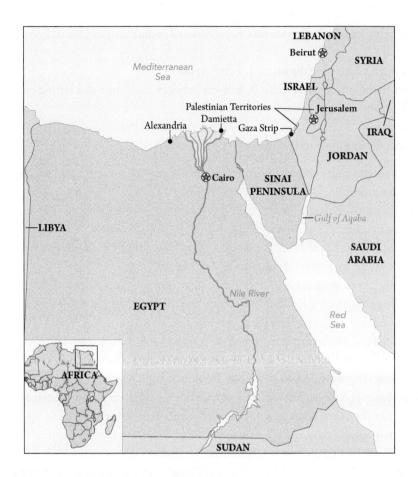

≡ **FIGURE 12.1**
Map of Egypt.

Musical Ideas and Practices
The Call to Prayer

Perhaps the most obvious example of the meaningful intersection between music and religion in Egypt is the call to prayer or *azān* that is addressed to all Muslims (Audio Example 12.1) (Marcus 2007). Performed five times a day from every functioning mosque, the call is indeed one of the most prominent and pervasive aspects of the Egyptian soundscape. Historically, the **muezzin** (the one who gives the call, **mu'azzin** in colloquial Egyptian Arabic) would present the call from the top of a mosque's minaret so as to be heard, ideally, by all in the surrounding neighborhood. Today, however, most mosques have microphones conveniently located inside and a number of loudspeakers both inside and on their outer walls. At prescribed times during the day, the *muezzin* approaches the microphone and recites the call's seven lines of text. Those times are as follows:

1. roughly an hour before sunrise (when the call includes an additional line of text)
2. at high noon when the sun is directly overhead
3. when the sun is half set, that is, halfway between high noon and setting on the horizon
4. at sunset
5. roughly one hour after sunset

The precise times will change throughout the year as the sun rises and sets at different times.

In Cairo, where there are mosques every few blocks, it is common to hear two to three or more calls at a time, coming from different directions. This is especially the case during the predawn call when the general quietness of the city allows the sound of the calls to travel far and wide. Additionally, many radio and TV stations regularly interrupt programming to broadcast the call. Thus, you may hear one or more *azān*s coming through your window from neighborhood mosques at the same time that you hear an *azān* on the radio or TV.

The call's text is fixed in both content and format; the first five lines are repeated, while the last two lines are presented only once. Further, each line is separated by somewhat lengthy moments of silence. Those unfamiliar with the call often think that it has ended, only to hear it resume with the next line after a few moments.

Usually the call is given in a florid melodic style with some syllables of the text given only a single note, but others are performed on dozens (even many dozens) of notes. The melodic rendition is different for each individual *muezzin*. Ideally it is improvised and therefore different each time, although many with less musical training have developed a rather fixed melody that they use each time they give the call.

What is confusing to some people about the distinguishing of the call to prayer from music is that the melody created by the *muezzin* is commonly based in one of the melodic modes (**maqām**; plural: *maqāmāt*) of Arab music, most often the mode named **maqām rāst**. This would seem to make it a "musical performance."

ACTIVITY 12.1

Follow the text in the recording of the call to prayer. As you listen, keep track of the repetition of lines of text. Note that the individual text phrases of the call are separated by moments of silence and that the melodic rendering of the text is improvised, with repeated text given unique renditions.

LISTENING GUIDE

The Call to Prayer

Starting times for each phrase in the recording are given at the left in the following table; brackets around a timing indicate repetition of a text phrase.

Time	Text	Translation
0:00 [0:08]	*Allāhu Akbar Allāhu Akbar* ×2	God is great God is great
0:30 [0:43]	*Ashhadu an lā ilāha illā llāh* ×2	I testify that there is no god but God
1:04 [1:23]	*Ashhadu anna Muḥammadan rasūlu llāh* ×2	I testify that Muhammad is the messenger of God
1:44 [1:55]	*Ḥayya ʿalā ṣ-ṣalāt* ×2	Come to pray
2:21 [2:38]	*Ḥayya ʿalā l-falāḥ* ×2	Come for success/salvation
	The predawn call includes the following additional line:	
	iṣ-Ṣalāt khayrun min in-nawm ×2	Prayer is better than sleep
3:08	*Allāhu Akbar Allāhu Akbar* ×1	God is great God is great
3:27	*Lā ilāha illā llāh* ×1	There is no god but God

However, it is not the details of musical practice that make religious practitioners view the call as distinct from "music" but its text and the religious purpose for which the text is being used.

In addition to explicitly calling the faithful to prayer, the text of the call also includes the three more important statements of Islam. *Allāhu Akbar* declares the faith to be based on a belief in God. *Ashhadu an lā ilāha illā llāh* declares the faith to be monotheistic (believing in one God), as Judaism and Christianity are. And *Ashhadu anna Muḥammadan rasūlu llāh* declares the uniqueness of the faith, that it follows the message of the prophet Muhammad, the Holy Qur'an.

One of the distinguishing features of the call to prayer in Egypt is the communal nature of the giving of the call. Unlike in many other Muslim communities, where the Arabic language is not commonly known and the *muezzin*, by necessity, must be a specialist (someone who has mastered the Arabic text of the call), in Egypt everyone knows the text as well as they know their own name. This has contributed to a tradition where, it seems, a majority of Egyptian men have given the call at one time or another. There are at least two reasons for this phenomenon: first, a given mosque's official *muezzin* cannot be expected to be at the mosque over the thirteen to seventeen hours that separate the multiple calls in a single day. Second, giving the call is understood to be both a privilege and a source of merit. In Islam, it is understood that one receives reward or merit for good deeds such as saying the *azān*. On the day of judgment, we all go before God and the good and bad deeds of our lives are weighed, resulting in each of us going either to heaven or hell. "For this reason," the head of a Cairo mosque explained to me, "many come and do the *azān* without it being an official position. Ahmad [a retiree who was sitting nearby] comes without being paid. He comes for God." A college student commented, "I love to come to pray and do the *azān*. I earn **sawāb**" (or reward for meritorious deeds). At a neighborhood grocery store, the man cutting cheese behind the counter confirmed, "Yes, I've given the *azān* many times, at the mosque near my house." Hearing this conversation, a young man who was mopping the floor in one aisle of the store, clearly from a lower working class than the cheese cutter, contributed, "Yes, me too! Any Muslim can say the *azān*. There are conditions for being an **imām** [the head of a mosque]," he said, "but any Muslim [man] can say the *azān*" (Figure 12.2).

≡ **FIGURE 12.2** A young college student giving the call to prayer from the *imām's* office at a Cairo mosque.

Madḥ, A Sufi Genre of Sung Religious Poetry

Life in Egypt is full of many examples of music traditions beyond the call to prayer that help create and maintain a vibrant Islamic presence in day-to-day life. One of the most common and widespread is a genre of Sufi sung poetry called *madḥ* (literally, praise) or more fully, *madīh in-nabī* (praise of the prophet; i.e., the prophet Muhammad) (Marcus 2007). Whereas conservative Muslims generally believe that one can only achieve union with God in the afterlife, followers of **Sufism**, the mystical branch of Islam, believe that one may attain union with God, here and now, if one follows a proper spiritual practice. *Madḥ* may play a part in this practice, and thus it is performed by hundreds of groups throughout Egypt, with the biggest singers achieving superstar status (e.g., Yāsīn al-Tuhāmī) (Frishkopf 2000a and 2000b).

Drawing on a variety of poetic forms, *madḥ* poetry praises God, the prophet Muhammad, and other revered figures of Islam, and thus communicates the mystical feelings and teachings of Sufism. Illustrating this are the lyrics of a song, "*id-Dunyā*," performed by the Cairo-based singer **Shaykh** Ramaḍān ʿUways and released c. 1981 on a commercial cassette (Audio Example 12.2). The song "*id-Dunyā*" praises the prophets Adam, Abraham, Moses, Jesus, and Muhammad, thus highlighting shared components of the Jewish, Christian, and Muslim faiths. Islam embraces the Jewish and Christian prophets, considering Jesus to be a prophet rather than the son of God. In the transcription of its lyrics in the Listening Guide, the first occurrence of the name of each prophet is underlined. The line "the world began with the name of God and Muhammad" expounds a mystical belief.

The song "*id-Dunyā*" is in the popular poetic form of **mawwāl** that is the most common genre of song in Shaykh Ramaḍān's *madḥ* performances. *Mawwāl* is characterized by seven lines with a distinctive AAABBBA rhyme scheme. Without any recurring textual or melodic material, the melodic lines are **through-composed**,

ACTIVITY 12.2

Follow along with the *mawwāl* text as you listen to the recording of "*id-Dunyā*." In the left-hand column of the Listening Guide just below, the timings that are bracketed pertain to text repetitions. Listen at least twice to recognize the occurrence of the prophets' names (underlined in the guide) and more times to anticipate the rhymes. Do you hear the percussion emphasizing any words? What relationships do you hear between the vocal melody and instrumental melody, and between the instrumental melodies?

Madḥ (Madīḥ in-Nabī): "id-Dunyā"

Performed by Shaykh Ramaḍān ʿUways

Studio cassette recording, c. 1981

Time	Text	Translation
Line 1 0:01 [0:24]	id-dunyā bada'it b-'ismi llāh wa Muḥammad	The world began with the name of God and Muhammad
0:10 [0:12 / 0:15 / 0:18 / 0:21]	id-dunyā	The world (repeated 5 times)
Line 2 0:34	min 'abl Ādam wa kān il-ʿahdi li-Muḥammad	Before Adam, the promise was given to Muhammad
Line 3 0:45 [1:02]	fīh raḥmah l-in-nās wa ynazzih dīnuh bi-Muḥammad	There is [God has] compassion/mercy for people and declares his religion through Muhammad
Line 4 1:25 [1:33 / 1:44 / 2:01]	min 'abluh ʿĪsā wa nuṭquh ramzı lı-t-tā līm	Before Muhammad, there was Jesus, His utterance was a symbol of instruction [referring to a story in the Qur'an in which Jesus speaks while still a baby]
Line 5 2:07	wa kalīmuh Mūsá ʿaṣāthu lamḥa li-t-taʿlīm	And His spokesman, Moses, his staff is a sign of instruction
Line 6 2:14 [2:18]	wa-l-kulli mur(u)sal samā ḥidā sayyid it-taʿlīm	All the prophets [Adam, Moses, Jesus, Muhammad] were sent from the sky from [God] the Lord of instruction.
Line 7 2:26	wa khalīluh kān Ibrāhīm wa ḥanānuh li-Muḥammad	His dear friend was Abraham and His affection was for Muhammad
2:32	Goes into the instrumental introduction to the following song	

that is, each successive line of text is generally set to new melodic material. The texts for Shaykh Ramaḍān's music are written by his longtime companion, the poet Muḥammad Muṣṭafá Burʿī. He then crafts the melodic lines himself, creating melodies that remain largely fixed but also allowing for a good deal of spontaneous improvisation.

Madḥ may be performed by a vocal soloist or by a vocalist with percussion accompaniment (e.g., a *riqq*, a single-headed frame drum [tambourine] with five sets of cymbals mounted symmetrically around the frame). However, performances at public events such as those associated with Sufi or family life-cycle rituals (e.g., birthdays or circumcisions) typically include a solo singer accompanied by a small instrumental ensemble, as in the performance of "*id-Dunyā*" (Audio Example 12.2). The melodic instruments include the **kawala** (end-blown flute made of a fairly thick, reed plant), violin, and *ʿūd* (short-necked plucked lute, pear-shaped body with deep back). Percussion is provided by the *riqq*, **ṭabla** (single-headed, metal goblet-shaped drum), and **ṭūra** (large finger cymbals). Recently, groups have added the electronic keyboard, called **org** in Arabic (Rasmussen, 1996).

Madḥ occurs in a number of different contexts. Shaykh Ramaḍān performed in a coffeehouse behind Cairo's famed Sayyidnā Ḥusayn Mosque every Friday for over forty years (Figure 12.3). Starting after the afternoon prayer, the music would continue past midnight, stopping only for short periods during each of the day's remaining two prayers (at sunset and about an hour after sunset).

A second and more common context for this same music is *zikr* events that occur with great regularity in countless places throughout Egypt. A *zikr* (literally,

≡ **FIGURE 12.3**
Ramaḍān ʿUways (with microphone) performs with a small version of his ensemble at a Cairo coffeehouse; note *kawala* player standing at the left; *riqq* player directly behind Ramaḍān; seated *ṭabla* player; and *ṭūra* player at right.

remembrance, i.e., remembering God) is a religious ritual within Sufism wherein believers seek to achieve a degree of union with God. In addition to the music, a *zikr* ritual involves a series of movements and communally chanted phrases that help to bring participants to the desired state of ecstatic union with God. Each Sufi order defines the nature of its own *zikr* ritual. In Cairo's *zikr*s, the music and movements commonly occur in cycles, each lasting ten to twenty minutes or more, starting calmly and peacefully, slowly rising in tempo and deliberateness, until a climax is reached with fast-paced music and highly energized movements.

While some *zikr*s are closed events that welcome only initiated members of a specific Sufi order, others are open to any and all who wish to attend. *Zikr*s might occur weekly, by a saint's tomb. They might also occur at annual public festivals that celebrate the birthday of a saint at his or her tomb, attracting from 100 to millions of people.

☰ FIGURE 12.4 A *zaffa* band at the beginning of a wedding procession at a Cairo five-star hotel. Note the bride and groom (at the top of the stairs), *mazhar* players (the top three musicians on each side of the stairway), *duff* players (on the lower stairs), and a *tabla* player (on the landing); the *tabla* and two *tomba* players (at the bottom of the picture, their instruments not visible) have shoulder straps that extend down their backs. Kāmil Mitwallī, the *mizmār* player, is at the bottom of the stairs.

Intersections of Music and Religion in Popular Culture
Zaffa Bands

As might be expected, music at Egyptian Muslim weddings often has a religious component, with lyrics of songs calling for God's blessings on the couple. Festivities commonly begin with a festive procession (*zaffa*) of the bride and groom (Figure 12.4) (Marcus 2007; Kent and Franken 1998). Beginning in the 1970s in the northern coastal city of Damietta and spreading to Cairo, a new type of ensemble was created for these processions, consisting of some twenty-plus drummers who also sing, one or two **trumpets** (a cylindrical brass tube with valves to produce pitches), a **trombone** (a cylindrical brass tube with telescoping slide mechanism to produce pitches), and a *mizmār* (a double-reed aerophone with a wooden tube body ending in a conical flare; Figure 12.5). The majority of the drummers play frame drums: either the *mazhar* or the *duff*, the former having five sets of large cymbals inserted around the frame of the instrument, rendering it a larger version of the *riqq* tambourine, while the *duff* is without cymbals.

≡ **FIGURE 12.5** A *zaffa* wedding procession: mizmār player Kāmil Mitwallī with two dancers (with finger cymbals) and three *mazhar* frame drummers.

In recent decades, this type of ensemble has been a standard feature of weddings celebrated in Cairo's many five-star hotels. The *zaffa* band assumes a long U-shaped formation, with the bride and groom and their parents at the open end, and slowly processes through the marble-floored halls, followed by dozens of wedding guests. The ensemble performs eight to ten songs, with all the

ACTIVITY 12.3

Watch Video 12.1 of a wedding *zaffa* that I made at a Cairo five-star hotel on November 26, 1998, featuring Kāmil Mitwallī and his *zaffa* ensemble. Because the video is 31:26 long, in this Activity I have provided a guide through it, with destination timings so that you can skim most of it, with focused watching and hearing at a sequence of central moments that mark the progression of such an event.

*Zaffa*s in five-star hotels begin at an elaborate stairway. The bride and her immediate family members begin at the top of the stairs while the groom waits below. A bagpipe player begins the performance, accompanying the bride and her father as they descend from the top of the stairs to a lower landing where the groom comes and takes the father's place. The couple then descends the rest of the stairs, accompanied by the bagpiper and his music. Below, the twenty-five-member *zaffa* ensemble, set in a U-shaped formation, greets the couple's arrival by beginning to perform. Note the moments in the Video Guide

drummers singing in forceful unison. Stopping occasionally for the bride, groom, and members of the wedding families to dance, the group finally ends up after some thirty minutes at the door of the banquet hall where the rest of the evening's festivities will take place. As the wedding families and guests enter the hall, the *zaffa* ensemble leaves, possibly heading for a second engagement elsewhere.

VIDEO 12.1 Guide

0:00	Our video begins as the bride and groom are led to the top of the U formation (NB: this is on the ground floor, at the bottom of the stairs), followed by six young women holding long candles and two young flower girls. We also see the bagpipe player who had begun the musical performance, playing while accompanying the couple down the stairs.
0:21	The brass players (trumpet and trombone) at the bottom of the U begin a fanfare melody that leads to a ceremonial *mizmār* solo improvisation (from 0:49–1:38).
1:38	The ensemble plays an instrumental introduction to the first of many songs, with the singing beginning at 2:28. Note the two *ṭabla* drummers in the center of the formation with their drums hanging from shoulder straps.
3:04	The ensemble goes through many different formations, adding to the entertainment value of its performance. As they move up to the bride and groom, note that the front six performers are playing *mazhar* frame drums (frame drums with cymbals), shaking them over their heads. Behind them twelve performers are playing *duff* frame drums (frame drums without cymbals).
6:13	Concluding the previous song, the ensemble takes up the eight-beat *zaffa* rhythm (D- TK T- T- D- T- T- --), beginning the next song with its instrumental introduction at 6:26, and bringing the bride and groom forward into the center of a circle formation. Note: the *zaffa* rhythm is used throughout the procession to introduce new songs.
12:40	The ensemble moves through a series of in-and-out and circling formations with the *mazhar* and *duff* players acting as two separate groups in the various formations.
16:25	Within a new song, Kāmil Mitwallī, the *mizmār* player, approaches first the groom and then the bride (17:44) performing an extended *zaghārīṭ*-like trill over each of their heads. (*Zaghārīṭ* is an extended high-pitched vocal trill, an expression of joy, performed by women on celebratory occasions.)
21:52	The entire *zaffa* party begins to process up the stairs toward the banquet hall led by the *zaffa* ensemble.
28:32	The *zaffa* rhythm begins the final song.
30:49	The bride and groom are directed into the banquet hall.
31:06	The *zaffa* ensemble performs its concluding melody and, following the last beat (31:18), quickly begins to leave the building.

LISTENING GUIDE

Refrain of the *Zaffa* Song *"Alfayn Ṣallā ʿa n-Nabī"*

Performers and instrumentation: Kāmil Mitwallī Kāmil, *mizmār*; Ahmed El Gamal, trumpet; Fathey Abd Rabou, trombone; Monir Mohamed, *mazhar*; Amin Abdou, *mazhar*; Mohamed Adel, *duff*; Mohamed Zaki, *duff*; Mohamed Samy, *duff*; Mohamed Zakariya, *duff*; Samy Mohamed, *duff*; Amr Mohamed, *duff*; Yasser Ahmed, *duff*; Tarek Fathey, *ṭabla*; Tamer El Gamal, *ṭabla*; Usama Khattab, *doholla* (a large-sized *ṭabla*); Amr Masoud, *ṭomba* (single-headed, elongated barrel drum); Essam Sayed, *ṭomba*.

Recorded at a Cairo recording studio, July 6, 2002; times indicate when each line is begun. The symbols "||:" and ":||" surround passages that are repeated.

Time	Text	Translation
Instrumental introduction:		
0:00		
refrain:		
0:30 [0:38]	‖:*Alfayn ṣallā ʿa n-nabī*	Two thousand blessings upon the Prophet.
0:34 [0:42]	*Alfayn ṣallā ʿa z-zayn*:‖	Two thousand blessings upon the beautiful one [here: the prophet and/or the groom].
0:46	*Dā ʿarīsnā ʿamar, win-nabī*	Our groom is radiant like the moon, by the Prophet.
0:49	*ammā l-ʿarūsa, ʿamarayn*	As for the bride, she is twice as beautiful [literally, two moons].
0:53	*Alfayn, alfayn, alfayn ṣallā ʿa n-nabī*	Two thousand, two thousand greetings upon the Prophet.

With references to Allah and the prophet Muhammad, *zaffa* songs are grounded in Muslim verbal expressions. The refrain of the wedding song *"Alfayn Ṣallā ʿa n-Nabī"* in the Listening Guide (Audio Example 12.3) provides an example. As a central rite of passage, weddings are indeed a time of religious affirmation.

The Mid-Twentieth-Century Long Song

Art and popular music in the Eastern Arab cultural sphere—centered in the cities of Cairo (Egypt), Beirut (Lebanon), and Damascus and Aleppo (Syria)—experienced major changes in the early decades of the twentieth century. At the beginning of the period, songs were performed by small ensembles called **takht** consisting, at their largest, of five musicians playing *'ūd*, violin, **nāy** (end-blown flute made of a long, thin tube of a reed plant), **qānūn** (trapezoidally shaped, plucked, box zither), and *riqq*, plus a small chorus, with the group fronted by a solo singer.

Beginning with the development of the then-new genre of musical theater and continuing with the birth of film, the size of the ensemble grew, including more instruments of the Western orchestra (multiple violins, cello, double bass). By the 1960s, the *takht* had grown to orchestra size, sometimes incorporating **saxophone** (single-reed aerophone with wide cylindrical brass tube that turns up on itself and widens slightly to the end), electric guitar, and/or **electronic keyboard** (which creates sounds through analog, digital, or hybrid electronic circuitry). It came to be called a *firqa*, commonly translated as "ensemble."

A succession of new media formats spread the music to an unprecedented degree. Beginning with commercial records from 1904, radio—with small local stations from the 1920s followed by Egyptian National Radio from 1934—and then films with musicals from the 1930s, a new type of star was created: a solo singer with far broader fame than had been possible prior to mass media technology. By midcentury, a few singers dominated across all media formats throughout the region, appearing on records, radio, as film stars, and singing with the newly created *firqas*—especially Umm Kulthūm (c. 1904–1975), Muḥammad 'Abd al-Wahhāb (1910?–1991), 'Abd al-Ḥalīm Ḥāfiz (1929–1977), and Farīd al-Aṭrash (1915–1974).

While love songs dominated the repertoire of the solo singers, religious songs were a common feature in keeping with a general religiosity that pervaded the region. Thus, Umm Kulthūm sang *"Inta 'Umrī"* ("You Are My Life"; 1964) (Danielson 1997 and 2002), perhaps the most famous of her hundreds of songs, a passionate love song with the following lines:

> O dearest of my days
> O sweetest of my dreams
> Take me, out of compassion, take me
> Away from all of this, take me far away
> Far away, far away, just you and me
> Far away, far away, all to ourselves
> Let our days awaken with love
> And our nights end with passion.

But she also sang *"il-'Alb Ya'shiq Kullī Gamīl"* (The Heart Yearns for Every Beauty"; 1971), an equally passionate religious song describing the experience of hearing the call of God and His prophet, Muhammad:

> The heart yearns for every beauty
> And, O my soul, how much beauty I have seen

Yet those who are faithful in love are few
And if love lasts it lasts but a day or two.
But He with whom I fell in love today
His tryst is everlasting.
He does not reproach any who repent
Nor does His nature know the meaning of blame
One — There is none other than He
His light has filled Creation
He invited me into his House
To the very threshold of his House
And when He revealed Himself to me
With tears in my eyes I confided myself to him.

Present-Day Pop Stars

The last decades of the twentieth century saw major shifts in music across the Eastern Arab world. With the death of the past greats—Umm Kulthūm, ʿAbd al-Ḥalīm Ḥāfiz, and Farīd al-Aṭrash, all in the mid-1970s—new generations of musicians took the stage. They brought a new configuration for the performance ensemble modeled on the Western rock band, new sounds, new technologies, and new levels of sensuality and sexuality. Music videos became a major component of every hit song, leading to an emphasis on young attractive singers wearing suggestive clothing and performing sexualized dance moves. Many objected to this breach of propriety; but by the late 1990s, the new songs, commonly upbeat and dance oriented, and their accompanying music videos became omnipresent.

While a vast majority of modern-day songs are about love relationships, many singers still include religious songs in their repertoire. This practice has had new relevance since the last decades of the twentieth century with the growth across the region of a more conservative and conspicuous interpretation of Islam. For example, aspects of Muslim dress, such as the *ḥijāb* (head scarf), rather uncommon in Egypt in prior decades, have become ubiquitous.

Musicians might present a religious song in an album (cassette or CD) otherwise devoted to love songs, or, occasionally, in an album entirely given over to religious songs. Examples of this are found in the releases of two of Egypt's most famous present-day singers, Hishām ʿAbbās (b. 1963) and ʿAmr Dīāb (b. 1961).

In a 2000 CD featuring a series of love songs, ʿAbbās included a setting of the 99 names of God according to Islamic tradition, *"Asmāʾ Allāh al-Ḥusnā"* ("The Beautiful Names of God"). Following an understanding that the 99 names of God occur in a standard progression, the song begins with al-Raḥmān (The Merciful)

ACTIVITY 12.4

Search the web for "99 names of God" in order to follow along with a list of the 99 names while listening to Hishām ʿAbbās's music video on YouTube.

and al-Rahīm (The Compassionate) and ends with al-Rashīd (The Righteous) and al-Ṣabūr (The Patient). While the song was composed decades earlier and occurred regularly as an audience favorite in concerts by a popular government music ensemble, Hishām ʿAbbās's recording launched the song to new levels of fame as Cairo-based DJs adopted it to start their wedding performances. This occurred in both lower-class weddings, where the DJ would have his equipment on a small wooden cart, and also in elaborate weddings in five-star hotels. ʿAbbās also produced a music video of this song (on YouTube at "Hisham Abbas - 99 Names of Allah"), the last frame of which has the following written in Arabic: "Whoever enumerates/recites [the names] will enter Paradise" (*man ahṣaha dakhal al jannu*) The names offer an insightful lesson about human values in Islam.

Religious songs—often new ones—are especially featured in celebrations during the annual holy month of Ramaḍān, a month of fasting (from sunrise to sunset) and—returning to the realm with which this chapter began—prayer. In 2016, ʿAmr Dīāb released a CD of twenty short prayers, each invoking one of the names of God (i.e., he picked twenty from the 99). The prayers also appeared as a series of twenty high-quality music videos (available on YouTube at "Amr Diab – *Mn Asmaa Allah Al Hosna*"), featuring scenes from nature and daily life, mosques in Cairo and the holy city of Mecca, and people praying. With audio and video releases, Hishām ʿAbbās and ʿAmr Dīāb continue a longstanding tradition of musicians contributing to a vibrant Islamic presence throughout the region.

Conclusion

Religion occupies a prominent place in Egypt's music traditions. The complex relationship between Islam and music is an important component for the call to prayer and all the musics and musicians discussed in this chapter. Whether devoted uniquely to religious genres or engaged predominantly with love songs, musicians join those who give the call to prayer in playing a vital role by helping to establish and maintain Islam as a vibrant force throughout Egypt, the larger Eastern Arab region, and beyond.

Bibliography

Danielson, Virginia. 1997. *The Voice of Egypt: Umm Kulthum, Arabic Song, and Egyptian Society in the Twentieth Century*. Chicago: University of Chicago Press.

Danielson, Virginia. 2002. "Snapshot: Opening Night for a Star Performer—Umm Kulthūm and Intá 'Umrī." In *The Garland Encyclopedia of World Music. Vol. 6: The Middle East*, 603–605. New York: Routledge.

Frishkopf, Michael. 2002a. "Islamic Hymnody in Egypt: Al-Inshād al-Dīnī." In *The Garland Encyclopedia of World Music. Vol. 6: The Middle East*, 165–175. New York: Routledge.

Frishkopf, Michael. 2002b. "Shaykh Yāsīn al-Tuhāmī in the Public Ḥaḍra: A Typical Layla Performance." In *The Garland Encyclopedia of World Music. Vol. 6: The Middle East*, 147–151. New York: Routledge.

Kent, Carlee, and Marjorie Franken. 1998. "A Procession Through Time: The *Zaffat al-'Arusa* in Three Views." In *Images of Enchantment: Visual and Performing Arts of the Middle East*, edited by Sherifa Zuhur, 71–80. Cairo: American University of Cairo Press.

Marcus, Scott. 2007. *Music in Egypt: Experiencing Music, Expressing Culture*. Oxford: Oxford University Press.

Rasmussen, Anne. 1996. "Theory and Practice at the 'Arabic *org*': Digital Technology in Contemporary Arab Music Performance." *Popular Music* 15(3): 345–365.

☰ FIGURE III.1 Map of Africa.

PART 3

Africa

Music in Ghana

Dagaaba Xylophone Music in a Ritual Context

JOHN DANKWA AND ERIC CHARRY

Chapter Contents

Introduction

Ghana is characterized by a wonderful diversity of music culture (see Figure 13.1). It is perhaps best known for its drum ensemble traditions, including those of the Akan, Ewe, Ga, and Dagomba peoples. Masters of those traditions have been teaching at universities in North America since the 1960s. In addition, those drum ensembles have been integrated into the national Ghana Dance Ensemble that tours regularly in Africa and also around the world. Featuring music from all corners of Ghana, the ensemble was formed in 1962 under the auspices of Dr. Kwame Nkrumah, the first president of the Republic of Ghana, as part of a postcolonial effort to create a national identity (Charry 2018). It has successfully promoted Ghanaian culture since.

Lest you think that drums are the only significant type of instrument in Ghana—or in West Africa (see Figure 13.2), or in the whole of Africa (see Figure III.1) for that matter, this chapter will introduce you to another aspect of musical diversity of Ghana: xylophone music. Like drum ensemble traditions, it is considered very significant for Ghanaian national identity and also in local regions. And like drum traditions, Ghanaian xylophones belong to a rich culture of related instruments spread out in the larger region of West Africa. Reaching beyond national borders, the Ghanaian xylophone known as the **gyil** and

≡ **Bernard Woma Ensemble:** Bernard Woma (left) plays the *gyil* with Kofi Ameyaw (center) and Mark Stone (right)

203

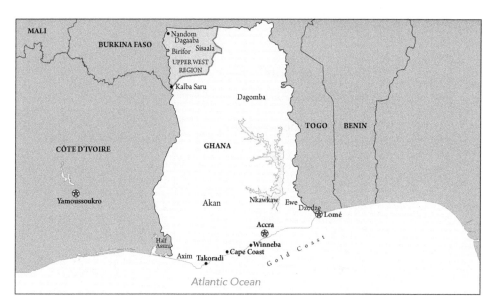

≡ **FIGURE 13.1** Map of Ghana.

its nearby relatives are part of a much more diffuse culture of xylophone music played across the breadth of the West African savanna (the green region between the dryer *sahel* to the north and wetter forest to the south). Burkina Faso, Ghana's neighbor to the northwest, for instance, hosts one of the richest xylophone playing regions in all of Africa (see Figure 13.2).

ACTIVITY 13.1

Diversity of Ghanaian Drums

Search for online images and videos of three different Ghanaian drum ensembles, using the following terms: Akan drum, Ewe drum, and Dagomba drum.

1. What kinds of drums are in each ensemble (e.g., their shape, size, and means of striking them)?

2. In what ways do these ensembles differ from one another?

3. How many different looking drums can you identify? For example, an Ewe drum ensemble can have five to seven different kinds of drums in it.

In West Africa, xylophones represent a precolonial past many generations old, one that predates arbitrary colonial borders and points to a broader tradition of African expressive culture. The xylophone played by hereditary professional musicians and oral historians (*griot*) in Mali and Guinea, called **bala or balafon**, has been associated with the Mande royal court since at least the thirteenth century. One of the oldest instruments in Africa, the Sosso bala, believed to be the original Mande xylophone, has been declared a site of Intangible Cultural Heritage by UNESCO.

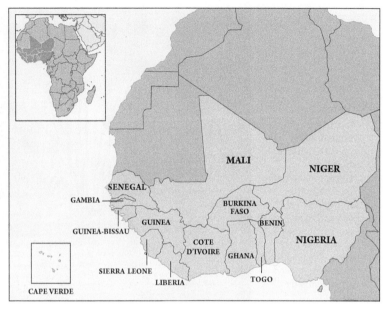

≡ **FIGURE 13.2** Map of West Africa.

Xylophone players have also toured internationally, bringing this tradition to a global audience. Kakraba Lobi, one of the most prominent West African *gyil* players, was lead xylophonist for the Ghana Dance Ensemble, was a regular performer at the Ghana Broadcasting Corporation in the 1970s and 1980s, and became renowned on the international stage as a concert soloist (see Figure 13.3). Information on albums of his music is easily found on the internet.

Like Kakraba Lobi, another top *gyil* player, Bernard Woma, got international exposure as a member of the Ghana Dance Ensemble (see Figure 13.4). He spent considerable time in the United States from 1999, receiving a BA in International Studies (State University of New York at Fredonia) and MAs in African Studies and Ethnomusicology (Indiana University). Residencies and performances in the United States—including of his compositions for *gyil* and orchestra (Gyil Jumbie Concerto and Gyil Yeru Concerto; see YouTube) sustained his musical presence in the United States. Bernard

≡ **FIGURE 13.3** Photo of Kakraba Lobi (d. 2007); Lobi's career opened the way for several *gyil* musicians from Ghana to build their careers abroad.

≡ **FIGURE 13.4**
Photo of Bernard Woma (d. 2018); born with clenched fists as if he was clasping *gyil* mallets, Woma's musical training began at a very early age. According to the Dagaaba belief system, clenched fists at birth is a sign of a predestined *gyil* player.

Woma's international legacy as a teacher is significant; from the Dagara Music Center that he established in Accra, he trained a number of international students in Dagaaba *gyil* playing (Lawrence, 2006). In an entirely different international vein and from another West African country, the Burkina-based group Farafina has brought the local sounds of xylophones, hunters harps, and goblet-shaped **jembe** drums to the international world music festival circuit, where they have toured extensively, including collaborating with the Rolling Stones and Ryuichi Sakamoto.

This chapter will introduce you to xylophones in Africa, focusing on one tradition in Ghana: xylophone music localized primarily in its rural Upper West region among just a few ethnic groups, primarily Dagaaba, Birifor (Hogan 2011), and Sisaala, numbering about one or two million people. They are but three of the many dozens of ethnic groups inhabiting Ghana, a nation of about twenty-eight million people, living in sixteen administrative regions. Mirroring both ethnic and linguistic diversity in most African nations, eleven languages are sponsored in government publications, and all share one national language (English). The Dagaaba people, the focus of this chapter, speak Dagaare, a language that forms part of the Gur language family of the Niger-Congo family (Mwinlaaru 2016).

Focusing on one kind of xylophone in one particular context enables us to explore the deeper significance of music in the lives of contemporary Ghanaians. In this chapter that context is Dagaaba funeral rituals. When someone passes away, xylophone music accompanied with song and dance is used to ease their transition to the spiritual world of the ancestors. The music transports the souls to this other world, provides the living with a proper forum for expressing their grief, protects them from potentially harmful spirits of the dead, and facilitates a kind of emotional balance moving forward. Xylophone players direct the funeral proceedings, including pacing the rituals and the intense emotional display. Here, xylophone music and the words that go along with it hold deep meaning in the community as an essential part of the life cycle that we all go through, especially the final transition out of the world of the living.

African Xylophones

Xylophones (the name is derived from xylo [wood] and phone [sound]), are found throughout Africa in many different forms. The simplest form is a wooden slat placed over a pit to give it resonance when struck; the more complex feature finely tuned slats attached to a frame made of bamboo, banana tree stalks, or some other kind of wood. This chapter focuses on **frame xylophones** that feature wooden slats placed on top of a frame and attached in some way. (Another major type of xylophone has the wooden slats suspended over a resonating case, without touching the case.) Found throughout Africa, they can be played solo or in large orchestras.

The specific way in which the slats are fixed to the frame differs according to region. Slats on the *timbila* of the Chopi people from Mozambique in East Africa are attached with cord running through a hole in it. Slats on the *akadinda* of the Baganda people of Uganda (also in East Africa) are kept in place by tall rods set on either side of them. Each slat on West African frame xylophones is attached by a cord wrapped around its circumference. Other ways in which they might vary are the shape of the frame, the number of wooden slats, the pitch range of the instrument, and the specific tuning, according to the preferences of the different ethnic groups.

The Dagaaba Xylophone (*Gyil*)

The xylophone is the most important and expressive instrument of the Dagaaba ethnic group. Its Dagaare language name of **gyil** (pronounced *jiil*, meaning "surround") may refer to the way that people often quite literally surround the *gyil* with the performer(s) in the middle in traditional performance contexts. In Dagaaba society, the *gyil* is the fulcrum around which musical activities revolve. It serves the purpose of recreation, also accompanying the Catholic Mass and rituals of traditional cults as well as rituals of everyday life such as funerals.

The Dagaaba use two types of *gyil*—the **lo-gyil** and **daga-gyil**—both of which are frame xylophones constructed in a similar manner (see Figure 13.5). The *lo-gyil* is relatively small and has fourteen slats. In contrast, the *daga-gyil* is bigger and has

FIGURE 13.5
The *Lo-gyil*.

typically eighteen slats. Both xylophones are tuned to a pentatonic scale, meaning that the tonal organization of the instruments is based on five pitches in an octave.

Dagaaba xylophones are permanently constructed with the slats secured to the wooden frame. Of varying lengths and sizes, the slats are attached firmly to the frame by either a leather cord or nylon rope wrapped around their ends. The wood used for the slats come from the *ligaa* tree, which is common in northwest Ghana where the Dagaaba live. It is a hard, long-lasting material. The frame on which the slats are fixed is made of wood that is stronger, durable, and resistant to attacks of wood insects.

A gourd resonator is suspended under each slat to amplify the sound. The gourd resonators have two or three holes carefully created and covered with a white membrane found in spiderwebs (*paapir*), to produce a buzzing sound quality. The buzz sounds define the timbral quality of the Dagaaba *gyil*. Among the Dagaaba, a *gyil* is considered bad when the buzzing quality is absent.

As shown in Figure 13.5, the *gyil* frame is not flat in structure. It slopes with one end higher than the other by several inches. The smallest and highest-pitched slats are fixed at the low end of the frame while the slats with lower pitches are placed on the higher end. Essentially, the sloped frame serves two purposes. First, it gives more room for suspending the large gourd resonators under the slats at the higher end of the frame that would be impossible on a flat structure. Second, the slope brings the bass slats fixed at the higher end within easier reach of the player than if they were stretched out on a flat frame. Thus, the distinctive sloped frame derives from the demands of construction and performance.

ACTIVITY 13.2

"*Gyil* Duet, Bewaa #2," performed by Rallio Kpampul and Sambaa Sopele from *Bewaare: They Are Coming: Dagaare Songs from Nandom*

Listen to the music and describe the sound of the *lo-gyil*. Note that the *lo-gyil* is heard in one speaker and a timeline in the other speaker.

1. Practice clapping the timeline.
2. How would you describe or notate the timeline? Can you clap a steady beat that might be used by dancers? Are you hearing the timeline and beats in a binary (even pulses) or ternary (triplet pulses) rhythm?

Gyil Music in Dagaaba Society
Music for Recreation

The *lo-gyil* is customarily used for **bewaa**, a popular recreational dance music of the youth in Dagaaba communities.

Music for Funerals

Like most West African societies, death is regarded as an occasion of the gravest crisis among the Dagaaba. Accordingly, the funeral ceremonies held to commemorate death are more complex and distinct from all other Dagaaba social events. The funeral is distinguished by its public dimension, duration, and the presence of many people outside the deceased's lineage who have varying degrees of social and ritual obligation to attend for the performance of certain roles. Dagaaba believe that death is the final episode of a person's life in this physical world (*tengzu*). After death, the soul of the deceased person enters the world of the ancestors (*dapaare-wie*). The funeral ceremony facilitates the transition of a dead person's soul into the otherworld. Due to the religious significance attached to the funeral, Dagaaba maintain that it must be accompanied by their most expressive and revered instrument, the *gyil*. The playing of tunes is crucial in disseminating the news of death. Other music serves as the vehicle for honoring, mourning, and praising the deceased as well as guiding his or her spirit into the world of the ancestors.

Not all deaths in Dagaaba society are publicly commemorated with *gyil* music. Integral in Dagaaba concepts of death are distinctions drawn between "bad death" and "good death." Bad death in its widest sense is any death that, in Dagaaba worldview, prematurely terminates the life of a person. These include deaths caused by suicides, accidents, and curses by gods. In principle, the death of anyone but an adult of considerable age is considered a bad death among the Dagaaba, and it is viewed with suspicion of supernatural interventions. These deaths are usually not celebrated publicly and, therefore, do not require *gyil* music. On the other hand, the Dagaaba talk of "good death" when the deceased is an older person or has lived a fulfilled life. The funeral of individuals who die "good deaths" are important events that include several ritual stages, both public and private, which may spread over a number of days depending on the status of the deceased. These funerals require *gyil* music; as Dagaaba strongly argue, there cannot be a funeral without *gyil* music. The *gyil* legitimizes the funeral as a public event because wailing, chanting of dirges, and death divination rituals—to mention a few of the important aspects of Dagaaba funerals—revolve around it (Dankwa, 2018).

Announcing Death on a *Lo-gyil*. Important ritual observances begin as soon as a person dies (Gbal 2013). Mourning commences immediately after death, but may remain informal while the family maintains a false sense of normality until the head of the deceased's family is informed of the death. Death announcements usually take two forms: wailing, and xylophone playing. The wailing is a loud projected cry recognized by the community as a mourning lament. It establishes the fact of death to members of the neighborhood who, upon hearing it, run to the house of the deceased. By informing the head of the family, the scene is set for the formal announcement of death, a rite designed to affirm the reality of the loss.

The formal announcement communicates the details of the funeral to the community. For this, the *lo-gyil* is used. The strong carrying power of the *lo-gyil* spreads the message to people farther away than can otherwise be reached by the wailing. The tunes played for this purpose are called ***lobri***.

Lobri melodies are short and repetitive and convey information, in the form of surrogate speech (without a singer) that indicates the gender of the deceased. The melodies are usually phrased around gender roles in Dagaaba society. For instance, the surrogate text announcing the death of a man revolves around farming activities. Farming is traditionally associated with men, and it is a role that all Dagaaba men fulfill at some point in their lives. Women, on the other hand, are generally responsible for housekeeping, and thus, texts announcing their death mainly center on culinary activities and motherly roles.

Audio Example 13.2 is purely instrumental. Nevertheless, it and other *lobri* tunes convey surrogate speech—a substitute for language—that is intelligible to the culturally trained listener. The tonal nature of the Dagaare language enables *gyil* musicians to simulate speech patterns to communicate important information. Dagaare is a two-tone language, meaning each syllable in a word has a high or low tone as in, for instance, **gàndáá** (pronounced *gundaa*), the Dagaare word for a strongman. The tones also serve to distinguish the meanings between words that have the same combination of consonants and vowels, as in the Dagaare verbs *dá* (push), and *dà* (buy)—pronounced with a high and low tone, respectively. In death announcements, the five-note sequence of the *gyil* scale allows the players

ACTIVITY 13.3

1. To experience how death may be announced to a Dagaaba community through the *lo-gyil*, listen to "*Gàndáá Yínà*" played by Gilbert Berese (Audio Example 13.3). Another of the top *gyil* players in Ghana, Berese was from northwestern Ghana, but he began a teaching career at age 17, in southern Ghana at the University of Education, Winneba, and the University of Cape Coast. He gained early prominence throughout Ghana by frequent appearances on the state radio, the Ghana Broadcasting Corporation (Dankwa 2013).

2. Practice humming the melody you hear and relate it to any song you know and see what kind of difference you can identify.

great flexibility to map words onto individual slats to optimally replicate speech patterns that can be understood by listeners. Sometimes, *gyil* speech surrogates may function to impart secret information intelligible to a limited audience. However, most Dagaaba people are culturally trained to understand the language of the *gyil* in death announcements. The underlying text of the tune played by Gilbert Berese is as follows (see Musical Example 13.1).

Gàndáá bé yínà	The hero lies forlorn
Gàndáá bé yínà	The hero lies forlorn
Kúkúr-nà gàndáá bé yínà	The hoe-chief hero lies forlorn

MUSICAL EXAMPLE 13.1 Excerpt of "*Gàndáá Yínà*" performed by Gilbert Berese.

This text announces the death of a man. The language is predominantly proverbial and not direct as found in ordinary speech; the word "death" is not even mentioned. Therefore, to understand the meaning of the text, people draw connections between the text and daily life in Dagaaba society. Terms such as *kúkúr-nà* and *gàndáá* denote not only specific economic activity among the Dagaaba but also the category of people who perform that activity. The primary economic activity among the Dagaaba is farming; and because of socially predefined gender roles, it is categorized as men's business. Due to the lack of mechanized farming, the major implement that farmers use in tilling the land is the hoe. A good, capable, and successful farmer is the man who tills the land with the hoe to feed his family. These men are described as *kúkúr-nà*, a term derived from "*kúkúr*" (the farming hoe), and "*na*" (chief). *Kúkúr-na*, thus, means "hoe chief," or chief farmer, a title that denotes honor and prestige. The chief farmer lying forlorn, on the surface, may be interpreted that he is physically incapacitated, an occurrence that can be attributed to ill health. However, no one publicly announces the ill health of an individual because it is a private affair. By this public announcement, a condition more serious than ill health is being stated. Thus, the message is quickly interpreted by listeners as an announcement of the death of a man based on these associations. Tunes announcing the death of women are expressed in similar terms, emphasizing their motherly roles.

Despite the accessibility of other means of spreading information—such as community radio stations in northwestern Ghana—the *gyil* remains the principal announcer of deaths in Dagaaba communities. There is good reason for this. The Dagaaba worldview is deeply permeated with spirituality. The *gyil* is believed to be supernaturally empowered and, thus, spiritually effective when used to broadcast death news. Additionally, the use of figurative expressions in the *gyil* surrogate speech is seen as psychologically more impressive, imperative, and compelling than ordinary human speech. Here is a classic case of a musical instrument being deeply imbued with meaning, and maintaining that meaning in modern society, even when faced with other means of communication that could have made it obsolete.

Death Dance Music Played on *Daga-gyil*. The bigger *daga-gyil* (typically with eighteen slats) is mainly reserved for funeral ceremonies. Music played on the *daga-gyil* during funerals is called **kuurbine**, from *kuur* (death) and *bine* (dance music). Thus, in a literal sense, *kuurbine* means "death dance music." The term is normally used in reference to the specific *gyil* music and dance form that accompanies Dagaaba funeral ceremonies.

Kuurbine is the most important category of *gyil* music in Dagaaba society and it forms the basis of training for xylophone students (Dankwa 2018, 61). A *gyil* player is said to be of no use to the society if he cannot play *kuurbine* music because funeral ceremonies are of such special significance.

After all necessary private rituals have been accomplished, the corpse is decorated in a beautiful outfit and seated on a chair mounted on a high platform. People gather around the arena where the corpse is displayed to mourn the deceased and to commiserate with the bereaved family. The activities of the mourners are largely dictated by the *kuurbine* music, which comprises a vast repertoire of songs.

≡ **FIGURE 13.6**
Photo of a *Kuurbine* ensemble led by Victor Ziem (facing camera), Nandom, Ghana.

The songs are performed by an ensemble that consists of two *daga-gyil*, a gourd drum called a **kuor**, and a chorus of dirge chanters (Figure 13.6). Chanting of dirges, playing of the xylophones, drumming, and dancing produce an emotionally charged atmosphere that depicts the seriousness of the occasion.

The *kuurbine* dirges are chanted by a chorus of men led by a cantor gifted in oration. The cantor is called a dirge crier (*langkōne*). The elegance of Dagaaba funerals leaves no room for commonplace expression. Therefore, dirge performances at the funeral calls for a lofty and ornate use of language. The cantor who leads the chants must have deep knowledge of Dagaaba oral art forms. Through proverbs, riddles,

ACTIVITY 13.4

1. To fully appreciate the skills of the dirge crier (*langkōne*), watch the "Dagaaba Funeral Music (*Kuurbine*)" video filmed by John Dankwa (Video Example 13.1). Note that there are two lead voices in the video. The man in the black cowboy hat is the dirge crier while the other in the "50 Cent" shirt (in the front) supports him.

2. How would you describe the dirge crier's style of singing? How similar or different is it from singing styles you are familiar with?

3. Practice humming the responses by the chorus.

ACTIVITY 13.5

1. Watch the *"Kuurbine* Music and Dance" video by John Dankwa (Video Example 13.2). Relate it to the video "Dagaaba Funeral Music (*Kuurbine*)" in Activity 13.4 and see what kinds of differences you can identify.

2. Listen attentively to the drum sound you hear in the video. Its distinctively deep sound penetrates the woody sound of the xylophones.

3. Observe closely the dance movements of the men and women and identify the similarities and differences between them.

4. How do the drum patterns relate to the dancers' feet movements?

and other figurative expressions, he effectively plays on the emotions of the funeral audience and address issues in ways that are deemed impossible in ordinary speech.

Each instrumentalist in a *kuurbine* ensemble plays a specific role that displays the familiar hierarchic organization found in many West African ensembles. First, there is a support xylophonist (*gyilkpagru*) who maintains a recurrent rhythmic motif called *kpagru*, which functions as point of reference for the rest of the instrumentalists. The player of the *kuor* drum occupies the next subsidiary role. The *kuor* is a very large gourd with a skin attached to the top, played by both hands, yielding a semi-deep tone. The drummer's role in the ensemble is to maintain, consistently, the pulsation pattern of the music on which dancers base their fundamental steps. The drummer may occasionally play variations during very hot or tense passages to intensify and reinforce the overall rhythmic complexity of the music.

At most funerals, the role of the lead xylophonist is played by a **gɔbaa** (pronounced gawba), a *gyil* player acknowledged in the community as master of the xylophone (Woma 2013, 45). The lead xylophonist directs the ensemble and establishes the themes that orient the dirge chanter. Through speech surrogates, the lead *gyil* player communicates relevant information to the funeral participants, gives situational comments about the event, queries the organizers when things go wrong, and gives commendations when appropriate.

Conclusion

Ghana, like all African nations, has a diverse array of musical traditions, matched by the linguistic diversity of its citizens. The *gyil* makes up one element of this dense network of traditions and has maintained its relevance in the modern world because of both its deeply embedded meaning among Dagaaba and its complex and aesthetically pleasing music that has enthralled listeners around the world. As *gyil* music is so fundamental to funerals—helping to ease the transition of the deceased to another world and helping with the grieving process of those left behind—its meaning is both time-honored, associated with generations reaching into the distant past, and also very contemporary. And so the *gyil* straddles worlds and generations, an extraordinary example of how tuned wooden slats tied onto a frame can hold such deep meaning among a group of people in one corner of one African nation.

Bibliography

Charry, Eric. 2018. "Music and Postcolonial Africa." In *The Palgrave Handbook of Colonial and Postcolonial History*, Vol. 2, edited by Martin S. Shanguhyia and Toyin Falola, 1231–1261. New York: Palgrave/Macmillan.

Dankwa, John Wesley. 2013. *What Makes a Gobaa? A Study of Musicianship and Aesthetics in Dagaaba Xylophone Music*. Master's thesis. Cape Coast, Ghana: University of Cape Coast.

Dankwa, John Wesley. 2018. *When the* Gyil *Speaks: Music, Emotions, and Performance in Dagaaba Funerary Rituals*. PhD diss. Middletown, CT: Wesleyan University.

Gbal, Tanson F. 2013. *Death and Funeral Rites of the Dagara People of Ghana in the Celebration of the Roman Funeral Liturgy: An Approach towards Inculturation*. Magister der Theologie. Austria: University of Vienna.

Hogan, Brian. 2011. *Enemy Music: Blind Birifor Xylophonists of Northwest Ghana*. PhD diss. Los Angeles: University of California.

Lawrence, Sidra Meredith. 2006. *Killing My Own Snake: Fieldwork, Gyil, and Processes of Learning*. Master's thesis. Bowling Green, OH: Bowling Green State University.

Mwinlaaru, Isaac N. 2016. *A Systematic Functional Description of the Grammar of Dagaare*. PhD diss. Hong Kong: The Hong Kong Polytechnic University.

Vercelli, Michael Biagio. 2006. *Performance Practice of the Dagara-Birifor Gyil Tradition through the Analysis of the Bewaa and Daarkpen Repertoire*. DMA diss. Tucson: University of Arizona.

Woma, Bernard. 2013. *The Socio-Political Dimension of Dagara Funeral Ritual, Music and Dirge*. Master's thesis. Bloomington: Indiana University.

Websites

https://www.farafina.com/en/home/

http://www.nebasolo.com/NebaSolo.com/Bio.html

https://ich.unesco.org/en/RL/cultural-space-of-sosso-bala-00009

https://ich.unesco.org/en/RL/chopi-timbila-00133

https://www.bbc.co.uk/programmes/p00d80qx

http://www.dagaramusic.org/bernard-woma/; https://www.fredonia.edu/news/suny-fredonia%E2%80%99s-bernard-woma-play-avery-fisher-hall

14

Music in South Africa

Language, Race, and Nation

GAVIN STEINGO

Chapter Contents

Introduction

This chapter demonstrates ways that music is meaningful to different people at different times, influenced by the interaction of geography, nationality, and race. Because the human voice is the instrument of choice in South Africa (Muller 2008), I will focus on the singer Miriam Makeba (1932–2008), affectionately referred to throughout the continent as "Mama Africa." Through a discussion of her first American hit song, "*Qongqothwane*," I will explore how Makeba used her African identity as a means of establishing herself as an international singing star.

South Africa and Its Languages

The southern region of Africa is unique for its many languages that use **click consonants**. To understand why this is the case, a survey of Africa's deep history is necessary. The dominant theory of human evolution is that humans originated in southern and East Africa between 200,000 and 100,000 years ago and gradually migrated from East Africa to other parts of the globe (Figure 14.1). The earliest human communities in southern

≡ **The South African singer Miriam Makeba in 1978**

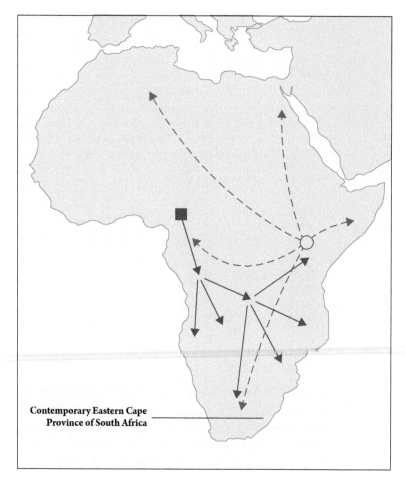

≡ FIGURE 14.1
Map of Africa with migrations; dashed lines represent the movement of the first humans out of East Africa and solid lines represent the far later migration of Bantu speakers.

Contemporary Eastern Cape
Province of South Africa

Africa were the San (hunter-gatherers) and Khoikhoi (semi-nomadic pastoralists). Over centuries of interaction, the separation between San and Khoikhoi blurred, and a hybrid group known as the **Khoisan** emerged.

Khoisan languages employ as many as 48 click consonants. When the first Europeans reached the area, they were fascinated by their "exotic" vocal "clicks." The French writer, historian, and philosopher Voltaire (1694–1778) found Khoisan speech so strange that he speculated that their "vocal organs are different from ours. . . . [T]hey make a stuttering and gobbling, that is impossible for other men to imitate." In the nineteenth century, another French writer argued—based entirely on secondhand travel accounts and having never heard a Khoisan language—that Khoisan speech, "by its hissing, its croaking, its shrill cries, its inarticulate sounds . . . appears to serve as the natural link between the language of men and that of animals" (as cited in Strother 1999, 3–4). Until the twentieth century, most Europeans referred to Khoisan peoples as "Hottentots," a word that is probably derived from the Dutch words *hateren* (stammer) and *tateren* (stutter).

Tragically, most Khoisan languages were wiped out by the mid-twentieth century due to long periods of slavery, genocide, and cultural assimilation. Today, speakers of Khoisan languages make up only a tiny fraction of the contemporary population in South Africa. The vast majority of people speak one of the many languages classified as "**Bantu**," a language *group* that includes **Xhosa**, as well as many other languages. Bantu-speaking peoples arrived in southern Africa long after the establishment of San and Khoikhoi communities; Bantu speakers probably reached the area that is today Johannesburg in around 300 AD. Another, larger wave followed around the year 1000 AD (Figure 14.1). As Bantu speakers came into contact with the Khoisan, they began to incorporate clicks into their languages. With a very few exceptions, the only Bantu languages that employ click consonants are those spoken in southern Africa.

Xhosa is spoken primarily in the Eastern Cape province of South Africa (Figure 14.2). It has three primary click consonants:

c: dental click produced by pulling the tongue from behind the top front teeth,

x: lateral click produced by pulling the tongue from the side of the mouth,

q: post-alveolar click produced by pulling the tongue from the alveolar ridge of the mouth.

There are also several accompaniments to each of these clicks. Here, however, only the unaccompanied clicks are considered.

ACTIVITY 14.1

Listen to the recording (Audio Example 14.1) and practice saying the three primary click consonants coupled with vowels.

ca, ce, ci, co, cu

xa, xe, xi, xo, xu

qa, qe, qi, qo, qu

Two important facts about Africa are evident in this brief history:

1. The peoples of Africa have been incredibly *dynamic* over the last thousands of years. Africa has a long history of migrations—it is a continent on the move.
2. Africa is a continent of **hybridity** (i.e., cultural mixing). For example, the San and Khoi peoples became nearly indistinguishable after hundreds of years of interaction.

An important factor in the evolution of African languages is that, until the nineteenth century, they were seldom written down or standardized. The border between two languages was often blurry. Later, languages such as Xhosa were forged out of the encounter between Bantu and Khoisan tongues. The mutual influence of languages was also commonplace—a good example being the adoption of clicks into Bantu languages. Most linguists estimate that over 2,000 languages are spoken on the African continent, an incredible amount of diversity. But language fluidity was cut off dramatically in South Africa in the twentieth century when Europeans began to aggressively colonize the region.

South Africa in the Twentieth Century

Europeans had settled in South Africa as early as 1652. The Boers—Dutch, German, and French Protestants who would become known as Afrikaners—came first, ruling the region until the British came to power in 1902. In 1909, the Union of South Africa was created as a dominion of the British Empire. In 1934, the country became a self-governing nation-state within the British Empire; then in 1961, a sovereign state named the Republic of South Africa (Figure 14.2).

In the twentieth century—with the discovery and aggressive extraction of natural resources (primarily diamonds and gold)—the White population began systematically controlling and exploiting the native populace. Racial

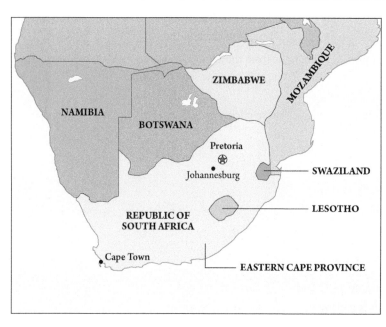

≡ **FIGURE 14.2** Map of present southern African region, with Republic of South Africa central.

segregation had been longstanding; but in 1948, it was systematically institution-alized (as **apartheid**, which literally means "apartness"), which would last until the early 1990s. Every aspect of African life was affected, as colonial and apartheid authorities controlled African cultures. Making up 90 percent of the population, Black South Africans were forced to use separate (and inferior) public facilities and attend separate (and inferior) schools. They also were barred from universities, government positions, and lucrative jobs. To uphold its laws, the apartheid govern-ment used any means necessary: police raided households at random, and activists were tortured and jailed. The Black populace lived in a state of constant fear.

Colonial and apartheid authorities also controlled African languages. Linguists have concluded that in South Africa, "language variation has been dramatically reduced on account of language standardization and the promulgation of standard languages over the past seventy-five years in South Africa" (Herbert and Bailey 2002, 65). The South African government recognizes eleven official languages: English, Afrikaans (a language derived from Dutch), and nine Bantu languages—Northern Sotho, Southern Sotho, Ndebele, Swati, Tsonga, Tswana, Venda, Xhosa, and Zulu. However, the designation of these nine Bantu languages in South Africa "is simply the output of historical accidents and design perpetrated by missionar-ies and government agents" (Herbert and Bailey 2002, 73).

Language standardization was part of the larger apartheid project. Using a divide and rule strategy, the apartheid government divided the Black populace into distinct language groups. The Xhosa language is just one example. Xhosa was originally the name of one small linguistic group. Over the course of the twentieth century, the word "was vigorously promoted as a cover for unifying the various Cape Nguni groups" (Herbert and Bailey 2002, 66). There was even a plan at one point to produce a single written standard for both Xhosa and Zulu. The plan seems to have failed because of competing *political* rather than linguistic interests (Herbert and Bailey 2002, 66).

Miriam Makeba's Early Career

Makeba's early career was shaped by the racial segregation and oppression in her home country. Her talents were first revealed through the work of documentary filmmaker Lionel Rogosin, who visited Johannesburg in 1958 in order to document the plight of Black South Africans and expose apartheid's crimes to the rest of the world. He did so at great risk. In order to avoid immediate deportation (or worse, arrest), Rogosin filmed clandestinely, often in the middle of the night, in a largely improvised fashion. One night, he filmed the young singer named Miriam Makeba at an informal drinking tavern. Wearing an elegant evening dress, Makeba sang

≡ **FIGURE 14.3**
Miriam Makeba in
performance, 1969.

two songs for Rogosin: "Lakutshon' Ilanga," by Mackay Davashe, and "Into Yam," by Dorothy Masuka (Figure 14.3). The lyrics of both songs are in Xhosa language, and Makeba performed them in the style of contemporary jazz. Jazz's influence on Makeba's music was not surprising. As Coplan (2008, 5) writes, "Among urban black South Africans, the sustained appeal of black American performance styles derives not only from similarities in song structure but also from the comparable experience of the two peoples under white domination."

Rogosin completed the film, "Come Back, Africa," the following year, and it became a minor hit. Audiences were especially enthralled by the young Miriam Makeba, who joined Rogosin for a screening of the movie at the Venice Film Festival. But the film's success was also Makeba's doom: On learning about Makeba's involvement in a film exposing the horrors of apartheid, the South African government revoked her passport and prohibited her from returning home. As a stateless person, Makeba went into exile in the United States in 1960, where she received assistance from Rogosin as well as the famous singer, actor, and activist Harry Belafonte.

Makeba began making a name for herself, performing in clubs around New York City. She drew larger and larger audiences and soon released her debut album with the major record company, RCA. It was a major success thanks to the hit song, "*Qongqothwane,*" which she sang in the Xhosa language (Audio Example 14.2).

"*Qongqothwane*" is striking for its use of "click consonants" that are commonly found in South African languages, including Xhosa. In her autobiography, Makeba later recalled: "In Xhosa, the tongue makes clicking sounds that one critic says are 'like the popping of champagne corks'. From this moment on I will be known as the 'click-click girl'" (1987, 86–87). In 1960, American audiences were delighted with this "click-click girl" all the way from South Africa—and Makeba knew it. The recording featured Makeba's spoken introduction: "In my native village in Johannesburg, there is a song that we always sing when a young girl gets married. It's called the 'Click Song' by the English, because they cannot say '*Qongqothwane*'." Makeba's choice of the song was strategic, as it helped establish her as a voice of Africa on the international stage (see chapter opener).

The "Click Song"

"*Qongqothwane*" shows how music becomes meaningful to different people at different times, influenced by the intersections of geography, nationality, and race. In South Africa, "*Qongqothwane*" was considered a sweet, playful tune that would be sung occasionally at weddings; it would not have been welcome at a concert hall, club, or tavern where jazz was the preferred form of musical expression. Only when she arrived in New York did Makeba turn to "traditional" African music (Pyper 2004). "*Qongqothwane*" may charm Xhosa audiences with its rich metaphors and delight American audiences with its effervescent sound—even when the American audiences do not understand a word of its lyrics:

> *Igqirha lendlela nguqongqothwane*
> *Seleqabele gqithapha nguqongqothwane.*

The use of click consonants brings percussive effects into vocal music. The percussive effect can be heard from the very beginning of "*Qongqothwane*" with the post-alveolar click on the letter "q" (see Activity 14.1). There is also the complex consonant cluster "nqg" in "*nguqoNGQothwane*" in the first line of text. Another sound that Western audiences may have found unusual is the guttural "rh" sound in the first word "*igqiRHa*."

The words compare the journey (*lendlela*) of a traditional healer (*igqirha*) to a beetle (*qongqothwane*) winding its way up a steep road. The literal meaning of the first line is, "The healer of the road is like a beetle." But this sentence can also be interpreted to mean that a healer's calling is arduous. The second line (*Seleqabele gqithapha nguqongqothwane*) literally means, "He climbed up a hill, the beetle," and can be interpreted as a metaphor for the steep incline a healer must ascend. According to one author, the song is based on a Xhosa proverb, "Don't look down on the knocking beetle"—a type of beetle that creates a "knocking" sound reminiscent of the "q" in Xhosa (Mbabi-Katana 1971, 28). The author goes on to suggest that "*Qongqothwane*" was originally derived from a children's game that consists of picking up a beetle and asking it to point in the direction of home. When the beetle moves its body to "point" in a certain direction, it is understood metaphorically as a "philosophical guide in hardships."

In her 1960 recording of the song, Makeba also interjects a few words into repetitions of line one, such as "*kuth'wa*" ("it is said") and "*haya*" (an exclamation without any literal meaning). The small change between lines five and six below ("*seleqabele*" vs. "*selequbule*") makes no semantic difference. Here are the lyrics as Makeba famously sang them in her 1960 recording of the "Qongqothwane."

Igqirha lendlela nguqongqothwane

Igqirha lendlela kuth'wa nguqongqothwane

Igqirha lendlela haya nguqongqothwane

Igqirha lendlela kuth'wa nguqongqothwane

Seleqabele gqithapha nguqongqothwane

Selequbule gqithapha nguqongqothwane

Miriam Makeba's Changing Worlds, 1958–1960

In her native South Africa, Miriam Makeba lived in a world in which apartheid ruled. Apartheid reversed the processes of hybridization that had characterized precolonial Africa. Supplanting fluidity and mixing, the apartheid system instituted fixity and separation. When she met Lionel Rogosin, Makeba was singing

ACTIVITY 14.2

Learn to sing the song "*Qongqothwane*" by listening closely to Audio Example 14.2. Listen particularly carefully for the subtle "accompaniments" to the post-alveolar click in the words "*ngu**qo**ngq**othwane*" and "*gqithapha*."

"Qongqothwane (The Click Song)"

Performed by Miriam Makeba

Recording location and year: RCA Victor, 1960; Catalogue number LSP 2267

Instrumentation: Guitar, double bass, percussion, vocals

Time	Something to Listen For
0:01	The female singer (Miriam Makeba) explains that "The Click Song" (so called by the English who cannot click their tongues in pronouncing the title), is sung in Black residential areas of Johannesburg for young girls who will be married.
0:17	A strummed guitar chord gives reference to the song's tonal center and starting pitch.
0:21	Makeba begins the melody in Xhosa language and is joined by a double bass.
	Xhosa: *Igqirha lendlela nguqongqothwane.*
	English Translation: The healer of the road is like a beetle,
0:34	Chorded guitar accompaniment begins, with the singer repeating the previous phrase.
0:36	Entrance of a chorus of male singers, first softly but gaining in volume, to back up the solo singer.
0:38	Makeba raises her voice from the melody to sound a call, "*haya*," and returns immediately to singing; the opening phrase is now in its third repetition.
0:48	Makeba's call, in a guttural voice, is immediately followed by two claps that mark the beginning of the second section with her leading the way.
	Xhosa: *Seleqabele gqithapha nguqongqothwane.*
	English Translation: He climbed up a hill, the beetle.
0:56	Two claps signal the start of the next phrase.
1:03	Two claps signal the start of the next phrase.
1:10	Two claps signal the start of the next phrase.
1:17	The female singer's call, in a guttural voice, leads to "ooh."
1:22	Makeba speaks rhythmically over the sound of the guitar, double bass, and percussion instruments, expressing "*iza*" in an exhaling of breath.
1:33	Makeba returns to the sung verse, and the male choir joins in.

Time	Something to Listen For
	Xhosa: *Igqirha lendlela nguqongqothwane.*
	English Translation: The healer of the road is like a beetle.
1:46	The verse is repeated, as before, including claps.
2:29	Two claps conclude the song.

in the style of American jazz, and was not interested in performing "traditional" African songs. The fact that she sang in Xhosa should not be misinterpreted as an affirmation of "tradition." Makeba (1987, 4) explained it this way:

> My mother is a member of the Swazi tribe. My father . . . is a Xhosa. Since I am his daughter, I am Xhosa, too. But in South Africa tribal differences are not important. We are all the same people. It was the British who first divided us. To be tribalist is to be a racist.

Makeba's development as a musician was defined by this basic tension between her desire to freely mix the different cultures she came into contact with, on the one hand, and the aim of the South African government to standardize, segment, and separate, on the other. As a child, she loved to gather with her friends "every Sunday to play jazz records from America. We [met] at somebody's house, make food, and sit for hours listening to Ella Fitzgerald and Billie Holliday on the wind-up record player" (Makeba 1987, 20). The apartheid government did not approve of these foreign influences. Makeba recalled one day in the 1950s: "Men come to each African house and install plastic radio speakers. There are no dials on these radios because there is only one station: the official station. All day and all night there is bland music and propaganda news broadcasts."

The "bland music" Makeba describes was probably the "standardized," "traditional" music produced by government agents. State radio stations "rigorously censored any music referring to explicit sex, the reality of urban experience, or social and political issues. African censors were employed to expunge any township slang or oblique reference to politics" (Coplan 2008, 250). The state "refused to play music that did not fit into one of the . . . rigidly defined 'tribal' styles of its stations" (Ansell 2007, 17).

By contrast, the first band that Makeba ever sang in was called the Cuban Brothers, a name of pure "fantasy, because no one is from Cuba. None of us have even met a Cuban. From the movies, though, we know they look like Cesar Romero and Carmen Miranda." Her second band name was equally fanciful: the Manhattan Brothers! It was in this group that Makeba first sang one of the songs she would perform in "Come Back, Africa," a Xhosa song about a man watching the setting sun (*"Lakutshon' Ilanga"*). When a recording of the song made its way to America and a producer asked Makeba to record a version in English for an international audience, apartheid again interfered because it was "forbidden for a Black person to sing on a record in the English language" (Makeba 1987, 53).

Considering Makeba's commitment to cosmopolitan music-making, it is surprising that her breakout song in America was the "traditional" song *"Qongqothwane."* However, it was her very foreignness that was most appealing to this new audience. When Makeba first performed *"Qongqothwane"* in America, audiences were spellbound. One writer for the *New York Times* referred to Makeba as a "young Xosa [*sic*] tribeswoman" who performs by "rolling her remarkably bright, large eyes and clicking like a field of beetles." Another *Times* writer foregrounded the "weird tongue-smackings of her native Xhosa language." Around the world, articles and reviews about the singer included the word "click" in the title, such as "Miriam Makeba Clicks" (*Jerusalem Post*) and "Makeba Clicks in L.A. Club" (*Los Angeles Times*). A critic for the *Boston Globe* emphasized Makeba's "devilishly beguiling knack of making a clicking sound with her tongue," and then added jokingly in parentheses "(Try it friend, and good luck on your swollen tongue)." In all of these reviews, we hear echoes of Voltaire and the other early European writers in their fascination with what to them was an "exotic" culture.

For contemporary music critics who dug a little deeper, Makeba's worldly approach to music—for example, her love of American jazz—was disconcerting. A writer for the *Washington Post* observed that Makeba had long listened to and performed American jazz, noting that this "destroys the image that she came from a thatched hut. If this is modern Africa speaking, the voice may be too familiar to us for some people's comfort." Performing a song like *"Qongqothwane"* was therefore a strategic choice for Makeba, who was careful not to sound "too familiar" for her American audience's comfort.

Miriam Makeba's Legacy

Makeba's displays of exoticism would cast a long shadow over subsequent South African musicians performing in the United States. When another singer, Letta Mbulu, traveled to New York for a concert in 1964, reviewers immediately compared her to Makeba, noting that, "Her native tongue, like that of her native compatriot Miriam Makeba, is Xosa [*sic*], which includes the celebrated click sound."

Makeba's "click" legacy has even lasted well into the twenty-first century both in South Africa and internationally. When I was researching **kwaito**—a South African genre of popular electronic music that emerged in the mid-1990s—I interviewed the famous *kwaito* musician Stoan in 2008. His immensely popular band Bongo Maffin was the first South African group to perform internationally "since those days of Miriam Makeba." Precisely because of songs like "*Qongqothwane*," Stoan felt pressure from American audiences to "give them the 'out of Africa' experience." Sometimes, he said, audiences will even "expect that you come through with loin cloths and stuff like that."

Makeba's legacy within South Africa is largely due to what ethnomusicologists call "reverse importation": the process through which a musician is "validated at home after gaining status on a foreign stage" (Novak 2013, 14–15). Bongo Maffin's first hit in South Africa was a song called "Makeba"—a reworking of one of Miriam Makeba's other hit songs, "Pata Pata," which opens with a loud and pronounced click consonant: "*Saguquka sathi bheka, nants' ipata pata.*" Thus, the popularity of click consonants in the United States was "imported" back to South Africa, even though in South Africa click consonants were simply part of language, of everyday speech.

Conclusion

Language and music are subject to constant change, and their meanings change as well. It would be pointless to write a sentence like, "In South Africa, languages have click consonants and these sounds are used in vocal music." It would instead be accurate to say "Some one thousand years ago, Bantu speakers migrating to southern Africa began to incorporate Khoisan clicks into their languages." In the twentieth century, Bantu languages with clicks (such as Xhosa) were standardized and codified by European administrators. In the second half of the twentieth century, these click sounds gained notoriety in the West largely through Makeba's performance of "*Qongqothwane*." Subsequently, South African musicians touring in Europe and America struggled to live up to Makeba's popularity, in part because they could not (or refused to) match her affecting "click" song. This emphasis on click consonants in vocal music was to some extent imported *back* into South Africa when Bongo Maffin released their song, "Makeba," which became an anthem of the post-apartheid South African youth. By studying the use of clicks in vocal music, the ever-shifting fault lines are revealed between music, language, race, and nation.

Bibliography

Ansell, Gwen. 2007. "Of Roots and Rhythms." In *Jazz, Blues, and Swing*, edited by Don Albert et. al., 15–30. Claremont: David Philip.

Coplan, David. 2008. *In Township Tonight! South Africa's Black City Music & Theatre*. 2nd ed. Chicago: University of Chicago Press.

Herbert, Robert, and Richard Bailey. 2002. "The Bantu Languages: Sociolinguistic Perspectives." In *Language in South Africa*, edited by Rajend Mesthrie: 50–78. Cambridge: Cambridge University Press.

Makeba, Miriam, with James Hall. 1987. *Makeba: My Story*. New York: NAL Books.

Mbabi-Katana, Solomon. 1971. "Qongqothwane." In *The World of African Song*, compiled by Miriam Makeba: 26–29. Chicago: Quadrangle.

Muller, Carol. 2008. *Focus: Music of South Africa*. 2nd ed. New York: Routledge.

Novak, David. 2013. *Japanoise*. Durham, NC: Duke University Press.

Pyper, Brett. 2004. "The Click Song: Representations of African Indigeneity in the Early Exiled Career of Miriam Makeba and Her Associates." *Papers Presented at the Symposium on Ethnomusicology*, No. 18, edited by Andrew Tracey. Grahamstown, South Africa: ILAM.

Strother, Z. S. 1999. "Display of the Body Hottentot." In *Africans on Stage: Studies in Ethnological Show Business*, edited by Bernth Lindfors: 1-61. Bloomington: Indiana University Press.

≡ **FIGURE IV.1** Map of Europe.

PART 4

Europe

15

Music in Spain

Flamenco, between the Local and the Global

**SUSANA MORENO FERNÁNDEZ AND
SALWA EL-SHAWAN CASTELO-BRANCO**

Chapter Contents

Introduction

This chapter takes us to Spain, one of the two countries on the southeastern edge of Europe, occupying the Iberian Peninsula. Bordered by the Atlantic Ocean and Portugal to the west, the Mediterranean Sea to the south and east, and France to the north (Figure 15.1), Spain is the second largest country in the European Union and the fourth largest country on the European continent. Including also the residents of the Balearic Islands in the Mediterranean, the Canary Islands in the Atlantic, as well as the North African cities of Ceuta and Melilla, Spain has a total population of approximately forty-six and a half million inhabitants.

Through several millennia, Spain was home to many different peoples, including Iberians, Celts, Phoenicians, Carthaginians, Greeks, Romans, Visigoths, and Moors.

In the sixteenth century, Spain embarked on maritime expansion, establishing colonies in North and South America, the Caribbean, and the Philippines. Thus, it has a great cultural and linguistic legacy: the 500+ million Spanish speakers make Spanish the world's second most spoken native language (after Mandarin Chinese). After its global power waned, it remained essentially a monarchy with intervals of republics.

≡ *Flamenco* **performance in Sevilla, Spain.**

≡ **FIGURE 15.1** Map of Spain, showing autonomous communities.

The Spanish Civil War in the twentieth century (1936–1939) brought to power the dictator Francisco Franco who ruled the country until his death in 1975.

Now a constitutional monarchy, Spain is governed as a "State of Autonomies" as decreed by the 1978 constitution. It comprises seventeen autonomous communities that have wide legislative and administrative independence (Figure 15.1). Claiming a distinct cultural identity informed by historical and cultural legacies, each autonomous community has an official name, capital city, flag, coat of arms, and anthem. In addition, the Spanish constitution recognizes—with Castilian Spanish—the co-official languages of the Basque, Valencian, and Galician autonomous communities and other territories.

This chapter focuses on *flamenco*, the music and dance genre that has been used the most to represent and market Spain overseas, although it is primarily associated with Andalusia in the south. *Flamenco* is deeply rooted in the culture of Andalusia's **Gitanos**, the Roma people formerly referred to as "Gypsies." Some researchers attribute the roots of the genre specifically to the Andalusian provinces of Seville, Cádiz, Málaga, and Granada (Figure 15.2). It also has roots in the neighboring autonomous communities of Extremadura and Murcia (Figure 15.1).

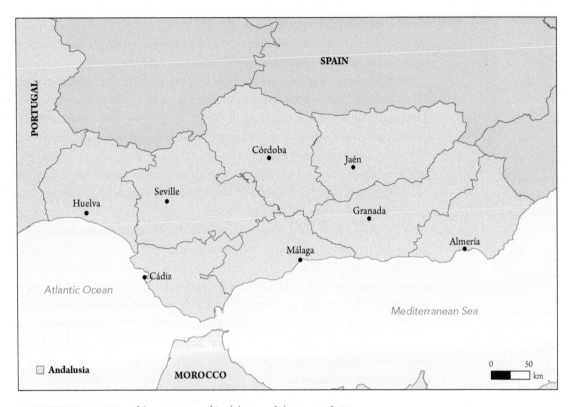

≡ **FIGURE 15.2** Map of the provinces of Andalusia and their capital cities.

Flamenco is a hybrid genre that can be traced back to the mid-nineteenth century. It incorporated the music and dance practices of *Gitanos* and non-*Gitanos*, as well as myriad influences from other regions of Spain and Latin America. ***Cafés-cantantes***—public venues offering regular *flamenco* performances as well as other music and dance shows—contributed to the consolidation, commercialization, and wide dissemination of *flamenco* among the middle class, as well as its professionalization. The wide popularity of the genre, and the bohemian behavior associated with the music and dance, provoked a negative reaction by some. In 1922, the composer Manuel de Falla, the writer Federico García Lorca, and other intellectuals and *flamenco* **aficionados** (devoted fans) organized the Cante Jondo Competition in Granada as an attempt to combat this negativity and commercialization of the genre, and to restore its "authentic" characteristics.

The *cafés-cantantes* lost their importance by the early 1920s, giving way to the ***ópera flamenca***, a commercial theatrical show intended to attract large middle-class audiences, which was predominant up to the 1950s. The development of *ópera flamenca* was largely supported by Francisco Franco's authoritarian regime. On the one hand, Franco's government suppressed *flamenco* in some settings and censored lyrics that were thought to express opposition to the regime (Machin-Autenrieth 2013, 99), but on the other hand, used the *flamenco* genre to express national identity and as a way of promoting tourism.

Ópera flamenca companies consisted of singers, dancers, and instrumentalists. They performed throughout Spain in large venues, and toured in Europe and the Americas. The repertoire consisted of "light" song types, and **copla andaluza** (a sentimental sung narrative often focusing on Andalusian themes and characters). Orchestral accompaniment displaced the central role of the guitar, and the singing and dancing emphasized exuberance and gaiety. Many prominent artists like La Niña de los Peines (whom you will hear in Audio Example 15.1) pursued their professional careers through *ópera flamenca*.

As La Niña's career was coming to an end in the 1950s, an artistic and ideological movement for the revitalization of traditional *flamenco* emerged. It was led by the *Gitano* singer Antonio Mairena partly as a reaction to the changes introduced through *ópera flamenca*. Highly influential between the 1950s and 1970s, it was anchored on the idea that "authentic" *flamenco* is grounded in *Gitano* communities in the provinces of Seville and Cádiz and that it is a quintessential expression of their ethnicity. He performed and recorded many songs emulating early *flamenco* singers and influenced several prominent singers, most notably José Menese, El Chocolate, and La Paquera.

In 1981, the Andalusian region was proclaimed an autonomous community, and its government subsequently reclaimed the genre as a distinctive element of its own cultural heritage and identity. The Andalusian autonomous community promoted the inscription of *flamenco* to UNESCO's representative list of Intangible Cultural Heritage. The vitality of the genre and its central place in the life of Andalusian cities remains strong. It is performed by and for local communities in taverns and private spaces, religious fiestas, and communal festivities, as well as weddings and christenings. One very special venue that can be found throughout Spain and abroad is a club where aficionados gather regularly to participate in *flamenco* sessions (**peña**). It is also performed at festivals, competitions, and concerts as well as commercial public venues such as **tablaos** and events linked to the cultural and tourist industries.

Although flamenco is by no means widespread throughout Spain, the dual sense of *flamenco*'s identity—as both local and global—is still present: both the government of the community and the national government have supported institutions for the preservation, study, and dissemination of the genre (Machin-Autenrieth 2017; Washabaugh 2012; Castelo-Branco and Fernández 2019). There are rich *flamenco* scenes in Madrid and Barcelona and their respective autonomous communities (see Figure 15.1). This chapter explores how, through its construction and dissemination, *flamenco* has been meaningful as the quintessential expression of Andalusian identity even as its hybrid nature has kept changing to the present.

Flamenco

The primary elements of the *flamenco* genre are the following:

1. Participatory performance involving the close interaction among musicians, and between musicians and devoted fans (aficionados).
2. The expression of intense emotions through
   a. singing (**cante**)
   b. dancing (**baile**, not discussed here)
   c. instrumental performance (**toque**). The instrument is mainly *flamenco* or Spanish guitar: a long-necked, plucked lute with a waisted-shaped body, a flat back, and six nylon strings.
3. Diverse song types (here, **palos**), each identified by musical elements such as melodic mode, metric cycle, tempo, and others.
4. Creative performance anchored in a set of fixed musical codes.

This chapter's primary focus is on *cante* and *toque*. The song types featured in musical examples are the traditional **bulerías**, **soleares**, and **tangos**, as well as the **rumbas**—a music and dance genre of Afro-Cuban origin that was appropriated by *flamenco* musicians.

The Expression of Intense Emotions through Participatory Performance

On the evening of October 22, 2011, we attended a *flamenco* session at the Peña Flamenca de Córdoba (PFC) in Andalusia (Figure 15.3). The walls of the PFC were covered with images associated with the beloved genre. In the middle, a plaque reads: *Aquí se vive el "cante"* ("Here 'cante' [*flamenco* singing] is lived"). Welcomed cordially by the owner, we joined a group sitting around a long table drinking and chatting. By the time the performance started at midnight, a total of about sixty people had gathered. The *peña's* owner started the session by singing briefly, accompanied by a guitarist (**tocaor**) and about eight hand-clappers (**palmeros**) who marked the metric cycle (**compás**). After a break, the session continued uninterruptedly for over an hour featuring several **cantaores** (singers) who sang festive *palos* (song types) in succession, accompanied by

≡ **FIGURE 15.3** *Flamenco* session at the Peña Flamenca de Córdoba, Andalusia, October 22, 2011.

guitarists and handclappers. Following the end of an emotionally charged cadence, one of the participants rose from his chair and started to sing and dance. The guitarists and *palmeros* intensified their accompaniment by playing faster and louder, drawing strong enthusiasm from all those present who cheered *olé* (**jalear**), applauded, and whistled in admiration. This was clearly the climax of the session.

The essence of *cante flamenco* performance lies in the singer's capacity to evoke intense emotions, from passion and joy to grief and pain, through the singer's vocal artistry in dialogue with the instrumental accompaniment (Chuse, 2003). The expression of emotions through *flamenco* unfolds in the course of performance toward an emotional transformation, as we witnessed in the *peña* session. A good *cantaor/a* interprets the words and melody creatively and decides on structural aspects of the *cante*. The singer might add emotional depth and force to the lyrics through expressive tools like ***tempo rubato*** (fluctuating speed), repetition or changes in the order of words, ornamentation, microtonal inflections, **dynamics** (changes in volume), changes in the quality of vocal sound or register, and/or shouts or sobbing-like singing. Lyrics are often difficult to understand, as they are sung in the Andalusian variety of Spanish, occasionally mixed with *caló*, the language of Spanish Gitanos. Singers emphasize vocal expressivity rather than clear diction. The emotional intensity of *flamenco* performance is also expressed through the singer's bodily posture and gestures, such as tense facial expressions, shut eyes, clenched fists, hands placed on the chest, or open arms. When the performance includes dance, emotions are also embodied through codified body movements including the torso, hips, legs, footwork, arms, and hands.

Flamenco Cante (Song)

Flamenco lyrics consist of a vast corpus of orally transmitted **copla**s—sung verses of poetry often inspired by Andalusian and *Gitano* themes—and traditional Andalusian songs by prominent writers. They tend to be brief, direct, and contain dramatic poetic statements that reflect *Gitano* and Andalusian values and worldviews. Many *coplas* describe life in Andalusia, or relate personal experiences. Love is the predominant theme and is often portrayed as joyful, passionate, painful, and tragic. One's mother and loyal wife are portrayed as the repository of virtue and the family's honor. Other women like the prostitute, the widow, or the mother-in-law are depicted negatively. Other themes of *flamenco coplas* include Catholic faith, superstition, death as the inevitable destiny, or the extreme consequence of deep passion; the hardship of daily life; injustice; the historical persecution of *Gitanos*; or life in prison (Manuel 1989, 52–53).

The basic form of a *flamenco cante* (song) consists of several verses (*coplas*) alternated with short guitar interludes (*falsetas/variaciones*). In traditional *flamenco*, a composition is a flexible, dynamic, and open-ended structure shaped in the course of performance where singers often **improvise**. An elaborated performance of a *cante* typically begins with a guitar introduction that establishes the metric cycle (*compás*), tempo, **tonality**, and mood. The singer usually then follows with a short vocal section in which the voice is warmed up and this sets the mood for the *copla* by vocalizing syllables like "*Ayayay*" (**ayeo**). One of the most important expressive tools in *cante*, the *ayeo* also has other uses such as expressing complaint, pain, or sadness. Following the final *copla*, the guitar closes with melodic patterns characteristic of the song type.

The *flamenco tangos* "*De color de cera, mare*" ("Of wax color, mother") illustrates several characteristics of the genre's lyrics and song performance (Audio Example 15.1). The song recalls the historic neighborhood of Triana in Seville where flamenco was cultivated especially among *Gitanos*. This recording features La Niña

≡ **FIGURE 15.4** La Niña de los Peines.

🔊))

de los Peines (artistic name of Pastora Pavón, 1890–1969), one of the founding figures of *flamenco*, and one of the most outstanding *cantaoras* of all times (Cruces Roldán 2009; Figure 15.4). She synthesized and expanded on the artistry of *cantaoras* who preceded her and on several local styles, consolidating song types like *flamenco tangos*.

Ideally, the *tocaor* follows and responds to the melody performed by the singer; providing a harmonic grounding for the melody is one of the main responsibilities. The guitarist also provides melodic figurations and short transitional rhythmic and harmonic patterns between stanzas. Those interludes (*falsetas/variaciones*) between stanzas are an important part of the song as performed. "*De color de cera, mare*" (Audio Example 15.1) illustrates the perfect fit between La Niña's vocal style and Melchor de Marchena's mastery of *flamenco* guitar. You can also hear this in "*Falseta de soleá*" (Audio Example 15.2). Initially used to accompany the voice, the *flamenco* guitar developed into a widely popular solo practice with virtuoso players like Paco de Lucía.

Tonality and Harmony

Vocal melodies and the harmonic accompaniment of many songs are based on a distinctive scale that *flamenco* musicians refer to as the "**Andalusian mode**". What makes it distinctive is that the interval between the second and third pitches of the scale can be either a whole step or the less usual interval in European music of an augmented second (aug2) that consists of three half steps. The two variants of the scale are shown in Musical Example 15.1 in staff notation, beginning on E.

MUSICAL EXAMPLE 15.1 Two variants of the Andalusian mode.

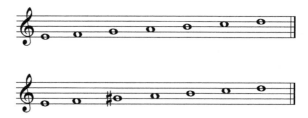

ACTIVITY 15.1

Listen several times to the *flamenco tangos* "*De color de cera, mare*" (Audio Example 15.1). Begin your listening by following the text. Then shift your attention to the form of the song as it is performed here. Photocopy the text and take notes on where you hear the vocables and the interchange between singer and guitar or the prominence of guitar.

"*De color de cera, mare*"	Of wax color, mother
0:00	Instrumental Introduction and ayeo
0:27	Stanza 1
A *De mare, de mare,*	Mother, mother
de color de cera, mare;	The color of wax, mother
B *De color de cera, mare*	Into the color of wax, mother
Tengo yo mis propias carnes,	My skin has turned,
C‖: *que me ha puesto tu querer*	Your love turned me this way
que no me conoce nadie ·‖	No one recognizes me:
0:55	Stanza 2
D *Pasa un encajero.*	A lacemaker is passing by.
Ay! Mare, yo me voy con él,	Oh! Mother, I'm going with him,
que tiene mucho salero.	He is very charming.
1:11	Stanza 3
E *Yo pasé por tu casita un día,*	As I passed by your house one day,
Y al passar por donde tú vivías	As I passed by where you lived
F *me acordaba yo de aquellos ratitos*	I remembered those moments
Ay!, que yo contigo tenía.	Oh! That I spent with you
1:39	Stanza 4
G *Hice un contrato contigo,*	I signed a contract with you,
la firma la tiré al mar;	I threw the signature into the sea;
H‖: *Fueron los peces testigos*	The fish were witnesses
Ay, de nuestra conformiá.:‖	Oh! To our agreement.
2:07	Stanza 5
I *¡Triana!*	Triana!
¡Qué bonita está Triana!	How beautiful is Triana!
J‖:*cuando le ponen al puente*	When they decorate the bridge
las banderitas gitanas.:‖	with Gypsy flags.
02:25–02:45	Stanza 6 followed by instrumental closure

K ¿Qué quieres de mí	What do you want from me
si a nadie miro a la cara	If I am unable to look into anyone's face
cuando me acuerdo de tí?	when I remember you?
K' ¿Si a nadie a la cara miro	If I am unable to look into anyone's face
cuando me acuerdo de tí?	when I remember you?

In addition to the Andalusian mode, some *palos* are set in the major mode of European music, while a few are in the minor mode. *Palos* tend to remain in the same mode, but some might briefly touch on another or alternate between two (Manuel 2006).

When the Andalusian mode is harmonized in the guitar accompaniment, a distinctive **chord progression** (sequence of chords) is formed. Occurring particularly frequently at cadences, the progression is so distinctive as to be called the **"Andalusian cadence"** (illustrated by Audio Example 15.3 and in Musical Example 15.2). This cadence is sometimes used in pop and rock music to evoke Andalusia, Spain, or Latin America.

MUSICAL EXAMPLE 15.2 Andalusian Cadence.

iv   III   II   I

Rhythm and Meter

Flamenco features both highly organized meter and rhythmic flexibility when performed. Its metric cycles (*compás*) are characterized by a number of counts and a specific distribution of accents that are emphasized through rhythm, melody, and harmonic changes. Most *palos* (but not all) are set to a metric cycle.

ACTIVITY 15.2

Listen again to *"De color de cera, mare"* (Audio Example 15.1) to focus on the melodic mode. It is predominantly in the "Andalusian mode," occasionally touching on the major mode or hovering between the major and "Andalusian" modes.

ACTIVITY 15.3

Until it becomes very familiar to you, listen to the Andalusian cadence (Audio Example 15.3). Then, continuing to focus attention on the guitar, listen to a different recorded song: a *soleá palo* titled "*Soleá de Alcalá*" (Audio Example 15.4) to assist you in identifying the recurrent use of the progression and to hear the complete cadence in the final chords.

The most characteristic *flamenco compás* consists of a cycle of twelve beats, divided into unequal units of three and two beats each. Within this cycle, the distribution of accents and the sequence of the beat units will vary, depending on the song type. The twelve-beat cycle for the widespread *palos* named *soleares* and *bulerías* is divided and accented as shown in Figure 15.5 (accents are shown in bold). The two song types are distinguished however, by tempo: *soleares* are performed in slow tempo, while *bulerías* are fast and lively.

Compás	1	2	**3**	4	5	**6**	7	**8**	9	**10**	11	**12**
Beat units			3			3		2		2		2

≡ **FIGURE 15.5** Schema of the twelve-beat *compás* of the *soleá* and *bulería* song-types.

In *flamenco*, both guitarist and *palmeros* (handclappers) guide the performance rhythmically. However, their parts are independent. While maintaining the *compás*, the instrumental accompaniment often results in **polyrhythmic patterns** (different rhythmic patterns played simultaneously) that sustain and complement the singing. In addition, dancers usually add a percussive component produced by foot stomping and castanets.

ACTIVITY 15.4

Following the schema of the twelve-beat *compás* shown in Figure 15.5, listen to the beat counting on "*Soleá de Alcalá*: Beat counting" (Audio Example 15.4), until you are comfortable with it. Then speak the counts of the *compás* with it, accentuating the beats indicated in bold. Note that the counting follows the convention used by *flamenco* musicians who usually start the cycle on beat 11 and count beats 11 and 12 as 1 and 2.

ACTIVITY 15.5

This Activity focuses on polyrhythmic patterns that are created even while the compass is maintained through a song. To begin, listen again to "*Soleá de Alcalá*: beat counting" (Audio Example 15.4), and count aloud the accented beats 3, 6, 8, 10, and 12. When you are comfortable with that, shift your listening to the guitar to hear the instrumentalist stress beats 3 and 10 through accent, harmonic changes, and percussive strumming with the fingernails. The guitarist also accents beat 12 by tapping on the soundboard, leading the singer into the stanza on beat 1.

Finally, listen to Audio Example 15.5 (*Soleá de Alcalá*: voice, guitar, and handclapping) to note how the **palmas** of the handclappers also accent beats 3, 8, 10, and 12 (see Figure 15.6; marked with an X). Palmas are also often heard on the half beats 1, 7, and 9 (marked with x). The (x) indicates the occasional occurrence of the *palmas*.

Compás	1	2	3	4	5	6	7	8	9	10	11	12
Palmas	x	x	X				x	x X	(x) x	X	x	X

≡ **FIGURE 15.6** Beat of *Soleá de Alcalá* (Audio Example 15.5).

Triple and quadruple metric cycles, with varying accents, are also common. Quadruple meter is illustrated by the *tangos* "*De color de cera, mare*" (Audio Example 15.1) with which you are already familiar.

Lyrics	De	ma	Re		de	Ma	re	
Compás	1	2	3	4	1	2	3	4

≡ **FIGURE 15.7** "De color de cera, mare" scheme.

Quadruple meter is also illustrated by Audio Example 15.6, the *rumba palo*, "*Entre dos aguas*" about which you will read in the next section of the chapter, along with one of the most popular triple meter *palos*, the **fandangos de Huelva**. Before

ACTIVITY 15.6

Listen again to the *flamenco tangos* "*De color de cera, mare*" (Audio Example 15.1) in the **quadruple meter** consisting of four-beat units divided into two pulses each. Refer to the start of the lyrics to locate the beginning of the pattern.

During much of the accompaniment, the guitar clearly stresses every beat, especially beat 1 (shown in bold in Figure 15.7), adding emphasis through strumming and percussive tapping on the soundboard while the *palmeros* mark the remaining beats.

LISTENING GUIDE

"De Color De Cera, Mare"

Performed by Pastora Pavón; artistic name: La Niña de los Peines (solo voice); accompanied by Melchor de Marchena (guitar)

Recording location and year: Barcelona, 1947

Instrumentation: Guitar, solo voice, *palmas* (handclaps)

Note: Bolded text indicates stress.

Time	Text	Something to Listen For
0:00		The guitar begins with three strummed (*rasgueado*) chords that are repeated, introducing the meter in fast tempo.
0:03		Clapping hands (*palmas*) enter, marking the meter throughout. Melodic figurations in the guitar follow, based on the Andalusian mode (on E) accompanied by calling out and cheering with "*Olé, Olé Pastora*" in invitation to the singer to begin.
0:13		The *cantaora* begins by vocalizing the syllable "ayayayaya . . . y," (ayeo) warming up her voice, setting the mood for the performance.
0:22		An instrumental interlude commences, consisting of melodic figurations on the guitar that are similar to the preceding ones.
0:27	A *De mare, de m**a**re,* *De color de cera, m**a**re; (Olé!)* B *De color de cera, m**a**re* *Tengo yo mis propias **carnes**,* C *Que me ha puesto tu querer* *Que no me conoce **nadie**.*	Stanza 1 opens with a quatrain on line 3 ("*De color de cera, mare*"), which is anticipated in the first and second lines. Three musical phrases (A, B, & C) unfold, each corresponding to two lines of the lyrics. Phrase A introduces the melodic idea. A call of "*olé*" is heard between phrases A and B, and Phrases B and C form an indivisible musical unit. The song lyrics address "mother," poetically speaking of the skin's turning to the color of wax, notably due to being in love.
0:55	D *Pasa un encaj**ero**.* *¡Ay! Mare, yo me voy con él,* *Que tiene mucho sal**ero**.*	Stanza 2 follows with no interruption, including a short expressive "ay!" in the beginning of line 2. It is set to a new musical phrase (D), which is, like phrase C, in the Andalusian mode (on E). The singer tells of a charming lacemaker passing by, and how she is "going with him."
1:04		An instrumental interlude commences, consisting of melodic figurations by the guitarist, accompanied by calls of "*Olé*"/"*Olé, Pastora*" that function to motivate the singer.

Time	Text	Something to Listen For
1:11	E *Yo pasé por tu casita un día,* *Y al passar por donde tú vivías* F *Me acordaba yo de aquellos ratitos* *¡Ay!, que yo contigo tenía.*	Stanza 3 consists of a quatrain set to two musical phrases (E & F) in which the singer recalls passing "by your house one day" . . . "where you lived" . . . and remembering moments spent together.
1:33	*Vamos, Melchor/olé primo*	An instrumental interlude consisting of melodic figurations on the guitar, accompanied by the encouragement of the guitar player by calling out *"Vamos, Melchor / olé primo"* ("Let us go Melchor / olé buddy").
1:39	G *Hice un contrato contigo,* *La firma la tiré al mar;* H *Fueron los peces testigos* *¡Ay!, de nuestra conformiá.*	In Stanza 4, the first line of phrase G touches on the major mode but returns to the Andalusian mode in phrase H, which is repeated with variation and contains another expressive short "ay!". The singer tells of signing a contract, then throwing it into the sea, and how "the fish were witnesses" to the agreement.
1:57		An instrumental interlude features the guitar's melodic figurations.
2:07	I *¡Triana!* *Qué bonita está Triana* J *Cuando le ponen al puente* *Las banderitas gitanas.*	In Stanza 5, phrases I and J remain in the Andalusian mode. Phrase J is repeated with variation. The lyrics refer to a place called "Triana," a beautiful place in which "they decorate the bridge with gypsy flags."
2:25	K *Qué quieres de mí* *Si a nadie miro a la cara* *Cuando me acuerdo de ti.* K' *Si a nadie a la cara miro* *Cuando me acuerdo de ti*	Stanza 6 features a new musical phrase, K, which is repeated with variation. The singer asks "What do you want from me if I am unable to look into anyone's face when I remember you?"
2:38		As closure, melodic figurations by the guitar in the Andalusian mode are followed by lively strumming of the final chords.

proceeding to the next section, however, following the Listening Guide will help you review much of what you have learned about flamenco thus far. Translation of the text is found in Activity 15.1.

New Paths: *Nuevo Flamenco*

Young artists and groups who were exposed to transnational popular musics in the 1960s and 1970s rejected the conservative movement of "authentic" *flamenco*. Part of a larger modernizing trend in Spanish popular music, they sought to revitalize the genre and attract new audiences. Since the late 1960s, *flamenco* artists and popular music groups in Spain have created new hybrids, mixing *flamenco* with rock, pop, blues, funk, soul, Latin American, Arabic, and Spanish popular musics. Groups and individuals like Smash, Lole y Manuel, Triana, Los Chunguitos, Los Chichos, Las Grecas, and Veneno pioneered this trend. In the 1980s, groups like Pata Negra and Ketama mixed *flamenco* with blues and salsa. Since the 1990s, many artists and groups, most notably La Barbería del Sur, Diego El Cigala, Estrella Morente, and Miguel Poveda have mixed the genre with a wide range of popular music styles. At the same time, many Spanish popular music groups have incorporated elements derived from *flamenco*.

The term ***nuevo flamenco*** was coined in the 1980s by the record company Nuevos Medios as a commercial label to promote artists and groups that created this new music. Scholars, musicians, and promoters adopted this and other labels including *flamenco fusión*, *flamenco pop*, and *flamenco rock* for productions that rejected a conservative approach to the genre (Steingress 2002, 2004). Since the 1980s, *nuevo flamenco* has gradually taken root and spread on a global scale, introducing new technologies in recording and performance (Berlanga 1997) that coexist with traditional *flamenco*. Three musicians especially—singer Camarón de la Isla, guitarist Paco de Lucía, and singer and composer Enrique Morente—created a new aesthetic that revolutionized the genre. All three musicians were steeped in traditional *flamenco* and also influenced by transnational music styles, and several of the earlier *nuevo flamenco* groups.

Icons of *Nuevo Flamenco:* Camarón de la Isla and Paco de Lucía

Camarón de la Isla (1950–1992)—the stage name of the legendary *cantaor* José Monge Cruz—was born to a *Gitano* family of *cantaores* in the province of Cádiz. In the late 1960s, he settled in Madrid where he formed an artistic partnership with Paco de Lucía, with whom he performed and recorded extensively. He also worked with other prominent *flamenco* musicians. In 1979, he released the landmark album *La leyenda del tiempo* (*The Legend of Time*), produced by Ricardo Pachón. It made a major contribution to shaping *nuevo flamenco*, mixing the *flamenco* idiom with stylistic elements from pop, rock, and Latin American music. Following this album, rock instrumentation and the electric sound became common in *nuevo flamenco*. The most popular track, "Volando Voy" (composed by Kiko Veneno), is a *rumba*.

Guitarist and composer Paco de Lucía (Figure 15.8)—the stage name of Francisco Sánchez Gómez (1947–2014)—formed several groups of which the most

ACTIVITY 15.6

Search online for a performance of *"Volando voy"* by Camarón, and sing along with the **refrain**— in a song, a stanza text that recurs with the same melody.

Volando voy, volando vengo
I go flying, I come flying
por el camino yo me entretengo
On the way, I entertain myself

≡ **FIGURE 15.8** Paco de Lucía in concert, Auditorio Kursaal, Donostia, Basque Country, Spain, November 2010.

successful was the Sexteto de Paco de Lucía, founded in 1981. It consolidated the flute and electric bass within the *flamenco* aesthetic and introduced the **cajón**, a box-shaped percussion instrument of Peruvian origin. Furthermore, he revitalized guitar accompaniment and placed the *flamenco* guitar at center stage, influencing younger *tocaores*. The best-known *flamenco* artist internationally, de Lucía gained wide national and international popularity through his album *Fuente y Caudal* (1973), especially the *rumba "Entre dos aguas"* (Activity 15.7). He performed and recorded extensively with different musicians, including the prestigious jazz guitarists John McLaughlin, Al Di Meola, and Larry Coryell and pianist Chick Corea.

Following an Introduction, this version *of "Entre dos aguas"* consists of three clearly marked sections of approximately equal length: Introduction: 00:00–00:21; Section 1: 00:22–02:22; Section 2: 02:23–04:13; Section 3: 04:13–06:00. Listen next to the entire composition to hear the sectional structure. Then listen again to answer this question: How are the transitions between sections marked?

"Entre dos aguas," a challenging example of *nuevo flamenco*, mixes melodic modes and introduces a new harmonic vocabulary such as ninth and eleventh chords and occasional dissonances (unstable or discordant chords). Drawing on those musical elements, each section is characterized by cyclically repeated chord progressions and distinct melodic and rhythmic material. The Listening Guide for *"Entre dos aguas"* will guide you through some of the detail.

LISTENING GUIDE

Rumba: "Entre dos aguas"

Performed by Paco de Lucía, composed by Paco de Lucía and José Torregrosa

Recording location and year: 1973, from the album *Fuente y Caudal*

Instrumentation: Guitar, bass, bongo drums

Something to Listen For	
0:00–0:21	**Introduction** Begins with each musician introducing a structural element of the composition: the bass line, the *compás* on the entrance of the bongo drums (00:06), and the chord progression on the guitar (00:11) that will be repeated throughout this section, each chord lasting for two measures: Am7 – Bm7 – Am7 – B7.
0:22–2:22	**Section 1** Following the introduction, the solo guitar plays the main melody that is repeated and elaborated in an improvisatory style through the remainder of the section, adding ornaments common in flamenco guitar. The section ends with a long held chord on B7.
2:23–4:13	**Section 2** This section consists of three melodic ideas (A, B, C) based on the chord progression Em – D7 – C7 – B7 corresponding to the "Andalusian cadence" that lands on B7 with additional chords, each lasting for two measures. The entire chord progression totals eight measures and is repeated throughout this section. The melodic ideas are presented and varied in the following sequence: 02:23–02:40 A, A1. 02:26–02:42 02:41–03:17 B, B1, B2, B3. 03:17–03:44 C, C1, C. 03:45–04:13 A, A1, A2.
4:13–6:00	**Section 3** This section is based on a two-chord harmonic progression (D7 – Em) extending over two measures. It is repeated and elaborated on up to the end, occasionally alluding to the sonority of the Brazilian *bossa nova*. Using an additive sequential structure, this section includes rapid melodic and rhythmic figurations. The composition culminates with a virtuosic section by the guitarist and then fades away to its conclusion.

ACTIVITY 15.7

Listen to the *rumba "Entre dos aguas"* (*Between Two Waters*), composed and performed by Paco de Lucía accompanied by a small instrumental ensemble (Audio Example 15.6). It is rhythmically grounded in the *rumba flamenca*, in quadruple meter and characterized by the accent on the first beat, allowing for syncopation (accenting a beat countering the regularly stressed beats in a meter). Your first listening should focus on that meter and rhythm through the whole composition.

Conclusion

Flamenco today is a highly dynamic local practice, cultural industry, tourist attraction, and world music phenomenon. Artists and community members maintain the core repertoire and "traditional" practices. In addition, a good number of artists are continually "renovating" *flamenco*, mixing it with myriad other styles. *Flamenco* and associated artifacts (guitars, costumes, and audio and video recordings, among others) are marketed in Spain and abroad, where one can find practitioners, schools, festivals, and performance venues. At the same time, *flamenco* continues to be constructed and disseminated as the quintessential expression of Andalusian and Spanish identities.

Bibliography

Berlanga, Miguel Ángel. 1997. "Tradición y Renovación: Reflexiones en torno al Antiguo y Nuevo Flamenco." TRANS: Transcultural Music Review (Special Issue TRANS Iberia). http://www.sibetrans.com/trans/articulo/311/tradicion-y-renovacion-reflexiones-en-torno-al-antiguo-y-nuevo-flamenco". Last accessed 06/10/2020.

Castelo-Branco, Salwa El-Shawan, and Susana Moreno Fernández, 2019. *Music in Portugal and Spain: Experiencing Music, Expressing Culture*. New York: Oxford University Press.

Chuse, Loren. 2003. *The Cantaoras: Music, Gender, and Identity in Flamenco Song*. London: Routledge.

Cruces Roldán, Cristina. 2009. *La Niña de los Peines. El Mundo Flamenco de Pastora Pavón*. Córdoba, Spain: Almuzara.

Machin-Autenrieth, Matthiew. 2013. *Andalucía Flamenca: Music, Regionalism and Identity in Southern Spain*. PhD diss. University of Cambridge.

Machin-Autenrieth, Matthiew. 2017. *Flamenco, Regionalism, and Musical Heritage in Southern Spain*. London: Routledge.

Manuel, Peter. 1989. "Andalusian, Gypsy, and Class Identity in the Contemporary Flamenco Complex." *Ethnomusicology* 33 (1): 47–65.

Manuel, Peter. 2006. "Flamenco in Focus: An Analysis of the Performance of Soleares." In *Analytical Studies in World Music*, edited by M. Tenzer, 92–119. New York: Oxford University Press.

Steingress, Gerhard. 2002. "Flamenco Fusion and New Flamenco as Postmodern Phenomena: An Essay on Creative Ambiguity in Popular Music." In *Songs of the Minotaur. Hybridity and Popular Music in the Era of Globalization. A Comparative Analysis of Rebetika, Tango, Rai, Flamenco, Sardana, and English Urban Folk*, edited by Gerhard Steingress, 169–217. Münster, Germany: LIT-Verlag.

Steingress, Gerhard. 2004. "La Hibridación Transcultural como Clave de la Formación del Nuevo Flamenco (Aspectos Histórico-sociológicos, Analíticos y Comparativos)." *TRANS: Transcultural Music Review* 8. http://www.sibetrans.com/trans/articulo/198/la-hibridacion-transcultural-como-clave-de-la-formacion-del-nuevo-flamenco-aspectos-historico-sociologicos-analiticos-y-comparativos. Last accessed 06/10/2020

Washabaugh, William. 2012. *Flamenco Music and National Identity in Spain*. Farnham, England: Ashgate.

16

Music in Ireland

Historical Continuity and Community in Irish Traditional Music

DOROTHEA E. HAST AND STANLEY SCOTT

Chapter Contents

Introduction

With roots in rural Ireland, Irish traditional music today has a strong link to history, identity, and heritage. As meaningful symbols of shared culture, traditional songs, tunes, and dances bring people together to celebrate and commemorate past experiences and events including centuries of political struggle under British rule, emigration, the formation of modern Ireland, and the creation of diasporic

≡ **Session at The Cobblestone, Dublin, October 2017. Musicians (R to L): Paul O'Shaughnessy, fiddle; Kate O'Shaughnessy, fiddle and Tom O'Shaughnessy (flute).**

FIGURE 16.1 Map of contemporary Ireland, including the twenty-six counties of the Republic of Ireland and, in the northeastern-most part of the island, the six counties of Northern Ireland.

communities around the world. Our emphasis will be on music and musical contexts that reflect this collective experience, demonstrating both the continuity and flexibility of the tradition over time and the dynamic interface between past and present.

This chapter begins with a glimpse of Ireland's turbulent political history as a way to contextualize the following traditions:

1. Songs in the Irish and English languages, many of which document historical people, places, and events. While songs in both traditions range from melancholy love ballads to boisterous drinking songs, we will focus on one genre of allegorical song in the Irish language and three emigration songs in English.
2. Dance tunes: the thousands of jigs, reels, hornpipes, and other tune types that are played as instrumental music at sessions, on recordings, and at concerts around the world and are also used to accompany two important dance traditions—Irish set and step dance.

We frame our discussion around a very old traditional music session in County Clare in the far west of Ireland. Although Irish traditional music has been influenced by professionalism and globalization, informal sessions are still at the heart of the tradition, providing a primary context for playing, singing, sharing, and passing on music and dance genres. We use this particular session as a springboard to further explore old and new repertoire in the Irish tradition.

History

The Celts controlled Ireland for over a thousand years, creating a rich legacy of language (Irish Gaelic), oral literature, and music. British colonialization of Ireland began in the twelfth century. Tightening their control, repressive legislation against the Irish began in the fourteenth century and intensified in the late sixteenth and early seventeenth centuries. By the eighteenth and nineteenth centuries, progressively stricter laws were enacted restricting the Catholic religion, the Irish language, land ownership, and voting rights. The Irish often responded with active resistance ranging from rhetoric to rebellion; every uprising had balladeers and poets who served to politicize issues, rally popular support, and chronicle history. Their ballads, often published on sheets called **broadsides**, commented on all aspects of the Irish struggle for religious and political freedom. As the renowned modern traditional singer and song collector Frank Harte said, "Those in power write the history, while those who suffer write the songs, and, given our history, we have an awful lot of songs" (Moloney 2005).

Irish emigration to North America began in the late seventeenth century, but increased in the eighteenth when many Irish were forced out of the country to escape religious discrimination, high taxes, and food shortages. The next large wave of emigration began in the early nineteenth century, when absentee landlords turned many Irish farmers off their lands. The widespread loss of land crippled the Irish economy. High taxes discouraged local industries, while anti-Catholic legislation and population growth spawned further economic depression. Over a million Irish emigrated to North America between 1815 and 1844 (Figure 16.2). "American wakes"—events that simultaneously celebrated and mourned the loss of a neighbor bound for North America—were important community rituals that included dances, instrumental tunes, and songs. Many farewell songs were composed as mementos of the familiar landscapes of home and loved ones.

The largest single wave of emigration occurred between 1845 and 1851 as a result of "The Great Famine" (*An Gorta Mór*: "The Great Hunger"). Originally caused by the failure of the potato crop over successive years due to a fungal blight, it was especially devastating because the potato was central to the Irish diet. The British colonial government mishandled the situation, with the result that over one million people died from starvation or diseases related to malnutrition. More than 1.6 million were forced to emigrate, the majority to North America; and many others to England, Australia, and New Zealand. Even after the famine ended, emigration continued to be a necessity due to the lack of industry and widespread poverty. Approximately three million more Irish came to America between 1855 and 1914.

In Ireland itself, the nationalist movement gained strength during the late nineteenth century and later turned into a fight for a free Irish state. During this

≡ **FIGURE 16.2**
Irish emigrants wait for their passage to Canada and America in the 1840s.

period known as the Gaelic Revival, traditional music, dance, literature, and the Irish language were harnessed to celebrate Ireland's rich cultural past and promote the ideal of Irish independence. Emigration songs—each praising a piece of the Irish landscape—contributed to the nationalist ethos. Taken collectively, this repertory inculcated love for the entire country among Irish at home and abroad—and stoked resentment against colonial policies that made emigration necessary.

After two years of a conflict known as the Irish War of Independence (1919–1921), a self-governing Irish state was finally achieved, but at a price: the country would be partitioned into two parts, north and south. The Irish Free State was established in 1922, giving twenty-six of Ireland's thirty-two counties independence within the British Commonwealth. The Free State, with its capital in Dublin, became the fully independent Irish Republic in December 1948. The remaining six counties were part of Northern Ireland, which had a distinct Protestant/pro-British majority and remained directly under British rule (see Figure 16.1).

Over time, politics in Northern Ireland became increasingly divided between Catholics and Protestants, leading to twenty-five years (c. 1969–1994) of sectarian violence and bloodshed known as "The Troubles." The 1998 Peace Accord brought home rule to Northern Ireland and a huge reduction in sectarian violence, but flare-ups continue to the present day. The ongoing political situation has spawned generation after generation of topical songwriters.

A Session in County Clare, Ireland

To illustrate the meaningful links between traditional music, history, and community, we turn to a session of traditional music and dance that thrived for generations in the hamlet of Coore, near Miltown Malbay in West Clare. It serves to show how all the strands of Irish traditional culture—music, dancing, singing, and the art of entertaining conversation—are inextricably bound together in an evening's entertainment. It reveals music as an essential part of a community, serving as a social magnet and a congenial background for the negotiation of local transactions. The community surrounding the music is vital to the overall musical experience. Because of its locale and mix of Irish and foreign participants, this session serves as a window into the culture of Irish traditional music, past and present: its perceived and actual base in rural Ireland, its strong link to community and history, the simultaneous present of old and new repertory, and the use of indigenous and adopted instruments.

Invitation to a Session

"Listen, Stan and Dora. There will be music, dancing, and singing tonight at Gleesons Pub in Coore," says Jerry O' Reilly. He leans over our table and draws a small map, providing directions for a twelve-mile drive along the western Irish coast and then inland on narrow, hedged country roads. We are sitting in a small restaurant in the coastal town of Ennistymon, where dozens of singers from Ireland and abroad have gathered for a weekend festival of traditional singing. It is Sunday evening, and the festival has begun to wind down. Jerry moves quietly between tables, inviting a handful of friends to the session.

Gleesons has hosted music, singing, and dancing on Sunday nights for four generations in the small farming hamlet of Coore. Today, festivals, schools, universities, clubs, competitions, and concert halls provide important venues for Irish traditional music; but those are, by definition, *contrived* occasions, created to promote the tradition. Gleesons provides a different kind of experience, in a community where the music has been patronized by local people and performed by local musicians for generations. Jerry's approach is therefore both welcoming and protective: he wants to share this special session, but is wary of drawing in people who would not respect its sensitive cultural ecology.

At half-past nine we set out. The Atlantic sparkles to the west, while the verdant hills of West Clare roll gently to the east. The narrow roads grow narrower still as we approach Coore. We dip and bounce over a short bridge and find ourselves before a farmhouse attached to a long, low pub with the words "Gleesons" and "Coore" above the door.

We park among a dozen cars and enter the pub. A small passageway leads into a spacious room; we find ourselves facing a large fireplace and two tables where a number of older patrons sit talking. A small stage with four empty chairs, an accordion, and several fiddle cases occupies the back corner. Photographs of musicians adorn the walls (Figure 16.3), alongside poems by Junior Crehan, the eighty-nine-year-old fiddler who has led these Sunday night sessions for more than fifty years. The remainder of the long back wall is taken up by the bar, where pub owners Jim and Nell Gleeson and their children serve drinks.

We are greeted by regular attenders of the session. Some, born within a mile of the pub, have danced to Junior Crehan's music all their lives. Others have moved here from Dublin, London, or the United States, drawn by West Clare's rich musical traditions. Some are expatriate Irish who return home from England and America during summer holidays. Local patrons include farmers (like the Gleesons themselves, and many musicians who have played in the pub over the years), old-age pensioners, teachers, students, and folklorists.

FIGURE 16.3
Musicians at Gleesons Pub in 1978. Members of the original house band include (L to R) Michael Downes, Junior Crehan, Josie Hayes and Pat Kelly; Barry Taylor far right.

After some minutes, the musicians move to the stage. Junior Crehan and Michael Downes are senior fiddlers, in their eighties. Kitty Hayes, whose late husband Josie played flute with Junior for seven decades, plays concertina. Eamon McGivney, fiddler, and Conor Keane, accordionist, represent a younger generation of players steeped in local traditions. Peter Labane (tin whistle and *uilleann* pipes) and Geoff and Gabi Wooff (fiddles), European continentals drawn to Clare by their love of the music, complete the ensemble.

They begin with a lilting **jig**, "The Mist Covered Mountain," composed by Junior Crehan. He has composed some forty tunes, many of which have entered the traditional repertoire (Munnelly 1998, 70). Every few minutes, the musicians switch to a new tune, moving seamlessly from one melody to the next. Finishing their first set of jigs, the musicians chat and refresh themselves with drinks Nell Gleeson has placed beside them: pints of Guinness stout, or glasses of soda water with lemon and a cherry. Their thirst temporarily quenched, the players launch into a set of reels. (To hear a set of reels, listen to Audio Example 16.1: "Maid Behind the Bar/Gregg's Pipes).

The music is lightly amplified; "anchor" players Junior, Eamon, and Connor play into microphones, but the music is kept down to a level that allows patrons at the bar to carry on conversations. Jimmy Gleeson explains:

> People that come in there want to come in and converse and talk and maybe sell a bullock or a heifer or something like that among themselves. It's a farming community. So it's very important that you can hold a conversation, listen to the music if you want to. If someone is singing then, that's the one time, the only thing I want to hear when someone is singing is the big clock ticking. And you know when you can hear the clock ticking that you have silence.

We talk with friends as the musicians continue to play, sip their drinks, and converse. Their playing is neither a concert nor background music; they are a complete unit among themselves, playing for each other and immensely enjoying one another's company. They make no announcements to the crowd, but joke with each other, enjoying the *craic* (chat) as they pause between two or more tunes that are played one after another without break. Their self-involvement makes no demands on the patrons, but their presence and music enliven and enrich the whole atmosphere of the pub.

Then several dancers gather before the stage and ask Junior to provide music for the "Caledonian Set." Conversation subsides, as all eyes move to the dance floor. The musicians launch into a fast reel for the first section of this traditional set dance and four couples begin moving gracefully through the figures, stepping in time to the music. As the dancers conclude their set, conversation resumes, and the musicians begin a new set of reels.

After this medley, a solo voice rises with the first notes of a song. Half a dozen tongues "shush" the crowd. Tim Dennehy is the singer; he moved from Dublin to West Clare some two decades back, drawn by music. A founder of Dublin's *Góilín* Singer's Club, he now broadcasts traditional music for Clare FM, a radio station based in the nearby town of Ennis. He frequently sings *sean-nós* ("old-style") repertoire in Irish Gaelic, but on this occasion he chooses an English-language song, "Farewell to Miltown Malbay." (To locate Miltown Malbay in County Clare, see Figure 16.1.) Tim continues his solo, unaccompanied performance through seven verses written by local poet, school teacher, and Gaelic scholar, Tomás O'hAodha (1866–1935). This song praises the beauty of West Clare, the kind hearts of its people, and local cultural traditions, including the piping of Garrett Barry—a cousin of Junior Crehan's grandmother. A powerful vein of praise for places and people (particularly musicians) runs through the culture of Irish traditional music, providing strong motivation to pass these songs, tunes, and stories on to future generations. Songs and dance tunes are so frequently linked to particular singers, players, places, and events that every step one takes toward the music (as a singer, player, dancer, or listener) seems to envelop one further among the threads of the culture that surrounds it.

As the night continues, more unaccompanied songs in both Irish and English are interspersed with dance tune **medleys** (two are more tunes most often in the same meter, that are played one after another without break), a solo step dance and another set performed by eight dancers. The musicians finally stop playing around 1 AM as the session winds down for the evening.

Many of the songs performed this evening were passed down orally, collected, published, and recorded. Contemporary collections, such as Terry Moylan's *The Indignant Muse: Poetry and Songs of the Irish Revolution 1887–1926* (2016), broaden our understanding of historical events from multiple perspectives. By performing these songs today, singers convey snapshots of history and tap into a powerful well of collective experience. The songs retain poignancy and relevance because they are frequently linked with particular singers who pass them down, as well as specific places and events, such as the Rising of 1798, the Easter Rising of 1916, the War of Independence, and centuries of emigration. Whether performed in the most traditional style by a single unaccompanied voice in free rhythm, as we heard at Gleesons, or repackaged with newer kinds of accompaniment, these songs create a powerful link between past and present.

Sean-nós: "Old-style" Songs in Irish

Sean-nós ("old style") songs in the Irish language constitute the bedrock of Irish traditional singing today, rooted in traditions that predate British rule and, in some instances, the arrival of Christianity. Like the Irish language, *sean-nós* singing became an important cultural symbol in the Gaelic revival of the late nineteenth century. There are several genres of *sean-nós*: love songs, lullabies, vision poems, laments, seasonal songs, drinking songs, humorous songs, bawdy lyrics, hymns, work songs, and topical songs.

Uirchill A' Chreagáin ("Creggan Graveyard"; Audio Example 16.2) demonstrates the sound of *sean-nós* through an ***aisling*** ("vision poem") composed by the eighteenth-century poet Art McCooey. In medieval *aislingí*, the poet recounted a dream meeting with a woman of supernatural beauty. In eighteenth century *aislingí*, the story became a political allegory, in which a series of questions and answers revealed the beautiful woman to be the personification of Ireland,

◁))

≡ **FIGURE 16.4** Singer Pádraigín Ni Uallacháin.

awaiting deliverance from foreign rule (Shields 1993, 74; Henigan 1999, 7; Ní Uallacháin, interview with authors, 2001).

"Creggan Graveyard" belongs to this allegorical tradition. In Audio Example 16.2, Pádraigín Ni Uallacháin (Figure 16.4) sings four verses of this song. In verse one, the poet is kissed by a beautiful fairy woman at daybreak, after spending a sorrowful night in a graveyard of poets, singers, harpers, and chieftains (Ní Uallacháin 2003, 254). In verse two, the fairy woman invites the poet to travel with her to a sweet land where "the foreigner has no hold." In verse three, the poet laments the loss of the "heirs of the Fews," the Gaelic chieftains of Ulster. Here the poet sings longingly of bygone days under Irish rulers and the generous patronage poets enjoyed before British rule. In verse four, he requests that when he dies, he be laid to rest beside the poets and chieftains of Creggan Graveyard. The full English translation is given in the Listening Guide .

Pádraigín's performance reveals several common characteristics of *sean-nós* singing. The texture is sparse: one unaccompanied voice. The timbre is warm and intimate, and the pitch and volume are slightly higher than that of a speaking voice—elevated enough to indicate that something more passionate than normal conversation is going on. The melody is richly ornamented, and its contour reinforces the meaning of the text. For example, in verse one, the highest note of line B (at 0:17, as noted in the Listening Guide below) renders the word *maidne,* "daybreak." Line C is musically identical to line A except for its final notes (at 0:36); its lower ending pitch calls attention to the words *mar or* ("like gold"), describing the hair of the young woman in the poet's vision. In line D, the highest notes (at 0:39) correspond to *íocshláinte an domhain,* the "cure" for the world's ills.

Perhaps the most remarkable aspect of this performance is its use of **free rhythm** (without pulse or meter so there is little or no sense of predictability about the organization of time), to emphasize the meaning and emotion of the text. Just as the timbre, pitch, and volume of this singing are closely related to those of a speaking voice, the cadence and timing of speech override other musical factors in its rhythm. As Irish musicologist Seán O'Boyle wrote:

ACTIVITY 16.1

Listen to the full recording of "Creggan Graveyard" (Audio Example 16.2) several times, until you can easily follow the flow of the text. Then shift your listening to other elements of the song. How would you describe the rhythm, timbre, pitch, and volume of this singing?

Even without knowing the Irish language, you can map the rhythm by listening closely to one verse. Take note of the timing for particularly long-held syllables. Listen further for moments when you imagine that you are hearing special expressivity. To hear a complete performance of this song, along with detailed commentary, go to https://www.orielarts.com/songs/uirchill-a-chreagain/

Whilst a *sean-nós* singer reflects the stresses of a poetic metre in his performance, he does not feel bound . . . [by that metre]. Being involved in the atmosphere and meaning of the song, he moves from stress to stress at his own pace which is really dictated by the feeling he puts into the words and by the amount of ornamentation and the number of stops he chooses to use in his gracing or "humouring" of a tune. (O'Boyle 1976, 17)

Instruments in the Irish Tradition

Musical instruments played at sessions similar to the one at Gleesons Pub often include the fiddle, harp, bagpipes, and flute, which became part of the Irish tradition by the eighteenth century. Of these, the harp and the *uilleann* (Irish "elbow") pipes are the most distinctly Irish representatives; the other instruments were found in similar forms throughout Europe. The Irish harp has been an important symbol of Irish identity for over 1,000 years, appearing on coins from the sixteenth century to the present day.

Uilleann pipes are a bagpipe type of aerophone: a set of reeds are enclosed in cylindrical pipes, which are attached to an air reservoir in the form of a bag. The **uilleann pipes** are smaller and quieter than the more familiar Scottish Highland pipes, bellows blown (rather than breath blown), and played indoors in a seated position. Air for the Uillean pipes is supplied from bellows held under the right arm, pumped by the elbow. A full set of pipes includes a chanter (fingered melody pipe), three drone pipes that play only one pitch each, and three regulator pipes that contain individual keys depressed by the heel of the player's right hand to add harmonic accompaniment.

LISTENING GUIDE

"Uirchill a' Chreagáin" (Creggan Graveyard)

Performed by Pádraigín Ní Uallacháin (1995)

Recording location and year: Dublin, Ireland, 1995

Instrumentation: Female voice

Time	Text	Translation	Something to Listen For
0:00	Line A: *Ag Úirchill a Chreagáin sea chodail mé aréir faoi bhrón,*	By Creggan Graveyard I slept last night in sorrow	Verse 1 begins: Entrance of vocalist
0:13	Line B: *'S le héirí na maidne tháinig ainnir fá mo dhéin le póig,*	At daybreak I was kissed by a young woman	
0:17	*maidne*	daybreak	Highest note reached in Line B on *maidne* (daybreak)
0:25	Line C: *Bhí gríosghrua ghartha aici agus loinnir ina céibh mar ór,*	With flaming cheeks and a golden lustre in her hair	Melody in Line C almost identical to Line A
0:36	*mar*	Like gold	Lower ending pitch on *mar* (like gold) in Line C
0:39	Line D: *'S gurbh é íocshláinte an domhain bheith ag amharc ar an ríoghain óir.*	One look of her would cure all the world's ills.	D begins with its highest notes on *íocshláinte an domhain* (the cure for the world's ills)
0:51	*Ó a fhialfhir charthannaigh, ná caitear thusa i néalta bróin, Ach éirigh go tapaidh agus aistrigh liom siar sa ród Go tír dheas na meala nach bhfuair Gaillibh inti réim go fóill, 'S gheobhair aoibhneas ar hallaí a' mo mhealladhsa le siansaí ceoil.*	My kind young man do not sleep in sorrow But rise swiftly and come along the road with me To the land of honey where the foreigner has no hold Where you will find happiness enticing me with sweet music.	Verse 2 begins

Time	Text	Translation	Something to Listen For
1:40	*'Sé mo ghéar-ghoin tinnis gur theastaigh uainn Gaeil Thír Eoghain* *Agus oidhrí an Fheadha gan se-aghais faoi líg dár gcomhai* *Géaga glandaite Néill Fhrasaigh nach dtréigfeadh an ceol,* *'S chuirfeadh éideadh fán Nollaig ar na hollaimh bheadh ag géil-leadh dóibh.'*	It is my great pain that we lost the Gaels of Tyrone And the heirs of the Fews now nearby in silent tombs Niall Frasach's good people who never rejected music But at Christmas would clothe the poets who served them well.	Verse 3 begins
2:32	*A théagair 's a chuisle más cinniúin duit mé mar stór* *Tabhair léagsa is gealladh sula ra-chaidh muid ar aghaidh sa ród* *Má éagaim fán tSionainn i gCríoch Mhanainn nó fán Éigipt Mhór* *Gurb' i gCill chumhra an Chreagáin a leagfar mé i gcré faoi fhód.*	My own my dear if you are fated to be my love Promise me before we go along the road That if I should die in Shannon, the Isle of Man or in great Egypt Bury me then in the fresh clay of Creggan Graveyard	Verse 4 begins

Free reed aerophones, such as the **accordion**, melodeon, and **concertina**, were introduced to Ireland in the nineteenth century and have become mainstays of the tradition. These "squeeze box" instruments are a family of aerophones with a box of some shape for a body, inside of which is encased a set of free reeds in a frame. The reeds are set into vibration by air that is supplied by a bellows. Individual notes are produced by the depression of buttons or keys. The concertina, the smallest member in this family, has a hexagonal shaped body with buttons on each side. The Anglo model, which plays a different note on the press and draw of the bellows, became especially popular in Ireland by the last decade of the nineteenth century and is a staple at sessions today.

Although whistle-like instruments have been found in archeological sites both in Ireland and throughout Europe, the modern form of the **tin whistle** was created in the early to mid-nineteenth century in England. A fipple style with mouthpiece, end-blown flute with six holes, it is in the same family as the recorder and was originally made of tin plate. Tin whistles today are made from a variety of materials, including brass, nickel plated brass, aluminum, plastic, and wood.

Other instruments were adopted in the twentieth century, including the *bodhrán*, guitar, mandolin, tenor banjo, and bouzouki. The **bodhrán** is a frame drum played with the fingers or a wooden beater. Originally a farm tool and ritual instrument, it only began appearing in sessions, concerts, and recordings in the 1960s. The **banjo** is a fretted, long-necked, plucked lute with a shallow circular frame body covered with a skin or plastic head. Rooted in African and African American traditions, the banjo became known on both sides of the Atlantic in the nineteenth century through minstrel shows. While both the four- and five-string banjos are played today in Ireland, the tenor banjo (invented c.1908–1915, with four strings and a shorter neck, and played with a plectrum) has been the more popular instrument in traditional music since the 1960s. The **bouzouki** is a fretted, long-necked plucked lute adapted from the Greek instrument by the same name. The Irish bouzouki has a flat back; four double, metal strings; and up to twenty-six frets.

Dance Types

Two genres of dances were performed at the session we attended at Gleesons Pub. A **set dance** is a genre of social dance that is performed by four couples in square formation. A **step dance** is a virtuosic solo or group dance characterized by a straight upper body and intricate footwork. Dancers use both hard and soft shoes in step dance performance: hard shoe dances allow for loud percussive footwork, while soft shoe dances are more aerial and graceful in nature. Step dancing became an international sensation with performances of the professional Riverdance troupe in the 1990s; a YouTube posting in 2013 titled "Riverdance, the final performance" has to date received over ten million hits.

Set dances were brought to Ireland by French dancing masters in the nineteenth century. Originally called "Sets of Quadrilles," these social dances were also exported from France to England and the United States. They were indigenized in Ireland by new choreography and the use of Irish dance tunes for accompaniment (Brennan 2001, 25–28). While set dances have enjoyed a remarkable revival all over Ireland during the last thirty years, areas like Coore have had an almost unbroken set-dancing tradition since the genre was introduced. Each figure or section of the set is associated with a specific dance tune type.

Dance Tune Types

The repertory of "dance" tunes types includes jigs, reels, hornpipes, slides, waltzes, and polkas. Each type consists of a single melodic line that can be played as a purely instrumental piece or to accompany step or set dances.

ACTIVITY 16.2

Watch a video of dancers performing the first figure of the Caledonian set, a popular set dance from Clare (Video 16.1). The context is a *"céilí"* (social dance event) in which there is live music performed by the Johnny Reidy Céilí Band. Before they begin, the dancers are grouped together in squares consisting of four couples each.

A set consists of a series of figures (usually between three and six), each consisting of a sequence of movements performed by the dancers. For example, in figure one of the Caledonian, the first sequence is "all join hands in a circle and advance and retire twice," performed to eight bars of music. The second sequence is for couples to swing or "dance at home" for another eight bars of music. Each subsequent sequence is clearly timed to eight-bar sections of the accompanying tunes. As you watch the entire first figure of the Caledonian set, notice that sequences include some movements in which all four couples are dancing in each square at the same time and other movements in which only two couples are dancing. All the couples move in prescribed patterns from a home position (called tops or sides) to which they always return. The first figure ends when the music stops and there is a brief break before the second figure begins.

The melodies of the majority of dance tunes (but not all) are in binary form, meaning that they have two sections (AB) of eight measures each. In performance, these sections are often repeated (AABB), and then the entire tune is repeated. Musicians typically play a single tune two or more times before switching to another one, thereby creating a medley. Tune types are differentiated by their meters.

The Jig

The first tunes played in the session at Gleesons Pub were jigs. Jigs are distinguished by their **compound meters** in which each beat consists of a subgroup of three pulses. Four variants of the jig exist in the Irish tradition: the single and double jig in 6/8, the slip jig in 9/8, and the slide in 12/8 (see Hast and Scott 2004, 66). "Garrett Barry's Jig," performed by *uilleann* piper Jerry O'Sullivan (Audio Example 16.3), is an example of a double jig characterized by two groups of three eighth notes per measure.

The Reel

The most popular tune type in the Irish tradition today is the **reel**. You can listen to an example of a reel that is played to accompany figure one of the Caledonian Set (Video 16.1). Reels are distinguished by their duple (4/4) meter, and are usually played at a quick tempo. When dancing to a reel, the feel is in two, with steps

ACTIVITY 16.3

Listen to "Garrett Barry's Jig." To hear the 6/8 rhythm, first clap with each eighth note—the shortest duration you hear, counting "**1**-2-3-**4**-5-6" (with stress shown by bolding). That is one bar of 6/8 meter, with emphasis on beat "1" and beat "4".

Then try clapping only on the accented first beat in each group of three, counting "**1**-and-a **2**-and-a"; this gives you the two-beat feel of 6/8 time.

When you count eight measures, you have gone through the A section of the tune. The A section then repeats.

At timing 0:21, the B section begins. Keep clapping the meter. At timing 0:31, the B section repeats. Then the whole tune repeats. Try to identify each section.

ACTIVITY 16.4

Listen again to "The Maid behind the Bar" and "Gregg's Pipes," two reels played by musicians at Gleeson's Pub (Audio Example 16.1). First, distinguish the instruments being played: fiddle, flute, and concertina.

Listen again to hear the rhythm and form of the first tune. It is in duple meter (4/4) and in binary form, with each section repeated in performance

(AABB). The musicians play the tune twice before switching to the second tune, "Gregg's Pipes." Unlike the first reel, "Gregg's Pipes" is a three-part tune (ABC) with eight-measure melodic sections that are not repeated. The entire tune is played three times. Notice that the meter and the tempo stay the same throughout the performance of the medley.

taken on beats 1 and 3 in each measure. Like the jig, reels are often in binary form with two sections of eight measures each.

Emigration Songs

Migration songs constitute another huge body of Irish traditional repertoire. These songs serve to document the history of emigration beginning in the late seventeenth century. We have selected three English language songs to illustrate this history over time. In contrasting performance styles, they demonstrate (1) how

ACTIVITY 16.5

Read the full text of the lyrics to "The Green Fields of Canada." First listen to the whole song to follow the text and imagine yourself in such a situation. Shifting then to the music, focus on these elements in order: (1) the rhythm, to identify what makes it "free"; (2) the melody, to identify what makes us describe it as "richly ornamented"; and (3) the combination of those two elements, to be able to say in detail how they "emphasize the text."

songs are vital in chronicling the emigrant experience, (2) how the theme of emigration remains relevant up to the present day, and (3) the flexibility of the tradition to absorb new elements and styles.

"The Green Fields of Canada"

The most traditional performance of the three selections is Paddy Tunney's unaccompanied rendition of "The Green Fields of Canada" (Audio Example 16.4), a song thought to date from c. 1810–1820. Tunney sings in free rhythm (characteristic of both Irish- and English-language traditional singing), emphasizing the text while richly ornamenting the melody. The song begins as a lament, outlining the tragic breakdown of community and economic life in Ireland, but its final verses brim with hope. The composer catalogues the wonders of the new world, where nature provides bounty instead of hardship and blight. These last stanzas convey a belief that fueled the Irish imagination throughout the nineteenth century:

ACTIVITY 16.6

Focus first on the song of "Edward Connor" (Audio Example 16.5), then on the instrumental accompaniment to answer these questions about the rhythm. How does the rhythm of this performance differ from that of "Green Fields of Canada"? Consider whether or not the presence of the instrumental accompaniment might influence the rhythm.

LISTENING GUIDE

"Edward Connors"

Performed by Andy Irvine (1989; vocals and bouzouki), Donal Lunny (harmonium and guitar), and Frankie Gavin (fiddle)

Recording location and year: Dublin, 1989

Instrumentation: guitar, bouzouki, fiddle, and harmonium

Time	Text	Something to Listen For
0:00		Guitar and harmonium
0:11	Come all you loyal Irishmen and listen all for a while All you that wants to emigrate and leave the Emerald Isle A kind advice I will give you which you must bear in mind How you will be forsaken when you leave your land behind.	Verse 1 Entrance of the singer with the first verse in a slow to moderate tempo, in 6/8 time, to chordal accompaniment from the harmonium; in this "Come All Ye" ballad, each verse consists of four lines of text, with a rhyming structure of AABB.
0:40	My name is Edward Connors and the same I'll ne'er disown I used to live in happiness near unto Portglenone I sold my farm as you will hear which grieves my heart full sore And I sailed away to Amerikay; I left the Shamrock Shore.	Verse 2 Bouzouki added to the harmonium accompaniment in verse 2; the *bouzouki* plays mostly countermelody over the chords of the harmonium.
1:06	For my mind it was deluded by letters that were sent By those that a few years ago to Canada had went They said that they like princes lived and earning gold galore And they laughed at our misfortunes here all on the Shamrock Shore.	Verse 3 Same accompaniment as verse 2.
1:34	So it's with my wife and my family to Belfast I went down I booked our passage on a ship to Quebec she was bound My money it was growing short when I laid in sea-store But I thought my fortune would be won if I reached the other shore.	Verse 4 The harmonium drops out in verse 4; by this time, the guitar has entered, weaving an intricate texture with the bouzouki's countermelodies to the vocal line.
2:03		Instrumental break: entrance of the fiddle playing the melody accompanied by guitar and bouzouki.

Time	Text	Something to Listen For
2:31	When we were scarce three days at sea a storm it soon arose It threw our ship on her beam-ends and woke us from our repose Our sea-store then it was destroyed by water that down did pour How happy we would then have been all on the Shamrock Shore.	Verse 5 Vocalist enters to sing verse 5 accompanied by fiddle playing the melody, bouzouki and guitar weaving countermelodies beneath.
2:59	And when we were nine long days at sea our sea-store was all gone And there upon the ocean wide with nowhere for to run But for our captain's kindliness he kindly gave us more We would have died with hunger ere we reached the other shore.	Verse 6 Same accompaniment as verse 5.
3:27		Short interlude played by guitar and bouzouki
3:40	And it's when we landed in Quebec the sight that met our eyes Three hundred of our Irish boys which did us sore surprise With a sorrowful lamentation charity they did crave And the little trifle we could spare to them we freely gave.	Verse 7 Fiddle plays melody during verse 7; the bouzouki plays countermelodies, while the guitar drops out.
4:08	We stayed three weeks in the town of Quebec hoping some work to find My money it was growing short which troubled my mind For I had friends when I had cash but none when I was poor I never met with friendship yet like this on the Shamrock Shore.	Verse 8 Same accompaniment as verse 7.
4:36	Well we stayed around in Quebec town till our money it was all gone Still hoping for employment but work we could find none And in that place it was the case with many hundreds more Who oft times wished that they were home all on the Shamrock Shore.	Verse 9 The fiddle drops out during verse 9, and the singer is accompanied by guitar and bouzouki.
5:03	So come all you who are intending now strange countries for to roam Bear in mind you have as good as Canada at home Before that you cross over the main where foaming billows roar Think on the happy days you spent all on the Shamrock Shore.	Verse 10 The singer is accompanied only by *bouzouki* in verse 10.
5:41		Instrumental conclusion features fiddle, bouzouki, and guitar.

that America was a land of promise, freedom, endless wealth, and unbounded opportunities.

"Edward Connors"

The performance of "Edward Connors" reflects the newer traditional style of solo singing over layered instrumental accompaniment (in this case, fiddle, **harmonium**, guitar, and bouzouki) that is popular today (Audio Example 16.5). Composed in the nineteenth-century genre of **"come all ye" ballads** that give warning or impart a moral lesson, "Edward Connors" is thought to date from after "Green Fields" but before "The Great Famine" (*An Gorta Mór*). While the composer of "The Green Fields of Canada" imagines a life filled with new possibilities, "Edward Connors" documents the painful process of selling his farm, packing up his family, and sailing to Quebec. Expecting to be greeted by successful compatriots upon arrival there, Connors instead meets unemployed Irishmen begging for charity. Unable to find work, he laments that as his money grows scarce, so-called friends abandon him. In the penultimate verse, he regrets making the trip, and like many other emigrants, sorrowfully wishes he were back at home.

This song resonated with nineteenth-century Irishmen on both sides of the Atlantic. It served as a warning and united emigrants who had experienced the hardships of exile. Over time, ballads like "Green Fields of Canada" and "Edward Connors" grew beyond personal stories; they became expressive symbols of shared positive and negative experiences, creating identity and reinforcing community. When sung today, these songs keep alive this sense of shared history and common roots.

"Thousands Are Sailing"

Our third example, "Thousands Are Sailing," was composed by Philip Chevron and recorded by the Pogues (Figure 16.5) in 1988 (Audio Example 16.6). Lyrically, its themes and imagery place it squarely in the lineage of emigration songs, continuing the conversation about being an outsider in a new world where strangeness, alienation, and success coexist, and "the hand of opportunity draws tickets in a lottery." Two centuries of emigrant experience are evoked: "coffin ships" on which famished nineteenth-century émigrés perished before reaching America and a catalogue of immigrant jobs from railway workers to policemen. But Chevron also treats emigration as an ongoing process in which contemporary Irish emigrants in New York not only deal with memories and "ghosts" of

exiles from the past, but also struggle with some of the same obstacles faced by their predecessors. In the process, we are reminded of a who's who of successful Irish and Irish Americans, from composer George M. Cohan to President John F. Kennedy.

ACTIVITY 16.7

Musically, "Thousands Are Sailing" fuses punk rock style with Irish traditional elements such as reel-like interludes. In the process, The Pogues create a truly modern emigration song, blending electric bass, drum set, and rough punk vocals with traditional acoustic instruments, including the tenor banjo, accordion, tin whistle, and guitar. Do you consider this to be a successful example of fusion music? If so, why? If not, why not?

Conclusion

Throughout its history, Irish traditional music has incorporated a variety of techniques, instruments, and styles from other parts of the world. Influenced by pop music and commercialism within the last sixty years, traditional music has been packaged successfully for the global marketplace, creating new contexts for performance and a variety of hybrid styles. But while change and innovation play a central role in the maintenance of the tradition today, musicians continue to be profoundly influenced by the past. Musicians feel linked to the rich repertory of songs and tunes; to the social world that surrounds performance; and to the people, places, and historical events that gave life to the music. This connection remains strong in large part because the majority of musicians still play in informal sessions where the traditional and social aspects of music-making play a dominant role. Seated in a semicircle around a group of tables in a pub, whether in Coore, Dublin, London, Sydney, or New York, and playing tunes together or taking time to listen to a solo singer, these musicians embody the heart of the tradition.

Bibliography

Brennan, Helen. 2001. *The Story of Irish Dance*. Lanham, MD: Roberts Rinehart Publishers.

Hast, Dorothea, and Stan Scott. 2004. *Music in Ireland: Experiencing Music, Expressing Culture*. New York: Oxford University Press

Henigan, Julie. 1999. "Aisling." In *The Companion to Irish Music*, edited by Fintan Vallely. Cork, Ireland: Cork University Press. P.7.

Irvine, Andy. 1989. *Rainy Sundays . . . Windy Dreams*. Wundertüte Musik CD Tüt 72.141.

Moloney, Mick. 2005. "'Those Who Suffer Write the Songs': Remembering Frank Harte 1933–2005." *The Journal of Music*.

Munnelly, Tom. 1998. "Junior Crehan of Bonavilla." *Bhéaloideras* 66: 59–161.

Munnelly, Tom. 1999. "Junior Crehan of Bonavilla" (Part Two). *Bhéaloideras* 67: 71–124.

Ní Uallacháin, Pádraigín. 2003. *A Hidden Ulster: People, Songs and Traditions of Oriel*. Dublin: Four Courts Press LTD.

Ní Uallacháin, Pádraigín. 2001. Interview with authors.

Ní Uallacháin, Pádraigín. 1995. *An Dara Craiceann (Beneath the Surface)*. Gael-Linn CEFCD 183.

The Pogues. 1988. *If I Should Fall From Grace of God*. WEA.

Shields, Hugh. 1993. *Narrative Singing in Ireland*. Dublin: Irish Academic Press.

Tunney, Paddy. 1982. *The Stone Fiddle*. Green Linnet SIF 1037 LP.

Tunney, Paddy. 1991. *The Stone Fiddle: My Way to Traditional Song*. Belfast, Ireland: Appletree Press.

≡ **FIGURE V.1** Map of the Americas.

PART 5

The Americas

17

Music in Cuba

Son and Creolization

ROBIN MOORE

Chapter Contents

Introduction

Although all parts of the Americas have unique music, the Caribbean represents an especially vibrant area. An enormous range of expression has developed there, particularly in Spanish-, French-, and English-speaking areas. This relatively small region, with a population of roughly 40 million, has proven to be a cultural force rivalling or even surpassing large nations of the developed world. Phenomenally popular commercial music from the Caribbean—merengue, reggae, salsa, and so on—is listened to around the world, and many noncommercial forms of music flourish as well. The islands also boast vibrant classical compositions, everything from music for the Catholic mass to nineteenth-century piano repertoire to avant-garde electronic composition. Some island communities perpetuate cultural forms brought to the region hundreds of years ago from Africa, Europe, and elsewhere; other groups blend traditional elements together in

≡ *Son* **band playing on the street in Trinidad, Sancti Spíritus, Cuba.**

FIGURE 17.1

Map of Cuba.

their music or fuse them with more modern musical styles. This chapter focuses on one Spanish-speaking island, Cuba, and on the blending of cultural forms.

Cuba is the largest and most populous island in the Caribbean (Figure 17.1). Culturally considered part of Latin America, it is a multiethnic country whose people, culture, and customs derive from diverse origins. The Ciboney and Taíno peoples, its earliest known inhabitants, lived on the island beginning in the fourth millennium BCE. From the late fifteenth century, Spanish colonizers ruled Cuba until the Spanish-American War of 1898. The Spanish brought countless African slaves to the country.

The United States occupied Cuba in 1898. Four years later, the islanders gained nominal independence as a Republic, but the United States remained a dominant political presence. In 1940, Cuba attempted to strengthen its democratic system, but increasing political radicalization and social strife led to the dictatorship of Fulgencio Batista in 1952. Batista's repressive government spawned more unrest and instability, and he was removed from office by the 26st of July Movement under Fidel Castro. Since 1965, Cuba has been governed by the Communist Party of Cuba. It ranks highly on the world's human development index, particularly strong in healthcare, education, and the arts. In recent years, there are signs of a lessening of communist influence and the development of a broader economic spectrum.

In Caribbean culture, the "blending of cultural forms" is best described by the concept of **"creolization."** The term refers to the fusion of different races and cultures over time and the creation of something new and different in the process. Creolization is evident in the varied color of people's skin and other aspects of their physical appearance. It is also apparent in local vocabularies, in ways of speaking and pronouncing, in cuisines that blend various influences, and in religious expression. Most scholars agree that Caribbean identity is neither European nor African but, rather, "in-between."

Caribbean musical forms that combine elements from Europe, Africa, and elsewhere represent another example of creolization. Most of the islands' national popular music—commercial forms of the twentieth century derived from the working classes but embraced by nearly everyone today—demonstrates cultural mixture. Consciously or unconsciously, residents understand that this music best represents their history and local experience in symbolic form. Through hybridity, Cuban peoples have used music to reconcile the multiple cultural influences in the region and to make them meaningful locally.

This chapter concentrates on one example of creolized music in Cuba, the **son** genre. In part because it effectively bridges the worlds of African and European aesthetics, it has been heralded as a national symbol in Cuba for many years. It is a unique style of Caribbean popular music. Elements of *son* that we will consider include song lyrics, musical structure/form, instruments, tonality/modality, and the organization of time. The chapter begins with brief commentary on the colonization of the Americas and the slave trade that brought about the conditions in which Cuban music emerged. Then it discusses the general characteristics of African-influenced music from the Caribbean. Finally, it explores the origins and early development of *son* music, and subsequent changes.

Colonization of the Americas and the African Slave Trade

The Atlantic slave trade began in earnest in the seventeenth century as colonial powers established large plantations, primarily to cultivate sugar cane. The colonization of the Americas is usually discussed as a European phenomenon; but in fact, the population of most settlements consisted primarily of Africans until about 1800—and, in some cases, they still represent the majority today. In all, approximately twelve million Africans were brought to the Americas under horrific conditions as laborers. Brazil and the Caribbean region imported most of them, about 40 percent of the total each, with the remainder distributed throughout Central, North, and South America. Only about 5 percent of all slaves brought to the Americas were taken to the United States.

For centuries, the Atlantic slave trade represented the center of all commerce in the Western Hemisphere. Slaving ships sailed a "middle passage" as part of a triangular trading route. The first leg involved travel from Europe to the West African coast carrying manufactured goods including weapons, textiles, and hardware. These would be sold to Africans in exchange for human captives. Next, the ships sailed to the Americas, trading slaves for tobacco, rum, coffee, sugar, and other products. Finally, the ships returned to Europe, turning a profit a third time on the sale of plantation goods before beginning the whole process again. It must be noted that slavery had existed for some time in Africa prior to the trans-Atlantic trade. But the European colonies created such tremendous new demand that they increased the practice exponentially, destabilizing large areas of West Africa as tribes attacked each other to provide captives.

The sizeable differences in the numbers of Africans brought to various regions had a strong impact on the sorts of music that would develop there. In Cuba, the slave trade peaked in the 1830s and ended officially in 1886. Large numbers of Africans arrived clandestinely even through the 1870s, yet shortly thereafter, large numbers of immigrants from Spain settled the island as well. Thus, one finds both strongly African-influenced and Spanish influenced music, together with creo lized forms. Relative to the United States, directly African-derived traditions are strong in Cuba (Figure 17.2; Hagedorn 2001).

≡ **FIGURE 17.2** The Conjunto Folklórico Nacional de Cuba, one of many groups in the Caribbean dedicated to preserving traditional forms of Afro-diasporic music and dance.

Musical Characteristics of African-Influenced Music from the Caribbean

African musical elements have greatly influenced the sound and style of many types of music from the Caribbean, including the Cuban *son*, along with its incorporation over time of instruments, harmonies, and other influences from Europe and elsewhere. (See Moore 2010 for the Hispanic Caribbean.)

Structure/Form

Much West African and Afro-Caribbean music is based on cycles and loops. It adopts an open-ended form that lasts as long as the performance requires.

Call-and-response singing is an African-derived characteristic in much of this repertoire. (Quite a number of musics in the world are structured by call and response, but in this instance the structure is derived from African practices.)

The layering of multiple, independent melodies or rhythms on top of one another is another African-derived characteristic.

Instruments

A wide variety of timbres, often non-pitched, are heard in any given ensemble. Many Afro-Latin musics incorporate a vast array of such sounds from metal, animal skin, plant material, and other sources.

African-influenced repertoire features groupings of instruments according to their musical role in an ensemble:

1. A group that tends to play relatively static, unchanging lines that serve to keep the pulse
2. A second group that varies their parts a bit more
3. A third group that features prominently as solo instruments, fighting the rhythms laid down by the rest

The Organization of Time

Pieces may be in duple or triple meter, or (at least as frequently) they may incorporate simultaneous rhythms that emphasize both groupings of two and three. Whatever the meter of a piece, the music usually demonstrates a high level of "rhythmic density" or **polyrhythm,** with many different beats sounding simultaneously.

Relationships between rhythms are very important. Many performers of traditional percussion music do not read Western notation and orient themselves solely on the basis of how their part fits with the others.

The Cuban *Son*

Cuban *son* developed in the nineteenth century in eastern Cuba, the largely mountainous region known as Oriente (the East). It was originally a rural dance music for parties and other informal gatherings, performed by the Afro-Cuban community in the hills surrounding cities such as Santiago, Baracoa, and Guantánamo (Figure 17.1). Following the Wars of Independence against Spain (1868–1898), there was a great deal of movement of people within Cuba that spread *son* throughout the country. Rural families whose homes and farms had been destroyed relocated to cities. Others found themselves displaced by the creation of huge sugar plantations and other commercial farming. The formation of a national army also brought many Cubans to new areas. These trends led to the gradual spread of the *son* to poorer neighborhoods in the capital, Havana, and other western cities. Soon it began to fuse with forms of music popular in these areas, including North American jazz and Afro-Cuban **rumba** (Acosta, 1991).

Accounts from around 1900 suggest that in its earliest manifestations, the *son* consisted only of a repeated chorus supported by very simple tonic-dominant chords played on a stringed instrument and percussion. The use of European harmony is noteworthy, and also the texture of a melody supported by harmonic accompaniment (**homophony**). Against this background, a lead singer might improvise brief phrases or perhaps a longer couplet or quatrain before the group sang the chorus once again. Those two characteristics—prominent vocal improvisation and leader-chorus structure—are likely influences from African music.

By the 1920s, an urban *son* variant had developed with a more elaborate structure and instrumentation, discussed following. The widespread popularization of this style of music helped break down many racial barriers, allowing working-class performers of color access to national audiences for the first time. Urban *son* sextets and septets (*sextetos, septetos*; see Figure 17.3) gained widespread popularity on the radio and through the sale of 78 records. *Son* was the first popular genre to incorporate performance on a drum played with the bare hands, previously considered by elites a "primitive" and unsightly practice.

Structure/Form of the Urban *Son*

The urban *son*'s formal structure, while more elaborate than earlier forms, is also hybrid. The beginning section derives from European models: a **strophic** song/verse section known as the ***tema,*** *verso,* or *canto*. The climactic finale comes from African models: a cyclic **montuno** section. Often a lead singer or instrumentalist improvises during a *montuno* in response to a chorus. *Montuno*s can also feature extended instrumental solos on a single instrument.

≡ **FIGURE 17.3** The Septeto Habanero (Havana Septet), a traditional Cuban *son* group performing in Havana in 2001. Instruments seen in the front row (L–R) are the *güiro*, *claves*, *maracas*, guitar, and *tres*. Instruments in the back row are the bass and *bongó* drum, though at this moment the *bongósero* is playing his bell.

Instrumentation of the Urban *Son*

The typical instrumentation of 1920s urban *son* bands was hybrid as well, including both stringed instruments derived from Spain and percussion from African models (see Figure 17.5). It reflected the preference for a wide variety of timbres, characteristic of African-influenced music from the Caribbean. In addition to voices, instruments in urban *son* ensembles included the following:

1. Guitar
2. **Tres**: A smaller guitar-like instrument with three courses of double strings, usually tuned to a major or minor chord
3. Acoustic bass
4. **Maracas**: Gourd rattles
5. *Güiro:* An open-ended hollow gourd with parallel notches cut into it; it is held in one hand and played with the other hand by scraping a stick along the notches
6. *Claves:* A pair of short, cylindrically shaped sticks of hard wood; one held, the other striking (see Figure 17.3)
7. *Bongó:* A pair of small drums (one slightly larger), with bodies yoked together, each single-headed with an open body, played with the hands (Figure 17.4)

≡ **FIGURE 17.4** Drum used in the performance of early urban Cuban *son: bongós*.

"La Negra Tomasa"

Performed by *Grupo el Órgano Pinareño*; Composed by Guillermo Rodriguez Fiffe (1934)

Recording location and year: Cuba, 1989, from the album *Pinareno: Music from Pinar del Rio*

Instrumentation: *Tres*, *clave*, cowbell, *bongó*, *maracas*, acoustic bass

"*La negra Tomasa*" (Audio Example 17.1) introduces you to the sound of the urban *son*. Listen to it several times just to "get it in your ears." Then listen to hear the *tema-montuno* structure. Try to identify the section changes yourself.

In addition to the overall structure of *tema* and *montuno*, concentrate on the singing, including the lyrics. On islands such as Cuba where the slave trade lasted much longer than in other countries, African communities retained a clearer sense of their heritage; many Afro-Cubans continued to speak African languages well into the twentieth century. Even today, religious songs continue to be sung in fragmented African languages brought to the island more than a century ago. Although "*La negra Tomasa*" is sung primarily in Spanish, African-derived words such as *bilongo*, *mandinga*, and *kikiribú* appear in it too.

Time	Text	Something to Listen For
0:01		The *tres* outlines an A minor-key chord in a syncopated rhythm, repeatedly.
0:04		The **claves** enters with its standard **son clave** rhythm (two strokes in one measure and three in another) along with the **bongós** and *maracas*. The *tres* switches to an **ostinato** pattern in which the "two-stroke measure" is less syncopated and emphasizes the downbeat, while the "three-stroke measure" emphasizes more offbeats. The *bongó* improvises, performing many flourishes.
0:11	*Estoy tan enamorado de la negra Tomasa.* *Que cuando sale de casa que triste me pongo.*	Section: *Verso* (or *canto*) First part: Two male voices enter on the two-side of *clave* to sing in parallel thirds of their love for "Tomasa the black woman," and their sadness when she leaves.
0:19		Verse: Previous line repeats.
0:29		Male voices sing "Ay, ay, ay" on three descending pitches, with a pause and a brief *tres* arpeggiation between each of them. All three emphasize beat 4 of the 4/4 measure, rather than beat 1.

Time	Text	Something to Listen For
0:34	*Esa negra linda, camará, que me hechó bilongo. Esa negra santa, camará, que me hechó bilongo.*	Second part of the *verso*: Male voices sing in parallel thirds, this time entering on the three-side of *clave*, about how "that beautiful black women, that saintly black woman, cast a spell on me."
0:42		The *tres* modulates to another key (C), the relative major, signaling the start of the final section of the *verso*.
0:43	*No más que me gusta e' la comida que me cocina.* *más que me gusta e' la café que ella me cuela.*	Final section of the *verso*: A solo male voice sings new lyrics in a higher range, beginning on the two-side of *clave*, about wanting to eat only the food Tomasa cooks and the coffee she makes.
1:01		Male voices sing "Ay, Ay, Ay," as earlier (0:29), and refrain (0:34).
1:13	(in Afro-Cuban Spanish): *Kikiribú, mandinga, kikiribú mandinga.* Translation: It's all over, Mandinga friend, all hope is gone.	New section: *Montuno* Singers break into a call-response section, the *montuno*, emphasizing the two-side of *clave* for the remainder of the piece. The *bongó* player switches to cowbell to mark the *montuno*.
1:36		Lead male voice improvises, while other male voices provide continuity with their "*kikiribú*" response.
2:04		An instrumental section featuring syncopated *tres* melodies interspersed with chords over percussion and bass; the bell player shifts back to the *bongó* heads.
3:07		Male voices return in a low register, singing in unison on "a la."
3:25		A new instrumental begins, a *bongó* solo over percussion and a repeated *tres* riff in *clave*.
3:46		Cowbell enters, signaling the return of call-response vocals.
3:47	"*Kikiribú mandinga.*"	Male chorus returns.
3:54		Lead male voice improvises over percussion, bass, and a *claved tres* riff, in alternation with the chorus.
4:52		*Tres* strum signals the start of the new section, a return to the verse.
4:53		New *verso*. Lead male voice sings a new verse.
5:10		Male voices sing "Ay, ay, ay," followed by "*mandinga*" and a slowing of the tempo followed by a final long *tres* strum and percussion flourishes.

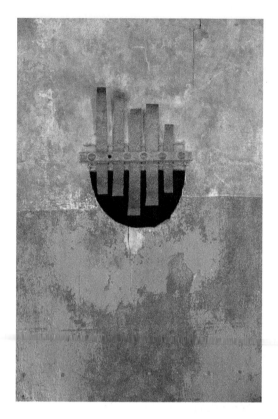

7.   Bell: A large cowbell that produces two different sounds on the low and high ends; it is played with a wooden stick

8.   Trumpet: A cylindrical brass horn formed into three parallel tubes connected by a valve mechanism to control pitch; the trumpet was added to the ensemble in the 1930s

In rural ensembles, various instruments substituted for the European acoustic bass. One of these was a ceramic jug called a **botija**, originally used to import oil from Spain (jug bands in the United States used similar instruments). *Botija* players blew over a small hole and moved their hand in and out of another in order to change the pitch. Another early bass instrument was the **marímbula**, a large "thumb piano" derived from Central Africa; it has a wooden resonator box to which metal strips (keys) are attached (Figure 17.5). But urban groups gradually came to view the *botija* and *marímbula* as "rustic" or "hick." They substituted the upright acoustic bass in an attempt to appeal to middle-class tastes and to allow for greater harmonic possibilities.

≡ **FIGURE 17.5** The *marímbula*, an African-derived instrument used in various forms of traditional music in Cuba, Puerto Rico, the Dominican Republic, and elsewhere. It consists of a wooden box to which metal strips are attached; performers pluck the strips to produce different pitches.

Instrumental Parts and the Organization of Time

Many instruments repeat their own riff or rhythm (*ostinato*) in cyclic fashion. In that way, each contributes to a complex, multilayered organization of time. This section of the chapter explores several of the ostinati that characterize the *son*.

One repeated rhythm—**son clave**—is the unique and foundational rhythm usually played on the *claves* (hard wood sticks) themselves. *Son clave* consists of a two-measure pattern with two strokes on one side (i.e., in one measure of 4/4 meter) and three on another; either side can be played first. The pattern beginning on the "two-side" is written in staff notation in Musical Example 17.1.

MUSICAL EXAMPLE 17.1 *Son clave* rhythm notation.

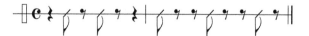

ACTIVITY 17.1

If you read notation, practice tapping out the rhythm pattern in Musical Example 17.1 until you can repeat it without thinking. If you can't read notation, find someone who can and do it together.

After you get a feel for it, try tapping it out while you (or a colleague) taps out all the quarter notes in two 4/4 measures: 1 2 3 4 / 2 2 3 4.

In addition to the *claves*, whose fundamental role you now understand, the *maracas* and the bell in the *son* ensemble tend to play relatively static, unchanging lines that serve to keep the pulse.

In many types of Afro-Latin repertoire, the rhythms performed on melodic instruments are at least as important as the pitches they play. A characteristic element of *son* is the rhythmic melody played on the *tres,* outlining or implying chords but not actually strumming them. Thus, the musical role of the *tres* is both rhythmic and harmonic, assisted by the usual tuning of the strings to a major or a minor chord.

One typical *tres montuno* pattern in a major key and one alternate are shown in Musical Examples 17.2 and 17.3 The chord pattern in both of them is I–IV–V–IV or G–C–D–C (tonic–subdominant–dominant–subdominant). Also in both, the first half of the *tres* pattern corresponds to the "two side" of the *clave,* emphasizing the downbeat of the measure. In the final *montuno* section, especially, rhythms on the *tres* often correspond to the *clave* pattern, with a somewhat "straighter" melodic/harmonic line played against the "two-side" of the *clave* and a more syncopated melody played against the "three-side."

ACTIVITY 17.2

Listen several times more to "*La negra Tomasa*" (Audio Example 17.1) and try to pick out the *claves,*

bell, and *maracas*—not only by the sound of each instrument but their repetitive rhythmic parts.

MUSICAL EXAMPLE 17.2 A typical *tres* pattern from the *montuno*, transcribed against the *clave*.

MUSICAL EXAMPLE 17.3 An alternate *tres montuno* pattern for the same implicit chord progression.

There are many different *montuno* patterns a *tres* might play, even over the rather simple chord progression implied in Musical Examples 17.1 and 17.3. "*La negra Tomasa*" (Audio Example 17.1) is in a minor key; the *tres* pattern shown in Musical Example 17.4 is taken from that piece. *Tres* patterns like these were important to the development of *salsa* music, influencing the style of keyboardists in commercial dance bands as early as the 1940s.

MUSICAL EXAMPLE 17.4 A *clave*d tres pattern in a minor key heard in the listening example "*La negra Tomasa*," 0:04–0:10.

The pattern played on the bass is probably the most unique aspect of the *son*. This pattern too is repeated continuously. The bass player uses an "anticipated bass" rhythm, meaning that the notes often sound slightly earlier than one might

ACTIVITY 17.3

Search for recordings or video clips of traditional Cuban *son* and listen to the performance style of the *tres* player. Try to hear the various patterns they play, then compare them to the freer patterns employed during solos. Songs on commercial recordings that might serve as a good point of departure include "*Son de la loma*" ("They're From the Hills")

on the Corason CD collection *Septetos Cubanos*; a slightly different piece in a minor key by the same name on *Routes of Rhythm. A Carnival of Cuban Music. Vol. 1* (Rounder Records); or "*Adios compay gato*" ("Goodbye Mr. Cat") on the Orfeón CD *Cuba: Guajira y son, caña tabaco y ron, Vol. 2.*

expect. For instance, in many types of music in the United States (most rock, country, polka) the bass plays mostly on strong beats: one and three of the 4/4 measure. In the *son*, by contrast, the bass plays on four (i.e., a full quarter note before the "normal" spot on beat 1) and on the "and-of-two" (an eighth note before the "normal" spot on beat 3) as shown in Musical Example 17.5. This lends the music a constant "uneven" **syncopated** feel with stress between the strong beats, or on offbeats.

MUSICAL EXAMPLE 17.5 *"Mueve la cintura,"* *clave* and *bass* patterns. These two instruments together with a maraca perform the rhythms played on the recording (Audio Example 17.3).

The recording "Bass, *clave*, and *maracas*" (Audio Example 17.2) provides a brief example of a typical *son* bass pattern played against the *clave* and *maracas*. The percussion enters first to establish the time, then the bass enters shortly thereafter. This example closely imitates the bass patterns and rhythms found in the song "*Mueve la cintura*" (Audio Example 17.3).

ACTIVITY 17.4

"Mueve la cintura" ("Shake Your Hips," Audio Example 17.3), from the Corason CD *Casa de la Trova de Santiago de Cuba*, serves as a good introduction to traditional *son* bass. Listen closely, focusing first on the *clave* and see if you can clap it out, noting that it begins on the "three-side" at the beginning of the piece. Focus next on the bass, hearing its pattern in relation to the *clave*. Try to hear how the *clave* creates constant tension and release with the bass pattern by first lining up with it and then deviating from it in alternating measures. Written against one another, the two lines would look something like the transcription in Musical Example. 17.5.

Improvisation

Balancing the repetitive ostinati that are basic elements of the *son* genre, some instrumental parts perform slightly more varied rhythmic patterns, while still others feature prominently as solo instruments, fighting the rhythm laid down by the rest. Even the slight variations represent a form of improvisation.

An illustration of slight variation is the part played by the *bongó* drum during the initial section of a piece, namely, the **martillo** or "hammer" pattern. The *martillo* in its most basic form consists of a constant eighth-note pulse, with accented strokes on the smaller head of the drum on beats 1 and 3 of each 4/4 measure and on beat 2 on the larger drumhead (Musical Ex. 17.6). *Bongó* players deviate from this basic pattern frequently, however, improvising in order to fill in spaces between the melodic lines and to generate excitement. The improvising is not entirely free, however; the **bongósero** listens and responds to vocals and instruments, filling in with embellished rhythms at particular times in order to complement rather than overshadow other performers. In the hands of an experienced player, the *bongó* is a decidedly virtuosic instrument.

MUSICAL EXAMPLE 17.6 The basic *bongó* drum pattern in Cuban *son*, known as the *martillo*. Higher notes are played on the smaller drumhead of the *bongó* and the lower notes, on the lower head. Slash noteheads indicate light touches or notes that are dampened.

ACTIVITY 17.5

Now that you have some feel for the basic elements of Cuban *son*, try performing a repeating vamp in this style with classmates, such as the one transcribed in Musical Example 17.7. You will need to imitate the *tres*, bass, and *clave* at the very least, ideally the *maracas*, *bongó*, and vocals as well.

When the *montuno* section begins, the *bongó* player typically switches to a bell, emphasizing the strong beats of the music in order to drive the tempo forward and generate excitement. In *"La negra Tomasa"* (Audio Example 17.1), this happens at 1:13.

Audio Example 17.4 provides a short excerpt of a *bongó* drum player performing against the *clave*. The transcription in Musical Example 17.6 should help you follow it. This combination of instruments is not traditional, but it clearly demonstrates the *bongó* performance style and its contribution to the overall sound. In the recording, the *bongó* performer begins by playing the basic *martillo*, but soon begins to vary and elaborate on it, as would be typical in an actual performance.

MUSICAL EXAMPLE 17.7 "La negra Tomasa" *montuno* vamp. The four measures of chorus transcribed here would traditionally be followed either by a four-measure vocal or instrumental improvisation, with the two sections then alternating repeatedly.

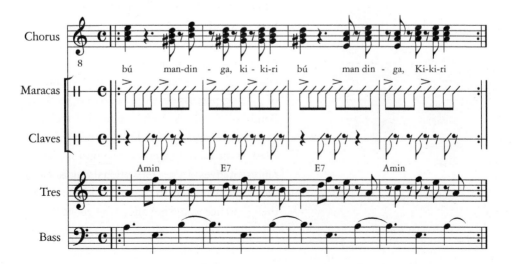

The Changing Sound of *Son*

From the 1910s through the late 1920s, groups typically consisted only of string instruments, percussion, and voices, more or less in the style of the "*La negra Tomasa*" (Audio Example 17.1). Then, about 1930, many groups added a single trumpet player. In this expanded ensemble (a septet instead of a sextet), the *tres* played a slightly less prominent role as soloist, with embellishments between vocal lines and solos often performed on the trumpet instead. In the 1940s and 1950s, a new *son* style became popular in Havana, known as **conjunto**. This new style introduced additional changes. For instance, a second and often a third trumpet were added to the bands, which required that written arrangements be created to coordinate the horn section's parts. Pianos became a standard part of *son* instrumentation, sometimes replacing the *tres*, sometimes playing alongside it. As more performers joined *son* bands who had formal training and knew how to read music, the pieces slowly became more elaborate in structural and harmonic terms.

By the 1950s, two additional instruments—the **conga** **drum** and *timbales*—were incorporated into these ensembles. One or two *congas* (tall, single-headed, barrel-shaped drums, played with the hands; Figure 17.6) were added to most ensembles. The **timbales** (a pair of shallow metal, cylindrically shaped, single-headed drums of slightly differing sizes held on a metal frame) along with two bells of distinct sizes (Figure 17.7) and a **woodblock** (a small piece of wood or plastic, hollowed out, struck with stick or mallet) were included in some groups as well: for instance, in the *Sonora Matancera* (Matanzas Sound). The *congas* and *timbales* each have an interesting history but were initially used in totally different kinds of ensembles.

≡ **FIGURE 17.6** Drum used in the performance of Cuban *son*: *conga* drums.

Congas originally accompanied slave dances and celebrations, but early in the twentieth century were also used by *rumba* percussion ensembles or carnival bands. Many middle-class Cubans refused to accept them in dance orchestras for some time, considering the practice of playing percussion with the hands barbaric. Bandleader Antonio Arcaño informed me (personal interview, July 1992) that during the early years of the *conga*'s incorporation into *son* bands representatives of some recreational venues asked the *conga* drummers to play behind a curtain so their presence would not offend the guests!

The *timbales* were introduced in Cuba through European military percussion practice and played during the nineteenth century by black and mulatto (mixed-race) soldiers. Since at least the 1830s, however, *timbales* also appeared in dance bands. In time, performers seem to have "re-Africanized" the instruments, playing various new rhythms with sticks on the sides of the drums as well as on the heads. They also began pressing on the head of the drum with one hand as they played, dampening the sound to change the head's timbre and pitch. *Timbales* were featured in late nineteenth-century **danzón** ballroom music and thereafter in **chachachá**, popularized about 1950.

Among the most influential musicians in the development of the *conjunto* format was *tres* player Arsenio Rodríguez (1911–1970), the first bandleader in that style to incorporate the *conga* drums (Garcia 2006). He was influential in defining the expanded format for playing Cuban *son* of the 1940s and 1950s that incorporated multiple trumpets, piano, and frequently *timbales* and *conga* drums as well. The 1950s gave rise to

≡ **FIGURE 17.7** Drum used in the performance of Cuban *son: timbales*.

scores of influential *conjunto* and other bands in Cuba that had a strong influence on dance music throughout Spanish-speaking Latin America and in the United States. Many musicians contributed to these developments, both in Cuba and in cities such as New York with large numbers of Caribbean immigrants.

With the onset of the Cuban Revolution in January 1959, relations between Cuba and the United States began to sour. The new Cuban leadership, including Fidel Castro and Ernesto ("Che") Guevara, began to nationalize foreign industries and to establish closer trade and military ties with the Soviet Union. In this Cold War era, fear of the spread of socialist ideals, among other factors, led the United States to impose an economic embargo on Cuba as well as a travel ban that prohibited most North Americans from visiting the island. The idea was to isolate Cuba economically and to force a change of government. In the latter sense, the US embargo proved decidedly ineffective, but it did isolate the country. Political tensions meant that Cuban artists could no longer travel freely abroad or sell their music to capitalist countries. As a result of all this, the center of commercial, Hispanic Caribbean music performance and recording shifted decisively from Havana to New York, with its large population of Puerto Rican immigrants.

ACTIVITY 17.6

Browse the web for a few audio recordings or videos to compare the sound of Cuban *son* from different periods. You might begin with the Corason album *Septeto Habanero: 75 Years Later* in order to hear roughly what *son* music with a single trumpet sounded like. Next, search for recordings of *conjunto* performers from later decades such as Arsenio Rodríguez or Félix Chappottín. Compare the repertoire in terms of overall form, instrumentation, harmonies, bass lines, and so on. Then consider the relationship between the *conjunto* sound and the music of New York salsa artists of the 1950s and 1960s like Puerto Ricans Eddie Palmieri or Tito Puente (Figure 17.8).

In Cuba, *son* performance remained central to musical expression, with new variants continuing to develop. During the 1950s and 1960s in Havana, flute and violin-based **charanga** bands became very popular as interpreters of *son*. They created a "sweeter" and somewhat less syncopated version of the music influenced by the *chachachá*. In the 1980s, by contrast, musicians began to fuse *son* with elements of rock, funk, jazz, and local Afro-Cuban drumming genres, resulting in the emergence of **timba** (Moore, 2006). *Timba* is still played widely, alongside reggaeton and more "classic" forms of *son*. The prominence of Afro-diasporic folklore and

≡ **FIGURE 17.8**
Puerto Rican percussionist Tito Puente (1923–2000), performing on the *timbales*. He and others helped establish *son*-derived music such as the mambo in the United States, and to popularize Cuban percussion there.

religious references in *timba* has resulted in what many describe as a "blackening" of the *son* tradition, more closely relating it to the Afro-Cuban community.

Conclusion

Most Cuban music incorporates European and West African elements. From Europe come instruments, scales, harmonies, and Spanish-language lyrics; West African influences include an emphasis on improvisation, spontaneity, and cyclic, open-ended performance, as well as the incorporation of new timbres, rhythms, and other elements such as the use of layered ostinati and call-response singing. Cuban *son* also features an "anticipated bass" pattern, use of the *son clave* rhythm, and instrumental melodies that are based on the *clave* rhythm. This sort of music effectively represents local sensibilities and the creolized aesthetics that developed in the aftermath of the slave trade.

Bibliography

Acosta, Leonardo. 1991. "The Rumba, the Guaguancó, and Tío Tom." Manuel, Peter, ed. *Essays on Cuban Music: North American and Cuban Perspectives: 49-74*. Lanham, MD: University Press of America.

García, David F. 2006. *Arsenio Rodríguez and the Transnational Flows of Latin Popular Music*. Philadelphia: Temple University Press.

Hagedorn, Katherine. 2001. *Divine Utterances: The Performance of Afro-Cuban Santería*. Washington, DC: Smithsonian Institution Press.

Moore, Robin. 2006. *Music and Revolution. Cultural Change in Socialist Cuba*. Berkeley: University of California Press.

Moore, Robin. 2010. *Music in the Hispanic Caribbean: Experiencing Music, Expressing Culture*. New York: Oxford University Press.

Music in Brazil

Samba, a Symbol of National Identity

JOHN MURPHY

Chapter Contents

Introduction

The three international symbols of Brazil are the country's natural beauty, particularly the city of Rio de Janeiro and the Amazon rainforest; the Brazilian style of playing soccer known as "the beautiful game" (*o jogo bonito*), represented by its star player, Pelé; and the musical genre of *samba*. It is not surprising, then, that the opening ceremony of the 2016 Summer Olympic Games in Rio de Janeiro featured *samba* as its musical theme. A century before the 2016 Olympics, the event's soundtrack would have been quite different because the popular music of the time included a wide range of styles, not one of which was considered the country's "national music." This chapter makes the point that *samba* is a meaningful symbol of national identity because it expresses Brazil's ethnic, racial, and cultural diversity. This is the result of a historical process

≡ **União da Ilha *Samba* School.** Musician of the *Bateria* with *Pandeiro* in the Sambadromo, Rio de Janiero, for the 2010 Carnaval.

through which a musical style practiced by musicians on the margins of society gradually moved to the center of the country's musical life.

Samba itself has taken several forms. They are distinguished by a mix of performance contexts each associated with a specific location, text, emphasis on melody or rhythm, and—significantly—ensemble instrumentation. Its earliest styles are the following:

1. **Samba de morro:** the foundational style that emerged in the Estácio neighborhood of the hills of Rio de Janeiro and established the basic musical characteristics of the genre. (See Figure 18.1.)
2. **Samba-enredo**: *samba* song that emphasizes rhythm and communicates the theme of a *Carnaval* parade.
3. **Samba-canção** (literally, *samba* song): developed for the theater, emphasizing melody more than rhythm.

≡ **FIGURE 18.1** Map of Brazil.

4. ***Samba-exaltação:*** a substyle of *samba-canção* that praises the Brazilian people, history, culture, or geography.
5. ***Bossa nova*** ("new wave")—a quieter, more intimate form of *samba*—came to the fore in the 1950s and 1960s. More recent styles include ***pagode***, a "backyard" style of *samba* for social gatherings; and ***samba sujo***, a so-called "dirty *samba*" style cultivated in the city of São Paulo.

To show the importance of *samba* for all Brazilians, this chapter traces the history of the genre from its geographical rootedness in Afro-Brazilian culture in first a region (Bahia, in Northeast Brazil) and then in the city of Rio de Janeiro; to its consolidation as a national popular music including varieties associated with other locations within Brazil; and the recent *pagode* style through which the global presence of *samba* grew—but always remaining identified with Brazil.

Four features have been consistent in *samba* since the beginning:

1. The prominence of rhythm in the music
2. The function of *samba* as music for dance
3. The importance of lyrics as an expression of the concerns of everyday Brazilian life
4. The composition of melodies that combine with the lyrics and rhythm to form an indelible musical message

Brazil and Its History

Brazil is the largest country in South and Latin America. Bounded by the Atlantic Ocean on the east, it borders all of South America's other countries except Ecuador and Chile, covering 47.3 percent of the continent's land area. In terms of territory, Brazil is the fifth largest nation in the world. Also one of the most multicultural and ethnically diverse nations, it is the sixth most populous in the world, with 210 million+ people. It has the eighth largest GDP (Gross Domestic Product) in the world.

Brazil was inhabited by numerous tribal nations prior to the landing in 1500 of explorer Pedro Álvares Cabral, who claimed the area for the Portuguese Empire. Brazil remained a Portuguese colony until 1808, when its capital was transferred from Lisbon, Portugal, to Rio de Janeiro. In 1815, the colony was elevated to the rank of kingdom. It became an independent nation in 1822 with the creation of the Empire of Brazil, a unitary state governed under a constitutional monarchy and a parliamentary system. The country became a presidential republic in 1889. From 1964, an authoritarian military junta was in power, after which civilian governance resumed. Brazil's current constitution, formulated in 1988, defines it as a democratic federal republic.

ACTIVITY 18.1

Evidence that *samba* came to express the identity of the entire nation on the world stage is demonstrated by the 2016 Olympics Opening Ceremony in Rio de Janeiro. The ceremony narrated the history of Brazil using video projection, large numbers of dancers and musicians, and sets in constant motion. By making music—and specifically *samba*—such a prominent part of this self-presentation of national identity to the world, musical directors Beto Villares and Antônio Alves Pinto confirmed the importance of musical experience in expressing the cultural identity of all Brazilians.

The ceremony began with Luiz Melodia singing *"Aquele Abraço"* ("That Embrace") by renowned Brazilian composer and singer, Gilberto Gil. *Samba* singer Paulinho da Viola was elected to sing Brazil's national anthem accompanied by a nine-member string ensemble and his guitar. A dramatic soundtrack for a video of aviator Santos Dumont flying over Rio at night was provided by composer Antonio Carlos Jobim's *"Samba do Avião"* (Airplane *Samba*). The **baterias** (percussion

groups) of Rio's twelve *Escolas de Samba* (*Samba Schools*) participated in the ceremony. During the parade of athletes, each country's athletes were accompanied by a small *samba* group.

Three "moments" of *samba* performance in the ceremony are particularly pertinent to this chapter, as you will see in licensed excerpts from the official video. In homage to Jobim (from 37:56–39:52 in the full official video but here, Video 18.1), the top-ranked model in the world, Brazilian Gisele Bündchen, crossed the floor of Maracanã Stadium to the sound of the composer's grandson, Daniel, singing the *bossa nova*, *"Garota de Ipanema"* ("The Girl from Ipanema"), an international hit in the late 1950s/early 1960s. From 41:08–41:54 in the full official video but here Video 18.2), Elza Soares sang *"Canto de Ossanha"* (music by Baden Powell, lyrics by Vinícius de Moraes), the song that rejuvenated the language of the Afro-Brazilian religion *candomblé* in *samba*. From 42:51–44:40 (here Video 18.3), Zeca Pagodinho sang his *pagode* hit *"Deixa a Vida me Levar"* ("Let Life Take Me") in alternating verses with rapper Marcelo D2.

Brazil is the only country in the world that has both the equator and the Tropic of Capricorn running through it. It has the greatest biological diversity in the world, and its topography is also diverse including hills, mountains, plains, highlands, and scrublands. Brazil has a dense and complex system of rivers, one of the world's most extensive, with eight major drainage basins, all of which drain into the Atlantic. Major rivers include the Amazon, the world's second-longest river and the largest in terms of volume of water. In addition to the Amazon and Iguaçu Falls, another great feature is the Pantanal, a natural region encompassing the world's largest tropical wetland area. Although mostly located in Brazil, it extends into portions of Bolivia and Paraguay (see Figure 18.1).

Early *Samba*

The roots of the *samba* lie in traditional forms of music for dance and for **candomblé** (an Afro-Brazilian religion) in Brazil's Northeast region, especially the Bahia state (see Figure 18.1). In the late nineteenth century, the end of legalized slavery (1888) led to a flood of Afro-Brazilian migrants from Bahia to the capital in Rio, bringing their music, dance, and religious practices with them. Bahian women—such as Tia Ciata (1854–1924) from the Praça Onze section of Rio de Janeiro—hosted musical and religious gatherings in their homes in the early decades of the twentieth century. Bahian migrants and their children gathered for observances of *candomblé* in which participants, by means of spirit possession, cultivate a personal relationship with a pantheon of deities (**orixás**). The dance and music associated with them were known as **batuque**. The early Bahian migrants also held informal music sessions during which the dance genres that were popular at the time were blended with this syncopated and percussive religious music by early *samba* musicians.

The first recorded *samba*, "*Pelo Telefone*" ("On the Telephone"), is a product of this musical community. Both the authorship of this piece (claimed by one of the five musicians) and its musical style label have been the subject of controversy, in part because *samba* had not yet emerged as a distinct genre. Despite the spoken identification of "*samba carnavalesco*" (Carnival *samba*) at the start of the recording, the music is closer to the **maxixe**, which combined elements of two other genres: *tango* and the polka. Despite these controversies, the date of

ACTIVITY 18.2

Watch Video 18.4 to understand more about this Afro-Brazilian religious practice from "Candomblé," chapter 9 in the video documentary *Rhythmic Uprising* by Benjamin Watkins (Video 18.4). Learn how *candomblé* has been present in Brazil since the era of slavery and has provided a spiritual foundation for people who live under difficult conditions. *Candomblé* centers play an important role in the social lives of participants of all ages that extends to family relationships and *Carnaval* celebrations. Note the importance of women as leaders in *candomblé*; the explanation of the *orixás* (deities), including references to Osain, also known as Ossanha; the musical instruments used in *candomblé* ceremonies; and the importance of *candomblé* as an expression of African cultural identity in contemporary Brazil. Compare this view of *candomblé* with faith-based communities you are familiar with.

"Pelo Telefone"'s copyright registration, November 27, 1916, was used as a basis for the celebration of the 100th anniversary of the *samba* in 2016.

The Emergence of Urban *Samba*

The circle of musicians of the **morros** or poorer hillside sections of the Estácio neighborhood of Rio (Figure 18.1), who were primarily of Afro-Brazilian descent, played an important role in the development of urban *samba*. In 1928, the first organized **escola de samba** ("*samba* school"), Deixa Falar ("Let them speak"), was formed there. Its name and designation as a "school" were signs of resistance to the middle class's disapproval of the music and the oppression by local authorities of *samba* musicians (Tinhorão 1998, 292–293). How oppressed were they really? Historian Marc Hertzman has questioned the accuracy of what he calls "the punishment paradigm." Referring to *samba* musicians in Rio de Janeiro in the 1930s, he writes, "Some musicians perpetrated illegal or violent acts, and others suffered arbitrary abuse. But individuals who played or composed music were rarely if ever arrested because they were musicians" (2013, 64).

SAMBA DE MORRO

With composers and other musicians of the Estácio neighborhood making important contributions to *samba* music and repertory, a style emerged that became known as *samba de morro*. In order to coordinate the tempo of a large group of dancers and musicians, the musician Bide introduced the practice of playing the second beat of a 2/4 measure strongly on the lowest-pitched drum of the ensemble. The **surdo** is a large, bass, double-headed cylindrical drum, bottom head not played, which is struck with a beater. He also introduced the use in the percussion section of the **tamborim**, a small tambourine without metal jingles in the frame (Tinhorão 1998, 293–294; Souza et al. 1988, 147). For images of instruments used in *samba*, see Figure 18.2.

Musicologist Carlos Sandroni calls the *samba* rhythmic feel established by these musicians "the Estácio paradigm" (2001, 32–37). The distinctive element of it is the composite rhythm played on four percussion instruments: the *surdo* and *tamborim*, along with the *cuíca* and the *pandeiro*. The **cuíca** is a friction drum of variable shape, single-headed, with a stick through the head, played with one arm inside, the other outside to manipulate the tension of the head to make a "laughing" sound rather than a percussive one. The **pandeiro** is a frame drum—tambourine—with metal jingles in the frame. The *cuíca* plays a syncopated, off-beat rhythm, while the *pandeiro* plays continuous sixteenth-notes with the third and fourth sixteenth-notes on each beat delayed slightly. The resulting musical texture of multiple rhythmic patterns performed simultaneously (**polyrhythm**)

Pandeiro   Tantã   Tamborim   Banjo   Repique de mão

Agogô   Tantã   Pandeiro   Tantã   Surdo

≡ **FIGURE 18.2**
Samba percussion
instruments. This
group playing
pagode-style
samba in Salvador
in 2019 includes
the following
instruments
(clockwise from
bottom left): *agogô,
tantã, pandeiro,
tantã, tamborim,
banjo, repique de
mão, surdo, tantã,*
and *pandeiro.*

is shown in staff notation in Music Example 18.1 and demonstrated by Audio
Example 18.1. These rhythms are examples of a rhythmic vocabulary characterized by basic patterns but with the expectation that they will constantly be varied
by the musicians.

MUSICAL EXAMPLE 18.1 Rhythms characteristic of the Estácio paradigm.

≡ **FIGURE 18.3** Ismael Silva plays the *pandeiro* with two *surdos* and one *caixa* (snare drum) in the foreground.

Putting all the musical parts of a *samba* together, the Estácio paradigm created the *samba*'s distinctive combination of a steady duple pulse with an accent on the second beat; layers of subtle syncopation in the percussion and also in stringed instrument parts; and a vocal line that floats above, following the speech accents of the lyrics (Murphy 2006, 10–11).

This foundational style of *samba* can be heard in the 1931 song "*Se Você Jurar*" ("If You Swear," using "swear" in the sense of promise or pledge) by Estácio composer Ismael Silva with Francisco Alves and Nilton Bastos. Silva was a founding member of the *samba* school Deixa Falar and one of the most prolific *samba* composers of the 1920s and 1930s (Figure 18.3). He collaborated with many important *samba* lyricists, including Noel Rosa, and the singer Francisco Alves, both of whom were of European descent. After a period away from the music business, he was active again from the 1950s, collaborating with and earning the admiration of a new generation of Brazilian composers, including Chico Buarque, until his death in 1978. His works have been performed and recorded often since that time.

The group *Velha Guarda da Mangueira* (Old Guard of Mangueira, a Rio de Janeiro neighborhood that is home to an important *samba* school) was founded in 1956 to keep the rootsy *samba de morro* style alive. The song "*Se Foi Bom Pra Você*" ("If It Was Good For You"), sung by Beth Carvalho on the group's 1999 release *Velha Guarda da Mangueira e Convidados* (Old Guard of Mangueira and Guests), is an example of this style (Audio Example 18.2). It was composed by Darcy Maravilha (b. 1947) and Darcy da Mangueira (1932–2008), *samba* composers and musicians from Rio.

Using mostly standard Portuguese language, the lyrics of "*Se Foi Bom Pra Você*" show how *samba* songs express the concerns of everyday Brazilian life. Sung from the perspective of a lover who was wronged, they urge the errant partner to reflect and to make amends. In verse 1 of this song, the narrator, who has been hurt by the actions of a former lover, urges the lover to reflect and to understand the narrator's feelings: "while our relationship might have been good for you" (*se foi bom pra você*), "for me

ACTIVITY 18.3

Listen to *"Se Foi Bom Pra Você"* (Audio Example 18.2) several times to familiarize yourself with this traditional *samba*. Once it sounds familiar, keep listening but focus your attention on the elements that establish the Estácio paradigm: 1) the low *surdo* drum on the second beat of the measure, 2) the layers of syncopation provided by other percussion and string instruments, and 3) the syncopated placement of the vocal phrases.

it wasn't, and that hurts." In verse 2, the narrator urges the former lover to recognize the good times they shared and ends with a plea: "let's erase the scar (*cicatriz*) of our failed romance." To hear where the verses begin, follow the Listening Guide.

Other Early *Samba* Styles

During the 1930s, a group of middle-class composers of European descent—including Noel Rosa, Ari Barroso, and Dorival Caymmi—made important contributions to another variety of *samba*: the *samba-canção* repertory. This style had been developed by composers for the musical theatre in Rio de Janeiro during the 1920s. **Samba-canção** (*samba* song) emphasizes melody more than rhythm and has a more varied harmonic accompaniment compared to *samba-enredo*, the up-tempo *samba* that would be used as the theme of each *samba* school for the *Carnaval* competition.

One of the best-known *sambas* is Ari Barroso's "Aquarela do Brasil" (1939), an example of a substyle of *samba-canção* called **samba-exaltação** ("exaltation *samba*") for the way it praises the Brazilian people, history, culture, or geography. Literally entitled "Watercolor of Brazil," and known in the English-speaking world simply as "Brazil," this song personifies Brazil as a "devious **mulato**" (person of mixed African and European descent; the term is considered derogatory) and paints a nostalgic image of the old Northeast during the time of slavery. At the end of list of idyllic descriptions in the lyrics is *"meu Brasil brasileiro/Terra de samba e pandeiro"* ("my Brazilian Brazil/Land of *samba* and *pandeiro*"). According to Shaw, Barroso wrote this *samba* in order to celebrate a more positive image of Brazil than that found in other *sambas*, which often focused on the figure of the **malandro**, and to praise the way of life found in Salvador, his favorite part of the country (1999).

"Se Foi Bom Pra Você"

Performers and instrumentation: Beth Carvalho, voice; Israel, harmonica; Márcio Vanderlei, banjo; Márcio Almeida, *cavaquinho*, plucked lute with four metal strings; Josimar Monteiro, 6- and 7-string guitar; Tuca, *ganzá* (shaker), *cuíca*, *pandeiro*, *repique de mão* (small, single-headed, cylindrical drum held on player's lap), *tamborim* (small, high-pitched drum), *tantã* (low-pitched, single-headed, elongated, barrel-shaped hand drum held on the player's lap), *surdo*; Mocinho, *reco-reco* (scraper); Darcy Maravilha, *pandeiro*; Sérgio Vieira, *surdo*; Roberto Marques, trombone; vocal chorus, uncredited.

Time	Something to Listen For
0:00	Ensemble begins its introduction with a stroke on the *repique de mão* on the "and" of beat 2. The introduction lasts eight measures, counted quickly in 2/4 at 104 beats per minute. The harmonica's melody is supported by syncopated strumming on the *cavaquinho*.
0:08	As the accompanying instruments pause for one measure, Carvalho begins verse 1 by singing the title phrase. The *pandeiro* joins the ensemble. The *cavaquinho* continues its active chordal accompaniment.
0:36	After reaching the end of the lyrics of verse 1, Carvalho repeats the last two lines.
0:44	As Carvalho reaches the word "*sorrir*" (smile), the accompaniment pauses for a two-measure melodic fill on a seven-string guitar. During the second measure, Carvalho begins singing verse 2.
0:46	As verse 2 begins, the *surdo* part begins. Listen for its low stroke on the second beat of each two-beat measure. The banjo enters, an element that links this performance to the rootsy style of *pagode*, discussed below. Listen for its rapid strumming in a register below that of the *cavaquinho*. The seven-string guitar continues to add melodic counterlines to the vocal part.
1:02	Carvalho ends verse 2 without repeating its last two lines.
1:04	The percussion parts pause while Carvalho sings the first line of verse 2. The seven-string guitar adds a counterline.
1:07	The banjo makes an upward slide while strumming rapidly.
1:22	Carvalho sings the *chamada* (call), a quick preview of the next lyric, which cues the entry of the vocal chorus.
1:24	As the chorus begins a repeat of verse 1, the *cuíca* joins the percussion accompaniment, providing high-pitched interjections that have a vocal quality.
1:26	Carvalho encourages the chorus by calling out, "*beleza* (beautiful), Velha Guarda!"
1:29	Carvalho calls out "*fala* (speak), Mangueira!"

Time	Something to Listen For
1:31	The trombone enters with a low-register counterline.
1:35	The trombone plays a quick melodic fill.
1:40	The *cuíca* plays a prominent fill, followed by a fill from the trombone.
1:47	The seven-string guitar, *cuíca*, and trombone add fills beneath the chorus's melody.
1:51	The chorus repeats the last two lines of verse 1.
1:59	The entire accompaniment pauses as Carvalho sings the first line of verse 2, supported by active counterlines in the seven-string guitar; *Cavaquinho* and banjo continue with syncopated chordal accompaniment over the percussion parts.
2:17	Carvalho sings the *chamada* to preview the first line of verse 2.
2:18	The chorus begins verse 2. Seven-string guitar and banjo continue their active accompaniment.
2:31	The *cuíca* adds a fill in its typical "laughing" style.
2:33	The trombone begins a series of fills between the final vocal phrases.
2:36	The chorus repeats the last two lines of verse 2 two more times.
2:44	An active trombone line leads to the final vocal phrase; over the trombone's held final note, Carvalho says "*Obrigada* (thank you), Velha Guarda da Mangueira."

Samba Schools and Carnaval

Carnaval in Brazil is a season of celebration that culminates in the three days preceding Ash Wednesday, the beginning of the Lent season that precedes Easter in the Christian liturgical calendar. *Carnaval* was celebrated in Brazil well before the founding of the first *samba* school. It developed from rowdy end-of-the-year celebrations that were practiced during the time of Portuguese colonialism from the sixteenth century until the early nineteenth century. By the early twentieth century, as the population of Rio de Janeiro grew and diversified, so did the participation in *Carnaval*. Groups from the middle and lower classes began parading together in costume, and eventually rhythms more appropriate for couple dancing in ballrooms were replaced with those such as the **marcha** that were developed for large processions (Tinhorão 1986, 121). The formation of the *samba* schools was an effort to legitimize the *Carnaval* groups formed by people who lived on the *morros*, most of whom were of Afro-Brazilian descent.

During the first administration of president Getúlio Vargas (1930–1945), the *samba* schools were given official recognition. In 1939, the government made it mandatory for them to use nationalistic themes for their parades (Souza et al. 1988, 149). Along with this official recognition came government subsidies for the *samba* schools, which were helping to make *Carnaval* into a major tourist attraction.

During their first decades, the *samba* schools were cooperative, community organizations:

> The leadership and membership were entirely indigenous, coming from each individual neighborhood. Members gave from their own near-empty pockets to meet the schools' needs, and artisans gave freely of their skills to build the schools' floats. Female school members sewed costumes, men made their own instruments, the children caught the cats whose skins covered the homemade drums used in the rhythm section. Rehearsals for the Carnival parade were held in the dirt lanes of the *favelas*; when headquarters were built, local carpenters provided the labor. (Raphael 1990, 77)

This is the seemingly idyllic time memorialized in the 1959 film *Orfeu Negro* ("Black Orpheus"), which has served as an introduction to Brazilian music and culture for generations of viewers.

By the 1960s, the *samba* schools had increased greatly in size and had come under increasing pressures from outside their communities. *Carnaval* performances became more competitive, with lucrative prizes for the winning schools. In 1960, when the Brazilian capital was shifted from Rio de Janeiro to the newly constructed city of Brasília, tourism became even more important to Rio's economy. The schools' activities became more commercialized as more middle-class Rio residents became involved in them. Professional designers known as *carnavalescos* made the parades and costumes ever more spectacular. The location of the *Carnaval* parade shifted among various avenues in downtown Rio until the construction in 1984 of the *Passarela do Samba*, known officially as the "*Praça da Apoteose*" ("Plaza of the Apotheosis," or "moment of crowning glory" in Charles Perrone's phrase [2001, 62]), but known popularly as the **Sambadrome** (Figure 18.4).

Each year, the *samba* schools select a theme for their presentations in the parade in the Sambadrome. The theme determines the design of costumes for hundreds of participants in the school, and the design of floats and other elements. The schools' composers compete to create the upbeat tempo **samba-enredo** that will constitute the entirety of the music for their presentation, including the lyrics that speak to the year's theme. The year's song will be repeated many, many times during the extremely slow, yet dramatic procession from one end of the space to the other, accompanied only by percussion. The hundreds of participants must

FIGURE 18.4
Carnaval samba at
Sambadrome in Rio
de Janeiro, featuring
the Portela *samba*
school, winner of
Carnaval 2017.

try to stay in absolute synchronization with each other. Competition among the schools is extremely keen and the *samba-enredo* is a crucial part of that competition. Selected within the schools well in advance of the *Carnaval* season, the songs are recorded and marketed to the public before the parade day. Performances of the winning song for each year can easily be found online, should you wish to hear a few.

ACTIVITY 18.4

With the help of your instructor, find videos that provide a sense of the experience of *Carnaval* in Rio de Janeiro. An excellent documentary is *O Samba* (directed by Georges Gachot, 2014), which profiles the prominent *samba* singer Martinho da Vila and shows how the *escola de samba* (samba school) Vila Isabel prepares for the competition in the Sambadrome.

To think about *Carnaval* in Rio in personal terms, compare the *Carnaval* parade to large-scale performances you are familiar with, such as marching band or drumline competitions. How do the community values and participation of the *samba* schools compare to your event?

Developments in the 1950s and 1960s

The *samba* tradition became more inclusive of all aspects of Brazilian life as a result of the collaboration between guitarist-composer Baden Powell (full name Baden Powell de Aquino; he was named after Robert Baden-Powell, the founder of the international scouting movement) and poet-diplomat Vinícius de Moraes. De Moraes had collaborated with Tom Jobim on songs including "The Girl from Ipanema" from the 1950s and 1960s that became classics of *bossa nova*. In that quieter, more intimate form of *samba*, the guitar (or piano) provides syncopated support for the voice. A Brazilian of European descent who called himself (in a song lyric) "the blackest white man in the country," de Moraes had been interested in Afro-Brazilian culture since the early 1940s when he wrote the play *Orfeu da Conceição*, a retelling of the Orpheus myth set in the world of *samba* and *candomblé* that was adapted into the film *Orfeu Negro*. The collaboration of Baden Powell with de Moraes resulted in the 1966 album *Os Afro-Sambas*.

Os Afro-Sambas was inspired by a recording of *candomblé* music. In his liner notes for the album, de Moraes wrote that the songs were intended to "Rio de Janeiro-ize Afro-Brazilian *candomblé* in the spirit of modern *samba*, and at the same time to give it a more universal dimension" (quoted in Kuehn 2014 [2002], 20). "*Canto de Ossanha*" opens the album. The Brazilian edition of *Rolling Stone* magazine named it number 9 in its list of the 100 best Brazilian songs, stating that it helped the sound of Afro-Brazilian religions—which had been systematically persecuted as late as two decades before—to enter Brazilian popular music "by the front door" (Espirito Santo 2009). In 1990, Powell received the opportunity to rerecord the album as a gift CD for a bank. He accepted, in order to honor de Moraes, who had died in 1980, and to take advantage of improved recording technology. He was so pleased by the result that he released it on a French and later a Brazilian record label. Audio Example 18.3 is from this later version.

In *candomblé*, Ossanha is the deity (*orixá*) of the earth and of plants that transmit the vital life force **axé**, and a rival of the *orixá* Xangô, the powerful deity who is noted for his anger (Kuehn 2014 [2002], 11). The lyrics evoke the treacherous nature of Ossanha with statements that are immediately negated, supported by a brooding minor key accompaniment with a descending chord pattern. The contrasting section, with conventional *samba* accompaniment in two major keys, deals with lost love.

This song has been covered by a wide range of artists, from *bossa nova* singer Elis Regina to jazz harpist Dorothy Ashby to the alternative hip-hop group Jurassic 5.

ACTIVITY 18.5

Listen several times to "*Canto de Ossanha*" to familiarize yourself with it. Note also the prominence of the call and response structure of Afro-Brazilian music.

Then try your own listening skills: review Audio Example 18.2 ("*Se Foi Bom Pra Você*") and then return to this example. Make a list of comparative statements that help to distinguish the two *samba*s.

Pagode: A "Backyard" Style of *Samba*

The style of *samba* that has received the most attention in recent decades is known as **pagode**. Ethnomusicologist Philip Galinsky traces its origins to the early twentieth century as music played at gatherings of lower-income people, but he links contemporary uses of the term to a movement in the 1960s and 1970s that resisted the entry of middle-class people and business interests into *escolas de samba* (1996). Ultimately, the entry of middle-class people and business interests resulted in the marginalization of the lower-income participants. *Pagode* exists in two forms: a rootsy, "backyard" style of *samba* that flourished in the 1960s–1980s, and a more commercial style that dates from the 1990s to the present.

Again, it was musicians in a particular suburb of Rio de Janeiro that established the style: the suburb of Ramos, where the important band *Grupo Fundo de Quintal* (The Backyard Group) was founded. The group performed older *samba*s and—in keeping with the *samba* genre—added new ones with lyrics that chronicled daily life. *Grupo Fundo de Quintal* collaborated frequently with Beth Carvalho, who you heard singing "*Se Foi Bom Pra Você*" (Audio Example 18.2).

As was the case with other varieties of *samba* through the twentieth century, *pagode* was distinguished by two particular musical features: instrumentation and a rhythm pattern. Along with the **cavaquinho** (a guitar-type plucked lute with four strings of wire or gut), **violão** (classical guitar with nylon strings), and *pandeiro*, *pagode* musicians added the four-string banjo; the **tantã**, a conga-like drum that rests on the player's lap and substitutes for the *surdo*; and the **repique de mão**, a small, high-pitched, single-headed cylindrical drum held in the lap that is played by hand on its skin and body.

LISTENING GUIDE

"Canto de Ossanha"

Recording location and year: Studio Sinth, Rio de Janeiro, October 1990

Performers and instrumentation: Baden Powell (guitar and vocals); Quarteto em Cy (Cyva, Cynara, Cybele, and Sonya, vocals); Ernesto Gonçalves (bass); Paulo Guimarães (flute); Aloísio Fagerland (bassoon); Flávio Neves (*surdo, atabaque,* **afoxé,** *ganzá*); Sutinho (drum set, *tamborim, agogô*); Alfredo Bessa (*atabaque, afoxé, ganzá, cuíca, tamborim*); Valdeci (*pandeiro, tamborim*)

Composed by Vinícius de Moraes and Baden Powell

Time	Something to Listen For
0:00	Powell plays a *rubato* (fluctuating tempo) introduction on guitar, establishing the D minor tonality, with rapid strokes on the *atabaque*.
0:15	The meter of two beats per measure, at a tempo of eighty-nine beats per minute, begins with steady sixteenth notes on the *afoxé* and the entry of the *surdo* on the second beat. When syncopated accents are added on the snare drum of the drum set, the basic elements of *samba* rhythm are in place: a layer of steady subdivisions, a low drum on the second beat, and syncopated patterns layered above.
0:21	Powell plays a low-register guitar line in D minor.
0:28	The *atabaque* joins the percussion section, producing a higher, ringing tone.
0:31	The four-chord progression that supports the first part of the song begins: D minor, moving up to F major, then descending through E major and E flat major, to begin again on D minor. This pattern is heard six times before the vocals begin.
1:02	Powell begins singing the first part of the song in call-and-response fashion with the Quarteto em Cy (a vocal group originally formed by sisters who had the letters "Cy" in their names); the lyrics establish a mood of uncertainty that is appropriate to an evocation of the *orixá* (Afro-Brazilian deity) Ossanha, a traitorous figure.
1:23	Quarteto em Cy sing the first line of the second section of the lyrics, which express pity for the man who is seduced by the song of the traitorous Ossanha; Powell sings the response, expressing pity for the man who goes after a love charm. The four-chord sequence in D minor continues through this section.
1:35	In the third section of the lyrics, Powell sings *"vai"* (go) at a lowered volume, to which the Quarteto em Cy respond that they won't go.
1:37	A flute counterline rises through the end of this eight-measure section that leads to the next section of the song.

Time	Something to Listen For
1:45	Quarteto em Cy sing the fourth section of the song in D major; this is a more conventional *samba* melody. The lyrics speak from the perspective of someone who has been unlucky in love and has learned from the experience. Brief woodwind interjections support the voice parts during the two phrases of eight and six measures.
2:03	The tonality returns to D minor as Powell sings the next section of the lyrics, which warn against following the song of Ossanha; bassoon doubles his vocal line, which spans a large interval.
2:10	The chord pattern in D minor returns, with bassoon playing a descending line.
2:14	In this final section of lyrics, Powell sings one of the song's most memorable phrases: ask your *orixá* if love is only good when it hurts.
2:19	That set of lyrics is sung again by Quarteto em Cy.
2:24	Powell sings "*vai*" (go) as the flute counterline returns.
2:35	The D major melody and its lyrics are heard, with woodwind backgrounds as before.
2:45	This time, however, the second phrase shifts upward to F major, which makes the major key section even brighter.
2:56	A return to D minor, with bassoon and flute counterlines; Powell improvises on guitar.
3:07	Powell sings the "*vai*" (go) lyric again, with responses by the Quarteto em Cy.
3:17	The D major section returns once more.
3:27	The second phrase shifts upward to F major as before.
3:37	The key shifts back to D minor, where it will remain; Powell improvises over the flute and bassoon counterlines.
3:50	The flute adds improvised phrases.
3:59	The song ends with a series of exchanges of the "*vai, vai, vai!*" (go, go, go!) phrase: first Powell, then the Quarteto em Cy, then the Quarteto an octave above, and finally Powell joins them on the upper octave.

Like other varieties of *samba*, *pagode*'s rhythmic texture is created by a complex weaving of on-beat and offbeat patterns. It is distinguished, however, by the use of a particular rhythm, the **partido-alto rhythm** that is notated in Musical Example 18.2 as played on the *pandeiro*; you can hear it played in Audio Example 18.4. You might notice that the tempo is slower compared to that of *samba-enredo* for *Carnaval*.

MUSICAL EXAMPLE 18.2 *Partido-alto* rhythm.

Early in his musical career, Jessé Gomes da Silva Filho was associated with the *pagode* scene in the Rio neighborhood of Ramos. His performing name—Zeca Pagodinho—associates him closely with the *pagode* style (Figure 18.5). He gained national prominence through his appearance on Beth Carvalho's 1983 album *Suor no Rosto*, and released his self-titled debut CD three years later. By the time he released his fifteenth CD, *Deixa a vida me levar* ("Let life take me") in 2002, he was an established figure in *pagode*. The title song, *"Deixa a Vida Me Levar"* (Audio Example 18.5), was composed by Serginho Meriti and Eri do Cais. The lyrics speak from the perspective of a person from a poor background who, despite life's challenges, maintains a grateful, positive attitude that is expressed in the song's refrain: let life take me, [because] I'm happy and I give thanks for everything God has given me. The song was adopted as the theme song by the Brazilian national **futebol** (soccer) team, which won its fifth World Cup title in 2002. In that year's Latin Grammy awards, the album won Best *Samba/Pagode* Album, and the song was nominated for Best Brazilian Song. The title was borrowed for a 2014 biography of the singer, which notes that the song has been used as a prayer and as an everyday motivational phrase among Brazilians (Barbosa and Bruno 2014).

Pagode was nationally popular during the late 1980s, before yielding to other popular musics such as **sertaneja**, **lambada**, and **axé-music** from Bahia. A more commercialized form of *pagode* emerged in the early 1990s, featuring romantic lyrics and an instrumentation that includes keyboards, drum set, and brass instruments.

≡ **FIGURE 18.5** Photograph of Zeca Pagodinho, (left) musician closely associated with the *pagode* style of *samba*.

Samba in Contemporary Brazilian Musical Life: Elza Soares and *Samba Sujo*

Styles of *samba* continue to emerge. Three examples of the vitality of *samba* in contemporary Brazilian musical life are

ACTIVITY 18.6

Listen to *"Deixa a Vida Me Levar"* (Audio Example 18.5) several times, focusing each time on one of these characteristics: tempo, instrumentation, the *partido-alto* rhythm pattern, and call-and-response structure. If you can, listen for rich harmonies as well. Some of the lyrics you hear might be improvised, as happens in *pagode*.

1. The growth of a roots *samba* scene in the Rio de Janeiro neighborhood of Lapa, illustrated by the music of Alfredo Del-Penho.
2. The popularity of participatory street *samba* groups in Rio de Janeiro, shown by the group *Monobloco*.
3. The ***samba sujo*** ("dirty *samba*") movement centered in São Paulo, exemplified by the album by veteran singer Elza Soares, *A Mulher do Fim do Mundo* ("The Woman at the End of the World").

This section of the chapter focuses on the third example.

Elza Soares (b. 1930) is a veteran *samba* singer who had a difficult early life (Figure 18.6). Born in a *favela* and obliged to marry early, she entered a radio talent show at age 16 wearing a borrowed dress. When host and composer Ari Barroso asked what planet she was from, she retorted "planet hunger" (Sherburne 2016). She won the competition and began her long career. Her personal life has included a tumultuous marriage to soccer star Garrincha and the death of five of her six children. The wide expressive range of her voice includes gravelly timbres and scat-singing passages that have led to comparisons to Bessie Smith, Billie Holiday, Ella Fitzgerald, Tina Turner, and Celia Cruz.

After decades of recording *samba*, often with jazz overtones, Soares made a series of experimental albums that began with *Do Cóccix Até Ao Pescoço* (2000) and *Vivo Feliz* (2003). Her 2015 CD *A Mulher do Fim do Mundo* ("The Woman at the End of the World") is an adventurous collaboration with musicians from the São Paulo *samba sujo* scene that frames her voice with distorted guitars, a string ensemble, and electronic sounds on a set of songs that, in the words of her record label, "tackles the burning issues of 21st century Brazil: racism, domestic violence, sex and drug addiction" (*Mais Um Discos* 2016). It won the 2016 *Prêmio da Música Brasileira* award for best pop/rock/reggae/hip-hop/funk album. Ben Ratliff of *The New York Times*

FIGURE 18.6
Photograph of Elza Soares, singer associated with the *samba sujo* ("dirty samba") movement centered in São Paulo.

called it "a devastating, late-career, vanguard-pop masterpiece about the parts of Brazilian life its popular music has tended to obscure" (Pareles et al. 2016).

The title song is told from the perspective of a woman who loses her identity in a *Carnaval* parade (Audio Example 18.6; Video 18.5). Supported by string ensemble, distorted electric guitar, and *samba* percussion, the song takes on a tone of impending doom. You can follow the lyrics through the link.

Conclusion

There are many forms of *samba*. However, they all have a prominent role in creating a sense of national identity. They all communicate something uniquely "Brazilian," rooted in national ways of making percussive music for dancing and using language to comment on daily life in artful ways. By making *samba* a prominent part of the opening—and closing—ceremonies of the 2016 Olympic Games in Rio de Janeiro, the organizers called the world's attention to Brazil's most important contribution to the world of music. By simultaneously preserving the classic *samba* style and blending it with contemporary popular music styles, current *samba* musicians ensure that their music speaks to the present while retaining its identity.

Bibliography

Barbosa, Jane, and Leonardo Bruno. 2014. *Zeca: Deixa o Samba me Levar*. São Paulo, Brazil: Sonora.

Espirito Santo, José Julio do. 2009. Text accompanying listing of "Canto de Ossanha" as no. 9 of "As 100 Maiores Músicas Brasileiras" (The 100 Best Brazilian Songs). *Rolling Stone* (Brazilian edition). https://rollingstone.uol.com.br/edicao/37/noticia-3947/

Galinsky, Philip. 1996. "Co-option, Cultural Resistance, and Afro-Brazilian Identity: A History of the *Pagode* Samba Movement in Rio de Janeiro." *Latin American Music Review* 17, no. 2: 120–149.

Hertzman, Marc A. 2013. *Making Samba: A New History of Race and Music in Brazil*. Durham, NC: Duke University Press.

Kuehn, Frank M.C. 2014 (2002). "Estudo sobre os elementos afro-brasileiros do candomblé em letra e música de Vinícius de Moraes e Baden Powell: os 'afro-sambas.'" In *Anais* do 3° Colóquio de Pesquisa em Música, Rio de Janeiro, Escola de Música da UFRJ.

Mais Um Discos. 2016. Bandcamp page for *A Mulher do Fim do Mundo*. Accessed January 21, 2017. https://elzasoares.bandcamp.com/album/the-woman-at-the-end-of-the-world-a-mulher-do-fim-do-mundo

Murphy, John. 2006. *Music in Brazil: Experiencing Music, Expressing Culture*. Oxford: Oxford University Press.

Pareles, John, Ben Ratliff, Jon Caramanica, and Nate Chinen. 2016. "The Essentials of Brazilian Music for Olympic Listening." *The New York Times*, August 2. https://www.nytimes.com/2016/08/03/arts/music/brazilian-music-playlist.html

Perrone, Charles. 2001. "Myth, Melopeia, and Mimesis: Black Orpheus, Orfeo, and Internationalization in Brazilian Popular Music." In *Brazilian Popular Music and Globalization*, edited by Charles Perrone and Christopher Dunn, 46–71. Gainesville, FL: University Press of Florida.

Raphael, Allison. 1990. "From Popular Culture to Microenterprise: The History of Brazilian Samba Schools." *Latin American Music Review* 11, no. 1: 73–83.

Sandroni, Carlos. 2001. *Feitiço Decente: Transformações do Samba no Rio de Janeiro (1917–1933)*. Rio de Janeiro: Jorge Zahar Editora/Editora UFRJ.

Shaw, Lisa. 1999. *The Social History of the Brazilian Samba*. Aldershot, England: Ashgate.

Sherburne, Philip. 2016. Review of *A Mulher do Fim do Mundo*. *Pitchfork*, July 29. http://pitchfork.com/reviews/albums/22173-a-mulher-do-fim-do-mundo-the-woman-at-the-end-of-the-world/

Souza, Tárik de, et al. 1988. *Brasil Musical/Musical Brazil*. Rio de Janeiro: Art Bureau Representações e Edições de Arte.

Tinhorão, José Ramos. 1986. *Pequena História da Música Popular: Da Modinha ao Tropicalismo*. 5th ed. São Paulo, Brazil: Art Editora.

Tinhorão, José Ramos. 1998. *História Social da Música Popular Brasileira*. São Paulo, Brazil: Editora 34.

19

Music in the Southwest United States

United States

Tales of Tradition and Innovation in Mariachi Borderlands

DANIEL SHEEHY

Chapter Contents

Introduction

This chapter is about mariachi, which developed in Mexico and spread, along with the Mexican people, into the United States. Rooted in rural life of western Mexico in the 1800s, the modern mariachi sound emerged during the first half of the twentieth century. Only in the 1950s, however, did it reach the form and sound in which it is well-known and appreciated today. With trumpets front and center, mariachi music is both expressive and rhythmic, exciting and easily engaging.

The term "mariachi" has had many different meanings. It has been applied to a type of Mexican American traditional ensemble; individual mariachi musicians; or, as an adjective, something identified with it, such as "mariachi repertoire."

We use the term "mariachi borderlands" to describe the expanding universe of meaning and sound that has occurred in mariachi music today, most particularly in the United States. Mapping these borderlands follows Mexican American **demography** (characteristics and movement of human populations) more than geography, although the arc-shaped area from Texas to Washington State continues

≡ **Mariachi Reyna de Los Ángeles.**

≡ **FIGURE 19.1** Mariachi ensembles are found in virtually every state of Mexico and in the majority of states in the U.S. This map does not intend to be comprehensive of mariachi presence; rather, it indicates a selection of cities historically important in the presence and cultivation of mariachi music.

to be a stronghold for the culture (Figure 19.1). Social circumstances often give music-making new meanings, and mariachi's interaction with the US musical environment often leads to new sounds. This chapter addresses the question, "How do people give meaning to mariachi music and make it useful in their lives?" In a seeming paradox, the answer is that, for the music to remain traditional— relevant and meaningful in people's lives—it must change.

In this chapter, three tales of tradition and innovation provide examples of how this tension between tradition and change has played out over the past half century of mariachi's presence in American society. The US-based mariachi pioneer Natividad "Nati" Cano (1933–2014) aptly described how this tension occurred in mariachi tradition:

ACTIVITY 19.1

Watch the two videos featuring Nati Cano. Take notes on what is striking to you and what you can learn about mariachi music from these visual sources. Make note of the different vocal styles and instruments that you hear. Be sure you include in your notes the major points made by Nati Cano about mariachi history in the United States.

You should not change things that are classic. You should leave them intact. . . . [At the same time], is not good for humanity for everything to be the same. . . . Here is how I put it. . . . On the taco, put *salsa de tomate*, *salsa verde*, *salsa de chipotle*, put whatever you like. But just don't put ketchup.

As a young man in Guadalajara and as leader of Mariachi Los Camperos in the United States, Cano and his music were discriminated against. In Guadalajara, Mexico, academic musicians referred to mariachi as low-class "**cantina music**." In the United States in the 1960s, Cano was confronted with racism in addition to the music being considered only fit for barrooms. He made it his life mission to elevate mariachi music to the highest artistic level possible, and earn it social respect through promoting mariachi music education.

Each of the tales told in what follows demonstrates that keeping music meaningful and useful often leads to a dynamic tension between continuity and uniformity on one hand and purposeful disruption and innovation on the other. This give and take of meaning in mariachi music plays out in several different social settings, generating new "borders" of meaning that reflect changing purposes and realities.

Mariachi History

In 1519, the Spanish conquistador Hernán Cortés sailed from the Gulf of Mexico toward Tenochtitlan in what is now Mexico City in order to seize control of the rulers of the Aztec empire. Among his 300 men were six musicians. One, a man named Ortiz, was a dance teacher and player of a bowed lute. While chordophones were nearly nonexistent among Mexican native peoples, the Spanish held them in high regard. During the three centuries of Spanish rule from 1521–1821, many types of guitar, harp, and violin were introduced to New Spain, as the area approximating much of today's country of Mexico was then called. Instrument making became widespread, and stringed instruments proliferated. In addition, musical and lyrical forms, important occasions for music-making, the social value of music, and many other basic building blocks of mariachi music, took shape. During that time, the population became mostly *mestizo*—people who emerged from the mix of cultures—in Mexico. Eventually, over three-quarters of Mexico's population had roots in the mixing of European, Indian, and African peoples.

Accepted as a symbol of regional Mexican culture by the first decade of the twentieth century, the sound of mariachi (particularly from the Jalisco region around Guadalajara; see Figure 19.1) was spread through visits of these ensembles to Mexico City and very early recordings by American phonograph companies. Sparked by the Mexican Revolution (1910–1917) that resulted in a less stratified society, the twentieth century would see a flood of interior migration. Along with many other regional *mestizos,* a number of mariachi musicians from rural areas migrated to cities, including to Mexico City, which became one of the largest cities in the world. This migration was an important step toward mariachi becoming an urban popular music.

Rampant urbanization created a demand for music that appealed to the tastes of the newly arrived people from rural areas. Eventually, as society evolved and as distinctly urban tastes emerged, the sound, repertoire, and role of the mariachi changed. In the 1930s, economic opportunities permitted mariachi groups to become full-time professional musicians, spurred on by an explosion of the entertainment industries in Mexico—radio and sound film in particular. Politically, mariachi was lifted to the position of national symbol—a position it still holds.

Besides immigrating within Mexico, many people crossed the border seeking economic opportunities in the United States. At the end of the twentieth century, the US population of Mexican origin had grown to more than 20 million, expanding the base of support for mariachi musicians. This audience lured many musicians from Mexico; fluid travel back and forth between the two countries contributed to maintaining a strong baseline of musical continuity across the political border.

At the same time, differing historical, social, and economic circumstances on the American side of the border have left their mark on the music and on the way people appreciate it. When Mexican Americans embrace mariachi music as an expression of their special, distinctive identity in a multicultural US society, they add a dimension of musical meaning and social status different from that in the Mexican context, where everyone is Mexican. As mariachi musicians have been integrated into the American cultural environment, changes in performance contexts, repertoire, the social meanings of the music, ways of learning it, and a rise in the status of the musicians have followed. Social movements, the popular music industry, and promotion of the music to the growing Mexican market have brought mariachi music to the fore of American life. Hundreds of US schools offer mariachi music performance programs, and dozens of annual mariachi festivals occur through the Southwest and other US regions.

Mariachi Music

Like most popular music, mariachi music is a product that is bought and sold: bought by audiences in a variety of contexts; sold by the musicians who work in a number of economic situations. Mariachis are hired by the hour by patrons for gigs (**chambas**), such as weddings and birthday celebrations. A variation of this is a **serenata** (a serenade of about a half hour to mark a special occasion)—a popular tradition in Mexican culture. They might be hired for a "regular gig" (**planta**) by a client such as a restaurant, hotel, or theater. Or, they might work *al talón* (literally, "on the heel") in which the musicians charge clients in bars or restaurants by the number of songs played. (See the segment in the video interview with Nati Cano [Video 19.2] from 7:17 to 10:53 for comment on performance contexts for his ensemble.)

As a non-Mexican American, my most memorable first experience with the modern mariachi sound occurred when I was sitting in a restaurant in Tijuana. When an eight-piece mariachi circled around my table, I was surrounded by the sound and power of the music. Being a trumpet player, I was deeply impressed by the energy, the volume, and the rhythmic punch of the two trumpets. The three violins produced a wall of three-part harmony that I could feel as much as hear. The strumming of the **vihuela** and the six-stringed guitar was tightly synchronized, crisp, and direct. And the **guitarrón**—the *guitarrón*!—what an amazing instrument! Its sheer quantity of low-end sound filled the room. Add to this a no holds barred, expressive singing style, and the result was an unmitigated, direct emotional expression that cannot be ignored. Sitting in the middle of all that, I was transformed. And when the mariachi played a fast-driving *son*, someone in the restaurant let out a loud **grito**—a yell—no more than two seconds into the piece, adding to the excitement.

The instruments and the way they are played are essential to the mariachi sound. The trumpet, violin, and nylon-stringed classical guitar are the same versions of the instruments used in European orchestras, bands, and guitar classes. The *vihuela* and *guitarrón* are special to the mariachi. They were created in Mexico; and though they were based on earlier instruments brought from Spain, they are unique in origin to western Mexico.

≡ **FIGURE 19.2** The spined, rounded, convex body of the *vihuela* sets it apart from other kinds of guitar. Its length is similar to that of a six-stringed guitar, though it may not look like it because its body is narrower than the guitar's. Most *vihuelas* are made of a cedarwood found in many parts of Mexico that is lightweight and resonates loudly. Master-luthier Roberto Morales, whose instruments are in demand throughout the world, puts the finishing touches on one of his *vihuelas*. Behind it on the work bench is a *guitarrón* in the making.

The *vihuela* takes its name from a sixteenth-century Spanish variety of guitar that was favored by the educated classes. Over time, "genteel society" came to prefer the six-stringed Spanish guitar; while, in western Mexico, the Mexican form of the *vihuela* remained in the hands of farmers, ranchers, traders—and mariachi musicians. Of the guitar family, the *vihuela* is a long-necked, waisted (figure-eight shaped), plucked lute with a spined, rounded, convex body (Figure 19.2). Its body is the same length as the six-stringed guitar, but narrower, and has five nylon strings. The *vihuela* provides a rhythmic pulse and chordal harmonic accompaniment to the melody instruments and singers. The *vihuelero* (*vihuela* player) uses defined hand patterns of strumming called *mánicos* to create a rhythmic background. Each genre has a distinctive *mánico* that sets it apart from the others.

The *guitarrón* looks like a big *vihuela*, except that its sound box is much bigger in proportion to its overall length than that of the *vihuela*. (The *guitarrón* can be seen in the video interview with Nato Cano [Video 19.2] at 5:57, 9:11, 12:47, 13.19, and at the end.) Also, it has six strings rather than five. Two are usually plucked at once

ACTIVITY 19.2

To get the sound of modern mariachi in your ears, listen to *"Las Olas"* ("The Waves"; Audio Example 19.1). Focus on the voice and then each instrument in turn as you listen several times. Try to hear the *vihuela* apart from the guitar and *guitarrón,* then the three of them together as the "rhythm section." Once you can identify the instruments by their sounds in "Las Olas," re-watch the videos of Nati Cano to identify them visually.

Do you agree with my characterizations of the musical parts? If not, how would you describe them?

There are two distinct differences between the mariachi performance you hear in *"Las Olas"* and the one you heard in the video "Nati Cano: What Makes a Good Mariachi." Can you figure out for yourself what those are?

in a pinching motion, thereby increasing the volume of the pitch. Like most bass instruments in Western European based musical traditions, it usually focuses on the main notes of the chordal harmony.

The *vihuela, guitarrón,* and guitar together form the "section" of the ensemble called **armonía**—meaning "harmony," but functioning as well as a "rhythm section." The musicians think of them as linked together in a single function, providing the rhythmic and harmonic structure and background for the rest of the music. In this spirit, the three instruments closely interlock, with their rhythms and harmonies complementing each other as a single unit.

Tales of Innovation and Tradition
Mariachi in Education

In contrast with Mexico—where mariachi musical skills have been passed on mainly within families—educational programs teaching mariachi have sprung up across a broad swath of the United States, starting with UCLA in 1961. In 1979, the First International Mariachi Conference in San Antonio, Texas, sparked an explosion of mariachi festivals and conferences throughout the Southwest, in tandem with the creation of hundreds of school teaching programs in the 1980s (see Figure 19.3).

Tucson, Arizona has long been a leader in mariachi-in-schools programs. Richard Carranza was a middle school mariachi student in Tucson when he attended the 1979 mariachi conference in San Antonio. He chose teaching as a

≡ **FIGURE 19.3**
Chula Vista High School mariachi class in Chula Vista, California taught by mariachi educator Mark Fogelquist.

career; and while teaching bilingual social studies at Pueblo High School, he started a mariachi ensemble there in 1991. As he explains, he knew both the value of mariachi to education and the value of education to mariachi:

> I saw students that were second or third-generation [immigrant] kids that were just in a bad way. They were involved with drugs or gangs, didn't live in the best part of town, and were disconnected to school. . . . Once they got really excited about the mariachi program, and they saw that they . . . could actually perform and get a ***traje*** [mariachi suit], then what we did was make sure that students knew that you just don't get a *traje*, you have to earn it. You represent your school, so you have to go to class, you have to keep your grades up, you can't get in trouble. So we raised the bar for our students, and every one of those kids met the bar. When I left the program and moved into administration about ten years later, our graduation rate was about 98% (Personal interview with Richard Carranza, December 11, 2016). Previously, the graduation rate was around 64 percent, so this was a dramatic difference.

Carranza also spoke to mariachi music-making as a means to bring greater cultural relevance to the school setting.

> We started doing things that were very culturally responsive and appro-
> priate. So for example, the spring concert . . . became the Mother's Day
> concert. . . . Mothers and grandmothers and aunts and neighbors, and
> everybody came out because they were going to get their Mother's Day
> serenade at this concert. And the kids knew what the significance of that
> was. The winter concert, which was the traditional winter concert that the
> band and orchestra does . . . became the feast of the Virgen de Guada-
> lupe [December 12]. . . . Again, the parents and the community came out
> in droves to support it. So, it really was culturally relevant in many, many
> very different ways, which was really beautiful to see (Personal interview
> with Richard Carranza, December 11, 2016).

The mariachi program's value was clear; and in 1996, Tucson's school board
adopted a mariachi curriculum.

Richard Carranza also saw the program's impact on music-making. As the number of mariachi school programs grew, he and his colleagues saw to it that the students gained a solid knowledge of both the fundamentals of their instrument and
basic traditional repertoire, and that they incorporated particular mariachi skill
sets into the curriculum:

> So violinists are playing in tune, they are playing with proper positioning.
> Guitar players know the names of their chords, the relationship of the circle
> of fifths so they know what key they are playing in. We wanted them to
> be musically solid. So the skill level, because of that, was incredibly high.
> . . . It got to the point that the kids were able to get the best of the both
> worlds. They were able to be very literate in music, know their fundamental
> musical theory, but they were also able, in the best traditions of the mari-
> achi art form, to improvise, and modulate [from one key to another], and
> transpose keys [play a selection in a key other than the one they have orig-
> inally learned or see notated] (Personal interview with Richard Carranza,
> December 11, 2016).

Carranza went on to launch new mariachi-in-schools programs as a high school
principal; a regional director in the Las Vegas, Nevada, schools; and superintendent
of the San Francisco Unified School District. In 2016, he became superintendent
of the Houston Independent School District, the seventh-largest in the country,
with 68 percent Hispanic student population and three mariachi-in-schools programs. In 2018, he was appointed Chancellor of the New York City Schools, the
nation's largest school district.

ACTIVITY 19.3

The recording of *"Las Olas"* (The Waves; Audio Example 19.1) by high school–level Mariachi Chula Vista shows the high level of skill attained by some student groups. When you first listened to it, did you guess from the music that it was being played by high school students? If yes, how? Their voices? Their instrumental technique?

To compare this performance with others, you might search the internet for sites such as the YouTube Mariachi Channel.

Mariachi Reyna de Los Ángeles: We're Women; We Do It!

Especially since the Chicano Civil Rights Movement in the 1960s, mariachi music has been on the forefront of the movement to assert cultural pride, adding new meaning and usefulness of the music in people's lives. It also has played a role in another major change in mariachi musical practice—the inclusion of women. The striking increase in the number of women performers in mariachi music has occurred thanks in large part to formal mariachi music education and its openness to students of any gender. (You did notice the presence of women performers in the video of my interview with Nati Cano [Video 19.2] at 12:05–13:45 and in the recording of *"Las Olas"* [Audio Example 19.1], didn't you?)

In 2011, UNESCO declared the mariachi tradition to be an important part of world heritage, stating that "the skill is usually passed down from fathers to sons." This acknowledgement of gender dominance is historically accurate, with occasional exceptions of female performers and groups dating back to the early 1900s. It was not until the 1970s in the United States that women moved to the front row of mariachi music-making in a big way. Pioneering achievements of Rebecca Gonzales and Laura Sobrino of California and Mónica Treviño of Arizona broke the gender barrier in top-flight mariachi ensembles in the 1970s and 1980s (Sheehy 2006, 57–60.) However, it took top-drawer professional, concert-savvy, all-female groups to drive a broader change. The group with the most impact was Mariachi Reyna de Los Ángeles (Figure 19.4), founded in 1994 by fifth-generation mariachi musician José Hernández.

José Hernández founded the Mariachi Heritage Society in 1991. After several successful years of teaching young people, he realized that the girls—half of his students—did not have the role models that the boys had. He decided to do something about that:

≡ **FIGURE 19.4**
Mariachi Reyna
de Los Ángeles
performing at
the Cielito Lindo
Restaurant in
South El Monte,
California.

Some young girls that were in the Heritage Society, that were already 13, 14 years old, played well. So I sent out a letter to different places where they had some female mariachis, like up in Fresno, in Tucson [that] I was going to hold an open audition to form America's first all-female mariachi group, Mariachi Reyna de Los Ángeles. . . . I ended up with the final 12 girls that I knew had to represent women in mariachi, but at a professional, high musical level. . . . I wanted them to project a sound that would blow everyone away. . . .I don't want them to say that . . . for being girls, they play pretty good. (José Hernández personal interview, November 2, 2016)

Luisa Fregoso joined Mariachi Reyna in 1995. Her mariachi trumpet-player father helped her take up the music. She played mariachi violin in school in East Los Angeles and also studied violin with Laura Sobrino at the Mariachi Heritage Society. There, she realized that, while girls played mariachi violin, she had never before seen girls playing *guitarrón, vihuela,* or trumpet. Reyna member Julie Murillo learned mariachi violin in public schools and looked up to violinist-singer Mónica Treviño, who played with Mariachi Los Camperos de Nati Cano. She told herself, "I want to be the next woman in that group." At the same time, she was bothered by what seemed to be a limit of one woman per group. When she joined Mariachi Reyna, she would, as Mahatma Gandhi famously said, "Be the change that you wish to see in the world."

ACTIVITY 19.4

Watch an interview I conducted with Luisa Fregoso and Julie Murillo, members of Mariachi Reyna de Los Ángeles, to hear more about their experiences in their own voices (Video 19.3). Take notes on points they make so that you can discuss this with classmates.

In addition, watch the video performance by Mariachi Reyna de Los Ángeles of *"El Pitayero"* ("The Dragon Fruit Harvester"; Video 19.4). From what you hear, can you tell that all the musicians are women? If so, how? To compare their sound with other groups male and female, listen to José Hernández's Mariachi Sol de México (http://soldemexicomusic.com/) or Nati Cano's Mariachi Los Camperos. (Find excerpts at https://folkways.si.edu/ by searching "mariachi.") How many all-female mariachi groups would you expect to find in the United States? How many can you locate via the internet—for example, on YouTube, Spotify, or mariachi blogs? Are there as many female groups as male groups?

For some, the male-dominated world of mariachi music is tradition; for others, it is gender bias. Both Luisa and Julie recalled the social challenges that came with being women in what was a male domain. Luisa said, "Before, women were just seen as like background, you know? Or, 'Just stand there and look cute.'" There were musical challenges as well. Since most mariachi songs were written in men's vocal keys, the original arrangements didn't work for women's higher vocal range. Luisa notes that José developed arrangements that fit the group's vocal and instrumental abilities: "José will arrange a whole intro for us, and he does it in such a way [that] it's classy. . . . It makes a big difference." Julie adds, "We have our own sound—keeping it traditional—but our own sound."

Both Luisa and Julie feel pride in having overcome so many social, personal, and musical challenges and being a role model for other aspiring women mariachis. As Julie put it, "We're women; we do it!" In "doing it," they look to parlay their own unique character into something on par with leading male groups, while playing to their own strengths as individuals and as an ensemble of women. Luisa speaks to the group's historical importance: "This group opened doors for women, made them believe that you *can* be professional and at the same level as men."

And many women have believed. Today, there are dozens of all-female mariachi groups throughout the United States. And women, though still outnumbered by men in the professional ranks, have carved out a more accepted and respected role in mixed-gender groups as well. They changed the social dimension of mariachi culture as they pressed to make gender bias a thing of the past.

The Mexican *Son*

The Mexican ***son*** is one of the many musical genres that are performed by mariachi ensembles. It is arguably the most important musical genre over the history of the mariachi, having defined the mariachi sound more than any other form of music. The term *"son"* (pl. *sones*) may be used generally to mean simply "tune" or "sound," reflecting its principal usage in pre-nineteenth-century Mexican colonial times. In Mexico, it may also refer to a regional style of *mestizo* music or to certain melodies of Indian cultural groups. A mariachi ensemble often includes in its repertoire several regional styles of *son*. Regional *mestizo son* traditions may be distinguished by instrumentation, instrumental technique, singing style, and repertoire. Use of the harp in the ensemble, for example, can be a distinction for the *son jalisciense* ("Jalisco-style *son*") from the western state of Jalisco, and the *son jarocho* from the eastern state of Veracruz. *"La Bamba"* is a well-known example. You might have noticed on the videos you have watched that some ensembles include a harp, an instrument that was popular in colonial times, died out in Spain, but flourished in many parts of Latin America with regional variants.

Musically, most regional *mestizo sones* are structured around *versos* (sung poetic stanzas) alternating with instrumental interludes. They have a rhythmic drive appropriate for dancing—produced by the *armonía* rhythm section that you are already familiar with.

ACTIVITY 19.5

"El Pitayero" ("The Dragon Fruit Harvester") shows the syncopated rhythm of the Mexican *son*, one of the most traditional of mariachi music rhythms. Listen to the tracks of the *vihuela, guitar,* and *guitarrón* playing an excerpt of this rhythm in *"El Pitayero demo"* (Audio Example 19.2), then then view Video 19.4 to hear the complete version of *"El Pitayero"* to see if you can tell how these instruments drive the forward motion of the piece.

As you listen again several times, pay attention to these musical elements:

- contrast provided by changing instrumentation including voice
- the use of **dynamics** (changes in volume) and sudden silence
- means of increasing the expressivity of the text

LISTENING GUIDE

"El Pitayero"

Performed by Mariachi Reyna de Los Ángeles

Recording location and year: California, 2017

Instrumentation: Mariachi (violins, trumpets, guitar, *vihuela*, *guitarrón*, vocals as instrumentalists sing)

Time	Text	Something to Listen For
Introduction		
0:01		*a:* Trumpets ascend octave + 5, in a tempo of increasing speed
0:03		Trumpets play melody, in thirds; guitar and *vihuela* strum; *guitarrón* plays bassline
0:10		*a:* Trumpets ascend octave + 5
0:13		Trumpets play melody, in thirds; guitar and *vihuela* strum; *guitarrón* plays bassline
0:20		*b:* Violins play melody, in thirds; guitar and *vihuela* strum; *guitarrón* plays bassline
0:27		Volume decreases and then increases
0:30	*¡Ahora, mi Reyna! ¡Ya toca rebonito! ¡Sí, señor!*	Woman's voice speaks to encourage the players (my *Reyna*) to "play it pretty"; violins, guitar, and *vihuela* play
0:33		Trumpets join with violins
Verse and Refrain		
0:38	*Soy pitayero señores* *Y ahora acabo de llegar* *Vengo de cortar pitayas, güerita* *Comenzando a madurar*	Two women sing in thirds a stanza about the role of a "*pitaya* (dragon fruit) cutter" coming from cutting *pitayas* that are beginning to ripen.
0:43–0:45		Trumpets signal three times
0:46		Verse repeats
0:55	*Ándale güerita, ándale güerita* *Vámonos al organal* *A cortar pitayas, a cortar pitayas* *Comenzando a madurar*	A chorus of women sing in harmony a refrain about a light-skinned girl whom they are encouraging to go to the cactus patch to cut *pitayas*.

Time	Text	Something to Listen For
Interlude		
1:12		*b*: Violins lead with the melody; guitar and *vihuela* strum; *guitarrón* plays bassline
1:13	*¡Eso, muchachas! ¡Tóquenle rebonito como allá en Pueblo Nuevo! ¡Sí, señor!*	Woman's voice speaks words of encouragement to the girls to "play it pretty like there in Pueblo Nuevo."
1:18–1:22		*Grito* begins with sustained "Ah" and develops into a stylized yell
1:23		*b*: Violins play melody
1:26		Trumpets join with violins
Verse and Refrain		
1:30	*Soy pitayero señores* *Que vengo de Manzanillo* *Vengo de cortar pitayas, güerita* *Del corazón amarillo*	Two women sing in thirds a stanza (as at 0:38) to express the role of the *pitaya* cutter, coming from Manzanillo, "cutting pitayas with a yellow heart."
1:35 1:37		Trumpets signal three times
1:38		Verse repeats
1:46	*Ándale güerita, ándale güerita* *Vámonos al organal* *A cortar pitayas, a cortar pitayas* *Comenzando a madurar*	Chorus of women sing in harmony a refrain (as at 0:55) of encouragement of the light-skinned girl to continue to cut *pitayas*.
1:55		Refrain repeats
Interlude		
2:03		*b*: Violins play melody, in thirds; guitar and *vihuela* strum; *guitarrón* plays bassline
2:11		Volume decreases and then increases
2:14		*b*: Violins play melody, in thirds; guitar and *vihuela* strum; *guitarrón* plays
2:18		Trumpets join with violins
Verse and Refrain		
2:21	*Soy pitayero señores* *Que vengo desde Sayula* *Voy a vender mis pitayas, güerita* *A este pueblo de Cocula*	Two women sing in thirds a stanza describing the *pitaya* cutter who comes from the town of Sayula to sell his *pitayas* in the town of Cocula.

Time	Text	Something to Listen For
2.27–2.29		Trumpets signal three times
2:30		Refrain repeats
2:36		Singers stretch the rhythm of the melody
2:40	*Ándale güerita, ándale güerita* *Vámonos al organal* *A cortar pitayas, a cortar pitayas* *Comenzando a madurar*	Chorus of women enter, singing in harmony a refrain calling for the light-skinned girl to "get along" to the cactus patch to cut *pitayas* that are beginning to ripen.
2:47		Refrain repeats
Interlude		
2:55		*b:* Violins play melody, in thirds; guitar and *vihuela* strum; *guitarrón* plays bassline
2:57	*¡Ahora, compañeras! ¡Vámonos,* *que se acabaron las pitayas!*	Woman's voice speaking, calling friends to go, as the "*pitayas* are all gone."
3:00		*b:* Violins with melody, in thirds; guitar and *vihuela* strumming; *guitarrón*
3:02–3:04		Volume decrease and then increase
3:05		*b:* Violins with melody
3:09		Trumpets join with violins
3:12		Sudden stop to silence
Closure		
3:14		*a:* Trumpets ascend octave + 5, in a tempo of increasing speed
3:16		Trumpets play melody, in thirds; guitar and *vihuela* strum
3:21		Sudden stop
3:22		Closing cadence ends the piece

Mariachi Arcoiris de Los Ángeles: The World's First LGBTQIA+ Mariachi

The remarkable tale of Mariachi Arcoiris de Los Ángeles (Mariachi Rainbow of Los Angeles), the world's first openly gay mariachi (Figure 19.5), offers yet another example of how mariachi has been transformed through its presence in the United

States. The group exists as a response to severe prejudice encountered by gay, lesbian, and transgender mariachi musicians. Carlos Samaniego founded it in 2000, first as a novel part of a gay pride celebration, and then again in 2014 as a "safe space" for **LGBTQIA+** mariachi musicians to play the music they loved. Eventually, the group became a visible advocate for LGBTQIA+ rights and freedom.

Carlos grew up loving mariachi music. It was a part of his family life in East Los Angeles. He studied mariachi violin in high school and played with the youth group Mariachi Voz de América, where he met his violinist friend Jay, who would eventually become the first known transgender female mariachi, Natalia Meléndez. Carlos knew early on that he was gay, but it wasn't until his college years that he openly expressed it. Carlos remembers:

> I was a music major, and I had just come out of the closet. And when you come out of the closet, you basically come, like, screaming out. And so, . . . I joined the gay and lesbian alliance, a club on campus at Cal-State L.A. . . . That year we were planning events for our Pride Week. . . . The biggest was going to be a mock wedding, . . . in protest that same-sex marriage wasn't allowed. . . . They knew I played in a mariachi, . . . so they said, . . . "Why don't we get a mariachi . . . for the mock wedding?" I said, "OK." (Personal interview with Carlos Samaniego and Natalia Meléndez, November 3, 2016)

Carlos decided to take the idea further, to put together an all-gay mariachi. The organizers were enthused, and after some calling around, Carlos assembled

≡ **FIGURE 19.5**
Mariachi Arcoïris de Los Ángeles meets up before playing at a house party.

a complete, all-gay mariachi for the event. The performance went well. He recalls that afterward, a man came up and offered the group a job playing regularly at a Latino gay nightclub. "So I ended up taking the mariachi there. . . . We played there, and we did gigs."

The group lasted only a year, but persistent prejudice and harassment kept the idea alive. Carlos reflects:

> So all of these years, until the year 2014 [when he relaunched the group], it's been in the back of my mind, because since then I have gone through a lot of bad things with mariachis, because I've come out, and I haven't been ashamed of the person that I am. . . . I've had a lot of discrimination and prejudices against me being in mariachi, and I haven't been allowed to be in certain groups. Unfortunately, it's so taboo within our culture and within the mariachi world, which is our subculture. . . . I invited Natalia to be in the group, . . . not only because . . . she's an amazing musician, . . . but frankly, [because] I thought that Natalia needed . . . to have a spotlight, for being the ground breaking person that she is. She's the first transgender woman in the history of mariachi, as a working musician. (Personal interview with Carlos Samaniego and Natalia Meléndez, November 9, 2016)

For her part, Natalia painfully recalls how when she was freelancing with various groups, she felt like a "dartboard" as she endured unwanted scrutiny and ridicule from other musicians. "For a while, it affected me really, really bad. . . . I would cry sometimes, and I'm like . . . why am I doing this? I don't need the money that bad. I need the music." In Mariachi Arcoiris, she was accepted for who she was. She remembers, "I had no idea that we would be considered to be a ground breaking group, first of all. . . . I thought, 'Yeah, we're just going to get a little group together and play and be at peace.'" She feels that the group has been a positive addition to the mariachi world: "People reach out to me a lot. . . . This group that we

▷

ACTIVITY 19.6

Watch Video 19.5 in which I interview Carlos Samaniego and Natalia Meléndez. It includes a performance at a birthday party by Mariachi Arcoiris. Watch and listen to the performance. Is there anything that differentiates their music from that of a non-LGBTQIA+ mariachi group? Why should or shouldn't there be?

formed, it has been such a necessity for the mariachi world. . . . We come from the mariachi world just like everybody else, . . . but we are not afraid to let you know what we are. . . . It's done so much good for people and for myself."

Carlos agrees that, through their music, Mariachi Arcoiris has contributed to greater tolerance for LGBTQIA+ people. Natalia and their group have been featured in stories on Univision television, National Public Radio, *The Los Angeles Times*, *La Opinion*, and *San Francisco Weekly*, among others. Carlos adds, though, "The most important thing for me, above everything else, is the music. There's no point of any of this without the music. Our mission and our goal is to be a good mariachi. That's it."

The tale of Mariachi Arcoiris de Los Ángeles is another story of making music meaningful and useful in life. In general, its members have embraced "mainstream" mariachi music-making, though they add their own touches, such as making one of their anthems the song "A Mi Manera": the Spanish-language mariachi version of Frank Sinatra's "My Way." In doing things their way, their message of tradition, change, and pride in being themselves is clear.

Conclusion

This chapter has explored the expanding universe of meaning and sound of mariachi music in the United States to make the point that, for the music to remain traditional—relevant and meaningful in the lives of Mexican Americans—some things have had to change. Significantly, a main goal that Nati Cano and other like-minded musicians had of elevating the social status of mariachi from "cantina music" to a respected form of cultural expression has been achieved. Especially since the Chicano Civil Rights Movement in the 1960s, mariachi music has been on the forefront of the assertion of cultural pride, adding new meaning and usefulness to the music in people's lives.

Three tales of innovation and change have illustrated the challenge of keeping the "mariachi" in mariachi music when it is learned in educational settings that differ from learning aurally from family members. Also important has been the expanded inclusion of who is accepted as a mariachi musician, including women and LGBTQIA+ musicians. Staying connected to the traditional repertoire and its special meaning in community life has been important for all.

Bibliography

Sheehy, Daniel. 2006. *Mariachi Music in America: Experiencing Music, Expressing Culture*. New York: Oxford University Press.

UNESCO Intangible Cultural Heritage website: https://ich.unesco.org/en/RL/mariachi-string-music-song-and-trumpet-00575. Accessed 05/06/2020.

Music in Native America

The Intertribal Powwow

JOHN-CARLOS PEREA

Chapter Contents

Introduction

Every **Native American** nation has its own songs and dances that are used for specific functions and contexts. However, over time, an interactive culture of **intertribal** exchange has inspired new musical and artistic forms. One location of that exchange is the **powwow**: intertribal Native American social gatherings built around a shared repertoire of songs and dances. Powwows provide opportunities for culturally diverse peoples to create "sounding communities." They are a space for negotiation of difference and the creation of communities among Native Americans. In addition, powwows have allowed Native and non-Native communities to educate each other and, as a consequence, to create new forms of culture and community relevant to the peoples' needs (Browner 2002; Ellis 2003; Ellis, Lassiter, and Dunham, 2005). (For other examples of contemporary intertribal and cross-cultural Native American music, see Diamond 2008.)

More than 500 Native nations are currently recognized by the US federal government and more than 200 are seeking federal recognition (Figure 20.1). When speaking generally about all of them, the terms "**American Indian**" and "Native American" are to a degree interchangeable in the continental US. Given their diversity, however, it is equally important that attention be paid to each person's affiliation(s) as expressed through reference to clan, tribe, and/or nation. It is common when attending Native

≣ Black Lodge singers perform at the 27th Annual Northern Colorado Intertribal Association Pow-Wow and Indian Market in Fort Collins, Colorado, April 2019.

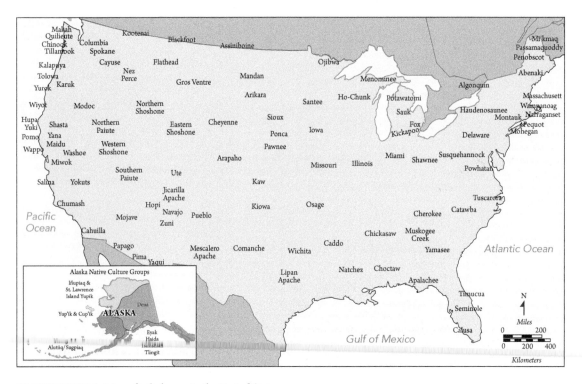

≡ **FIGURE 20.1** Map of tribal areas in the United States.

ACTIVITY 20.1

Are you familiar with the Indigenous lands you live on? When addressing questions of Indigenous presence and naming practices, these are some necessary topics that may require a bit of research

- Name(s) of the Indigenous Peoples who serve as stewards of your homelands
- Name(s) of the Indigenous Peoples' language and place names (with translations or explanations)
- Correct pronunciation for the name(s) of Indigenous Peoples and places

- Names of living Indigenous People from these communities
- Past and present relationships between the Indigenous People and your homeland

Part 1

Do an internet search to find information on each of these topics. Some existing resources may include:

- Local Indigenous organizations
- Indigenous communities and Elders
- Online information and official public websites (such as nativeland.ca)

American gatherings to be asked, "Where are you from?" In response, I personally will say that "I am John-Carlos Perea; I was born in Dulce, New Mexico. My father is Mescalero Apache and Chicano from Las Cruces, New Mexico, and my mother is German and Irish from Long Island, New York. Not long after I was born, my parents moved from Dulce to San Francisco, California, where I have spent most of my life. While I identify with and respect all of my different cultural heritages, I identify primarily as urban Mescalero Apache."

Some of my earliest childhood memories involve my parents taking me to powwows in the San Francisco Bay Area. However, it was not until I went to college at San Francisco State University (SFSU) that I began studying and singing with Dr. Bernard Hoehner-Pȟeží, D.V.M. (Húŋkpapȟa, Sihásapa). Among many other things, Dr. Hoehner-Pȟeží was a **Northern Plains** singer, Northern Traditional dancer, emcee, and lecturer in American Indian Studies at SFSU (Figure 20.2). He invited me to sing with his **drum** group; those experiences form the core of my knowledge about the contemporary intertribal powwow and the role of music at these gatherings as a sonic marker of community.

The Powwow

Every powwow is put on by a committee. The committee designs an agenda and then invites various head staff members to participate, including the **master of**

≡ **FIGURE 20.2** Photo of Dr. Hoehner-Pȟeží at Three Rivers Powwow, c. 1980.

ceremonies, **arena director**, **head dancers**, and **host drums**. The committee will also interact with craft and food vendors in order to have those services available. On the day of the gathering, the public voice of the committee is sounded through the master of ceremonies, or emcee. It is their responsibility to keep the event moving by providing explanations of the different dances; introducing honored guests and dancers; and making sure that all the participants, whether they are Native or non-Native, are kept aware in a respectful way of what is taking place. The master of ceremonies is also expected to keep the powwow atmosphere from getting overly competitive by using humor and teasing to ensure that all participants are in a good mood and having a good time.

The relationship between individual, tribal-specific practices and intertribal sharing relating to music, dance, arts, crafts, and lifeways means that, as Native communities grow and change, so too will powwows change every time they are held. An intertribal powwow may be run according to the practices of a single tribe but take its direction from the constantly renegotiated practices of many different tribes. An intertribal dance may draw together into the arena dancers from all parts of the country representing different dance categories. Depending on the interaction between the committee and the master of ceremonies, the dance might also involve participation from Native and non-Native spectators. Intertribal dancing thus becomes a space where difference is negotiated and community is created through the social activity of **musicking** together. This means that there are potentially as many different ways to powwow as there are tribes in the United States. In my experience, this is why powwows continue to remain relevant: they provide space for the creation and negotiation of culture through intertribal music and dance for successive generations of participants.

It is through collective ownership of and shared responsibility for cultural practices that are incredibly specific at local and also individual levels that powwows provide opportunities for culturally diverse peoples to create "sounding communities" (Perea 2014). It is also important to note that—given contemporary histories of Native relocation—many Native people do not have immediate access to their tribal-specific ways of being. Intertribal culture provides a point of access for those individuals to experience and construct their identities on a macro level through social interaction.

Music in the Social Space of the Powwow

In order to visualize the place and function of music within the social context of a powwow, Dr. Hoehner described the event, from his Lakȟóta worldview, as taking place within four circles, as illustrated in Figure 20.3.

ACTIVITY 20.2

To truly experience the social interaction that occurs during a powwow, you ideally would attend a powwow yourself. To explore the possibilities, go to powwows.com and make a list of powwows in your area. If a powwow being held near you has a website, use it as a source to prepare yourself by reading about the powwow's history, head staff members, schedule, and rules of etiquette.

When attending your first powwow, always follow the directions the emcee gives at the event. If the emcee asks the spectators to stand up, you stand up, unless physically unable to do so. If the master of ceremonies asks you to remove your head covering, remove your head covering—unless keeping it on is part of your religious practice. By following the emcee's directions, you are showing respect.

The drum (*čháŋčheğa*) represents the first circle of the powwow. The drum is placed at its center because its voice gathers singers, dancers, and other community members together. The drum is also placed at the center out of respect for the symbolism embedded in its construction (e.g., see Vennum 1982). Drum frames may be made from different woods and drumheads are made from the hides of specific animals. Those woods, hides, and other natural materials are symbolic of the relationship between human beings and the environment of which they are a part. If the sound of the drum may be heard as the sound of those natural elements, then that sound is not just a sound to motivate dancers; it is the sounding of the relationships between human beings and the world around them. It reminds powwow participants that they do not live in control of or apart from, but very much in relation to and as part of, the world. These ways of thinking illustrate the importance of the drum to a powwow and explain its placement at the center.

The male singers (*ȟʼokȟá wičháša*) who sit around the drum represent the second circle of the powwow. They have the responsibility of supplying the powwow's "heartbeat": by striking the drum, they sound the relationship between human beings and the world of which they are a part. In

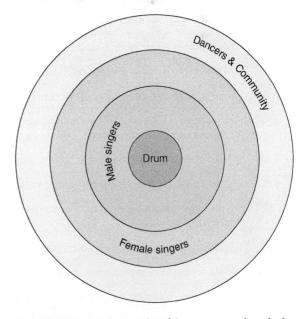

≡ **FIGURE 20.3** Four circles of the powwow as described by Dr. Bernard Hoehner.

LISTENING GUIDE

"Straight Intertribal"

Performed by Black Lodge Singers

Recording location and year: Live at White Swan, 1996

Instrumentation: Powwow drum and singers

Time	Something to Listen For
0:01	Drum begins sounding a steady pulse as multiple drummers play in unison (cough is heard from a singer preparing his entrance).
0:04	First **push-up**: singing of the full powwow song begun by solo lead singer starting at high pitch and descending
0:09	Multiple male voices enter, matching the previous melody of the lead voice.
0:20	Male voices drop to a medium pitch region.
0:31	Male voices drop to a low pitch region.
0:36	With a quick call from lead male voice, male singers begin a new phrase at a high pitch, descending.
0:41	Honor beats are performed as accents on the drum as male singers continue with the B section that starts high and descends.
0:56	Second push-up: lead male singer starts a song repetition, beginning high and descending.
1:00	Male voices enter, matching the previous melody of the lead voice.
1:25	Male voices drop to a lower pitch range and sing a long "hey."
1:32	Honor beats are performed as accents on the drum, with male singers continuing to sing.
1:44	Low pitched vocal "ooh" sounds above drum and singers; drummers crescendo and increase the speed of the song slightly as they move to third push-up.
1:48	Third push-up: lead male voice starts another repetition of the full song.
1:53	Male voices sing in response to lead male voice and continue onward.
2:17	One singer encourages the other singers. Honor beats are not performed on the third push-up.
2:36	Fourth push-up: lead male voice starts another repetition of the full song.
2:39	Male voices sing in response, and continue onward.
3:07	With honor beats on the drum, the male voices continue singing.
3:12	Drum dynamic becomes very soft, while male voices sing (the drum never drops out).
3:17	Drum dynamic builds, first softly and then prominently amid the singing voices.

Time	Something to Listen For
3:24	Fifth push-up: lead male voice starts another repetition of the full song.
3:28	Male voices sing in response, and continue onward.
3:57	Honor beats are performed as accents on the drum, with male singers continuing.
4:00	The drum's dynamic level becomes very soft, male voices continuing.
4:05	The drum's dynamic builds as male voices continue to sing.
4:10	Drum and singing stops, followed by a vocal shout.

order to respect that relationship, singers must take on the responsibility of singing and behaving "in a good way." "In a good way" is a phrase heard at many Native events; there is no one specific "good way," but there are aspects of singer comportment that are intertribally shared. For many singers, a "good way" begins with a commitment to sobriety, as it is often considered extremely disrespectful to sing while under the influence of alcohol and/or drugs.

State of mind is also an important part of male singer behavior. I remember asking Dr. Hoehner to explain why Northern Plains singers sing as high as they do (as in "Straight Intertribal"; Audio Example 20.1). He responded that Northern Plains–style singing was meant to emulate the cry of a newborn baby. As a younger man, I was not always clear on the significance of that image, but after the births of my daughter and son, I had a different insight. When my children cry, they are communicating with me in a language without words. They are telling me they need to be fed or held and I have to be able to hear and understand their needs in the moment. As a singer, I have to communicate with that same emotional intensity. This is not to say that words are not important, but those words or **vocables** must be communicated with an intensity and focus that draws listeners in and makes them pay attention to whatever is being communicated at that moment.

The female singers (*wičháglatA*) who stand behind the drum represent the third circle of the powwow, surrounding the singers and the drum. Many people assume that women are made to stand behind the drum because their musical and social role is less important than that attributed to men. However, Dr. Hoehner explained that women stand behind the drum out of respect for the power of their role as mothers; they encircle the male singers and the drum in the same way that a pregnant mother encircles her baby. The place of women within the four circles should not be read as a gendered slight but instead as a recognition of the balance and complementarity between men and women in the activity of producing music at a powwow (Diamond, Cronk, and Rosen 1994).

My own drum group, the Sweetwater Singers, follows the example of Dr. Hoehner's Blue Horse Singers in which women and men sat and sang together. The Sweetwater Singers understand that the social relationships between male, female, and Two-Spirit musicians in drum groups are represented in many different ways, reflecting individual, tribal, and intertribal influences. People exercise their own agency in negotiating these influences in order to make music. For every drum group that gives people the choice to sit or stand, another may choose to enforce rules regarding sitting and standing. The issue comes in the interpretation of the rationale behind these decisions and respecting the fluidity of practices from one community to another.

Dr. Hoehner emphasized the importance and responsibilities of the singers, without whom the dance cannot take place. While singers occasionally sing **solo**, at powwows you are most likely to see large groups of singers gathered around a drum or singing as part of a group of hand drummers. Once a drum "sets up" at a powwow, Dr. Hoehner expected that drum to stay for the entire day, making that commitment for the benefit of the dancers and the powwow as a whole. Singers should not sing for themselves or for the accolades they receive, or to take advantage of their position for personal gain. Instead, they must give selflessly of time and talents for the health of the fourth circle, made up of dancers (*wačhí wičháša* [male dancer], *wačhí wíŋyaŋ* [female dancer]), and other community (*oyáŋke*) members gathered to participate in the event. So, powwow music is not just a performance: it provides a sonic foundation for the larger social activity of the gathering. It is an example of sound structuring and modeling social relationships.

What's Going On: Opening Sequence

While every powwow is unique, a somewhat standard order of events characterizes most powwow agendas. A **Gourd Dance** may begin the event as a means of purifying or cleansing the dance arena before the powwow "officially" begins. The cleansing takes place through the gourd dancers' special status as warriors/military veterans. The **Grand Entry** follows, marking the beginning of intertribal dancing. All the assembled dancers enter the arena in a specific order, presided over by the **arena director** whose responsibility it is to oversee and adjudicate protocols.

Powwow songs narrate the events taking place within the dance arena. During the Grand Entry, they will sing about coming to dance and having a good time, as seen in the lyric excerpt from Elk Soldier's Grand Entry song entitled "Hoka Hey" (Audio Example 20.2), given with translation at the end of this paragraph. The song begins with the voice of the master of ceremonies asking participants to rise and remove their hats before the lead singer enters with the lead, sung with vocables, and then the A section, which includes words in the Dakhóta language. The words are repeated during the song's B section. (see Figure 20.4) Then, the whole form of lead, A section, and B section is repeated in what is called a **push-up.** The voice of the master of ceremonies continues throughout, explaining the significance of the different dancers as they enter the arena.

"Hoka Hey" by Elk Soldier

Tȟéhaŋtaŋhaŋ wahíyelo	We came from afar.
Hókahey! Eš wauŋči ptaȟwá	Let's go. Are we going to dance?

The Grand Entry concludes after all of the dancers have made their way into the arena. At that point, an elder or honored guest is invited to give a prayer. This prayer refers to the sacred component of powwow participation and asks for a good day, for good feelings, and a good time to be had by all. The prayer may be given in a Native language, in English, or in a combination of both.

After the prayer, the master of ceremonies calls on the host drums for a **Flag Song** and **Victory Song.** These accompany the posting of the colors that were carried at the beginning of the Grand Entry procession by the flag bearers. The responsibility of carrying in a flag is considered an honor, and veterans are often selected for this duty given their service and status. The number of flags leading a

ACTIVITY 20.3

Listen to "Hoka Hey" (Audio Example 20.2) several times. Be sure you can identify which text consists of vocables. Follow the text in the Dakhóta language, including being sure where the text repeats. Note each time the lead singer is heard.

Grand Entry can vary from community to community; in my experience growing up, the most commonly seen were the United States flag (Stars and Stripes), the Prisoner of War/Missing in Action flag (POW/MIA), and the Eagle Staff. Other powwows may bring in flags from other Native nations, state flags, and flags representing the individual branches of military service. The Flag and Victory songs are sung to respect these flags and the sacrifices they represent. Every Native nation has their own flag and victory songs for posting colors.

In order to balance Northern and **Southern Plains** representation at large powwows, it is common to have Northern and Southern drums share the responsibility of performing these opening songs. So, if a Northern drum is requested to sing the Grand Entry, then a Southern Plains drum will be given the responsibility of singing the Flag and Victory songs. This sharing is another way community is sounded to balance the sonic and cultural characteristics of Northern and Southern Plains singing.

The opening events may be seen and heard as functioning to provide a ceremony, fusing sacred and secular. They remind all participants to remember the many reasons why we are able to practice these ways and to make sure they remain available for future generations. A variety of social and contest dancing follows the opening segment.

Song Form, Singing Styles, and Drum Rhythm

Powwow songs are sung for unique social, ceremonial, and contest dances. They can be characterized by function and also by singing **style:** Northern Plains or Southern Plains. While many elements differentiate the two styles, the best ways for the novice listener to differentiate them are pitch and **timbre** (tone quality). Northern Plains singing is characterized by a much higher overall starting pitch than Southern Plains singing. Because of the higher pitch, there is also a sharper timbral quality to Northern Plains singing, as opposed to the lower voices used by Southern Plains singers.

ACTIVITY 20.4

Listen again to "Straight Intertribal" (Audio Example 20.1) sung by the Black Lodge Singers (Blackfeet) and to "Road Warrior" (Audio Example 20.3) sung by the Young Bird Singers (intertribal, Pawnee, Oklahoma), paying attention to the different pitches and vocal timbres used. Be sure you identify the style of each song. How would you describe the sounds of Northern and Southern Plains style singing to someone who had never experienced it before?

Then, listen to each of these songs at least one more time to hear more detail (for example, focusing on form, dynamics, or language).

LISTENING GUIDE

"Road Warrior"

Performed by Young Bird Singers

Recording location and year: Shakopee 2001

Instrumentation: Powwow drum and singers

Time	Something to Listen For
0:01	Steady pulse sounds from the drum as multiple drummers play in unison (cough is heard from a singer preparing his entrance).
0:04	First push-up: singing of the full powwow song begun by solo lead singer, starting at middle-range pitch and descending
0:08	Multiple male voices enter, matching the previous melody of the lead voice.
0:16	Male voices continue singing, with a notable descending direction of their melody; female singers standing behind drum enter just a little after the male singers start, then sing throughout the song.
0:18	Solo male voice interjects "heys" alongside the singing voices.
0:31	Honor beats sound as accents on the drum (three), signal change between sections.
0:32	Male voices begin B section, prompted by the "heys" of a solo male voice.
0:46	Second push-up: lead male voice begins new repetition of the full song.
0:51	Male voices imitate lead voice, then continue onward.
1:02	Five accent beats played.
1:09	Crescendo into three honor beats appear as numerous strong beats on the drum, without singing voices.
1:12	Male voices begin B section, prompted by the "heys" of a solo male voice.
1:21	Tempo changes are signaled by group accents on the drum, as the voices continue singing to strong drum pulses.
1:26	Third push-up: lead male voice begins new repetition of the full song, starting at new and slightly higher pitch.
1:28	Male voices imitate lead voice, then continue onward.
1:48	Voices drop out briefly while drums play honor beats.
1:50	Male voices reenter, singing a descending melody.
1:58	Accents on the drum (three) are followed by male voices.

continues

Time	Something to Listen For
2:02	Fourth push-up: lead male voice begins repetition of the full song.
2:04	Male voices imitate lead voice, then continue onward.
2:13	Male voices shout "heys" above other singing male voices.
2:23	Singers stop at the honor beats, the sound of accents on the drum (three).
2:25	Male voices return to singing.
2:36	Drum beats are prominent above the singing, ending cadence.
2:40	One singer voices a closing "hey ya."

Figure 20.4 graphically illustrates the powwow song form with which you have become familiar through the chapter. A full powwow song consists of a "lead, or call," sung by a solo voice, followed by the "second" (the A section in Figure 20.4), which is a response to the "lead" by the rest of the assembled singers. The B section normally reworks some variant of the A section melody. A full repetition of the song (a push-up) is loosely equivalent to the concept of a verse in Western music. You will always know when you have reached a new push-up when you hear the sound of the lead singer singing again. The only time you will hear a solo voice during a song is when the lead is sung.

You may find it useful to keep track of push-ups by listening to **honor beats**. Honor beats, or "hard beats," take place during the B section of a Northern Plains song, while in Southern Plains songs they divide the A and B sections. In Figure 20.4, this is represented by solid lines to indicate the discrete sections of a Northern Plains song and by dashed lines to indicate the flow between A and B sections in a Southern Plains song. Upon hearing the honor beats, dancers in the arena will acknowledge the drum by raising their dance fans, bowing toward the drum, or

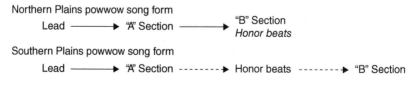

≣ **FIGURE 20.4** Visual Representation of Northern and Southern Plains Powwow Song.

ACTIVITY 20.5

Listen to "Straight Intertribal" (Audio Example 20.1) and "Road Warrior" (Audio Example 20.3) at least three more times to complete the following three tasks:

1. With copies of each Listening Guide and the diagram in Figure 20.4 side by side, label the start of A and B sections for each song.

2. Now that you have distinguished between the A and B sections for each song, listen again and label the placement of the Honor Beats for each song on its respective Listening Guide.

3. Your final task is to label any changes in dynamics of the drumming and singing for each song by drawing them in order to visually represent your perception of where and how much the drumming and singing get louder and softer over the course of the song.

Once you have completed all three tasks, compare your labels with that of a colleague. Discuss any differences in how you chose to label the results of each task.

performing other movements. Dr. Hoehner taught that these beats are meant to remind all powwow participants to keep good feelings inside while dancing and to respect the drum.

For the foundational drum rhythm, many (but not all) **intertribal songs** are sung with "**straight beats**": a regular pulse 1 2 1 2 1 2, with the second beat slightly

ACTIVITY 20.6

Listen again to all three Audio Examples for the "straight beat" practice. It might be a challenge to reorient yourself to listen for breaths rather than beats, but it is important to feel this in the style. As you listen, take breaths with the singers—all the way through each selection. Then pick one of the examples and listen to answer this question: How many beats does it take for a singer to sing a musical phrase before they take a breath and begin another phrase? Is it regular through a selection?

accented. Listeners with backgrounds in Western music theory might be tempted to parse the beat or pulse into groups of two or four in order to try and understand the rhythmic structure of the song. While this is one way to get acquainted with powwow drum rhythms, I would also encourage you to think not in groups of two or four but in breath lengths. This kind of thinking/hearing will give you multiple senses of how powwow music fits together.

Conclusion

Intertribal Native American powwow music can be heard as sounding communities. These communities are located by place (where the powwow occurs), function within the powwow (singers, dancers, vendors, spectators, etc.), and social function within the powwow community writ large (e.g., differing conceptions of the role of veterans or women from one powwow community to the next). These communities interact to create the fluid, constantly changing nature of contemporary powwow experience. In addition, powwows have also become interactive spaces for Native and non-Native communities to educate each other and to create new forms of culture and community relevant to the needs of the people. The intertribal Native American powwow is thus a space for negotiation of difference and the creation of communities. Powwow music sounds and structures these actions in a way that is simultaneously both traditional and contemporary.

ACTIVITY 20.7

Earlier, we noted that powwows change every time they are held. As of March 2020, the type of powwow written about in this chapter changed greatly due to the necessities of sheltering in place and physical distancing during the COVID-19 pandemic. Some innovations during this time period include the formation of social media groups, such as the Social Distance Powwow, and prerecorded contest dancing hosted online during virtual powwows. Many more innovations will surely follow by the time this text is published.

How are powwow communities in your local area responding to the COVID-19 pandemic? Search for local powwow websites and/or news articles to read about how powwow committees are explaining their decisions to go online or to postpone their gatherings. Keep in mind that the goal here is not to judge one event against another but instead to keep track of how powwow committees are responding in different ways and, in the process, how powwows are changing during the pandemic.

Bibliography

Browner, Tara. 2002. *Heartbeat of the People: Music and Dance of the Northern Powwow*. Urbana: University of Illinois Press.

Diamond, Beverley. 2008. "Contemporary Intertribal and Cross-Cultural Native American Music." In *Native American Music in Eastern North America*, edited by Bonnie Wade and Patricia Shehan Campbell, 117–136. Global Music Series. New York: Oxford University Press.

Diamond, Beverley, M. Sam Cronk, and Franziska von Rosen. 1994. *Visions of Sound: Musical Instruments of First Nations Communities in Northeastern America*. Chicago: University of Chicago Press.

Ellis, Clyde. 2003. *A Dancing People: Powwow Culture on the Southern Plains*. Lawrence: University Press of Kansas.

Ellis, Clyde, Luke E. Lassiter, and Gary H. Dunham. 2005. *Powwow*. Lincoln: University of Nebraska Press.

Perea, John-Carlos. 2014. *Intertribal Native American Music in the United States*. Edited by Bonnie C. Wade and Patricia Shehan Campbell. Global Music Series. New York: Oxford University Press.

Small, Christopher. 1998. *Musicking: The Meanings of Performing and Listening*. Middletown, CT: Wesleyan University Press.

Vennum, Thomas Jr. 1982. *The Ojibwa Dance Drum*. Smithsonian Folklife Studies. Washington, DC: Smithsonian Institution Press.

Glossary

Abe, Keiko (see Keiko Abe).

Acceleration (ch. 1) Speeding up.

Accenting/stressing (ch. 1) In music, articulating emphasis.

Accordion (ch. 16) Family of aerophones with a box of some shape for a body, inside of which is encased a set of free reeds set in a frame. The reeds are set into vibration by air that is supplied by a bellows. Individual notes are produced by the depression of buttons or keys.

Aerophone (ch. 3) Instrument whose primary sound medium is a vibrating column of air.

Aesthetics (Intro) What makes a sense of beauty.

Affect (Intro) Capacity for expressivity.

Aficionados (ch. 15) Devoted fans.

Aforé (ch. 18) Brazilian gourd shaker covered by beaded net, also known as *cabaça* or *shekere*. Also exists in metal version.

Agama Hindu Bali (Balinese Hindu religion) or *Agama Tirtha* (holy water religion). A synthesis of pre-Hindu beliefs and practices with elements of Indian Hinduism and Buddhism which reached Bali via the neighboring island of Java.

Aisling (pl. *Aislingí*) (ch. 16) Vision poem, a category of Irish *sean-nós* song.

Akadinda (ch. 13) Frame xylophone of the Baganda people of Uganda in East Africa.

Ālāp (ch. 1) Unmetered prelude to a selection of Indian classical music.

American Indian (ch. 20) Generalized term used to refer to Indigenous individuals and/or communities living in the contiguous United States.

Anatolia (ch. 11) The portion of the West Asian subcontinent located within the borders of the Republic of Turkey.

Andalusian cadence (ch. 15) The descending chord progression Am G F E characteristic of the Andalusian mode that marks the end of musical sections.

Andalusian mode (ch. 1, ch. 15) Diatonic scale type in Spanish *flamenco* music. An adaptation of the Phrygian mode, starting on E, harmonized with a raised third on the first degree of the scale.

Angsel (ch. 9) A cue, sign, or articulation of a dance movement and music marked by a sudden, rhythmic break or accent (Bali).

Apartheid (ch. 14) System of racial segregation in South Africa that began (officially) in 1948 and lasted until 1994.

Arena Director (ch. 20) Powwow staff member responsible for overseeing dancing and other events taking place within the dance arena.

Armonía (ch. 19) Rhythm section of the mariachi ensemble—*vihuela, guitarrón,* and guitar.

Arpeggiated (ch. 2) Pitches of a chord played in succession.

Arrangement (ch. 11) The process of orchestrating rural and art-music repertoires for performing ensembles or recording-studio productions.

Asymmetrical meter (ch. 1) A musical meter with subdivisions of unequal length.

Augmented second (ch. 1, ch. 15) Melodic interval comprised of three half steps.

Axé (ch. 18) Vital life force in Brazilian *candomblé.*

Axé-music (ch. 18) Music style from Bahia that blends elements of Brazilian and Caribbean popular music styles.

Ayeo (ch. 2, ch. 15) In Spanish *flamenco,* improvised melody using the syllable *ay.*

Azān (Egyptian colloquial; *adhān* in standard Arabic) (ch. 12) The Islamic call to prayer.

Baile (ch. 15) Spanish *flamenco* dance.

Bala, balafon (ch. 13) Xylophone played by Mandinka (Mande) *griots.* Also the name of an old form of xylophone played by the Sosso people of West Africa.

Bamar (Burman) (ch. 8) Largest ethnic group in Myanmar.

Banjo (ch. 16) A fretted, long-necked plucked lute with a shallow circular frame body covered with a skin or plastic head. While both the four- and five-stringed banjos are played today in Ireland, the tenor banjo (c. 1908–1915 with four strings, a shorter neck, and played with a plectrum) has been the more popular instrument in traditional music since the 1960s.

Bantu (ch. 14) Language (and sometimes cultural) umbrella group encompassing many distinct languages widely distributed in West, Central, East, and southern Africa.

Bar See **Measure**

Bateria (ch. 18) Brazilian *samba* ensemble percussion group.

Batuque (ch. 18) Dance and music event associated with Afro-Brazilians in Rio de Janeiro, Brazil in the late nineteenth century.

Beat (ch. 1, ch 11) In rhythm, consistent, equal-length durations of time; in some systems, relatively longer or shorter than equal-length durations of time.

Bell (generically) A hollow object, typically metal, struck by clapper, hammer, or some other tool.

Bewaa (ch. 13) Popular recreational dance form among the Dagaaba of Ghana.

Biwa (ch. 7) Japanese short-necked, ovoid/pear-shaped, plucked lute with high wooden frets.

Blues progression (ch. 2) Common sequence of chords in blues music.

Bodhrán (ch. 16) Irish frame drum consisting of a shallow hoop of wood covered on one side with a stretched skin and reinforced with cross pieces of wood, cord, or wire; played with bare fingers or a wooden beater.

Bongo (ch. 17) Cuban pair of small drums (one slightly larger) with bodies yoked, each single-headed with open body, hand-played. It is spelled *bongó* in Spanish.

Bongosero (ch. 17) Player of the Cuban *bongo* drum.

Bossa nova (ch. 18) Quieter, more intimate form of Brazilian *samba* in which the guitar provides syncopated support for the voice.

Botija (ch. 17) A ceramic jug, bass aerophone used in traditional Cuban *son* music.

Bouzouki (ch. 16) Greek fretted long-necked plucked lute. Adapted into Irish traditional music, the *bouzouki* has four double, metal strings, a flat back, and up to 26 frets.

Broadside (ch. 16) Ballad text published on sheets of paper.

Bulerías (ch. 15) A Spanish *flamenco palo* in twelve-beat metric cycle.

Bunraku (ch. 7) Seventeenth-century Japanese puppet theater.

Cadence (ch. 2, ch. 10) Musical term for an ending.

Cafés-cantantes (ch. 15) In the late nineteenth and early twentieth centuries, commercial venues in Spain offering shows of *flamenco* and other music, dance and theatrical genres.

Cajón (ch. 15) In Spanish *flamenco*, a box-shaped percussion instrument of Peruvian origin.

Call-and-response (ch. 2, ch. 5) Generally, the alternation of solo with group; more specifically, a musical repartee between parts.

Candomblé (ch. 18) Afro-Brazilian religion based on spirit possession by *orixás*.

Cantaor (ch. 15) Male *flamenco* singer; *cantaores* (plural masculine); *cantaora* (female *flamenco* singer); *cantaoras* (plural feminine).

Cante (ch. 2; ch. 15) A generic term that refers to Spanish *flamenco* singing, a "song," or song type.

Cantina music (ch. 19) Often a pejorative term meaning "low-class bar music," used by some to disparage the quality and social status of mariachi music and musicians. The Mexican *cantina*, an important institution of social life, especially for men, has long been a place for music-making.

Carnaval (ch. 18) Celebrations that precede the start of Lent in the Christian calendar, the most lavish of which takes place in Rio de Janeiro.

Cavaquinho (ch. 18) Brazilian guitar-type plucked lute with four strings of wire or gut.

Céilí (ch. 16) An Irish social dance event.

Chachachá (ch. 17) A style of Cuban dance music popularized about 1950 and derived from the *danzón* that featured the *timbales.*

Chakradār tihāī (ch. 10) In North Indian rhythmic practice, nine occurrences of a cadential *tihāī*, ending on high pitch *sa.*

Chambas (ch. 19) Gigs (Spanish).

Charanga bands (ch. 17) Cuban dance groups playing *son*-style music but featuring flute and violins as the lead melodic instruments.

Chauk lon batt (ch. 8) "Six-drum set" of tuned drums in *hsaing waing* ensemble of Myanmar.

Ceng-ceng (ch. 9) In Balinese *gamelan gong kebyar*, a series of overlapping, small, bronze discs facing upward along a stand that is often a carved wooden turtle (related to an important Balinese origin myth). Player holds a cymbal in each hand to strike those on the stand.

Chord (ch. 2) In tonal music, intervals stacked vertically (or, produced simultaneously).

Chord progression (ch. 2, ch. 15) A sequence of chords.

Chordophone (ch. 3) Instrument whose primary sound medium is a vibrating string.

Clapper (ch. 8; see ***wa***) Pair of wooden sticks hit against each other in China, Myanmar.

Claves (ch. 3, ch. 17) Percussion idiophone; thick sticks of hard wood that are struck together (Cuba).

Click consonant (ch. 14) A method of producing consonants in spoken language by "clicking" the tongue against different parts of the mouth. (The clicking is in fact a rapid sucking action that releases a pocket of air temporarily trapped in the buccal cavity.)

"Come all ye" ballads (ch. 16) Nineteenth-century song type that gives warning or imparts moral lesson.

Compás (ch. 1, ch. 15) In Spanish, a generic term indicating meter. Metric cycle in Spanish *flamenco* music.

Compound meter (ch. 1, ch. 16) Recurring groupings of beats, but with each beat consisting of a subgroup of three pulses with equal duration.

Concertina (ch. 16) Hexagonal button operated free-reed instrument with bellows, in the same family as the accordion. Originally developed in England and Germany, it became widespread in Ireland by the late 1800s.

Concerto (ch. 7) A piece for solo instrument and orchestra.

Conga drums (ch. 17) Tall single-headed, barrel-shaped drums played with hands; developed in Cuba during the colonial period.

Conjunto (ch. 17) "Group" or "ensemble"; an expanded format for playing Cuban *son* of the 1940s and 50s that incorporated multiple trumpets, piano, and frequently *timbales* and conga drums as well.

Copla (ch. 2, ch. 15) In Spanish, including *flamenco*, a sung verse characterized by its poetic structure and melody, in some cases alternated with a refrain.

Copla andaluza (ch. 15) Literally, Andalusian *copla*. In Spain, a sentimental sung narrative created by poets, composers, and playwrights since the first half of the twentieth century, often focusing on Andalusian themes and characters.

Copy thachin (ch. 8) Burmese revision of foreign popular songs.

Corpophone (ch. 3) The human body as a musical instrument.

Craic (ch. 16) Modern Gaelic language term for conversation and fun; derived from the English word "crack" having the same meaning.

Creolization (ch. 17) A central element of Caribbean culture, the term refers to the fusion or blending of different racial and cultural elements over time and the creation of something new and different out of those components.

Cuíca (ch. 1, ch. 3, ch. 18) Brazilian friction drum that makes a "laughing" sound by means of a stick attached to the underside of the drum head.

Cymbal (ch. 9) Type of idiophone: lightly concave, round, metal plate.

Dagaaba (ch. 13) Ethnic group from the Upper West Region of Ghana.

Daga-gyil (ch. 13) Ghanaian Dagaaba frame xylophone; relatively large, typically with eighteen slats.

Dalang (ch. 9) Balinese shadow puppet master.

Danzón (ch. 17) A style of ballroom dance music popular in Cuba beginning in the late nineteenth century that features the *timbales*.

Dapu (ch. 1) In Chinese music, individual process of interpretation notation in sound.

Davul (ch. 3) Cylindrically shaped, double-headed frame drum (Turkey).

Deceleration (ch. 1) Slowing down.

Demography (ch. 19) Characteristics and movement of human populations.

Devr-i hindi (ch.1, ch. 11) A three-beat *usul* (short+ short+long) notated in 7/8, used in music in Turkey.

Dha (ch. 1, ch. 10) Syllable for the sixth of the basic seven pitches in the Indian pitch-naming system (in ascending order).

Diatonic scale (ch. 1) Seven-pitch scale type in the European system of music.

Didjeridu (ch. 3) End-blown aerophone (Australia).

Digital Audio Workstation (DAW) (ch. 11) A computer-based audio recording, editing, mixing, and mastering system.

Dizi (ch. 6) Side-blown bamboo flute with a thin membrane placed on the top of the flute between the blow hole and the first finger hole to modify the soft bamboo sound to more nasal (China).

Dominant (ch. 1) Pitch 5 in a diatonic scale; the second most important pitch in tonal music.

Dominant chord (ch. 2) Chord (V) built on pitch 5 of a scale or key in tonal music.

Double-tracking A kind of studio-produced overdubbing used in Turkey. The process of manually creating subsequent performances of the same part on the same instrument, usually done to create the illusion of an ensemble texture.

Downbeat (ch. 1) In Western meter, count 1.

Drone (ch. 2, ch. 10) One or more pitches sounding persistently.

Drum (ch. 20) One type of membranophone; drum may also refer to a powwow singing group.

Duff (ch. 12) A frame drum (Egypt).

Duple (ch. 1) In musical meter, beat groupings of 2 and multiples of 2.

Durak (ch. 11) "Resting place"; in Turkish music, the final note of a musical work, and a defining note of a *makam*.

Dynamics (ch. 15, ch. 19) In music, changes in volume.

Electronic keyboard (ch. 12) Keyboard instrument that creates sounds through analog, digital, or hybrid electronic circuitry.

Electronophone Instrument whose primary sound medium is electricity. Sub-types: keyboards, lutes.

Emweyir (ch. 5) Genre of exclamatory chants in Chuuk (Micronesia).

Erhu (ch. 6) Chinese two-stringed, long-necked, bowed spiked lute.

Escola de samba (ch. 18) Brazilian *samba* school, the organization that sponsors the yearly *Carnaval* Parade in Rio de Janeiro.

Ethnography (ch. 4) In ethnomusicology, the research method of learning about culture primarily from people. Also, the written account of what has been learned.

Éwúwénú (ch. 5) Genre of sitting dances for men and women, also called *pwérúkún faan maram* (Chuuk, Micronesia).

Expressive culture (ch. 3) Objects that are useful for the expression of cultural beliefs and values, for some function such as signaling in warfare, or for entertainment or trade.

Falsetas/variaciones (ch. 2, ch. 15) In Spanish *flamenco*, an instrumental interlude played on the guitar.

Fandangos de Huelva (ch. 15) A Spanish *flamenco palo* in triple meter.

Favelas (ch. 18) Poor hillside neighborhoods in Brazil.

Field notes (ch. 4) While doing fieldwork, keeping careful track of observations and information for later study and reference.

Fieldwork (ch. 4) Research in ethnomusicology, usually assumed to be largely (but not only) ethnographic, located wherever needed for a particular project. This can extend to library research in preparation for out-of-station research.

Firqa (ch. 12) "Ensemble"; used to refer to the orchestra-sized performance ensembles of eastern Arab music that emerged from the 1930s.

Flag Song (ch. 20) Type of powwow song used to honor and recognize the flags carried in at the beginning of the American Indian powwow Grand Entry processional.

Flamenco (ch. 1, ch. 2) A style of music associated with the region of Andalusia in Spain.

Flute (ch. 3) Subtype of aerophone on which a stream of air is directed against an edge on the instrument.

Frame drum (ch. 3) Membranophone whose head(s) are wider than the width of the frame that holds it (them).

Frame xylophone (ch. 13) Xylophone with wooden slats placed on top of a frame and attached in some way.

Free rhythm (ch. 1, ch. 16) Music with little or no sense of predictability about the organization of time.

Frequency (ch. 1, ch. 2) The number of times a sound vibrates per second; in acoustics of music, rate of vibration (cycles per second) in a string, column of air, or other sound-producing body.

Functional harmony (ch. 2) Chords as used in the European tonal system.

Futebol (ch. 18) Soccer.

Ga (ch. 1, ch. 10) Syllable for the third of the basic seven pitches in the Indian pitch-naming system (in ascending order).

Gagaku (ch. 2, ch. 7) Japan's largest traditional music ensemble; music of the imperial court and Buddhist temples.

Gamelan (ch. 2, ch. 3, ch. 9) Term for "ensemble" in Balinese (and other Indonesian) musics.

Gamelan balaganjur (ch. 9) Balinese processional (marching) *gamelan*.

Gamelan gambuh (ch. 9) Balinese dance drama and *gamelan from which many genres are derived.* Melody is played on large, vertical, bamboo flutes (see *Suling*).

Gamelan gender wayang (ch. 9) A quartet of ten-keyed metallophones that accompanies the Balinese shadow play.

Gamelan gong gedé (ch. 9) "*Gamelan* of the large gong"; an ancient, ceremonial, large bronze Balinese ensemble of up to sixty players.

Gamelan gong kebyar (ch. 2, ch. 9) Balinese *gamelan* with an "explosive" sound, developed in the early twentieth century.

Gamelan semar pagulingan (ch. 9) A Balinese court *gamelan*, originally played in the king's bed chamber.

Gàndáá (ch. 13) Word for a strongman in Dagaare language (Ghana).

Gangsa (ch. 9) Balinese metallophone with bamboo resonators.

Ganzá (ch. 3) Cylindrical rattle-type idiophone (Brazil).

Garmon (ch. 11) A family of small accordion-type instruments, including both piano and button accordion types, originally from Azerbaijan but introduced to Turkey in the twentieth century. The *garmon* performed in a few Eastern Black Sea villages is the piano type.

Gat (ch. 10) Generic term for an instrumental fixed composition in a *rāg*. The term is more generally used to describe the entire part of an instrumental performance of North Indian classical music that is accompanied by *tablā*.

Gender (ch. 4) The ways maleness and femaleness are constructed in a context.

Gineman (ch. 9) A freestanding prelude usually played by a soloist or group of soloists: metrically and rhythmically free, in Balinese *gamelan*; in *gamelan gong kebyar*, features instrumental group "solos."

Gɔbaa (pronounced gawba) (ch. 13) A *gyil* player acknowledged in the community as master of the xylophone.

Gitanos (ch. 15) The Roma people of Spain, formerly referred to as "Gypsies."

Gong A metal disc with deeply turned rim and, on Indonesian gongs, with a bulbous raised boss (for controlling vibration) in the middle of the disc; usually suspended.

Gong-chime (also called "kettle gong"). In Balinese music, a set of tuned gongs, laid horizontally on a rack with the raised boss facing up. Played with a damping technique, it is used in sets for melody either as a soloist (*trompong*) or with four players playing interlocking parts and percussive patterns with the drums (*reyong*).

Good intonation (ch. 1) Pitch produced at desired frequencies in a pitch system.

Gourd Dance (ch. 20) Southern Plains American Indian veteran's society dance that, in some areas, has been incorporated into the opening sequence of events at a powwow as a means of acknowledging military service and preparing the dance arena for a powwow.

Grand Entry (ch. 20) Opening processional at an American Indian powwow, during which all assembled dancers dance into the arena together. Some nations see Grand Entry as having been borrowed from Wild West shows. Grand Entry line-up order is determined by local protocol as mediated by the Arena director.

Griot (ch. 13) Hereditary professional musicians and oral historians, primarily found in West Africa (e.g., Senegambia, Mali, Guinea).

Grito (ch. 19) A yell (Spanish).

Guitar (acoustic) family (generically) (ch. 15, ch. 19) Long-necked, wooden, waisted/eight-shaped hollow body with neck attached; flat cover and back; with fixed frets. Usually steel strings but examples with nylon strings.

Guitarrón (pl. *guitarrones*) (ch. 19) The bass instrument of the mariachi; chordophone. Its eight-shaped soundbox, with a spined, convex back, is much larger than that of the guitar or *vihuela*. Its six strings are tuned A¹-D-G-c-e-A. The *guitarronero* (*guitarrón* player) plays most notes by plucking two strings at a time, producing either a unison or an octave. Together with the *vihuela* and six-stringed guitar, it forms the mariachi instrumental rhythm section called *armonía*.

Guqin (ch. 1, ch. 3, ch. 6) Historic Chinese, seven-stringed, long zither.

Gûru (Intro, ch. 10) In Hindu and Buddhist culture, a revered teacher and guide.

Gyil (Pronounced *jiil*, meaning "surround.") (ch. 13) Gourd resonated frame xylophone used by several ethnic groups in northwestern Ghana. Dagaaba play the *lo-gyil* and the *daga-gyil*.

Half step (ch. 1) An interval of which there are twelve in an octave.

Ḥarām (ch. 12) Forbidden or unlawful in Islam.

Harmonium (ch. 16) Small keyboard instrument that consists of a series of reed pipes encased in a box that sound when a key is pressed to open a valve that allows air from a bellows to pass through.

Harmony (ch. 1) Generically in music, two or more pitches heard simultaneously.

Head Dancers (ch. 20) Dancers invited by American Indian powwow committee members to lead the dancing at a given powwow and, in doing so, to act as public representatives of that powwow in publicity and on the day of the event. Depending upon powwow size, head dancers may also be selected across different ages and/or genders (head man, head woman, head golden age, and others).

Hertz (hz) (ch. 1, ch. 2) Number of times a pitch vibrates per second.

Heterogeneous sound (ch. 2, ch. 3) Timbral variety.

Heterophony (heterophonic) (ch. 2, ch. 6, ch. 8, ch. 9) "Different voices"; musical texture of one melody performed almost simultaneously and somewhat differently by multiple musicians.

Ḥijāb (ch. 12) A head scarf (Arabic).

Hindustani (ch. 10) Of the northern part of the subcontinent of India (Hindustan), through which runs one of the longest rivers in Asia—the Indus/Sindhu/Sind.

Hne (ch. 8) Conical wooden multiple-reed aerophone with loose flare in Burmese *hsaing waing* ensemble.

Homogeneous sound (ch. 3) Timbral similarity.

Homophony (ch. 2, ch. 17) Musical texture of melody accompanied by chords or fully chordal.

Honor Beats (ch. 20) Accented beats performed by one drummer in the course of an American Indian powwow song. Usually inserted during the B section in a Northern Style Powwow song, but they can be placed according to the tribal or intertribal practices of the drum in question. Honor beats are sometimes described as moment in which dancers "honor" the drum.

Horon (ch. 11) Line dances done in the Black Sea region of Turkey, most commonly involving music using asymmetrical beat structures such as *devr-i hindi*, that are performed on the *kemençe, tulum* (bagpipe), *garmon*, or *kaval*; related to the Bulgarian *horo*.

Host Drums (ch. 20) Similar to head dancers, host drums are drum groups invited to lead the singing at an American Indian powwow and, in doing so, to publicly represent that powwow in publicity and on the day of the event. Depending on powwow size a committee might invite one or multiple host drums.

Hsaing waing (ch. 8) Outdoor ensemble of Myanmar.

Hybridity (ch. 14) Theoretical term used to describe mixing and fluidity between cultures, languages, and population groups.

Hymn (ch. 5) Musical genre often associated with unaccompanied, multipart Christian songs in Chuuk (Micronesia).

Idiophone (ch. 3, ch. 9) Instrument in which the primary sound-producing medium is the body of the instrument itself.

Imām (ch. 12) Head of a Muslim mosque (Egypt).

Improvise (ch. 15) To create music and/or lyrics in the course of performance, usually on the basis of pre-existing ideas.

Intertribal (ch. 20) As opposed to pan-Indian, a term derived from American Indian powwow practice to describe the various processes of cultural exchange that inform powwow practices.

Intertribal Song (ch. 20) Type of powwow song used for social dancing where dancers of all dance styles participate together.

Interval (ch. 1) In music, distance between pitches.

"In tune" (ch. 1) Matching a desired pitch.

Jalear (ch. 15) Cheering in Spanish *flamenco*.

Jembe (ch. 13) (also transliterated as *djembe*) Ghanaian goblet-shaped hand drum.

Jhālā (ch. 10) "Sparkling"; the concluding rapid section of a North Indian instrumental performance that uses repeated striking of the drone strings.

Jiangnan sizhu (ch. 2, ch. 6) Instrumental ensemble of the Jiangnan region of east central China.

Jig (ch. 2, ch. 16) Solo or group step dances performed to the music of a tune type by the same name. Four variants of the jig exist in the Irish tradition, all in compound meter: the single and double jig in 6/8, the slip jig in 9/8, and the slide in 12/8.

Kabuki (ch. 7) Seventeenth-century Japanese popular theatrical form.

Kaja and Kelod (ch. 9) Cardinal directions on the Indonesian island of Bali: toward the (sacred) mountain and toward the sea, north and south respectively. Because the mountains are toward the center of the island, *kaja* and *kelod* vary according to where in Bali the speaker is.

Kapasen le mataw (ch. 5) "Language of the sea," and a broad term for songs and chants for ocean wayfinding (Chuuk, Micronesia).

Karen (ch. 8) Ethnic group in Eastern Myanmar.

Kathak (ch. 10) A form of North Indian classical dance, one that emphasizes rhythmic play.

Kaval (ch. 11) End-blown wooden or reed flute used in rural Anatolian folk music.

Kawala (ch. 12) An end-blown flute made of a fairly thick reed plant, with six fingerholes, common in Egyptian *madh* music

Kawitan (ch. 9) Introductory section of a piece (the "head") (Bali).

Kebyar section (ch. 9) An explosive section of a Balinese composition for *gamelan gong kebyar* in which all parts move together in an asymmetrical, syncopated melody; usually at the beginning of a composition, often during the piece and at the end as an explosive finish.

Kéénún etiwetiw (ch. 5) Welcome songs (Chuuk, Micronesia).

Kéénún namanam (ch. 5) Christian songs (Chuuk, Micronesia).

Kéénún nóómw (ch. 5) Songs (and music) from the past (Chuuk, Micronesia).

Kéénún núkún (ch. 5) Love songs (Chunk Micronesia).

Keiko Abe (ch. 7) Superstar Japanese marimbist.

Kemençe (ch. 1, ch 11; Greek: *Pontos lyra*) Short-necked, three-stringed, bowed box lute played in the Black Sea region of Turkey and historically performed primarily by Laz and Pontic Greeks.

Kendang (ch. 9) Balinese conical drums with two playing heads; held horizontally, played in pairs or solo, with the hands or mallets.

Key (ch. 2) In tonal music, a tonality named after the main pitch (tonic).

Khoisan (ch. 14) A somewhat imprecise term used to describe the amalgamation of various autochthonous population groups—both San and Khoikhoi—in the southern part of Africa.

Kotekan (ch. 2, ch. 9) Texture of interlocking instrumental parts in Balinese music.

Koto (ch. 2, ch. 7) Long zither-type chordophone of Japanese traditional music, with 13 strings (or, recently, more), each supported on a moveable bridge.

Kúkúr-nà (ch. 13) Term in Ghanaian Dagaare language derived from "*kukur*" (the farming hoe), and "*na*" (chief).

Kuor (ch. 13) Very large Dagaaba gourd drum with a skin attached to the top, played by both hands, yielding a semi-deep tone (Ghana).

Kuurbine (ch. 13) Dance music played on the *daga-gyil* during Dagaaba funerals; from *kuur* (death) and *bine* (dance music) (Ghana).

Kwaito (ch. 14) South African genre of popular electronic music from mid-1990.

Kyi waing (ch. 8) Set of tuned gong chimes resting horizontally on a circular rack, in Burmese (Myanmar) *hsaing waing* ensemble.

Lalambatan (ch. 9) [slow music] played in Balinese temple ceremonies, traditionally on *gamelan gong gedé*.

Lambada (ch. 18) Dance music from northern Brazil that grew into an international craze in the 1980s.

Language standardization (ch. 14) A politically driven process (used, e.g., by the apartheid government) that halts linguistic hybridity and change, and that concretizes boundaries between overlapping languages.

Larant (ch. 10) In North Indian music, melody that uses the repeated pitch *sa* as a springboard for neighbor-note motion around it.

LGBTQIA+ (ch. 19) A common abbreviation for the Lesbian, Gay, Bisexual, Pansexual, Transgender, Genderqueer, Queer, Intersex, Agender, Asexual, and Ally community.

Lingwin (ch. 8) Cymbal pair (Myanmar).

Literati (ch. 6) Culturally elite scholar-bureaucrats of Imperial China.

Lobri (ch. 13) Tunes played on the *lo-gyil* that announce the death of a Dagaaba man or woman (Ghana).

Lo-gyil (ch. 13) Dagaaba frame xylophone; relatively small, with 14 slats (Ghana).

Lute (ch. 3) Subtype of chordophone with strings running along a body and a neck.

Ma (ch. 1, ch. 10) Syllable for the fourth of the basic seven pitches in the Indian pitch-naming system (in ascending order).

Madḥ (*or madīḥ in-nabī*) (ch. 12) Literally "praise" or "praise of the prophet," a genre of Egyptian Sufi religious music.

Major chord (ch. 2) Chord that has a root note, a major third above the root, and a perfect fifth above the root note.

Major scale (ch. 1) In the European melodic system, diatonic scale with interval distribution W W H W W W H (W = whole step, H = half step).

Makam (plural: *makamlar*) (ch. 1, ch. 11) Turkish melodic modes used in urban art music and in some Anatolian rural folk music traditions.

Malandro (ch. 18) Hustler figure celebrated in lyrics of early *samba*.

Maqām (plural: maqāmāt) (ch. 12) General term for the melodic modes of Arab music.

Maqām rāst (ch. 12) The "first" of the modes according to modern Arab music theory, frequently used in Egypt, including for the Islamic Call to Prayer.

Maracas (ch 3, ch. 17) Gourd rattle type of idiophone; shaken by a handle.

Marcha (ch. 18) March (Brazil).

Mariachi (ch. 3, ch. 19) Refers mainly to an individual *mariachi* musician; to a *mariachi* ensemble; or, as an adjective, to something identified with either of these, such as "*mariachi* repertoire" (Mexico, United States). The *mariachi* ensemble's instrumentation typically includes two to five violins, one or two trumpets, *guitarrón*, *vihuela*, six-stringed guitar. A large harp might be included in a large-scale mariachi or in an old-style *mariachi tradicional*. Term's etymological link to the French word *mariage* has been proven to be false.

Marimba (ch. 7) A xylophone-type instrument with keys/bars tuned chromatically, each with resonator pipe below each bar/key to amplify the sound. Pitched relatively lower than the orchestra xylophone.

Marímbula (ch 17) Bass instrument played in some traditional Cuban *son* ensembles; it is patterned after the African *mbira* or "thumb piano," a wooden resonator box with metal strips (keys) attached.

Martillo pattern (ch. 17) A rhythmic *ostinato* played by the bongo drum during the initial *tema* section of a *son*.

Master of Ceremonies (ch. 20) Also referred to as the MC or emcee, an individual who is invited by an American Indian powwow committee to narrate, explain, and to some degree mediate the similarities and differences between the various tribal and intertribal events taking place at a powwow to dancers and spectators.

Material culture (ch. 3) Physical objects produced by a certain group of people.

Maung (ch. 8) Set of tuned gong chimes resting horizontally on a straight rack; in *hsaing waing* ensemble of Myanmar.

Mawwāl (ch. 12) A genre of Egyptian sung poetry characterized by rhyme scheme.

Maxixe (ch. 18) Early twentieth century Brazilian dance genre that combined features of the tango and the polka.

Mazhar (ch. 12) Large frame drum with five sets of cymbals set around the rim, especially featured in Egyptian wedding processions.

Mbira (ch. 3) Plucked idiophone; "thumb piano" with thin metal prongs (Zimbabwe).

Measure (ch. 1) In Western music and notation, one metric group of beats (also called "bar").

Medley (ch. 16) Two or more tunes played one after another without break.

Melodic mode (ch. 1) Pitch set with musical traits and non-musical associations.

Melody (ch.1) Generically, any selection of pitches in succession.

Membranophone (ch. 3) Instrument on which a vibrating membrane stretched over a resonator or frame produces the sound.

Mestizo (ch. 19) People who emerge from the mix of cultures (Spanish language).

Metallophone (ch. 3, ch. 9) Percussion idiophone-type instrument; set of tuned metal bars. In Bali, each suspended over a bamboo tube resonator played with a hard mallet and made in multiple pitch registers (low, mid, high) with different numbers of keys.

Meter (ch. 1) A regular recurring grouping of beats.

Metric cycle (ch. 1, ch.10) Metrical unit system in which units are brought to an end on a next count 1.

Michio Miyagi (ch. 7) Twentieth-century Japanese *koto* player known as the "father of modern *koto* music."

Microtones (ch. 1) Intervals that deviate from those of the European system of whole steps and half steps.

Minjian yiren (ch. 6) "Artists among the folk" (China)

Minor chord (ch. 2) Chord that has a root note, a minor third above the root, and a perfect fifth above the root note.

Miyagi Michio (ch.7) See Michio Miyagi

Minzu yinyue (ch. 6) Term for Chinese traditional music since the 1950s, sometimes known as *minyue* for short.

Mizmār (ch. 12) A cylindrical double-reed aerophone with a wooden tube ending in a conical flare (Egypt).

Monophony (ch. 2) Texture in music of a part performed solo or by multiple people in unison.

Montuno (ch. 2, ch. 17) "From the mountains or rural areas"; term used to describe the final climactic section of Cuban *son* music (and also *rumba*). *Montuno*s typically involve cyclic, repeated melodies and rhythms. Often a lead singer or instrumentalist improvises during a *montuno* in response to a chorus. *Montuno*s can also feature extended instrumental solos on a single instrument.

Morros (ch. 18) Poor hillside neighborhoods (Brazil).

Muezzin (*mu'azzin* in colloquial Egyptian Arabic; *mu'adhdhin* in standard Arabic) (ch. 12) caller of the Islamic call to prayer.

Mukhrā (ch. 10) "Face"; the first phrase of a North Indian vocal composition that is used as a refrain or point of return to a fixed composition.

Mulato (ch. 18) Person of mixed African and European descent; the term is considered pejorative (Brazil).

Munshid (ch. 12) An singer of religious song (*nashīd*) (Egypt).

Musical form (ch. 2) The overall structure or plan of a piece of music.

Musicking (Intro, ch. 20) The activity of taking part, in any capacity, in musical performance.

Musicker (Intro) A person who participates in musicking.

Musiqa (Intro) In Egypt, instrumental music now; in Middle Ages, theoretical discussions of music.

Nād Brahmā (ch. 10) "The language of God"; the ancient Indian concept that sound (*nād*) is a sacred manifestation of the universe, that is, that sound itself is divine.

Nat (ch. 8) Animistic spirit (Myanmar).

Nat pwe (ch. 8) Ceremony to facilitate communication with *nats* (Myanmar).

Native American (ch. 20) Generalized term used to refer to Indigenous individuals and communities living in the United States.

Natural minor scale (ch. 1) In the European music system, diatonic scale with interval distribution W H W W H W W. (W=whole step, H=half step).

Nāy (ch. 12) Reed end-blown flute with six finger-holes on top, one on underside. Featured especially in eastern Arab art music, including in Egypt.

Na yi si (ch. 8) Four-beat rhythmic pattern common in Burmese music (Myanmar).

Ngiring (ch. 9) To escort or accompany; describes music's function as "guiding along" and "accompanying" ceremonial and theatrical performance (Bali).

Ni (ch. 1, ch. 10) Syllable for the seventh of the basic seven pitches in the Indian pitch-naming system (in ascending order).

Noh theater (ch. 7) Fifteenth-century type of music drama of the Japanese *samurai* class.

Norot (ch. 9) "Neighbor-tone" type of *kotekan* (Bali).

Northern Plains (ch. 20) Geographic distinction used in American Indian powwow singing practice to indicate a higher-pitched style of singing, as opposed to Southern Plains. Can also be used in reference to tribal or intertribal powwow practices emerging from states on the Northern Plains of the United States up into Canada.

Nuevo flamenco (ch. 15) A commercial label created in the 1980s to promote artists and groups with new approaches to *flamenco* (Spain).

Nyog-cag (ch. 9) "Leaping" type of *kotekan* (Bali).

Observation (ch. 4) During ethnomusicological fieldwork, research by asking questions, holding discussions, watching musical performances, and other activities pertinent to the project.

Odalan (ch. 9) Temple anniversary, celebrated every 210 days in the Bali Hindu Çaka calendar year.

Offbeat (ch. 1) In musical rhythm, stress between the beats.

Ópera flamenca (ch. 15) A commercial theatrical *flamenco* show intended to attract large, middle-class audiences that was predominant in Spain between the 1920s and the 1950s.

Org (ch. 12) The electronic keyboard instrument (Egypt).

Orixás (ch. 18) Deities in *candomblé* (Brazil).

Ostinato (pl. ostinati) (ch. 17) Repeated, cyclic melodic or rhythmic figure.

Ozi (ch. 8) Goblet-shaped drum of various sizes (Myanmar).

Pa (ch. 1, ch. 10) Syllable for the fifth of the basic seven pitches in the Indian pitch-naming system (in ascending order).

Pagode (ch. 18) "Backyard" style of samba that includes *tantã*, *repique de mão*, and banjo in the instrumental group. The song form is characterized by call-and-response and lyric improvisation.

Paixiao (ch. 6) Type of aerophone often referred to as a panpipe; set of end-blown bamboo pipes of different lengths bound together (China).

Pali (ch. 8) Historic language of Theravada Buddhist texts (Myanmar).

Palmas (ch. 15) In Spanish *flamenco*, handclapping.

Palmeros (ch. 15) In Spanish *flamenco*, handclappers.

Palo (ch. 15) In *flamenco*, song type.

Pandeiro (ch. 1, ch. 18) Brazilian drum (tambourine) with metal jingles, played by hand.

Pangawak (ch. 9) "Main body" of a piece: the longest section.

Pangecet (ch. 9) "Legs and Feet"; short, compressed, final section of a piece. Pieces may have more than one *pangecet*.

Pa-O (ch. 8) Ethnic group in East Central Myanmar.

Participation (ch. 4) During ethnomusicological research, taking part in musicking, often by receiving music instruction and performing.

Partido-alto (ch. 18) Song form characterized by call-and-response and lyric improvisation.

Partido-alto rhythm (ch. 18) A syncopated rhythm that distinguishes *pagode* style of Brazilian *samba*.

Patt ma (ch. 8) Large, double-headed, barrel-shaped drum in *hsaing waing* ensemble of Myanmar.

Patt sa (ch. 8) "Drum food." Tuning paste for *patt waing* drums in *hsaing waing* ensemble of Myanmar.

Patt waing (ch. 2, ch. 8) Set of twenty-one double-headed, tuned drums suspended vertically on a circular frame; in *hsaing waing* ensemble of Myanmar.

Paya pwe (ch. 8) Festival held at a Buddhist pagoda in Myanmar.

Pélú (ch. 5) Master mariner (Chuuk, Micronesia).

Peña (ch. 15) In Spain, pub where aficionados gather regularly to participate in *flamenco* sessions.

Pentatonic scale (ch. 13) Scale consisting of a selection of five pitches in an octave.

Perfect pitch (ch. 1) Identifying or producing a pitch from aural memory.

Pitch (ch. 1) The relative quality of "highness" or "lowness" of sound; in music, usually some purposefully placed sound on a continuum from low to high.

Pitch frequency (ch. 2) In acoustics, rate of vibration (cycles per second, or Hertz) in a string, column of air, or other sound-producing body.

Pitch register (ch. 3) An area within a pitch range.

Pitch set (ch. 1) A group of pitches.

Plantas (ch. 19) Regular gig for a mariachi ensemble (United States and Mexico.).

Pokok (ch. 9) The basic skeletal melody of a Balinese musical composition.

Polos (ch. 9) "Basic, simple"; one of two interlocking melodic parts in Balinese music; the half of *kotekan* usually on the beat.

Polyphony (ch. 2, ch 8) Texture in music of simultaneous combining of multiple melodies.

Polyrhythm (ch. 1, ch. 17, ch. 18) A musical texture of multiple rhythmic patterns performed simultaneously.

Polyrhythmic patterns (ch. 18) Multiple rhythmic patterns performed simultaneously.

Power chord (ch. 2) Influence of heavy metal music in Turkish studio arrangements, the overtracking of multiple instruments playing the same chords simultaneously to produce a "powerful," oversaturated sound.

Powwow (ch. 20) Intertribal Native American social gatherings built around a shared repertoire of songs and dances.

Powwow drum (ch. 3, ch. 20) Bass frame drum, played with membrane facing upward by multiple singers at a Native American powwow.

Powwow songs (ch. 20) Songs performed at powwow events for social, ceremonial, and contest dances.

Pulse (ch. 1) Rhythm of consistent, equal-length durations of time.

Push-up (ch. 20) One iteration of a complete Native American powwow song melody.

Pwe (ch. 8) Burmese performance, celebration, or event (Myanmar).

Pwérúkún faan maram (ch. 5) "Dances under the moon," genre of Chuukese sitting dances for men and women, also called *éwúwénú* (Micronesia).

Qānūn (ch. 12) The trapezoid-shaped, plucked box zither common in eastern Arab art music, including in Egypt.

Quadruple meter (ch. 1, ch. 15) Meter consisting of four beat units divided into two pulses each (4/4).

Qur'an (Intro) Sacred text revealed to the Prophet Muhammad.

Rāga/rāg (ch. 1, ch. 3, ch. 10) System of melodic maps/formats/modes of classical music in India.

Ramé (ch. 9) "Full, boisterous, active"; the desired soundscape for Balinese ceremonies.

Range (pitch) (ch. 3) Span of pitches.

Rebab (ch. 9) Long-necked, bowed, spiked lute with a small resonating chamber covered in skin, and long, thin lateral pegs to tune its two strings. Imported to Bali from Java.

Reed (ch. 3) Subtype of aerophone on which a piece of reed has been placed at the head of the instrument or inside.

Reel (ch. 16) Solo or group step dances performed to the music of a tune type by the same name. The most popular tune type within the Irish tradition, it is in duple meter (4/4).

Refrain (ch. 15) In a song, a recurrent stanza with the same melody.

Relative pitch (ch. 1) The ability to sing a pitch in reference to any another.

Repertoire (Intro, ch. 9) A group of pieces that are linked in some way.

Repique de mão (ch. 18) High-pitched, single-headed drum, held on player's lap and played by hand in Brazilian music.

Representation (ch. 4) In ethnomusicology, having a voice to present oneself or another.

Reverberation (reverb) (ch. 11) The propagation of sound in an acoustic environment; in recording studio productions, typically refers to artificial reverberation, or the simulation of the propagation of sound in an acoustic environment through electro-mechanical or digital means.

Reyong (ch. 9) Gong-chime type of idiophone in Balinese music: straight row of kettles played by four musicians producing complex interlocking melodic parts and percussive articulations by striking the rims with the wooden part of the mallets.

Rhythm Generically in music, the management of time into durations of musical sounds.

Rhythmic recitation (ch. 5) A rhythmic and speech-derived delivery of expressive poetry.

Ri (or **re**) (ch. 1, ch. 10) Syllable for the second of the basic seven pitches in the Indian pitch-naming system (in ascending order).

Riqq (ch. 12) A single-headed frame drum with five sets of cymbals mounted symmetrically around the frame (Egypt).

"Rokudan" ("Six Sections"; ch. 7) Seventeenth-century composition for solo *koto*, Yatsuhashi Kengyō, composer.

Root (ch. 2) The pitch on which a chord is based in tonal music.

Rubato (ch. 1) Generically in music, fluctuation in tempo.

Rumba (ch. 15, ch. 17) A secular drumming and dance style in Cuba associated with the black community. Its two-part form (a strophic verse section followed by a *montuno*) is said to have influenced the development of the *son*. In Spain, appropriated and adapted to *flamenco* as a *palo* in quadruple meter.

Sa (ch. 1, ch. 10) Syllable for the first of the basic seven pitches in the Indian pitch-naming system (in ascending order).

Sahel (ch. 13) The semi-arid zone of transition in Africa between the Sahara to the north and the Sudanian Savanna to the south and between the Atlantic Ocean and the Red Sea.

Sahib (ch. 10) A polite form of address for a man, here attached to the surname of Khan as *Khansahib*.

"Sakura, sakura" ("Cherry Blossoms") (ch. 7) Emblematic Japanese folk song.

Samba de morro (ch. 1, ch. 18) Style of Brazilian *samba* originated by 1930s composers of the *Estácio* neighborhood of Rio de Janeiro, using percussion instruments *surdo*, *pandeiro*, and *tamborim*.

Samba-canção (ch. 18) *Samba* song that emphasizes melody more than rhythm and has a more varied harmonic accompaniment compared to *samba-enredo*.

Samba-enredo (ch. 18) *Samba* song that communicates the theme of the year's *Carnaval* parade in Rio de Janeiro, Brazil.

Samba-exaltação (ch. 18) *Samba* song that praises the Brazilian people, history, culture, or geography.

Sambadrome (ch. 18) Stadium in Rio de Janeiro, Brazil where *samba* schools parade.

Samba sujo (ch. 18) So-called "dirty *samba*," style cultivated in São Paulo that addresses gritty urban themes and can include elements of rock and electronic music.

Samurai (ch. 7) Warrior; military class in premodern Japan.

Sangha (ch. 8) Order of Buddhist monks (Myanmar).

Sangsih (ch. 2, ch. 9) "Differing"; one of two interlocking melodic parts in Balinese *kotekan*; the half of *kotekan* usually off the beat that fits between the pitches of the *polos* part, completing the composite figuration.

Sārangī (ch. 10) Short/broad-necked bowed lute with sympathetic strings (India).

Sargam (ch. 1, ch. 10) Term for solfege in Indian music; syllables for naming the seven basic pitches—*sa ri ga ma pa dha* and *ni* (in ascending order)

Sarod (ch. 1, ch. 2, ch. 10) North Indian, long-necked, plucked lute. Slightly waisted-shaped wooden resonating body is covered with goatskin. Its fretless neck tapers from wide at the body to narrower and is covered with a smooth steel fingerboard; has steel playing, drone, and sympathetic strings.

Saung gauk (also *saung*; ch. 1, ch. 2, ch. 8) Burmese arched harp (Myanmar).

Savanna (ch. 13) A green ecozone characterized by scattered trees and continuous grassland.

Sawāb (Egyptian colloquial; *thawāb* in standard Arabic) (ch. 12) Reward for meritorious deeds.

Sawāl-jawāb (ch. 10) In North Indian practice, a "repeat the motive" exchange between two artists, the exchanges becoming shorter and quicker until the performance ends with a thrilling *tihāî* played together.

Saxophone (ch. 12) Single-reed aerophone with wide cylindrical brass tube that turns up on itself and widens slightly to the end.

Saz (ch. 1, ch. 11) "Instrument"; a family of long-necked plucked lutes of different sizes with movable frets and three courses of strings (a total of three to eight strings) (Turkey).

Scale (ch. 1) A set of pitches presented in straight ascending or descending order.

Sean-nós (ch. 1, ch. 16) Literally, "old style." A singing style developed in the Irish language most often performed unaccompanied and in free rhythm.

Serenata (ch. 19) Mariachi serenade of about a half-hour or a fixed number of pieces to mark a special occasion such as Mother's Day (United States and Mexico).

Sertaneja (ch. 18) Brazilian country music.

Set dance (ch. 16) Genre of Irish social dance performed by four couples in square formation, originally brought to Ireland by French dancing masters in the nineteenth century.

Sexuality (ch. 4) A human's capacity for sexual feelings, understood broadly and without precise definition as the ways a person might experience and express themselves sexually.

Shakuhachi (ch. 2, ch. 7) Long, wide, end-blown, bamboo flute with notched rim (Japan)

Shamisen (ch. 7) Long-necked, three-stringed, spiked plucked lute with lateral pegs; square wooden body closed by catskin "head"; without frets.

Shan (ch. 8) Second largest ethnic group in Myanmar.

Shaykh (ch. 12) A man respected for his piety or religious learning (Egypt).

Shō (ch. 2) Free-reed aerophone with multiple bamboo pipes ("mouth organ") in the Japanese imperial court music ensemble.

Si (ch. 8) Two small metal bells struck against each other, paired with the *wa* clapper (Myanmar).

Sitār (ch. 2, ch. 10) Long-necked plucked lute with a bowl-shaped, gourd resonating chamber attached to the wooden neck; high metal frets movable to accommodate the North Indian *rāga* being performed. Its metal playing, drone, and sympathetic strings create a distinctive sound.

Soleá/Soleares (ch. 15) A *flamenco palo* in twelve-beat metric cycle (Spain).

Solfege (ch. 1) Generically, a set of syllables for naming pitches.

Solo (ch. 20) Performance by one person; a musical part meant to stand out.

Son (pl. *sones*) (ch. 2, ch. 17, ch. 19) A cognate with the word "song" in English, "*son*" in Spanish can refer generally to a song or songs, or to particular kinds of regional repertoire.

Son (Cuban) (ch. 17) A unique style of Caribbean music that emerged in eastern Cuba in the late nineteenth century. Its characteristic features include an "anticipated bass" pattern, use of the *son clave* rhythm, and "claved" instrumental melodies. This style of music influenced the development of modern salsa in New York City and elsewhere.

Son (ch. 19) In Mexico, may refer to a regional style of mestizo music or to certain melodies of Indian cultural groups. In both cases, most *sones* have a rhythmic drive appropriate for dancing. Regional mestizo *son* traditions may be distinguished by instrumentation, instrumental technique, singing style, repertoire, and other traits. A mariachi ensemble often includes in its repertoire several regional styles of *son*, especially the *son jalisciense* "Jalisco-style *son*," but also the *son jarocho* from Veracruz and *son huasteco* from the Huastecan regional of eastern Mexico.

Son clave (ch. 17) In Cuban *son*, two-measure rhythmic pattern consisting of two strokes in one measure and three in another. Either side of the pattern can be played first. *Son clave* serves as a guiding rhythm or timeline, organizing those played by many other instruments in the ensemble.

Southern Plains (ch. 20) Geographic distinction used in Native American powwow singing practice to indicate a lower-pitched style of singing, as opposed to that of the Northern Plains. Can also be used in reference to tribal or intertribal powwow practices emerging from states on the Southern Plains of the United States.

Step dance (ch. 16) A virtuosic solo and group dance genre in Irish tradition characterized by a straight upper body and precise footwork, performed in either hard or soft shoes. The most common dances are reels, jigs and hornpipes, accompanied by tunes types of the same name.

Straight Beat (ch. 20) American Indian powwow song dance beat characterized by a "straight" or regular pulse: 1 2 1 2 1 2. The second beat is slightly accented.

Stratified "Layered"; (ch. 9) In Balinese *gamelan* music, correlation of pitch register of an instrument with density of the musical part.

Stressing See accenting.

Strophic song (ch. 2, ch. 17) Song in which the tune repeats, each time with new lyrics.

Style (ch. 20) The combination of qualities that create distinctiveness.

Subdominant (ch. 1) Pitch 4 in a diatonic scale; the third most important pitch in tonal music.

Subdominant chord (ch. 2) Chord (IV) built on pitch 4 of a scale or key in tonal music.

Sufism (ch. 12) The mystical branch of Islam.

Suling (ch. 9) Held vertically, end-blown Balinese bamboo flute of various lengths and widths.

Surdo (ch. 1, ch. 18) Large double-headed bass drum in Brazilian popular music; lowest-pitched drum in *samba* percussion group, played on one head only with a beater.

Sutras (ch. 8) Buddhist blessings and prayers.

Syllabic (ch. 8) Text setting of one pitch per syllable.

Sympathetic strings (ch. 10) Strings underneath the playing strings that vibrate in sympathy rather than being plucked (North India).

Syncopated (ch. 1, ch. 17) With rhythmic stress between the beats (termed "offbeat").

Ṭabla (ch. 12) A single-headed, metal goblet-shaped drum (Egypt).

Tablā (ch. 10) A North Indian pair of single-headed, hand-struck drums played by one musician—the left one (*bayan*) bowl-shaped with a deep sound, the right one (*tablā*) conical, the shape of two truncated cones bulging at the center and carefully tuned to higher pitch with a special paste.

Tablao (ch. 15) Performance venue for *flamenco* associated with the tourist industry (Spain).

Tablature (ch. 1) Music notation that gives instructions for playing.

Takht (ch. 12) A small performance ensemble prevalent in eastern Arab art music of the late-nineteenth century into the twentieth century.

Tāla/tāl (ch. 1, ch. 10) Term for India's system for organizing musical time into metric cycles.

Tamborim (ch. 1, ch. 18) Small Brazilian frame drum without jingles played with a beater.

Tān (ch. 10) A melodic pattern used to expand the *rāga* in performance after the fixed composition; often used in the sense of a fast, melodic run/flourish.

Tangos (ch. 15) A *flamenco palo* in quadruple meter (Spain).

Tānpūrā (ch. 10) Plucked composite lute-zither chordophone, used solely for drone pitches in Indian classical music.

Tantā (ch. 18) Low-pitched, single-headed drum held on the player's lap and played by hand (Brazil).

Tārānā (ch. 10) A North Indian rhythmic vocal composition in which vocables, some derived from drumming and dance as well as melodic pitches, are set to a particular *rāg* and *tāl*.

Tema (ch. 2, ch. 17) "Theme"; term for the initial verse-like section in Cuban *son*, prior to the *montuno*. The *tema* can also be referred to as the *canto* (chant, song) or *verso* (verse).

Tempo (ch. 1) Italian term for "speed."

Tempo rubato (ch. 15) Expressive technique that features slight speeding up or slackening of tempo.

Tessitura (ch. 3) Most comfortable pitch range for a singer.

Texture (ch. 2, ch. 9) Musical relationships among multiple parts.

Theravada (ch. 8) "The Way of the Elders." Tradition of Buddhism found in Sri Lanka, Myanmar, Thailand, and Cambodia.

Through-composed (ch. 2, ch 12) Music with new material from beginning to end.

Tihāī (ch. 10) "One-third"; In North Indian performance practice, a rhythmic or melodic pattern played or sung three times, often returning either to the beginning of the composition or to the downbeat of the *tāl* to end a musical unit.

Timba (ch. 17) A fusion of traditional Cuban *son* with influences from local Afro-Cuban drumming styles as well as rock, funk, and jazz.

Timbales (ch. 17) A percussion instrument associated with Cuban *son* and modern salsa music; two single-headed tom tom–like drums of slightly differing sizes held on a metal frame, along with two bells of distinct sizes and a woodblock.

Timbila (ch. 13) Frame xylophone of the Chopi people from Mozambique in East Africa.

Timbre (ch. 2, ch. 3, ch. 20) The quality or character of sound produced by an instrument or voice, whether naturally or by intentional cultivation.

Tīntāl (ch. 1, ch. 10). A North Indian metric cycle of 16 beats subdivided 4 + 4 + 4 + 4.

Tin whistle (ch. 16) An end-blown Irish flute originally made from tin sheeting but often made today from brass or nickel plated brass tubing; a "fipple" type of flute with mouthpiece. A plug inside the fipple forms a windway that directs the player's breath alternately above and below a sharp edge, thereby setting the air in the column in motion.

Tocaor (ch. 15) *Flamenco* guitarist (Spain).

Tonal center (ch. 1) Pitch in a pitch set to which melody is oriented.

Tonal system (ch. 2) The European harmonic system that emphasizes the relationships between chords and the way to progress from one chord to another.

Tonality (ch. 1, ch. 15) In Western music, the organized relationships of tones with reference to a center, the tonic.

Tone cluster (ch. 2) Set of simultaneously sounded multiple pitches that make no reference to the tonal harmonic system .

Tonic (ch. 1) Term for tonal center in the European music system; the most important pitch in tonal music.

Tonic chord (ch. 2) Chord (I) built on the fundamental pitch of a scale or key in tonal music.

Toque (ch. 15) In *flamenco*, guitar playing (Spain).

Traje (ch. 19) Suit worn by mariachi musicians (United States)

Transposition (ch. 2) In music, shifting to another key in the tonal system.

Tres (ch. 17) A medium-sized guitar-like instrument with three courses of double strings, usually tuned to a major or minor chord, and featured prominently in traditional Cuban *son* music.

Triad (ch. 2) Generally, in tonal music, simultaneous sounding of pitches a third and a fifth above the root of a chord.

Triple (ch. 1, ch. 15) In musical meter, beat groupings of 3 and multiples of 3.

Trombone (ch. 12) A cylindrical brass tube with telescoping slide mechanism to produce pitches.

Trumpet (ch. 12) A cylindrical brass tube with valves to produce pitches.

Tukuyá (ch. 5) Stick dances performed by men in Chuuk (Micronesia).

Tulum (ch. 11) Anatolian bagpipe without drone pipe, with two chanters.

Ṭūra (ch. 12) Large finger cymbals (Egypt).

Türkü (ch. 11) Turkish-language folk songs of unknown authorship.

ʿŪd (ch. 12) Short-necked plucked lute, pear-shaped body with deep bowl; without frets; bent scroll with lateral peg attachment (Egypt).

Uilleann pipes (ch. 16) From the Irish *uilleann* meaning elbow; bagpipe with a chanter, three drones and three regulators, with air supplied by bellows. Originally called the Irish union bagpipes.

Unison (ch. 2) Multiple people singing or playing the same part simultaneously.

Ustad (Intro) Urdu language; in Indian Muslim culture, honorific title for a master, usually of music.

Usul (ch. 1, ch. 11) Metric system of Turkish music; a named, ordered pattern of long and short beats that defines the metrical structure of a musical piece in Turkey.

Vādi-samvādi (ch. 10) Strong tonal centers found in some North Indian *rāgs*.

Victory Song (ch. 20) Type of Native American powwow song used to honor and reenact deeds of bravery in battle.

Vihuela (pl. *vihuelas*) (ch. 19) Along with the *guitarrón* and six-stringed guitar, supplies the rhythmic and chordal framework for the music played by the mariachi (United States and Mexico). It has an 8-shaped soundbox with a spined, convex back and five strings tuned A-d-g-B-e. The *vihuelero* (vihuela player) employs defined hand patterns of strumming called *mánicos* to create a rhythmic background.

Violão (ch. 18) Brazilian classical guitar with nylon strings.

Vistār (ch. 10) An improvised developmental section played by the melodic artist in a North Indian *rāg* performance.

Vocable (ch. 1, ch. 5, ch. 10, ch. 20). Syllable that usually does not convey a linguistic meaning. In the case of powwow songs using vocables (ch.20), the usage of vocables does not connote a linguistically meaningless song as singers are still tasked with the responsibility of calling and supporting the dancers in their efforts.

Wa (wa let kouke) (ch. 8) Slit node of bamboo or pair of stubby wooden sticks, paired with the *si* bells (Myanmar).

Wayang (ch. 9) "Shadow" puppet theater; intricately carved puppets made of rawhide; at night performed with a coconut-oil lamp projecting shadows on a white screen and during the day in sacred contexts with no lamp or screen.

Wayang lemah (ch. 9) Daytime ceremonial *wayang*.

Wayfinding (ch. 5) A means of orienting and finding one's way through an environment (Micronesia).

Weriyeng (ch. 5) A patron spirit of ocean voyaging and also a traditional school of wayfinding (Micronesia)

Whole step (ch. 1) In tonal music, an interval equal to two half steps; a major second.

Woodblock (ch. 17) A small piece of wood, hollowed out, struck with a stick or mallet (Cuba).

Xhosa (ch. 14) South African language that uses click consonants.

Xin minyue (ch. 6) New traditional music (China).

Xylophone Percussion idiophone; set of tuned wooden bars struck with a mallet.

Yangqin (ch. 6) Chinese trapezoidally shaped box zither. Hammered with padded bamboo hammers.

Yatsuhashi Kengyō (ch. 7) Sixteenth-century *koto* player who set elite Japanese *koto* music on a popularized path.

Zaffa (ch. 12) "Procession," term commonly used to refer to wedding processions; also, the rhythmic mode commonly used in wedding processions (Egypt).

Zapateado (ch. 3) Rhythm of the footwork in Spanish *flamenco* dance.

Zikr (*dhikr* in modern standard Arabic) (ch. 12) "Remembrance," that is, remembering God; a Sufi ritual wherein believers seek to achieve a degree of union with God (Egypt).

Zither (ch. 3) Subtype of chordophone without a neck, with strings running along almost the length of the body.

Credits

PHOTO

INTRODUCTION
Figure 0.2 Photo by Julie A. Wolf; Figure 0.3 Courtesy of the author

Chapter 1
Figure 1.0 © Hiltrud Schulz, 2017. Reproduced by permission of photographer; Figure 1.1 Gift of Lawrence Creshkoff, 1990. The Metropolitan Museum of Art; Figure 1.2 Courtesy of Frederick Lau; Figure 1.3 Chart by Jane Chiu, Viet Nguyen, and Pamela Han; Figure 1.4 Chart by John Groschwitz; Figure 1.5 Chart by John Groschwitz; Figure 1.6 Chart by Kin Hang Lam; Figure 1.7 Chart by Kin Hang Lam; Figure 1.8 Notated by Susana Moreno Fernandez and Salwa El Shawan Castelo-Branco; Figure 1.9 Notation by John Murphy; Figure 1.10 Notation by John Murphy

Chapter 2
Figure 2.0 Shutterstock/Melanie Lemahieu; Figure 2.1 Courtesy of Frederick Lau; Figure 2.2 Photograph by Lisa Gold

Chapter 3
Figure 3.1 Zoonar GmbH/Alamy Stock Photo; Figure 3.3 Photograph by Eliot Bates

Chapter 4
Figure 4.0 Photo: Andrew Stuart

Chapter 5
Figure 5.0 Photograph by Hikaru Koide. Used with permission from the photographer; Figure 5.3 Photograph by Brian Diettrich, 2007; Figure 5.4 Photograph by Brian Diettrich, 2006; Photograph by Brian Diettrich, 2006; Photograph by Brian Diettrich, 2016

Chapter 6
Figure 6.0 Mario Savoia/Shutterstock; Figure 6.3 Courtesy of ROI and Frederick Lau; Figure 6.4 Photo by Lei Ouyang Bryant, 2005

Chapter 7
Figure 7.0 Shutterstock/Makoto_Honda; Figure 7.2 Museum of Fine Arts, Boston, William Sturgis Bigelow Collection; Figure 7.3 Gift of Mrs. Howard Mansfield, 1948. The Metropolitan Museum of Art; Figure 7.4 Museum of Fine Arts, Boston, William Sturgis Bigelow Collection; Figure 7.5 Bain Collection, Library of Congress

Chapter 8
Figure 8.0 Charles O. Cecil/Alamy Stock Photo; Figure 8.3 Photograph by Gavin Douglas; Figure 8.4 Photograph by Gavin Douglas; Figure 8.5 Photograph by Gavin Douglas

Chapter 9
Figure 9.0 Photograph by Lisa Gold; Figure 9.2 Photograph by Lisa Gold; Figure 9.3 Drawing by I Dewa Putu Berata; Figure 9.4 Photograph by Lisa Gold; Figure 9.5 Drawing by I Dewa Putu Berata; Figure 9.6 Photograph by Lisa Gold

Chapter 10
Figure 10.0 Photo by Chuck Fishman/Getty Images; Figure 10.4 Photo by Keystone Features/Hulton Archive/Getty Images; Figure 10.5 Photo by Benzmann/ullstein bild via Getty Images

Chapter 11
Figure 11.0 Photograph by Yeliz Keskin; Figure 11.3 Photograph by Ladi Dell'Aira; Figure 11.4 Photograph by Yeliz Keskin; Figure 11.5 © chrisstockphoto/Alamy Stock Photo

Chapter 12

Figure 12.0 World Religions Photo Library/Alamy Stock Photo; Figure 12.2 Photograph by Scott Marcus; Figure 12.3 Courtesy of Scott Marcus; Figure 12.4 Photograph by Zaveeni Khan-Marcus; Figure 12.5 Photograph by Zaveeni Khan-Marcus

Chapter 13

Figure 13.0 Photo courtesy of Jumbie Records and the Dagara Music Center; Figure 13.3 Photograph by Salvino Campos. Courtesy of Valerie Naranjo; Figure 13.4 Photograph by Annie Garau. Courtesy of the Indiana Daily Student; Figure 13.5 © 2001 Carla R. González Photography, courtesy of the Grinnell College Musical Instrument Collection; MusEx 13.1 Transcription by John Dankwa; Figure 13.6 Photo by John Dankwa, July 2013

Chapter 14

Figure 14.0 MARKA/Alamy Stock Photo; Figure 14.3 AF archive/Alamy Stock Photo

Chapter 15

Figure 15.0 Shutterstock/Marcin Krzyzak; Figure 15.1 Courtesy of Maria José Roxo and Gonçalo Santos Antunes; Figure 15.2 Courtesy of Maria José Roxo and Gonçalo Santos Antunes; Figure 15.3 Photograph by Susana Moreno Fernández; Figure 15.4 Courtesy of the Centro Andaluz de Flamenco, Jerez de la Frontera, Spain; Figure 15.8 Photo by El humilde fotero del pánico, CC

Chapter 16

Figure 16.0 Dorothea Hast; Figure 16.2 Pictorial Press Ltd/Alamy Stock Photo; Figure 16.3 Courtesy of Nell Gleeson; Figure 16.4 Photograph courtesy of the artist; Figure 16.5 CBW/Alamy Stock Photo

Chapter 17

Figure 17.0 Image Professionals GmbH/Alamy Stock Photo; Figure 17.2 Danita Delimont/Alamy Stock Photo; Figure 17.3 Photograph by Robin Moore; Figure 17.4 Anthony Brown/Alamy Stock Photo;

Figure 17.5 Herb Quick/Alamy Stock Photo; MusEx 17.5 Notation by author Robin Moore; MusEx 17.7 Notation by author Robin Moore; Figure 17.6 Wilawan Khasawong/Alamy Stock Photo; Figure 17.7 Dorling Kindersley ltd/Alamy Stock Photo; Figure 17.8 Craig Lovell/Eagle Visions Photography/Alamy Stock Photo

Chapter 18

Figure 18.0 imageBROKER/Alamy Stock Photo; Figure 18.2 Stefano Ember/Shutterstock; Figure 18.3 Collection of the National Library of Brasil; Figure 18.4 Andre Luiz Moreira/Shutterstock; Figure 18.5 Foto Arena LTDA/Alamy Stock Photo; Figure 18.6 Foto Arena LTDA/Alamy Stock Photo

Chapter 19

Figure 19.0 Photograph by Michael G. Stewart; Figure 19.2 Photograph by Dan Sheehy, 1997; Figure 19.3 Photograph by Dan Sheehy; Figure 19.4 Photograph by Dan Sheehy; Figure 19.5 Photograph by Dan Sheehy

Chapter 20

Figure 20.0 Stephen Butler/Canyon Records; Figure 20.2 Photo by Margaret Hoener Ryle; Figure 20.3 Designed by Monica Magtoto; Figure 20.4 Designed by Monica Magtoto

AUDIO

"Áách Kapwongen Etiwa Áámi," courtesy of Brian Diettrich.

"Bu Düya Bir Pencere (Aytekin's arr.)," Performed by Şevval Sam, arranged by Aytekin Gazi Ataş from Kalan CD 454, c. 2008. Used with permission from Kalan Ses Görüntü Film ve Yapim San.Tic.Ltd.Şti.

"Bu Düya Bir Pencere (Marsis's arr.)," Performed by Marsis from Kalan CD 470, c. 2009. Used with permission from Kalan Ses Görüntü Film ve Yapim San.Tic. Ltd.Şti.

"Call to Prayer," Shaykh Mohammed Gebril. Courtesy of Scott Marcus.

"Edward Connors," performed by Andy Irvine from *Wundertude* CD TUT 72.141, 1989. Trad. Arr. Andy Irvine/Donal Lunny.

"El pitayero (The Pitaya Cutter)" by Mariachi Reyna de Los Angeles from the recording entitled Mariachi Reyna de Los Angeles, SFW40579, courtesy of Smithsonian Folkways Recordings. (p) (c) 2018. Used by permission.

"Erééta Meyinuku (excerpt)," Meichik Amon, Toleison Island, Chuuk State, 2001. Courtesy of Brian Diettrich.

"Garrett Barry's Jig (Versions 1 and 2)" performed by Jerry O'Sullivan, recorded by Dora Hast and Stanley Scott. Courtesy of Jerome O'Sullivan.

"*Gyil* Duet, Bewaa #2," performed by Rallio Kpampul and Sambaa Sopele. *Beware: They Are Coming: Dagaare Songs from Nandom*, Pan Records PAN 2052CD. © Pan Records.

Junior Crehan (fiddle), Michael Tubridy (flute), Tommy McCarthy (concertina) and Eamon McGivney (fiddle), "The Maid Behind the Bar/Gregg's Pipes" (reels). *Set Dances of Ireland, Volume 1.* Séadna 001. 1992. Produced by Larry Lynch.

"Green Fields of Canada," performed by Paddy Tunney. Used with permission from the Tunney family and Mick Moloney.

"Hoka Hey" from *A Soldier's Dream* (CR-6418) by Elk Soldier, courtesy Canyon Records.

"In praise of the Burmese harp" by Inle Myint Maung and Yi Yi Thant from the recording entitled Mahagitá: Harp and Vocal Music of Burma, SFW40492, courtesy of Smithsonian Folkways Recordings. (p) (c) 2003. Used by permission.

"La Negra Tomasa" performed by Grupo el Ogano Pinareño (appears on *Piñareno: From the Tobacco Road of Cuba*): Alula #ALU-1011, 1998. © Piranha Records, c/o Piranha Arts AG.

"Las Olas," Mariachi Chula Vista, Mark Fogelquist. Courtesy of Mark Fogelquist.

"Mueve La Cintura Mulata." Composed by Alejandro Enis Almenares Sánchez and performed by El Cuarteto Oriente. Source: D, *Casa de la Trova Santiago de Cuba*,

CODCD 120. © Discos Corason SA, México, www.corason.com.

"Navigators of Puluwat," performed by Navigatrs Hipour and Tawochu, Track 24 from Saydisc CDSDL414, *Navigators of Puluwat.* © Saydisc Records, England.

"Rag Chandranandan," performed by Ali Akbar Khan. AMMP Records, CD 90001, 1990. Courtesy of Mary Khan.

"Road Warrior" from *Down 4 Life* (CR-6334) by Young Bird, courtesy Canyon Records.

"Rokudan: 16th Century Kengyo Yatsuhashi" by Shinichi Yuize from the recording entitled The Japanese Koto, COOK01132, courtesy of Smithsonian Folkways Recordings. (p) (c) 1955. Used by permission.

"Sakura, Sakura (Dreams of Cherry Blossoms," performed by Keiko Abe. Used with Permission from Xebec Music Publishing Co., Ltd.

"Se Foi Bom Pra Você," performed by Beth Carvalo with the Velha Guarda da Mangueira Se Foi Bom Pra Você. Track 4 from the 1999 album, *Velha Guarda da Manguiera e Convidados.* © Nikita Music.

"Straight Intertribal" from *Pow Wow Songs, Recorded live at White Swan* (CR-6273) by Black Lodge, courtesy Canyon Records.

"Tarānā," performed by Asha Bhosle. AMMP CDF 9601, 1996. Courtesy of Mary Khan.

"Tongue Twister," performed by and courtesy of Joanna de Souza and drummer Ritesh Das.

"The Click Song," performed by Miriam Makeba. RCA LSP 2267 1960. © Sony Music Entertainment.

"The Maid Behind the Bar/Gregg's Pipes," performed by Junior Crehan (fiddle), Michael Tubridy (flute), Tommy McCarthy (concertina), and Eamon McGivney (fiddle). Seadna 01. Courtesy of Larry Lynch.

"Úirchill á Chreagáin (Creggan Graveyard)" performed by Pádraigín Ní Uallacháin, Gael Linn CEFCD 174. Courtesy of Pádraigín Ní Uallacháin.

"*Wúwa nómw wóón Fénú neey*" (I am on my Island), A village group from Feefen Island, Chuuk State, 2006. Field recording courtesy of Brian Diettrich.

VIDEO

Chuuk Team, College of Micronesia—FSM Founding Day 2015. © Takuya Nagoaka/NGO Pasifika Renaissance.

"Candomoblé" performance from *Rhythmic Uprising*. © Director, Benjamin Watkins.

College of Micronesia—FSM Founding Day 2017. © Takuya Nagoaka/NGO Pasifika Renaissance.

"'El pitayero (The Pitaya Cutter)" by Mariachi Reyna de Los Angeles," 2018, CFV11079, courtesy of Smithsonian Folkways Recordings

Gagaku: The Court Music of Japan. © 1989, Center for Music Television, University of Oklahoma.

Haru no Umi, performed by Shirley Muramoto Wong (koto) and Kaoru Kakizakai (shakukuhachi), 2013. Courtesy of Shirley Kazuyo Muramoto.

"Interview With Nati Cano," 2015, CFV10707, courtesy of Smithsonian Folkways Recordings

"The Quarter-Century Reign of Mariachi Reyna," 2019, CFV11121, courtesy of Smithsonian Folkways Recordings

"Rokudan" performed by Shoko Hikage.

Sacred Vessels: Navigating Tradition and Identity in Micronesia, Part I. Used with permission from Moving Islands, Vicente M. Diaz, Producer. Men's chants (in order of appearance): Fai, Hokaiu, "Sleeping With Father," performed by Sosthenis Emwalu. Women's chant—Pon Weresak, performed by women of Relong, Polowat.

"Sakura, Sakura," performed by Shoko Hikage.

"What Makes a Good Mariachi?," 2007, CFV10073, courtesy of Smithsonian Folkways Recordings

"The World's First LGBTQ Mariachi," 2018, CFV11078, courtesy of Smithsonian Folkways Recordings

Index

376